of Modernity

FR- 26096

Anthropologies of Modernity
Foucault, Governmentality, and Life Politics

Edited by Jonathan Xavier Inda

Blackwell
Publishing

© 2005 by Blackwell Publishing Ltd

BLACKWELL PUBLISHING
350 Main Street, Malden, MA 02148-5020, USA
9600 Garsington Road, Oxford OX4 2DQ, UK
550 Swanston Street, Carlton, Victoria 3053, Australia

The right of Jonathan Xavier Inda to be identified as the Author of the
Editorial Material in this Work has been asserted in accordance with the
UK Copyright, Designs, and Patents Act 1988.

First published 2005 by Blackwell Publishing Ltd

1   2005

Library of Congress Cataloging-in-Publication Data

Anthropologies of modernity: Foucault, governmentality, and life politics/edited by Jonathan
Xavier Inda.
p. cm.
Includes bibliographical references and index.
ISBN-13: 978-0-631-22826-4 (hard cover: alk. paper)
ISBN-10: 0-631-22826-8 (hard cover: alk. paper)
ISBN-13: 978-0-631-22827-1 (pbk.: alk. paper)
ISBN-10: 0-631-22827-6 (pbk.: alk. paper)
1. Political anthropology—Philosophy, 2. Politics and culture. 3. Culture and globalization.
4. Foucault, Michel, I. Inda, Jonathan Xavier.
GN492.2.A57 2006
306.2—dc22 2005003400

A catalogue record for this title is available from the British Library.

Set in 10.5/13pt Galliard
by SPI Publisher Services, Pondicherry, India
Printed and bound in the United Kingdom
by T J International Ltd, Padstow, Cornwall

The publisher's policy is to use permanent paper from mills that operate a
sustainable forestry policy, and which has been manufactured from pulp
processed using acid-free and elementary chlorine-free practices. Furthermore,
the publisher ensures that the text paper and cover board used have met
acceptable environmental accreditation standards.

For further information on
Blackwell Publishing, visit our website:
www.blackwellpublishing.com

Contents

Notes on Contributors

João Biehl is Assistant Professor of Anthropology at Princeton University.

James Ferguson is Professor of Cultural and Social Anthropology at Stanford University.

Akhil Gupta is Associate Professor of Cultural and Social Anthropology at Stanford University.

Deborah Heath is Associate Professor of Anthropology at Lewis and Clark College.

David G. Horn is Professor of Comparative Studies at the Ohio State University.

Jonathan Xavier Inda is Assistant Professor of Chicana/o Studies at the University of California, Santa Barbara.

Diane M. Nelson is Associate Professor of Cultural Anthropology at Duke University.

Aihwa Ong is Professor of Anthropology and Southeast Asian Studies at the University of California, Berkeley.

Adriana Petryna is Assistant Professor of Anthropology at the Graduate Faculty of New School University.

Paul Rabinow is Professor of Anthropology at the University of California, Berkeley.

Rayna Rapp is Professor of Anthropology at New York University.

Peter Redfield is Associate Professor of Anthropology at the University of North Carolina, Chapel Hill.

David Scott is Professor of Anthropology at Columbia University.

Karen-Sue Taussig is Assistant Professor of Anthropology and Medicine at the University of Minnesota, Minneapolis.

Acknowledgments

Special thanks go to Gerardo Aldana, João Biehl, Jim Ferguson, David Horn, Diane Nelson, Aihwa Ong, Adriana Petryna, Peter Redfield, and Ann Stoler. They all contributed greatly to the development of this volume. I would also like to express my gratitude to Jane Huber, my editor at Blackwell, for her enthusiastic support of the project. Finally, I am quite grateful to the Ford Foundation. I began this book while on a Ford Postdoctoral Fellowship.

Analytics of the Modern:

An Introduction

Jonathan Xavier Inda

This book is intended as a reflection on the question of modernity. It has two general orientations. One is anthropological. What this means, simply put for now, is three things. First, it means that the essays gathered here treat modernity not in abstract terms but tangibly as an ethnographic object. Their aim, in other words, is not to come up with some grand, general account of modernity but to analyze its concrete manifestations. Second, it means that these essays examine the materialization of the modern not just in the West, as tends to be the case in most disciplines, but worldwide. Indeed, the bent of the volume is determinedly global, its empirical sites ranging from Italy and Ukraine to India, Brazil, and French Guiana. Finally, to be anthropological in orientation means that at the stake in the analysis of modernity is the value and form of the *anthropos* or human being (Collier and Ong 2003; Rabinow 2003). Said otherwise, the book is centrally concerned with the modern constitution of the social and biological life of the human.

The other orientation of the book is Foucauldian. This means that the intellectual point of departure for the essays in the volume is the work of French philosopher Michel Foucault. Particularly central to these analyses of modernity are Foucault's (2000) reflections on modern government. In these reflections, the term "government" generally refers to the conduct of conduct – that is, to all those more or less calculated and systematic ways of thinking and acting that aim to shape, regulate, or manage the comportment of others, whether these be workers in a factory, inmates in a prison, wards in a mental hospital, the inhabitants of a territory, or the members of a population. Understood this way, "government" designates not just the activities of the state and its institutions but more broadly any rational effort to influence or guide the conduct of human beings through acting upon their hopes, desires, circumstances, or environment. Sketched out in these reflections is thus a particular approach to analyzing modern political power – one that treats the state as only one element, albeit a rather important one, in a multiple network of actors, organizations, and entities involved in exercising authority over the conduct of individuals and populations. The essays gathered here pursue, each in their own way, the particular style of investigation Foucault brought to bear on contemporary rule. They are concerned with analyzing what has been dubbed the "will to govern" (Rose 1999: 5). Of particular importance to such an analytics are three dimensions of government. First, there are the reasons of government. This dimension encompasses all those forms knowledge, expertise, and calculation that render human beings thinkable in such a manner as to make them amenable to political programming. Second, there are the technics of government. The technical is that domain of practical mechanisms, instruments, and programs through which authorities of various types seek to shape and instrumentalize human conduct. Finally, there are the subjects of government. This dimension covers the diverse types of individual and collective identity that arise out of and inform governmental activity.

All told, then, the essays gathered here amount to what could be called Foucauldian anthropologies of modernity. They are concerned with subjecting modern government – as a heterogeneous field of thought and action – to ethnographic scrutiny in a variety of empirical settings. In this introductory chapter, I would like to shed light on these Foucauldian anthropologies. I will start by detailing a bit more thoroughly Foucault's thinking on the subject of modern government or what he calls governmentality. Some attention will be paid to how political power has assigned itself the duty of administering life. I will then elaborate on the three analytic dimensions that are the main concern of the essays – these are the reasons, technics, and subjects of government – as articulated in a body of interdisciplinary literature developing around Foucault's work. And in the final section, I will provide a discussion of the anthropologies that make up the volume. The discussion will be focused around five main themes: colonialism, globalization, science, biosociality, and necropolitics.

Foucault and the Art of Government

Foucault's thinking on the subject of modern government is best articulated in a series of lectures given at the Collège de France in 1978 and 1979. The most important of these lectures is one entitled "Governmentality" (2000).[1] In this lecture, Foucault undertakes a genealogical analysis of the art of government. His opening move is to locate the emergence of this art in sixteenth-century Europe. There, as signaled in numerous political treatises of the time, certain questions regarding government exploded with particular force. These questions – which had to do with who can govern, how best to govern, how to be governed, and how to govern oneself and others – were discussed with respect to a broad array of issues: from that of the proper management of one's self and the good government of children to that of the correct administration of the state by the sovereign. This intense interest in questions of government arose largely on account of two major social developments. One was the breakdown of feudal institutions, which led to the formation of the modern state; the other was the Reformation and Counter-Reformation, which resulted in the spread of religious dissidence. As Foucault articulates it: "There is a double movement, then, of state central-ization, on the one hand, and of dispersion and religious dissidence, on the other. It is . . . at the intersection of these two tendencies that the problem comes to pose itself with this peculiar intensity, of how to be ruled, how strictly, by whom, to what end, by what methods, and so on" (2000: 202).

This raising of questions with respect to government signals, for Foucault, a major shift in thinking about political rule. The shift is from a sovereign notion of power to an art of government. Foucault explores this shift through an analysis of Machiavelli's *The Prince*. What he does is show that the idea of the art of government arose in explicit opposition to the theory of sovereign rule articu-lated by Machiavelli. In Machiavelli's thinking, the prince's chief goal in the exercise of power must be to protect and strengthen the principality. This last is understood not as "the objective ensemble of its subjects and the territory" but instead as "the prince's relation with what he owns, with the territory he has inherited or acquired, and with his subjects" (2000: 205). The idea here is that sovereignty is first and foremost exercised on a territory and only as a conse-quence on the subjects who populate it. Indeed, it is the territory that is the fundamental element in Machiavelli's principality. Everything else is a mere variable. This is not to say that subjects do not really matter. They do, but only as it concerns the law. At work here is the idea that the sovereign's right to rule should be grounded in the notion of the common good. This notion "refers to a state of affairs where all the subjects without exception obey the laws, accomplish the tasks expected of them, practice the trade to which they are assigned, and respect the established order insofar as this order conforms to the laws imposed by God on nature and men" (2000: 210). The common good means, in other words, compliance with the law, either that of the worldly sovereign or that of God, the supreme ruler. This suggests that when it comes to the inhabitants of a territory what matters is that the law be observed. It indicates that the good for the prince is essentially that people should obey him. For sovereignty, then, the object is to preserve the principality (or territory) and concomitantly to subject the people to the law. Its end is really self-preservation through the force of law.

The idea of the art of government stands in sharp contrast to this sovereign notion of power articulated in *The Prince*. In the anti-Machiavellian political literature, being able to hang on to one's principality is not quite the same thing as enjoying the art of governing. One crucial difference is that whereas sovereignty is exercised over a territory and, consequently, over the subjects who dwell in it, government is effected on a complex made up of men and their relation to things. As Foucault puts it:

> What government has to do with is not territory but, rather, a sort of complex composed of men and things. The things, in this sense, with which government is to

be concerned are in fact men, but men in their relations, their links, their imbrication with those things that are wealth, resources, means of subsistence, the territory with its specific qualities, climate, irrigation, fertility, and so on; men in their relation to those other things that are customs, habits, ways of acting and thinking, and so on; and finally men in their relation to those still other things that might be accidents and misfortunes such as famine, epidemics, death, and so on. (2000: 208–209)

The key point here is that, for government, the issue of territory is only a secondary matter. What really counts is this complex of men and things. Indeed, it is this complex that is the fundamental target of government. Everything else, including territory, is simply a variable. A second key difference is that whereas the end of sovereignty is the common good, the object of government is the efficient and productive disposition of things. This means that with government it is not a matter of imposing law on people but of arranging things so as to produce an end appropriate to and convenient for each of the things governed. Entailed in this disposal of things is a multiplicity of specific goals: "For instance, government will have to ensure that the greatest possible quantity of wealth is produced, that the people are provided with sufficient means of subsistence, that the population is enabled to multiply, and so on" (2000: 211). Said otherwise, to dispose things means to properly manage wealth and resources, modes of living and habitation, and all those eventualities – accidents, epidemics, death, and the like – that tend to befall humans. For government, then, neither territory nor law hold much significance. The important thing is that men and things be administered in a correct and efficient way.

This thinking as regards the art of government, according to Foucault, was not to remain a purely theoretical exercise. From the sixteenth century on, it became linked directly to the formation of the territorial, administrative state and the growth of governmental apparatuses. At first, the practice of the art of government was concerned with introducing economy – "economy" here harks back to its original definition and signifies the wise management of individuals, goods, and wealth within the family – into political practice. That is to say, it was preoccupied with setting up at the level of the entire state "a form of surveillance and control as attentive as that of the head of a family over his household and his goods" (Foucault 2000: 207). However, with the expansion of capitalism and the demographic growth of the eighteenth century, the practice of the art of government experienced a recentering: the theme of the family was supplanted with that of the population. What happened is that, through statistical forms of representation, population was identified as a specific objectivity: as an entity that had "its own regularities, its own rate of deaths and diseases, its cycles of scarcity, and so on" (2000: 216). As such, the domain of population was shown to involve a range of aggregate effects – such as epidemics, mounting spirals of wealth and labor, and endemic levels of mortality – that were not reducible to the dimension of the family. The consequence of such representation was to establish population as a higher-order assemblage of which the family formed only one component. It was to dislodge the family from its supreme position as model of government and to resituate it as an element internal to population. Significantly, once this dislodging took place, the practice of the art of government grew to be above all concerned with populations. Its primary end became to manage such assemblages in ways that augmented their prosperity, longevity, safety, productivity, and so forth. As Foucault notes:

> In contrast to sovereignty, government has as its purpose not the act of government itself, but the welfare of the population, the improvement of its condition, the increase of its wealth, longevity, health, and so on; and the means the government uses to attain these ends are themselves all, in some sense, immanent to the population; it is the population itself on which government will act either directly, through large-scale campaigns, or indirectly, through techniques that will make possible, without the full awareness of the people, the stimulation of birth rates, the directing of the flow of population into certain regions or activities, and so on. (2000: 216–217)

Starting in the eighteenth century, then, population emerges as the terrain par excellence of government. It becomes the object that government must bear in mind – where knowledge and practice are concerned – in order to be capable of managing rationally and effectively.

Important to note here is that, as the care and growth of population becomes a fundamental concern of government, a novel technology of power takes hold. Foucault names this technology biopower. In *The History of Sexuality*, he remarks that biopower designates "what brought life and its mechanisms into the realm of explicit calculations and made knowledge-power an agent of transformation of human life" (1980: 143). The point is that at stake in the management of populations is essentially nothing other than life itself. It is that the vital processes of human existence are what really matter when it comes to governing. This technology of biopower has assumed two basic forms. One form, which Foucault calls a biopolitics of the population or simply biopolitics, is concerned with population at "the level of its aggregate effects" (2000: 219). Here biopower takes as its target the population regarded as a species body: "the body imbued with the mechanics of life and serving as the basis of the biological processes: propagation, births and mortality, the level of health, life expectancy and longevity, with all the conditions that can cause these to vary" (1980: 139). Put otherwise, biopolitics attends to the biological processes of the collective social body. It is concerned with regulating the phenomena that typify groups of living human beings: reproduction and human sexuality, the size and quality of the population, health and illness, living and working conditions, birth and death, and the like. The goal: to optimize the life of the population as a whole. The second form, which Foucault calls an anatomo-politics of the human body or simply discipline, "implies the management of population in its depths and its details" (2000: 219). Here biopower centers not on the population per se but on the individual bodies that compose it. Indeed, the target of discipline is not the collective mass but the individual human body: the body taken as an object to be manipulated. The goal of discipline is to produce human beings whose bodies are at once useful and docile. It is to optimize the life of the body: to augment its capabilities, extort its forces, and increase its utility and docility. Biopower thus amounts to nothing less than the taking charge of life by political power. It points to how government has assigned itself the duty of administering bodies and managing collective life.

Such, then, is Foucault's genealogical analysis of the art of government. What we get with this analysis is a rather particular understanding of modern political power. The name Foucault gives to this understanding is governmentality. There are at least three important elements to governmentality. One element is that the term "government" is assigned the rather broad meaning it enjoyed in the sixteenth century. It refers essentially to the conduct of conduct – to the more or less considered and calculated ways of thinking and acting that propose to shape, regulate, or manage the conduct of individuals or groups toward specific goals or ends. Said otherwise, government points our attention very broadly to any rational effort to influence or guide the comportment of others – whether these be workers, children, communities, families, or the sick – through acting upon their hopes, desires, or milieu. A second element is that there is a refusal to reduce political power to the activities of the state. Indeed, for Foucault, governing – that is, the regulation of conduct – is not merely a matter of *the* government and its institutions but involves a multitude of heterogeneous entities: from politicians, philanthropists, and state bureaucrats to academics, clerics, and medics. What thus counts in thinking about governmental power is not simply the state but also all these other actors, organizations, and agencies concerned with exercising authority over the conduct of human beings. The point here is simply that government takes place both within and outside state contexts. The third element is that the principal target of government is population. This means that political and other authorities have come to understand the work of governing as requiring them to act upon the particulars of human conduct so as to enhance the security, longevity, health, prosperity, and happiness of populations. All told, then, governmentality draws attention to all those strategies, tactics, and authorities – state and nonstate alike – that seek to mold conduct individually and collectively in order to safeguard the welfare of each and of all.

An Analytics

Significantly, the work of Michel Foucault on modern government has produced a burgeoning corpus of political, social, and cultural analysis. For simplicity's sake, we shall refer to this interdisciplinary literature as governmentality. Scholars of governmentality – as might be expected given foregoing discussion – have been most concerned with exploring those practices that take as their target the wealth, health, security, and happiness of populations. More specifically, they have been occupied with studying those assemblages of authorities, knowledges, and techniques that endeavor to shape the conduct of individuals and populations in order to effect individual and collective welfare. They have thus drawn attention to the intrinsic links between strategies for knowing and directing large-scale entities and schemes for managing the actions of particular human beings – to how the conduct and circumstances of individuals are connected to the security and well-being of the population as a whole. Focusing along these lines, scholars from a variety of disciplines have produced important studies on a broad range of subjects including: space and urban planning (Rabinow 1989); psychiatry, medicine, and psychology (Castel 1981; Ong 1995; Rose 1998); poverty and insecurity (Dean 1991; Procacci 1993); social insurance and risk (Ewald 1986; Defert 1991); the regulation of pregnancy and reproduction (Horn 1994; Weir 1996; Ruhl 1999; Greenhalgh 2003); programs for self-esteem and empowerment (Cruikshank 1999); criminality (O'Malley 1992; Rose 2000; Horn 2003); globalization (Ong 1999; Ong and Collier 2004); colonialism (Stoler 1995; Kalpagam 2002); and the regulation of unemployment (Walters 2000). The perspective of these studies does not amount to a formal methodology or a unifying theory of government. It is actually a perspective that draws attention to government as a heterogeneous field of thought and action – to the multiplicity of authorities, knowledges, strategies, and devices that have sought to govern conduct for specific ends. Nonetheless, it is possible to single out at least three closely related analytical themes along which their analyses are organized. A review of these themes will help better establish the aims and limits of the essays in this book.

Reasons

The first analytical theme of the governmentality literature involves the political reasons or rationalities of government. According to Nikolas Rose and Peter Miller, two of the foremost proponents of the governmentality approach, this domain designates:

> the changing discursive fields within which the exercise of power is conceptualized, the moral justifications for particular ways of exercising power by diverse authorities, notions of the appropriate forms, objects and limits of politics, and conceptions of the proper distribution of tasks among secular, spiritual, military and familial sectors. (1992: 175)

Political rationalities may thus be generally conceptualized as intellectual machineries that render reality thinkable in such a manner as to make it calculable and governable. They point to the forms of political reasoning ensconced in governmental discourse, the language and vocabulary of political rule, the constitution of manageable fields and objects, and the variable forms of truth, knowledge, and expertise that authorize governmental practice. Political rationalities, in short, name that field wherein lie the multiplicity of endeavors to rationalize the nature, mechanisms, aims, and parameters of governmental authority.

With respect to this first analytical theme, governmentality scholars generally have a couple of important concerns. One concern is with the epistemological character of political reasons (Rose and Miller 1992; Dean 1999). They are interested in how these rationalities both foster and rely upon assorted forms of knowledge and expertise – such as psychology, medicine, sociology, public policy, and criminology. Knowledges of this kind embody specific understandings of the objects of governmental practice – the poor, the vagrant, the economy, civil society, and so forth – and stipulate suitable ways of managing them. Moreover, such forms of knowledge define the goals and purpose of government and determine the institutional location of those authorized to make truth claims about governmental objects. Governmentality scholars, then, are occupied with how the practices of government are intertwined with specific regimes of truth and the vocation of numerous experts and authorities. They are concerned with "analyzing what counts as truth, who has the power to define truth, the role of different authorities of truth, and the epistemological, institutional and technical conditions for the production and circulation of truths" (Rose 1999: 30). These scholars thus highlight how, in order to govern efficaciously, it is necessary to "know." They show that the activity of governing is possible only within particular epistemological regimes of intelligibility – that all government positively depends on the elaboration of specific languages that represent and analyze reality in a manner that renders it amenable to political programming.

The other important concern of governmentality scholars is with the problem-oriented nature of political reasons (Rose and Miller 1992; Dean 1999). They note that government is inherently a problematizing sphere of activity – one in which the responsibilities of administrative authorities tend to be framed in terms of problems that need to be addressed. These problems are generally formulated in relation to particular events – such as epidemics, urban unrest, and economic downturns – or around specific realms of experience: urbanism, poverty, crime, teenage pregnancy, and so on. The goal of governmental practice is to articulate the nature of these problems and propose solutions to them. Guided with this perspective on government, the governmentality literature tends to explore how certain events, processes, or phenomena become formulated as problems. Moreover, they are often concerned with investigating the sites where these problems are given form and the various authorities accountable for vocalizing them. To focus on government, then, is to attend, at least on some level, to its problematizations – to the ways intellectuals, policy analysts, psychiatrists, social workers, doctors, and other governmental authorities conceptualize certain objects as problems. It is to focus on how government is bound to the continual classification of experience as problematic.

Technics

The second analytical theme of the governmentality literature involves the technics or technologies of government – that is, how government takes on a technological and pragmatic form. The technological is that domain of practical mechanisms, devices, calculations, procedures, apparatuses, and documents "through which authorities of various sorts have sought to shape, normalize and instrumentalize the conduct, thought, decisions and aspirations of others in order to achieve the objectives they consider desirable" (Miller and Rose 1990: 8). It is that complex of techniques, instruments, measures, and programs that endeavors to translate thought into practice and thus actualize political reasons.

Governmentality scholars' concern with the technological domain reveals itself best in two ways. One way is through the attention paid to specific technical instruments. These instruments encompass such things as: methods of examination and evaluation; techniques of notation, numeration, and calculation; accounting procedures; routines for the timing and spacing of activities in specific locations; presentational forms such as tables and graphs; formulas for the organization of work; standardized tactics for the training and implantation of habits; pedagogic, therapeutic, and punitive techniques of reformation and cure; architectural forms in which interventions take place (i.e., classrooms and prisons); and professional vocabularies (Miller and Rose 1990; Rose 1996, 1999; Dean 1999). Particularly important technical instruments are what Bruno Latour (1986) calls material inscriptions. These are all the mundane tools – surveys, reports, statistical methodologies, pamphlets, manuals, architectural plans, written reports, drawings, pictures, numbers, bureaucratic rules and guidelines, charts, graphs, statistics, and so forth – that represent events and phenomena as information, data, and knowledge. These humble technical devices make objects "visible." They render things into calculable and programmable form. They are the material implements that make it possible for thought to act upon reality. The governmentality literature's concern with technologies of government, then, draws attention to importance of technical means in directing the actions of individuals and populations. Without such means, the government of conduct cannot take place.

The other way governmentality scholars manifest their concern with the technological domain is through a focus on the programmatic character of government – that is, on how government tends to be conceptualized into existence in programmatic form. The programmatic may be taken to be that:

> realm of designs put forward by philosophers, political economists, physiocrats and philanthropists, government reports, committees of inquiry, White Papers, proposals and counterproposals by organizations of business, labor, finance, charities and professionals, that seek to configure specific locales and relations in ways thought desirable. (Rose and Miller 1992: 181)

Government is programmatic in the sense that it assumes that the real can be programmed – that it can be made thinkable in such a manner as to make it amenable to diagnosis, reform, and improvement. This programmatic character manifests itself most directly in specific programs of government – that is, in practical schemes for reforming reality. Governmentality scholars tend to train a good deal of attention on these programs of government. They focus on how such governmental schemes conceptualize, manage, and endeavor to resolve particular problems in light of specific goals. They attend to how specific programs go about shaping the environment and circumstances of specific actors in order to modify their conduct in very precise ways. All in all, this emphasis on the programmatic calls attention to the eternally optimistic disposition of government – to its firm belief that reality can be managed better or more effectively and thus achieve desired ends.

Subjects

The third analytical theme of the governmentality literature involves the subjects of government – that is, the diverse types of selves, persons, actors, agents, or identities that arise from and inform governmental activity. In relation to this final theme, as Mitchel Dean puts it, governmentality scholars tend to ask:

> What forms of person, self and identity are presupposed by different practices of government and what sorts of transformation do these practices seek? What statuses, capacities, attributes and orientations are assumed of those who exercise authority (from politicians and bureaucrats to professionals and therapists) and those who are to be governed (workers, consumers, pupils and social welfare recipients)? What forms of conduct are expected of them? What duties and rights do they have? How are these capacities and attributes to be fostered? How are these duties enforced and rights ensured? How are certain aspects of conduct problematized? How are they then to be reformed? How are certain individuals and populations made to identify with certain groups, to become virtuous and active citizens, and so on? (1999: 32)

To focus on the subjects of government is thus, on one level, to direct attention to how governmental practices and programs seek to cultivate particular types of individual and collective identity as well as forms of agency and subjectivity. It is to emphasize how government is intimately involved in making modern subjects – whether it be as workers, citizens, consumers, students, or the like. The importance of such subject-making is that through it – that is, through attaching individuals to particular identities, through getting them to experience themselves as specific kinds of beings with certain kinds of capacities and qualities – government is able to mold human conduct in such a way as to bring about individual and collective wellbeing. On another level, to focus on the subjects of government is to deal with how particular agents cultivate "their own" selves and identities. The idea here is that while governmental practices might seek to create specific kinds of subjects, it does not mean that they necessarily or completely succeed in doing so. Individuals can and do negotiate the processes to which they are subjected. For governmentality scholars, then, it is important to look not just at the forms of collective and individual identity promoted by practices of government, but also at how particular agents negotiate these forms – at how they embrace, adapt, or refuse them.

Anthropology and the Practices of Modernity

Taking their inspiration from Foucault and the governmentality literature, the essays in this volume are fundamentally concerned with examining the modern will to govern.[2] The approach they take to this will to govern is anthropological in nature. To be anthropological means, first of all, that these essays deal with modern government principally as an ethnographic object. "Ethnographic" here has a rather particular connotation. The concern of the essays is not with describing a place and its people – that is, with analyzing an ethnos. Nor is it with searching for meaning – that is, with investigating culture. This is what one usually thinks of when the word "ethnography" is evoked. Rather, the concern of the chapters is with materiality. It is with examining the concrete manifestations of modern government – the way it is materialized in very specific practices. The practices these essays generally focus on correspond to the three analytical themes presented above. These are the reasons, technics, and subjects of government. Accordingly, the essays, to varying degrees, pay attention to the problematizations, forms of expertise, and assorted types of knowledges that render human beings thinkable as governable objects; to the practical mechanisms, instruments, and programs through which authorities seek to actualize particular political rationalities; and to the sundry types of individual and collective identity that specific practices of government attempt to mold in order to instrumentalize human conduct. To be anthropological also means that the essays gathered here are not content to limit their analyses of modern government simply to "Western" settings (e.g., the United States, Europe). Instead, they are collectively global in scope. Their empirical locations encompass Sri Lanka, French Guiana, France, Malaysia, Indonesia, India, Africa, Brazil, Guatemala, Italy, Ukraine, and the United States. The concern here, I should note, is not with "describing" these places, but with these places as milieus or environments in which and through which government occurs. Indeed, we will see that milieu – proper environment, setting, local particularities – matters very much when it comes to governing. Finally, to be anthropological in nature means that at the heart of the examination of modern government is the *anthropos* or human being. Indeed, a central concern of the essays is with how practices of government put the social and biological life of the human in question. It is with the problematization of human beings as citizens, objects of knowledge, living entities, targets of regulation, and so forth. All in all, then, as I noted earlier, the texts in this volume are preoccupied with bringing ethnographic scrutiny to bear on the practices of modern government in an array of empirical sites. They add up to what I have called Foucauldian anthropologies of modernity.

Colonial Reasons

The volume is divided into five thematic sections. The first section is largely engaged in expanding the geographical vision of modernity Foucault presents in his genealogy of governmentality. The problem with this genealogy is that it is disconcertingly silent about the emergence of modern government outside the geography of the West. It is as if governmentality were simply a product of modern Europe – fully constituted within its borders. The essays in this section rectify this Eurocentric conceit by focusing on the career of governmentality in the colonies. They draw attention to how Europe's colonial outposts were key sites in the development of modern governmental practices.

In chapter 1, David Scott tackles the relocation of governmentality in a colonial context through spotlighting the case of British rule in Sri Lanka. A main concern of the essay is to show "that to understand the project of colonial power *at any given historical moment*, one has to understand the character of the political rationality that constituted it." To illustrate this point, Scott discusses two political rationalities operating in colonial Sri Lanka. One was mercantilism or sovereignty. Under this rationality, which held sway between 1796 and 1832, the principal object of colonial power was the "extraction of tribute" – tribute for the defense and aggrandizement of the state and monarch. Accordingly, the ways of life of the colonized population – their habits, distinctions, and religious obser-vations – did not figure prominently in colonial calculations. What mattered was simply that colonial subjects "knew their place" and "obeyed when com-manded." The second political rationality was governmentality. Under this ra-tionality, which came to prominence after 1832, colonial power was no longer directed at extracting wealth. Instead, it was aimed at improving the social conditions of the population. This improving entailed the alteration of the conduct or habits of the colonized. The goal was to produce – through new technologies, institutions, and forms of knowledge – self-interested subjects with "a progressive desire for industry, regularity, and individual accomplishment."

In chapter 2, Peter Redfield confronts the colonial relocation of governmen-tality through an exploration of the penal colony in French Guiana. The starting point for this exploration is Foucault's *Discipline and Punish* (1979). In this book, which focuses on the birth of the prison, Foucault mentions that the deportation of criminals to overseas colonies constituted an alternative to their detention in prisons. However, he offhandedly dismisses this practice as a "rig-orous and distant form of imprisonment" that achieved little as regards colon-ization or economy (1979: 272, 279). Redfield questions this dismissal and takes seriously the emergence of the penal colony as a viable colonial alternative to the prison. His basic argument is that the penal colony, as instantiated in French Guiana, constituted a negative form of governmentality. The logic of this argument is as follows. A key goal of French administrators was to foster the life of the penal population. They sought to achieve this end through arranging the social and physical environment in such a way as to favor the production of rehabilitated subjects capable of survival and proper self-management. However, far from being a technology that cultivated the wellbeing of the populace, the penal colony wound up as a machinery of infirmity that produced high mortality rates and low norms of health. There was thus a major gap between stated goals and actual effects. What this suggests, according to Redfield, is that "rather than governmentality we have something like its negative impression: a deployment of the possibility of government without its fulfillment." It indicates that political rationalities of colonial power contain within them the possibility of inefficiency, mismanagement, imperfection, and failure.

Global Governance

The second section of the book is concerned with situating the practices of modern government in a global frame. The inclination in the governmentality literature has been to disregard how global processes are affecting the nature of contemporary government.[3] Indeed, their analyses tend to proceed as if the intensification of global interconnectedness were of little relevance to how the activity of managing individuals and populations is conducted. The essays in this section remedy this neglect through exploring specific ways in which globalization is reshaping the terrain of government (Perry and Maurer 2003: xiii).

In chapter 3, Aihwa Ong examines this reconfiguration of governmental practice through the example of South-East Asia. Her basic argument is that, in this area of the world, globalization has led to the development of what she calls "graduated sovereignty." This concept refers to how, in order to remain globally competitive, South-East Asian countries – Malaysia and Indonesia, for example – have had to cede some aspects of state power and authority to corporate entities and supranational organizations. Significantly, this has produced a situation in which, depending on the particular mix of state and nonstate agencies involved in governing a particular domain, "different sectors of the population" have become "subjected to different technologies of regulation and nurturance." The result of such differential technological treatment has been to endow different populations with very different kinds of rights, caring, and protection. It has been to create a system of uneven distribution, or "variegated citizenship," in which some subjects are nurtured and afforded rights and resources, while others are largely neglected.

In chapter 4, James Ferguson and Akhil Gupta take up their exploration of how global developments are reshaping the territory of government through a focus on India and Africa. One of their main observations, particularly as regards Africa, is that many contemporary states are not quite able to carry out the functions typically associated with the modern nation-state. In this context, the work of governing has not just ceased. Rather, it has been outsourced, at least in part, to an array of nonstate transnational organizations. For example, with respect to state economic policy, entities such as the IMF (International Monetary Fund) and the World Bank have a direct hand in shaping many of its aspects. And as regards education, there are a good number of grassroots groups, such as Christian development NGOs (nongovernmental organizations), which partake in building and operating schools. All across Africa, then, state regimes are operating within a larger assemblage of governance composed of transnational NGOs and other large-scale nonstate agencies. Ferguson and Gupta refer to this larger assemblage as an "emerging system of transnational governmentality."

Technico Sciences

The third section of the book underscores the technological nature of scientific knowledge. The basic assumption here is that knowledges cannot be understood simply as contemplative pursuits. Rather, they have to be viewed as eminently practical phenomena. Or, to phrase it in Nikolas Rose's terms, they have to be viewed as "intellectual technologies" – as specific ways of seeing and diagnosing that represent and analyze reality in a manner that renders it not only intelligible but also amenable to political programming (1998: 120). The point, simply put, is that knowledges are in themselves technical means that enable interventions into social processes.

In chapter 5, David Horn engages this understanding of knowledge as technical means by focusing on the "invention of the criminal anthropologist" in nineteenth-century Italy. Emphasized in the essay is how this figure emerged "as a new kind of scientific expert, qualified to read the deviant body and to diagnose social dangers." Two key points are worth noting here. One is that the ability of the criminal anthropologist to establish scientific authority rested fundamentally on tools and techniques. These ranged from mundane instruments like compasses, eye charts, measuring tapes, and magnets to more exotic mechanisms such as the Anfosso tachianthropometer, Broca's auricular goniometer, and Sieweking's esthesiometer. What these instruments enabled the criminal anthropologist to do is measure the body and claim the capacity to produce objective knowledge about it – particularly about its normality and pathology. The second point is that the criminal anthropologist "measured, palpated, shocked, sketched, photographed, and displayed" bodies not for the sake of creating abstract knowledge but "in order that judges, penologists, educators, and social planners might be guided in the identification and treatment of individuals, and in the development of appropriate measures of social hygiene." Otherwise said, the knowledge that this scientific expert produced was fundamentally practical: designed to intervene in social life.

In chapter 6, Adriana Petryna undertakes her exploration of knowledge's technological character by focusing on the management of the aftermath of the Chernobyl (Ukraine) nuclear disaster. One of her main arguments is that, "with Chernobyl, science left the domain of the experiment and became central to . . . regulating the terms in which individuals are included in the public realm of citizenship." When the Chernobyl catastrophe took place, Ukraine was still part of the Soviet Union. Consequently, it was the Soviet administration that initially managed the fallout. Their response can generally be described as technically lax. They established a high threshold of allowable radiation dose intakes; significantly restricted the size of the area considered contaminated; and only selectively measured individual and population-wide exposures. Following the break-up of the Soviet Union, the responsibility for managing the Chernobyl aftermath shifted principally to the new state of Ukraine. Ukrainian officials promptly denounced the Soviets as having willfully disregarded the lives of exposed populations, and then set a new course of intervention. This new course entailed lowering the radiation threshold dose, expanding the territories judged contaminated, and stepping up efforts to collect knowledge about and identify exposed populations. Perhaps more significant though, in a context where the state was generally downscaling its social welfare system, a large number of newly designated Chernobyl sufferers were afforded compensation – in the form, for example, of preferential and free medical treatment. The significant thing about this is that, in this downscaled welfare context, claiming biological injury – through the medium of scientific knowledge – becomes one of the few legitimate ways for individuals to get access to social protection: that is, citizenship.

Biosocial Subjects

The fourth section focuses on how contemporary genetic knowledges and technologies are giving shape to new practices of life. What has generally happened is that, as a result of new understandings of vital processes at the molecular level, life has become open to all kinds of calculated intervention and reformation. The ramifications of this capacity to know and manipulate the basic elements of life are tremendous. It essentially means that: "Existence is being lived according to new coordinates, a new game of life is now being played" (Rose 2001: 16).

In chapter 7, Paul Rabinow refers to this new game of life as biosociality. Or, to be more specific, biosociality names how the new genetics is operationalizing nature in such a manner as to model it "on culture understood as practice." The idea here is simply that biological life is no longer regarded as destiny or fixed endowment but as something to be reworked. It is that the vital order is coming to be "known and remade through technique" and thus turning overtly artificial. One important instantiation of biosociality that Rabinow highlights is the "formation of new group and individual identities and practices" out of new genetic truths. What he shows is that, through genetic screening practices, individuals can now be revealed to be at risk of developing certain genetic disorders. Notably, these individuals, as well as those actually living with particular maladies, are joining into groups and demanding recognition, calling for civil rights, and making claims on the use of biomedical research and technologies. For example, there are "neurofibromatosis groups who meet to share their experiences, lobby for their disease, educate their children, redo their home environment, and so on." As vital processes become an object of technical manipulation, then, we end up with the cultivation of new subjects – which one might call biosocial – who understand themselves through their biology and engage in all sorts of new life practices aimed at fostering individual and collective health.

In chapter 8, Karen-Sue Taussig, Rayna Rapp, and Deborah Heath similarly take up the question of biosocial subject formation. The biosocial subjects they focus on are Little People (LPs) – that is, people living with various forms of heritable dwarfism. Highlighted in their analysis is how LPs deploy an ethics of self-care in order to resist the normalizing practices of modern power. In the contemporary United States, LPs live in a society characterized by what Taussig et al. call flexible eugenics. This term refers to how advances in biotechnology – such as gene therapy, prenatal testing, and genetic diagnosis – are making it possible for people to improve, and desire to improve, their biological assets and achieve individual perfectibility. A key implication of flexible eugenics is the possibility of the United States becoming a genetically normalized society: a society where the ability to intervene into life processes and detect "abnormal" genetic states – such as dwarfism – will lead to the elimination of such states. In this context, one thing that LPs are doing – specifically those associated with the Little People of America (LPA), a national advocacy organization for people of short stature – is resisting "the push to perfectibility." They are resisting this push through rejecting the stigma associated with atypical bodies and affirming the value of dwarf children and of dwarves having babies. What we have here again, then, are subjects who understand themselves through biology. In this case, though, their desire is not necessarily to overcome this biology but to engage in life practices that affirm it.

Necropolitical Projects[4]

The final section of the book explores what could be called the underside of biopower. We can call this underside "necropolitics" (or perhaps hygienic governmentality). Foucault, of course, famously defined biopower as "what brought life and its mechanisms into the realm of explicit calculations" (1980: 143). Thus defined, scholars have generally interpreted this technology of power as simply a life-affirming power – one aimed at investing life and making it grow. However, Foucault also noted that there was another side to biopower. It is often the case, he suggested, that "entire populations are mobilized for the purpose of wholesale slaughter in the name of life necessity" (1980: 137). This means that biopower does not just foster life; it also routinely does away with it in order to preserve it. The reasoning here is that the death of the other – that is, of those deemed dangerous, unfit, or diseased – will make life in general more healthy and pure.[5]

The idea, then, is that under the logic of biopower, it is possible to simultaneously protect life and to authorize a holocaust.

In chapter 9, Diane Nelson explores the underside of biopower by focusing on the waging of war in Guatemala. She discusses two wars: one is the civil war (1962–96) that took place between the right-wing military state and, roughly speaking, leftist revolutionaries; the other the war against malaria (1955 to the present). From the perspective of the state, the goal in each instance was to eliminate the enemy. In the case of the civil war, the state sought to accomplish this end largely through techniques of terror and violence – massacres, torture-murder, and disappearance. The result was very much a genocidal politics: thousands upon thousands of people were put to death. In the case of the war against malaria, the state pursued its objective through organizing "brigades to fan out across the countryside to test for malaria, hunt mosquitoes, destroy breeding areas, administer quinine for free, and spray down walls." The result was, if not the elimination of malaria, the definite improvement of the health of the population. The situation we end up with in Guatemala is thus one in which the state is at once a purveyor of death and life. There is no contradiction here though: the elimination of revolutionaries, like the elimination of malaria, is done in the name of protecting the life of the social body.

In chapter 10, João Biehl takes up his examination of the underside of biopower through the case of AIDS policy in Brazil. Highlighted in this account is Brazil's creation – with the help of activists, politicians, economists, and scientists – of an impressive administrative apparatus designed to contain the spread of AIDS through community-mediated prevention projects and to extend the lives of people afflicted with the disease by making drug therapies freely available. These efforts, according to officials, have produced vital results: they have led to a decline in both new AIDS cases and AIDS mortality rates. This is not all there is to the story though. Biehl also shows that the AIDS apparatus does not target all populations alike. A large number of the poorest of the poor, for example, have only sporadic contact with AIDS testing services and medical care. These individuals are just not objects of prevention and treatment programs. Their lives are not deemed worthy of being extended. The result: numerous poor people with AIDS are dying in abandonment. The implicit logic here is that the death of these unhealthy elements will lead to a more vigorous and productive citizenry.

Such, then, are these Foucauldian anthropologies of modernity. And such is this volume. Provided here is essentially an introduction to a particular way of thinking and style of analysis: one that draws attention to the heterogeneous forces – forms of knowledge, types of authorities, and practical mechanisms – that seek to shape the conduct of individuals and populations in order to effect certain ends. What we get is a concern with how practices of modern government are materialized in specific times and places. The hope is that readers will find productive this attempt to make our present intelligible.

Notes

1   The work of several scholars informs the reading of Foucault presented here: Rabinow (1984), McNay (1994), Hindess (1996), Dean (1999), and Rose (1999).
2   The anthropological concern with the "will to govern," as will become clear, is somewhat different from that of Foucault. In his periodization of the modern, Foucault reaches back to and assigns a great deal of significance to sixteenth-century arts of government. By contrast, the essays in the volume concentrate on the post-Enlightenment period and most actually deal with current events. So for anthropologists what matters about the modern is not so much its emergence as its present-day manifestations.
3   Notable exceptions include Perry and Maurer (2003) and Ong and Collier (2004).
4   I'm borrowing the term "necropolitical" from Achille Mbembe (2003).
5   This death does not have to be direct death (or the literal act of putting to death). It could also be indirect death: the act of exposing to death, of multiplying for some the risk of death, or simply political death, expulsion, rejection, or exclusion.

References

Castel, Robert
    1981   La gestion des risques: De l'anti-psychiatrie à l'après-psychanalyse. Paris: Editions de Minuit.
Collier, Stephen J., and Aihwa Ong
    2003   Oikos/Anthropos: Rationality, Technology, Infrastructure. Current Anthropology 44(3): 421–426.
Cruikshank, Barbara
    1999   The Will to Empower: Democratic Citizens and Other Subjects. Ithaca: Cornell University Press.
Dean, Mitchell
    1991   The Constitution of Poverty: Toward a Genealogy of Liberal Governance. New York: Routledge.
    1999   Governmentality: Power and Rule in Modern Society. London: Sage Publications.
Defert, Daniel
    1991   "Popular Life" and Insurance Technology. In The Foucault Effect: Studies in Governmentality. Graham Burchell, Colin Gordon, and Peter Miller, eds. Pp. 211–233. Chicago: University of Chicago Press.
Ewald, Françoise
    1986   L'état providence. Paris: Grasset.
Foucault, Michel
    1979   Discipline and Punish: The Birth of the Prison. New York: Vintage Books.
    1980   The History of Sexuality, vol. 1: An Introduction. New York: Vintage Books.

2000   Governmentality. *In* The Essential Works of Foucault, 1954–1984, vol. 3: Power. James D. Faubion, ed. Pp. 201–222. New York: New Press.

Greenhalgh, Susan
2003   Planned Births, Unplanned Persons: "Population" in the Making of Chinese Modernity. American Ethnologist 30(2): 196–215.

Hindess, Barry
1996   Discourses of Power: From Hobbes to Foucault. Malden, MA: Blackwell.

Horn, David G.
1994   Social Bodies: Science, Reproduction, and Italian Modernity. Princeton: Princeton University Press.
2003   The Criminal Body: Lombroso and the Anatomy of Deviance. New York: Routledge.

Kalpagam, U.
2002   Colonial Governmentality and the Public Sphere in India. Journal of Historical Sociology 15(1): 35–58.

Latour, Bruno
1986   Visualization and Cognition: Thinking with Eyes and Hands. Knowledge and Society 6: 1–40.

McNay, Lois
1994   Foucault: A Critical Introduction. New York: Continuum.

Mbembe, Achille
2003 Necropolitics. Public Culture 15(1): 11–40.

Miller, Peter, and Nikolas Rose
1990   Governing Economic Life. Economy and Society 19(1): 1–31.

O'Malley, Pat
1992   Risk, Power, and Crime Prevention. Economy and Society 21(3): 252–275.

Ong, Aihwa
1995   Making the Biopolitical Subject: Cambodian Immigrants, Refugee Medicine, and Cultural Citizenship in California. Social Science and Medicine 40(9): 1243–1257.
1999   Flexible Citizenship: The Cultural Logics of Transnationality. Durham, NC: Duke University Press.

Ong, Aihwa, and Stephen J. Collier, eds.
2004   Global Assemblages: Technology, Politics, and Ethics as Anthropological Problems. Malden, MA: Blackwell.

Perry, Richard Warren, and Bill Maurer
2003   Globalization and Governmentality: An Introduction. *In* Globalization Under Construction: Governmentality, Law, and Identity. Richard Warren Perry and Bill Maurer, eds. Pp. ix–xxi. Minneapolis: University of Minnesota Press.

Procacci, Giovanna
1993   Gouverner la misère: La question sociale en France, 1789–1848. Paris: Editions du Seuil.

Rabinow, Paul
1984   Introduction. *In* The Foucault Reader. Paul Rabinow, ed. Pp. 3–29. New York: Pantheon Books.
1989   French Modern: Norms and Forms of the Social Environment. Cambridge, MA: MIT Press.

2003   Anthropos Today: Reflections on Modern Equipment. Princeton: Princeton University Press.

Rose, Nikolas

1996   Governing "Advanced" Liberal Democracies. *In* Foucault and Political Reason: Liberalism, Neo-Liberalism, and Rationalities of Government. Andrew Barry, Thomas Osborne, and Nikolas Rose, eds. Pp. 37–64. Chicago: University of Chicago Press.

1998   Inventing Our Selves: Psychology, Power, and Personhood. Cambridge: Cambridge University Press.

1999   Powers of Freedom: Reframing Political Thought. Cambridge: Cambridge University Press.

2000   Government and Control. British Journal of Criminology 40: 321–339.

2001   The Politics of Life Itself. Theory, Culture & Society 18(6): 1–30.

Rose, Nikolas, and Peter Miller

1992   Political Power Beyond the State: Problematics of Government. British Journal of Sociology 43(2): 173–205.

Ruhl, Lealle

1999   Liberal Governance and Prenatal Care: Risk and Regulation in Pregnancy. Economy and Society 28(1): 95–117.

Stoler, Ann Laura

1995   Race and the Education of Desire: Foucault's *History of Sexuality* and the Colonial Order of Things. Durham, NC: Duke University Press.

Walters, William

2000   Unemployment and Government: Genealogies of the Social. Cambridge: Cambridge University Press.

Weir, Lorna

1996   Recent Developments in the Government of Pregnancy. Economy and Society 25(3): 372–392.

Part I
Colonial Reasons

Part I
Colonial Reasons

1

Colonial Governmentality

David Scott

Maybe what is really important for our modernity – that is, for our present – is not so much the étatisation *of society, as the "governmentalization" of the state.*

Michel Foucault, "Governmentality"

Within the modern world which has come into being, changes have taken place as the effect of dominant political power by which new possibilities are constructed and old ones destroyed. The changes do not reflect a simple expansion of the range of individual choice, but the creation of conditions in which only new (i.e., modern) choices can be made. The reason for this is that the changes involve the re-formation of subjectivities and the re-organization of social spaces in which subjects act and are acted upon. The modern state – imperial, colonial, post-colonial – has been crucial to these processes of construction/destruction.

Talal Asad, "Conscripts of Western Civilisation"

Reformulating the Question about Colonialism

The above remarks on modernity by the late Michel Foucault and Talal Asad mark out the problem-field in which the argument in this chapter is to be situated. I want to inquire into what appears to me a problem in the now considerably advanced discussion about colonialism – a problem that turns very much on the question of what is distinctive about the political rationality of forms of power, on the one hand, and on the other, on those transformations effected by *modern* power, the consequence of which is that the old, premodern possibilities are not only no longer conceptually approachable except in the languages of the modern, but are now no longer available as practical historical options. Stated baldly (and therefore at the risk of some simplification) the problem that animates this

Reprinted from David Scott, "Colonial Governmentality," in *Refashioning Futures: Criticism After Postcoloniality.* Princeton: Princeton University Press, 1999, pp. 23–52.

chapter is the following: If it is the case, as many critics of colonialism now agree, that Europe has been too much at the center of our theoretical knowledges of the colonial and postcolonial world – and that, in virtue of this, these knowledges typically privilege the colonial state's autobiography, its cultural values, its presumption of an all-pervasive and totalizing influence, its marginalization of resistance and the many local ways of incipient anticolonial refusal – what then is the *conceptual* level to be assigned to "Europe" understood not merely as a geographical space but as an apparatus of dominant power-effects? My question, it is easy to see, presupposes that the critique of European hegemony in the construction of knowledges about the non-European world – the "decentering" of Europe – ought not to be confused (as I think it very often is) with programmatically ignoring Europe, as though by doing so one would have resolved the problem of Eurocentrism.[1] My question presupposes, in other words, that there is a difference – and a consequential one – between the polemical dismissal of Europe and its conceptual repositioning, between the Fanonian rhetoric of forgetting Europe and an investigation in which those structures and rationalities through which Europe's colonial projects were organized come more prominently into view.[2] My question, in short, is aimed at interrupting that conceptual formulation that seeks little more than an inversion of the colonial habit of deploying "Europe" as the universal subject of all history.

In recent years, a good deal of the discussion about colonialism has tended to center on colonialism's *attitude* toward the colonized and the question of its *exclusionary* discourses and practices – whether these discourses and practices have to do with exclusion of the colonized from humanity (colonialism's racism), or their exclusion from the institutions of political sovereignty (colonialism's false liberalism). Thus, one strand of the critique of colonialist discourse, for instance, one which owes much to Edward Said's *Orientalism*, has been centrally concerned to demonstrate how colonialist textuality works at the level of image and language to produce a distorted representation of the colonized. This strategy has sought to expose the devices through which the colonized have been denied voice, autonomy, and agency. Another strategy, less concerned with the rhetorical economy of texts and more with the institutional mechanisms of colonial dominance, has sought to show the hollow – indeed, the ideological – content of colonialism's claim to have introduced the colonies to liberal-democratic political principles, the principles of good and humane government, and thus to have enabled that modernizing transition from the "rule of force" to the "rule of law." It has been easy to demonstrate that these exalted liberal principles never entailed a political equality between colonizer and colonized.[3] In large measure, therefore, the critique of colonialist discourse has constituted itself as a kind of *writing back* at the West, as a critical practice of making visible, on the one hand, the internal economy of this discourse, as well as, on the other, the active resistances of the colonized. Assuredly, these strategies have operated different thematic domains, but they both share the field of a general problematic in which what is at stake is the way colonialism as a practice of power works to include or exclude the colonized.

I should like to set this problematic aside and introduce in its place one that is not centrally concerned with whether or how power works to include or exclude portions of the colonized, and that in consequence is not concerned with the arrogance or even with the "epistemic violence" of colonialist discourse as such. The problematic with which I am concerned takes as its object what I shall call the *political rationalities* of colonial power. By this obviously Foucauldian formulation I mean those historically constituted complexes of knowledge/power that give shape to colonial projects of political sovereignty. A colonial political rationality characterizes those ways in which colonial power is organized as an activity designed to produce effects of rule. More specifically, what I mean to illuminate are what I call the *targets* of colonial power (the point or points of power's application; the object or objects it aims at; and the means and instrumentalities it deploys in search of these targets, points, and objects) and the *field* of its operation (the zone that it actively constructs for its functionality). What this reformulation of the question of colonialism is seeking to do, therefore, is to suggest a way of bringing into conceptual view, of bringing into critical thought, the problem of the formation of historically heterogeneous rationalities through which the political sovereignties of colonial rule were constructed and operated. Conceived in this way, the problem about "Europe" for colonialism ought to be re-posed. Because if, as I argue is the case, what ought to be understood are the political rationalities of colonial power, then what now becomes important is not a "decentering" of Europe as such, but in fact a critical interrogation of the practices, modalities, and projects through which *the varied forms of its insertion* into the lives of the colonized were constructed and organized.

In this chapter, then, what interests me about the problem of colonialism in relation to the political forms of modernity is the emergence at a moment in colonialism's history of a form of power – that is, therefore, *a form of power not merely coincident with colonialism* – which was concerned above all with disabling old forms of life by systematically breaking down their conditions, and with constructing in their place new conditions so as to enable – indeed, so as to *oblige* – new forms of life to come into being. I am concerned with a way of understanding colonial power that brings *this* transformation into focus. For what is at stake in this transformation is not merely the notion of a "break" with the past. After all, such a notion is very familiar to us in the liberal and nationalist narratives of modernization. What is at stake is *how this break is configured* and *what it is understood to consist in.* And where the stories of modernization conceive of this break as producing an expansion of the range of choice, the expansion of freedom, the problematic with which I am concerned is interested in the *reorganization* of the terrain in which choice as such is possible, and the political rationality upon which that reorganization depended.

Reiterating, then, the provisional nature of my explorations, what I propose to do is the following: First, I will spell out some aspects of one recent argument about colonial power with a view to setting off the kinds of questions I think are important. Here, it should be clear that what I am attempting to do is to focus on the problem of power and the modern in their colonial career in such a way as to cast into relief the *conceptual level* at which they have often been thought out. Second, I try to say how the problem of modern power might more usefully be thought for my purposes and why I think Foucault's notion of "governmentality" and the kind of investigation it is concerned to illuminate might be helpful in this. And third, I will attempt to rethink in these terms the story of the formation of modern colonial power in Sri Lanka.[4]

The Problem about Colonial Power

The thrust of my argument can be clarified if I set it off against a recent intervention to which it is allied but with which it differs in certain important respects. Partha Chatterjee has criticized with considerable force the liberal historiography of colonialism that reproduces the view "that colonial rule was not really about colonial rule but something else." He begins by posing the following questions:

> Does it serve any useful analytical purpose to make a distinction between the colonial state and the forms of the modern state? Or should we regard the colonial state as simply another specific form in which the modern state has generalized itself across the globe? If the latter is the case, then of course the specifically colonial form of the emergence of the institutions of the modern state would be of only incidental, or at best episodic, interest; it would not be a necessary part of the larger, and more important, historical narrative of modernity.[5]

In this formulation of the problem of colonial power, Chatterjee marks a distinction between colonial and modern power in such a way as to bring into focus the specificity of the former. In Chatterjee's view, unless we produce this conceptual distinction we shall be left with no recourse but to see the colonial as little more than an episode in modern – *Europe's* – history. We shall see in a moment why Chatterjee feels obliged to formulate the relation between colonialism and modernity in the way he does, that is, as a simple opposition. On my view, however, this formulation is not a conceptually adequate one. This is not because I think the question – What is the specificity of *colonial* power? – irrelevant, but because, as I shall suggest, I think that unless the formulation of that question is made to depend upon a prior reconstruction of the historically differentiated structures and projects of colonial rule (the discontinuities *within* the colonial, in other words), we run the risk of a too-hasty homogenization of colonialism as a whole. In other words, my worry is that in formulating the question as he does (in a simple counter-position of colonial and modern), Chatterjee preempts an inquiry that would allow us to sort out those political rationalities that constituted colonialism in its *historically varied configurations*, and therefore enable us to mark the modernity *of a turn* in the career of colonial power.

Chatterjee's argument – carried out on the terrain of the historiography of colonial India – is perhaps most importantly directed not so much at older schools of blatantly colonialist historians as at more recent "revisionist" schools – and the "new Cambridge" school in particular.[6] On his account of it, there are two parts to the revisionist argument. The first involves a periodizing distinction between earlier and later phases of colonial rule in which the crucial period of "transition" is roughly 1780–1830.[7] On the revisionist view, the earlier colonial regimes are argued to be largely "continuations" of prior indigenous regimes. What seems to be suggested is that colonialism, far from constituting a complete break with the past (as had hitherto been assumed by both colonialist and nationalist historians), can be shown to have an organic, internal connection to it. The second part of the revisionist argument turns on the assignment of "agency" in the establishment of empire. The revisionists, influenced by recent trends in historical writing (world-systems theory, for example) and mindful of recent criticisms made by radical Third World scholars (regarding the question of *making* history), are explicitly concerned to show that contrary to the conventional colonialist view, Indians have always been the active subjects of their own history and not the mere passive victims of it. Ironically however, Chatterjee argues, their seemingly benevolent bestowal of agency only has the effect of making the colonized the authors of their own domination and, in so doing, safely deflects the force of anticolonial politics. On the whole, then, Chatterjee maintains that in this revisionist view, colonialism as a distinctive formation all but disappears. For what this view does, he says, is to "spirit away the violent intrusion of colonialism and make all of its features the innate property of an indigenous history."[8]

It is evident, then, that Chatterjee interposes the questions with which he begins in order to take issue with a very prominent view in the contemporary historiography of colonial India. They are meant to operate as a critique of the persistence into the present of an ideological *erasure* in liberal historiography by means of which the assumptions of universal history work to displace – indeed one might say, to *repress* – the specificity of colonial power. This is all very well. But, its polemical cash value aside, it is not clear to me why this kind of critical move need hang on a conceptual opposition that makes colonialism a singular reiterated instance. It seems to me important to insist upon a certain kind of historicization of Europe's power, one that clarifies the distinctiveness of – and the transformation entailed in – the making of *modern* power in its colonial career. On my view, therefore, the distinction between earlier and later forms of colonial rule *is* a potentially useful one, though what is crucial for me is the *kind* of elaboration of the structure and project of colonial power it is made to turn on.[9]

For Chatterjee, what is distinctive about colonial power is its deployment of what he calls a "rule of colonial difference," the rule or principle by which, across differently inflected ideological positions within the field of colonialist discourse, the colonized are represented as inferior, as radically Other. And on his view, "race" is the defining signifier of this rule of difference. It is "race" that marks the specificity of colonial power. As he puts it, "the more the logic of a modern regime of power pushed the processes of government in the direction of a rationalization of administration and the normalization of the objects of its rule, the more insistently did the issue of race come up to emphasize the specifically colonial character of British dominance in India."[10] But this very formulation itself (with its accent on temporality, and suggestive therefore of the historicity of the colonial) urges us to ask at least three questions. First, did this rule of difference operate *in the same way* across the entire length of colonial dominance? Or ought there to be a way of understanding this rule *in relation to* differently configured modes of organization of power, different political rationalities, over the historical period of colonial dominance? Part of the point here is that as a classificatory signifier, what constituted "race" (and therefore what uses it was available for) altered between, say, the eighteenth and nineteenth centuries, and, most important, within the latter. Second, if the rule of colonial difference is a rule of exclusion/inclusion (and all power may be said to operate through the construction of such a principle of difference) what are the specific power-effects of "race"? In other words, even if as a system of representation "race" can be shown to operate across the colonial period, what also needs to be understood and specified is when and through what kind of political rationality it becomes inserted into *subject-constituting* social practices, into the formation, that is to say, of certain kinds of "raced" subjectivities.[11] But third, to even assert that "race" can be said to characterize the Othering practices of colonialist discourse as such – that is, in *all* its historical instantiations – is, to begin with, a very shortsighted claim. As a number of students of the European encounter with peoples in the New World in the sixteenth century have argued, for instance, it was not "race" but "religion" (or more properly, the lack of one) that constituted the discursive frame within which the "difference" of the non-European was conceived and represented.[12]

The point, therefore, is that the crucial question is not whether there is a difference between the colonial state and forms of the modern state in Europe, but how to impose an historicity on our understanding of the rationalities that organized the forms of the colonial state. This is because on my view, something called "*the* colonial state" cannot offer itself up as the iteration and reiteration of a single political rationality. Rather what is necessary to understand, it seems to me, is that within the structures and projects that gave shape to the colonial enterprise as a whole, there were discontinuities in which different political rationalities, different configurations of power, took the stage in commanding positions. To be sure, modern power in its colonial career may indeed have operated by "rules of difference" nonidentical with those in its European career. But for me, approaching this entails a prior understanding of the alteration that brings into being the distinctively "modern" in which this rule of difference was to produce its effects. So that, on my view, side by side those questions in which the central problem about colonial power is whether or not and by what sign of difference power included or excluded portions of the native population, there are another set of questions. And these take the following form: In any historical instance, what does colonial power seek to organize and reorganize? In other words, what does colonial power take as the *target* upon which to work? Moreover, what *project* does it require that target-object for? And how does it go about securing it in order to realize its ends? In short, what in each instance is colonial power's *structure* and *project* as it inserts itself into – or more properly, as it *constitutes* – the domain of the colonial? These questions, it seems to me, do not deny the relevance of the idea of a rule of colonial difference, but its comprehension is now framed by a differently inflected problematic. And what is crucial to this problematic is historicizing European colonial rule in such a way as to distinguish different modes of organizing colonial power and the different political rationalities they depended upon. The important questions, in other words, have to do with the nature of the terrain available for the colonized to produce their responses. For what is important to understand, as I shall try to outline in a moment, is that with the formation of the political rationality of the *modern* colonial state, not only the rules of the political game but *the political game itself* changed[13] – not only did the relation of forces between colonizer and colonized change, but so did *the terrain* of the political struggle itself. And therefore, on my view, not only accommodation but resistance as well would have to articulate itself in relation to this comprehensively altered situation.

The Problem about Modern Power

In effect, then, not *less* Europe, but a differently configured one; not a reified Europe, but a problematized one. The point is that an understanding of the non-Western world's modernities ought to be informed by a more nuanced and discerning understanding of Europe's pasts and its modernities, grasping especially "its peculiar historicity, the mobile powers that have constructed its structures, projects, and desires."[14] The reason for this is obviously not because the modernities of the non-Western world are somehow "derived" from Europe's and that *therefore* an understanding of the "original," as it were, would repay the effort. Rather it is because those "structures, projects, and desires" of Europe generated changing ways of impacting the non-Western world, changing ways of imposing and maintaining rule over the colonized, and therefore changing terrains within which to respond. Needless to say, this is not the place to pursue an elaborate discussion of European modernities. But it is important to note, I think, that recently, and across a variety of intersecting theoretical discourses, the story of those modernities has been undergoing a considerable critical reexamination and revision. This has started to alter the picture we have of Europe's pasts in a manner that interrupts, indeed sweeps away, the consoling fable of the Enlightenment's long developmental march of reason and freedom.[15] What I should like to do here, however, is to foreground two distinctive features of the political rationality of modern power that have a special bearing on the problem of the colonial modern that I take up in the following section of this chapter. Following on my earlier remarks on political rationality, the first of these features will have to do with the point of application of modern power; the second, with the field of its operation. My argument is that historicizing Europe by way of an attention to these features is indispensable for a more discriminating inquiry into the modernities of the colonial and postcolonial world because it will enable us to understand the specificity of the terrain – including, most crucially, the specificity of the apparatus of power – in relation to which the colonized constructed their own very varied forms of response.

As Talal Asad has suggested, modern power is distinctive not so much – as varieties of modernization theory would have it – for its relation to capitalism or to the social and institutional differentiation that expands the possibility for individual freedom.[16] Rather, modern power is distinctive for its *point of application*. And the point of application of modern power is not so much the body of the sovereign's subject (we are all familiar with the stunning image of Michel Foucault's "body of the condemned")[17] as the *conditions* in which that body is to live and define its life. This is, of course, because of modern power's relation to Enlightenment reason. As we know, the Enlightenment belief in progress rested on an idea of reason that was irreconcilably opposed to forms of understanding and action that depended upon what it called superstition and prejudice. For these, it argued, by disabling individual rational judgment and encouraging timidity and fear, left people in blind obedience to the capricious tyranny of despots and priests. However, the emancipation from this moral slavery and the eradication of benighted ignorance could not be carried out by the mere alteration of a few false notions and the superficial tinkering with behaviors. What was required instead was first, their fundamental uprooting by means of a broad attack on the *conditions* that were understood to produce them, and second, their systematic *replacement* by the inducement of new conditions based on clear, sound, and rational principles.[18]

At the end of the eighteenth century and beginning of the nineteenth, this view was engaged in argument with an older way of thinking best exemplified perhaps in the "traditionalist" thought of Edmund Burke. For Burke, as he asserted nowhere more viscerally than in the *Reflections on the Revolution in France*, the institutions of political society were not to be understood by means of a handful of abstract maxims regarding the general nature of society as such. These institutions, being the product of the accumulation of generations of specific experience built up slowly over the course of uncountable years, changing and adjusting as contingencies warranted, could only be judged with reference to this immemorial usage, with reference, that is, to custom. This is not to say that Burke was hostile to reform as such – he was hostile only to what he considered a dogmatic, arrogant, and dangerous spirit of reform which believed that by the application of a priori principles, a society which had existed time out of mind could be suddenly, irrevocably, pulled down and constructed anew in conformity with reason.[19] To this, of course, Enlightenment reason responded with confident scorn. For on the view it advanced – and one sees this, for instance, as much in Jeremy Bentham's early work, *A Fragment on Government*, published more than a decade and a half before Burke's *Reflections*, as in Thomas Paine's *Rights of Man*, which was a response to it – reason, seeing as it did into the very nature of things, had a prescriptive and an aggressively programmatic mission, the accomplishment of which entailed striking uncompromisingly at the presumed foundation of error.[20] This, then, is the first distinctive feature of modern power that needs to be foregrounded. And it is in this sense too – the sense of an alteration of grounds, of fundamental bases – that it is important to speak of the modern as forming a *break* with what went before, a break beyond which there is no return, and in which what comes after can only be read in, read through, and read against the categories of the modern. This is the point, I think, that Zygmunt Bauman is urging in the following very striking passage regarding the inauguration of the modern:

> This world which preceded the bifurcation into order and chaos we find difficult to describe in its own terms. We try to grasp it mostly with the help of negations: we tell ourselves what that world was not, what it did not contain, what it was unaware of. That world would hardly have recognized itself in our descriptions. It would not understand what we are talking about. It would not survive such understandings. The moment of understanding would be (and it was) the sign of its approaching death. And of the birth of modernity.[21]

At the same time, if modern power is concerned with disabling nonmodern forms of life by dismantling their conditions, then its aim in putting in place new and different conditions is above all to produce governing-effects on conduct. Modern power seeks to arrange and rearrange these conditions (conditions at once discursive and nondiscursive) so as to oblige subjects to transform themselves in a certain, that is, *improving*, direction. And if this is so, if the government of conduct is the distinctive strategic end of modern power, then the decisive (which is *not* to say the only) locus of its operation is the new domain of "civil society." The idea of civil society, now enjoying something of a revival, belongs, of course, to an old, premodern tradition of political thought reaching back at least to Aristotle's *Politics*.[22] In its modern career, however (that is, roughly since those remarkable moral philosophers of the Scottish Enlightenment like Adam Ferguson, whose *Essay on the History of Civil Society* appeared in 1767), it has come to mark off a domain separate and distinct from the state. In other words, the modern concept of civil society amounted to an attempt to think the emerging forms of relation that were organized by new regularities, new forms of skeptical knowledge, new grounds for judgment, and new communicative technologies – the emerging forms of a relation that signal, in a phrase, "the rise of the social," as Hannah Arendt aptly called it.[23]

This is, of course, the great theme of Jürgen Habermas's early work, *The Structural Transformation of the Public Sphere*.[24] It will be recalled that what Habermas is concerned to do in this now much discussed book is to provide an historical and sociological account of the emergence – and subsequent decomposition – of a domain distinctive, even constitutive, of the European modern: the bourgeois "public sphere."[25] This public sphere emerges in the eighteenth century as a product of new commercial relationships that involve a traffic in commodities and news – and indeed in news as a kind of commodity. It forms a component of that wider realm of civil society that is establishing itself at the same time as a corollary of the depersonalized state and as the realm of commodity exchange and social labor governed by its own regularities in such a way that what is effected is a convergence between private interest and public good. The public sphere, Habermas argues, is preeminently that sphere in which private individuals come together as a public to make use of their reason as the ground of critical authority and judgment. However, since for Habermas this story of the public sphere of civil society is by and large a chapter in the story of the progressive emancipation of an enlightened domain of unrestricted and rational discussion of matters of general interest (and of the contemporary threat to that progress in the widespread advance of technocratic consciousness), it still reads like the familiar improving story of modernization.[26] And therefore, sociologically rich as it may appear to be as an historical account, what gets elided from its comprehension of modernity is of course *power* – power understood not as the antithesis of freedom and reason (in which freedom emerges as a product of the progressive rationalization of power), but power as the general name of a relation in which differential effects of one action upon another are produced. More specifically, what gets elided is the emergence of a new – that is, *modern* – political rationality in which power works not *in spite of* but *through* the construction of a subjectivity normatively experienced as the source of free will and rational, autonomous agency. It is this conception of a form of power, not merely traversing the domain of the social, but constructing the normative (i.e., enabling/constraining) regularities that positively constitute civil society, that Michel Foucault tries to think in his work on "governmentality."[27]

In some of his later lectures at the Collège de France and elsewhere (in a period in which, as we know, the entire *History of Sexuality* project was being rethought),[28] Foucault devoted a good deal of attention to the theme of modern political power – its rationality, its sources, its character, its targets – constructing a story, as one can well imagine, as much historical as historiographical, as much substantive as critical.[29] Part of the point of this work is to invite us to rethink the story told by liberalism and Marxism alike, according to which the state is the privileged site of an immense and magical power standing in opposition to a civil society imagined as the absence of power and the fulfillment of freedom.[30] What interests Foucault is the emergence in early modern Europe of a new form of political rationality that combines simultaneously two seemingly contradictory modalities of power: one, totalizing and centralizing, the other individualizing and normalizing.[31] This form of political rationality he calls "governmental" rationality of "governmentality." "How to govern oneself, how to be governed, how to govern others, by whom the people will accept being governed, how to become the best possible governor – all these problems," writes Foucault, "in their multiplicity and intensity, seem to me to be characteristic of the sixteenth century, which lies, to put it schematically, at the crossroads of two processes: the one which, shattering the structures of feudalism, leads to the establishment of the great territorial, administrative and colonial states; and that totally different movement which, with the Reformation and Counter-Reformation, raises the issue of how one must be spiritually ruled and led on this earth in order to achieve eternal salvation."[32] Now on his account, the first threshold of this governmental form of political rationality is that complex early modern ensemble of power known as mercantilism. However, while there emerges in the late sixteenth and seventeenth centuries systematic disciplinary techniques for working upon latent individual capacities and reconstructing individual behaviors,[33] and the institution of "police" for the detailed regulation of order and the maintenance of good conduct in the community,[34] mercantilism by and large remains within the objectives of an older political rationality, that of "sovereignty." This is because the problem of politics remains above all the preservation and strengthening of the state, the enhancement of the prince's wealth and power against his military and commercial rivals through the conquest, colonization, and exploitation of the non-European world. It is in fact only with the emergence of "population" as an object of political calculation at the end of the eighteenth century that there comes into being the historical conditions for the displacement of the problematic of sovereignty by "government."

Now, I want to draw out two distinctions in Foucault's conceptualization of the political rationality of government. The first is between sovereignty and government; and the second between discipline and government. Within the political rationality of sovereignty, individuals are dependent upon the absolute authority of the prince; they are subjects of, and subject to, his power and protection. Here law is deployed as an instrumentality, a direct means toward the primary political end of commanding obedience. With government, by contrast, says Foucault, "it is a question not of imposing law on men, but of disposing things: that is to say, of employing tactics rather than laws, and even of using laws themselves as tactics to arrange things in such a way that, through a certain number of means, such and such ends may be achieved."[35] That is to say, with the political rationality of government it is a question, as that preeminent "governmentalist" Jeremy Bentham had suggested, of artificially so arranging things that people, following only their own self-interest, *will do as they ought.*[36] And if with sovereignty, the relation between ruler and ruled is such that power reaches out like an extension of the arm of the prince himself, announcing itself periodically with unambiguous ceremony, with government, governor and governed are thrown into a new and different relation, one that is the product not merely of the expanded capacity of the state apparatus but of the emergence of a new field for producing effects of power – the new, self-regulating field of the social. It is here that the new problem of government (of which the specific problem of the state is now but one component) is articulated. For it is here, by the arrangement and disposition of the instrumentalities and institutions that sustain it – public opinion, private property, the division of labor, the market, the judiciary – that the tendency toward the identification of interests operates to ensure that the new rights-bearing and self-governing subjects do as they ought.[37]

Foucault's discussion of discipline – to turn now to the second distinction I want to focus on – belongs to a period in his work when he was elaborating the "micro-technology" of power. Disciplinary power typically operates at the micro-level and through technologies and apparatuses. Specifically, discipline has to do with habituating the mind or body to a particular activity. It does this by systematically working upon mental or physical capacities and building these up into discrete abilities by the continual repetition of complex actions broken down into simple operations. The rationality of government operates differently. Whereas discipline is concerned to work actively upon subjects (the intellectual discipline of school, the bodily discipline of the workhouse or factory, or the social discipline imposed by police), government does not regulate in this kind of detail. As James Tully has lucidly suggested, for writers of the late eighteenth century, the most striking feature of commercial society was the seeming self-sustaining character of its basic institutions. This they attributed to the division of labor and specialization. "In virtue of being caught up in the practices of division of labour in economic, political, and military life," Tully writes:

> [I]ndividuals were constrained to behave in ways which – willy-nilly and unintentionally – led to the overall improvement and growth of these societies. In addition, individuals constrained to act in this way would gradually become "polished," "disciplined," "civilized," and "pacific." If behaviour within the causal constraints of divisions of labour within commercial society explained the growth of European society, then the regulation and governance of every area of life in the seventeenth century could be seen as unnecessary.[38]

Now to be sure, between the Whig protagonists of the *natural* identification of interests and the Benthamite theorists of the *artificial* identification of interests there was disagreement regarding the degree of coordination these autonomous governmental processes required. But they were all agreed, as Tully says, on their existence and their effects.

The important point about these distinctions, tentative and overlapping as they may be, is that here as elsewhere, what Foucault is engaged in is tracing in outline the sources of the modern form of political reason, as well as interrupting those political histories in which the object is taken to be a singular evolving reason for which each instance is but the reiteration of an identical functionality. The *kind* of investigation Foucault undertakes (in however sketchy and incomplete a manner, and with however narrow a geographical focus) encourages those of us interested in the problem of the specific effects of colonialism on the forms of life of the colonized to historicize European rule in a way that brings into focus the political rationalities in relation to which this rule was effected. For of course the colonial enterprise spans precisely these centuries in which there are significant alterations and discontinuities in European conceptions and practices of political power. Again, the point here is not the banal one that the forms of the state in Europe are simply replicated in the colonies (and that therefore one need only inquire into the former to grasp the latter). The point is that to understand the project of colonial power *at any given historical moment*, one has to understand the character of the political rationality that constituted it. And what is crucial to such an understanding is not what the attitude of colonialism was toward the colonized nor whether colonial power excluded or included natives as such. Rather what is crucial is trying to discern what the point of application – the target – of colonial power was, and what the discursive and nondiscursive field it sought to encompass was.

Governing Colonial Conduct

The general line of my argument should now be clear enough. Critically rethinking the problem about the modern in its relation to the colonial ought to entail displacing the modernization narrative such that not only can modernity no longer appear to us as the normalized *telos* of a developmental process, *but consequently* colonialism can no longer seem to consist in the mere historical reiteration of a single political rationality whose effects can be adequately assessed in terms of the "more or less" of force, freedom, or reason. And in a refigured narrative such as I would wish to commend, the formation of colonial modernity would have to appear as a discontinuity in the organization of colonial rule characterized by the emergence of a distinctive political rationality – a colonial governmentality – in which power comes to be directed at the destruction and reconstruction of colonial space so as to produce not so much extractive-effects on colonial bodies as governing-effects on colonial conduct.

Part of the point I am making here is the one made many years ago by Eric Stokes in his classic work, *The English Utilitarians and India*. Readers of that book will recall that its argument turns on a significant if subtle distinction between two historically successive moments in the insertion of English political ideas into colonial rule in India, moments linked to the alteration of the raison d'être of colonial rule effected by the Industrial Revolution, the Reform movement, and Evangelicalism. The first moment is that associated with the names of Cornwallis and Munro and their reforms in Bengal and Madras respectively; and the second with that of the liberals, Evangelicals, and Utilitarians. On Stokes's account, the important difference between these moments does not have to do with the mere adoption of English political ideas as such – the rule of law, for example, or the fundamental place of the institution of private property rights in land. Rather the important difference has to do with the *spirit* and *target* of the colonial power whose ends they participated in – that is, the colonial *project* into which these were inserted. Cornwallis's and Munro's reforms were far from identical, but inserted as they were into the mercantilist colonial project of tributary extraction, they were, as Stokes puts it, essentially "defensive" and "conservative," power seeking to make changes as expediency and experience dictated. The liberal and Utilitarian reforms, on the other hand, were inserted into a colonial project in which the mercantilist end of the aggrandizement of the state was being displaced, as one nineteenth-century writer put it, by the "surer foundation" of a "dominion over the wants of the universe."[39] Now colonial power came to depend not merely upon inserting English ideas here and there, but upon *the systematic redefinition and transformation of the terrain on which the life of the colonized was lived*. It became, in short, "revolutionary," inasmuch as, guided by abstract, universal principles regarding the supposed relation between moral conditions and moral character, it now saw as integral to its task the rational possibility of so altering those conditions as to alter fundamentally that character in an improving direction. And with the assumption of this project, colonial power came to be, as Stokes so acutely puts it, "consciously directed upon Indian *society* itself."[40] It is, it seems to me, in the discerning articulation of this transformation in the *structure* and *project* of colonial power that the whole genius of Stokes's book lies. What his book does not do, however, is elucidate the principle of the new political rationality that required and indeed constructed the domain of "society itself."[41]

I now wish to turn briefly to one historical instance, that of Sri Lanka, and to the story of the making of its colonial modernity. What interests me here, I should emphasize, is not by any means a full historical account, but an attempt to shift the conceptual *register* or alter the narrative *frame* in which such an account of modernity might be resituated.

In the writings of colonialist and nationalist historians alike, the story of Sri Lanka's insertion into the regime of British colonialism has been told and retold through a familiar set of events and a familiar narrative plot. That story is generally told as a succession of three episodes that chart a progressive journey of transition from the medieval to the modern.[42] The first episode in this transition to the modern (1796–1802) is the brief story of the capture of the maritime provinces of the island from the Dutch, its unsettled fate as a colony during the Anglo-French War, and its mismanagement at the hands of the Madras administration of the English East India Company. The second episode (1802–32) takes the story from the beginnings of Crown Colony status and plots the early building up of the apparatuses of the colonial state, the political resolution of the problem of territorial integrity with the ceding of the Kandyan Kingdom, the construction of the institutions of civil and judicial administration, the growth of plantation agriculture, and the development of the infrastructure of communication in roads and bridges and canals and post. In the overall economy of the colonialist and nationalist narratives, these first two episodes form a sort of backdrop: they enumerate the cumulative improvements that will culminate in the third episode which tells the story of that watershed of reform when the recommendations of Commissioners W. M. G. Colebrooke and C. H. Cameron were implemented and modernity, a mere glimmer until now, burst in upon the colony.[43]

In the story of the formation of Sri Lanka's modernity, the reforms known historiographically as the Colebrooke-Cameron Reforms established the definitive moment of the break with the "medieval" or "feudal" past. These reforms were far-reaching and comprehensive: they led to the unification of the administration of the island, the establishment of executive and legislative councils, judicial reform, the development of capitalist agriculture, and of modern means of communication, education, and the press. Emphasizing the progressivist direction of the transition the reforms made possible, G. C. Mendis – first of the modern professional (and liberal-nationalist) Sri Lankan historians – wrote as follows in his introduction to *The Colebrooke-Cameron Papers*: "[T]he reforms recommended by Colebrooke and Cameron have contributed greatly to the advancement of Ceylon. They have turned the course of the history of Ceylon in a modern direction and enabled Ceylon to fall in line in many ways with modern developments and ultimately to attain to the stage to which it has risen today as an equal member of the Commonwealth of Nations."[44] In this kind of account, therefore, the Colebrooke-Cameron Reforms form the crucial moment in an approved journey of progress in which modernity and the nation are linked stages of attainment.

My problem with this story is not the proposition of a "break" as such, the idea of a "discontinuity" that inaugurates the modern, but rather the progressivist plot into which the modernization narrative inserts it. Because, working as it does through the familiar counter-positioning of power and freedom (the modern as the rationalization of power), what it invites us to suppose is the unfolding trajectory of the teleological path of a single political rationality. And in so doing what it masks is the nature of the transformation that the modern seeks to induce, and the new political rationality by which it seeks to accomplish this. If, however, we take the important point about colonial power to be its structure, its project, and its target, then a different sort of story ought to be told about the formation of Sri Lanka's colonial career, one whose principal axis is the displacement of one kind of political rationality – that of mercantilism or sovereignty – by another, that of governmentality. On this view, colonial power in Sri Lanka between 1796 and 1832 will be understood to be largely organized around the mercantilist rationality of sovereignty. The principal object of this colonial project was the extraction of tribute – tribute for the security and aggrandizement of the state and crown. In marking off this period, the crucial point is not the degree of oppressiveness or corruption of colonial officials (as in the period of East India Company administration), nor even the steady, as it were, incremental rationalization and humanizing of absolutist-autocratic colonial rule (as during the early phase of crown colony administration). Therefore, the increase or decrease of the level of taxation or the variety of things taxed may have been more or less oppressive; the officials who collected revenues may have been more or less corrupt; forms of forced labor may have been administered in such a way as to have been more or less onerous. But none of this changes the *point of application of power.* Power deployed through this form of political rationality is directed principally at the points of extraction of wealth. This is because tributary power was largely concerned to ensure that bodies knew their place, that they obeyed when commanded, but it did not need to work on reorganizing the conduct or habits of subjects themselves. What is important about sovereignty from the point of view of the modern then is that in this strategy of rule, the "lives" of the colonized population – their "local habits," their "ancient tenures," their "distinctions," and "religious observations" – were not a significant variable in the colonial calculus (at least so long as they did not interfere with the immediate business of extraction). And what is crucial about the Colebrooke-Cameron Reforms is that, with their implementation, colonial power came to depend precisely upon the systematic attempt to intervene at this level of what Stokes calls "society itself."

To understand the new political rationality that was now about to displace the old, it is necessary to open up the Colebrooke-Cameron recommendations for reform to a *reading* that, partial though it will necessarily be, aims to make visible the altered project of colonial power. I would suggest that the configuration of that project of colonial power – the new target it would now aim at bringing within its reach, the new knowledges it would now depend upon, the new technologies it would now seek to deploy, the new domains it would now need to construct as the field of its operations – can be discerned if we inquire into the kinds of effects that Colebrooke and Cameron sought to produce in each of three domains whose systematic reform they recommended. These domains – government, the economy, and the judiciary – which they marked out (or rather, which were marked out for them in their "Instructions" from the Earl of Bathurst)[45] as preeminently warranting attention, were of course domains that the late eighteenth and early nineteenth centuries were constructing as distinct if integrated domains, each with its own level of rationality, its own laws of motion, and its own corresponding sciences. They were, moreover, precisely those domains that the political rationality of governmental power sought at once to *construct* and *work through* in order to induce its improving effects on colonial conduct.

In his report on the administration of government, W. M. G. Colebrooke, for the most part a Whig liberal, vigorously opposed the absolute and autocratic control exercised by the governor. It hindered, he maintained, the development of commerce, the movement of voluntary labor, and the development of a press. Colebrooke recommended instead the formation of executive and legislative councils (the latter of which would admit native representation) to limit the arbitrary power of the governor. Much of this was argued in relation to the principle of the "natural" rights of the people. The people, said Colebrooke, "are entitled to expect that their interests and wishes may be attended to, and their rights protected; and although the ignorance and prejudice which still prevail generally throughout the country may preclude the adoption of their views upon all subjects, it would be consistent with the policy of a liberal government that they should have an opportunity of freely communicating their opinions of the effects of the legislative changes that may be proposed."[46] But we ought, I think, to avoid reading this claim from within the narrative of the progress of democratic principles and institutions, and not only for the obvious reason that native members (who only began sitting in 1835) were nominated rather than elected and had no control of government expenditure. The crucial point here is not whether natives were included or excluded so much as *the introduction of a new game of politics* that the colonized would (eventually) be obliged to play if they were to be counted as political. And one of the things the new game of politics came to depend upon was the construction of a legally instituted space where legally defined subjects could exercise rights, however limited they were.

This is why Colebrooke was concerned with the creation of the instrumentalities and technologies of "public opinion" – specifically, those great Whig principles of an English education and a free press. The old form of the colonial state had no need of "public opinion" because then colonial power did not depend upon the productivity and consumption of an improving public. By contrast what the new form of the colonial state required was not self-aggrandizement but a form of power that could exercise a "dominion over the wants of the universe." What it needed, therefore, was to seek to produce the conditions of self-interest or desire in which these wants would tend to be of certain kinds and not others. Or to put it another way, if the new form of colonial power depended upon the idea of the identification of interests, it was necessary to provide the means of inducing an understanding of what those interests were (or ought to be). For this, a press involved in the diffusion of useful knowledges (and with the criticism of ignorant and prejudicial ones) would be indispensable.

> The very limited operation of these presses [i.e., those run by the government and the missionary societies] has tended to check the progress of moral and intellectual improvement; and in those parts of the country where there is little intercourse with Europeans the ignorance and prejudices of the people have been perpetuated, and have greatly tended to obstruct the improvement of the country and the amelioration of its institutions.[47]

At the same time, there is another reason besides the direct effect on the moral conduct of people whose want of intercourse with Europeans was the source of the perpetuation of their prejudices. The institutionalization of the public use of reason, on Colebrooke's view, would in turn also have an effect on the government of the state itself:

> In a political point of view the unrestricted operation of the colonial press would have a direct tendency to promote good government in the island, and to diminish

the influence of those classes who are interested in upholding the ignorant prejudices of the people, and who retain them in servile dependence on themselves.[48]

By creating a rational public, the press would promote good government so that
not only would public opinion depend upon the liberal government of the state,
but the state would also depend upon the play of a reasoned public opinion. In
other words, a more public circulation of reason would serve to undermine and
break down the supports of native knowledges, to disqualify them. It would, in
effect, help to put in place a public sphere in which only certain kinds of
knowledges – and not others – could circulate with any efficacy; a sphere in
which fluency in these knowledges (in part determined by the ability to point
out the unreason in the old) would be a condition of participation; and in which
participation would be the only rational and legal way of exercising influence in
what now counted as politics.[49]

By the early nineteenth century "economy," no longer understood at the level
of "family" but, as Foucault suggests, on the biopolitical level of "population,"
was becoming a distinctive domain of reforming intervention articulated through
the emergence of the new science of political economy – "the governmental
discourse of the modern world," as Denis Meuret puts it (echoing Adam Smith's
famous characterization of political economy as "a branch of the science of the
statesman or legislator").[50] This was because in that representation of "economy"
that Smith's *The Wealth of Nations* did so much to establish, a new relation was
being constructed among the state, the economy, and that new comprehensive
domain of the social in which "the principle of population" operated.
"The emergence of political economy," Meuret suggests a bit later, "is inseparable
from the movement by which, in the eighteenth century, the public, which in the
seventeenth century was still only an object of discourse, begins to intervene as an
explicit actor in an intellectual debate for which it was, at the same time, the
stage."[51] It was only to be expected then that Colebrooke would seek to interrupt
and transform the existing relation between economy and the state, that relation
that had been constructed through the idea of the state's responsibility for commercial strength. His design, of course, was to introduce conditions for the
development of private property, market relations, and capitalist agriculture. As
we know, Colebrooke particularly objected to the government's mercantilist monopolies of cinnamon and salt. They were, he said, "injurious to commerce and to
the influx and accumulation of capital." And most particularly it is why he objected
to the system of "compulsory service" known as *rājākāriya* upon which these
monopolies rested. Indeed, both in his general report and in the special report on
"compulsory services," *rājākāriya* appears as a sort of key to the structure of the
old society. Colebrooke objected to *rājākāriya* on several grounds. Principally it
was, he said, "unfavourable to agricultural industry and improvement,"[52] insofar
as it prevented people from attending continuously to their own cultivation and
hindered the development of a free market in labor. Colebrooke was also of the
view that *rājākāriya* exposed the people to undue hardships because of the manner

of its administration. Moreover, he argued, it rested on and worked to maintain "absurd distinctions" based on "race" and "caste." Now again, this ought not to be read as the rationalization of the economy, the breakup of "feudal" forms of economic relation. It ought instead to be read as a concern to introduce the conditions for a new order of social power wherein conduct was enabled and disabled by the automatic regulation of free exchanges.

These new conditions amounted, in fact, to new social and legal conditions of property and labor, a new social and legal space for the desiring subject. To create them colonial power had to direct itself at breaking down those "ancient usages" that irrationally connected people to obligations of service (those, in fact, that it had itself formerly made use of) and, through the construction of a notion of rights, to shift the site of agency such that it now came to be assigned to the private sphere of an individuality regulated not by the personal discretionary demands of a sovereign extracting tribute but by the internal volitional agency of a rational free will. In other words, the new order of private landownership and market relations that was to be promoted required that new habits of social discipline be acquired by the native population, in particular, the improving habit of self-propelled industry. Now the native would be obliged to learn the new relation between temporality and voluntary productiveness, but not by the old forms of authority and hierarchy that *rājākāriya* entailed, those based principally on caste. For now the only principles of economic authority and distinction to be allowed were those defined by the abstract and self-regulating demands of the market, which operated not on such aggregates as caste but on individuals responding only to the rational or natural pressure of want and self-interest. Here, in short, was a new organization of social power in which the division of labor and the exchange mechanism of the market were to operate in such a fashion as to oblige a progressive desire for industry, regularity, and individual accomplishment.

For Utilitarians, important as public opinion and schooling were in effecting a progressive improvement in human conduct, nothing could be as instrumental in this endeavor as the scientifically arranged technologies of the legal and judicial establishments. And here, on Bentham's juridical theory, the task of arriving at that identity of interests requisite for a harmonious society could not be left to the spontaneous working of Adam Smith's hidden hand, but rather depended upon a calculus of pleasures and pains artificially established by the legislator and the magistrate.[53] Charles Hay Cameron – "ultimately the last disciple of Jeremy Bentham," as Sir Leslie Stephen called him, and who was charged with reporting on the judicial establishments in Ceylon – was a legal scholar keenly preoccupied with this Benthamite principle of inducing desired effects on conduct by a careful and economic weighting of rewards and punishments.[54] In his meticulously systematic report, he repeatedly returned to this theme. In Cameron's view, moreover, Ceylon was an especially favorable field for experimenting with legal reform because, unlike India (where he would work alongside Macaulay on the penal code some four years later),[55] "the courts of justice in that island, and the forms of their procedure are, without exception, the creations of the British

Government, and have not in the eyes of the natives anything of the sanctity of religion or of antiquity."[56] There was therefore little to fear in disabling existing practices since, on this view, they were neither deeply entrenched nor legitimized by native religion. And so, with that cheerful expectation of wonderful improvements that characterized liberalism in the first blush of its youth, he declared: "A fairer field than the island of Ceylon can never be presented to a legislator for the establishment of a system of judicature and procedure, of which the sole end is the attainment of cheap and expeditious justice."[57]

In the opening paragraph of his report Cameron set down the rationale for what was to follow (some twenty-five sets of recommendations in all). "The condition of the native inhabitants of the Island of Ceylon," he wrote, "imposes upon a government which has their improvement at heart, the necessity not only of providing cheap and accessible judicatures for the relief of those who have suffered injury, and the punishment of those who have inflicted it, but also of guarding with peculiar anxiety against the danger that the judicatures themselves should be employed as the means of perpetrating that injustice which it is the object of their institution to prevent." The precise "danger" which provoked this "peculiar anxiety" stemmed from the colonial view that in Ceylon the "restraints" on "bad passions" were "deficient to such a degree" that "each individual owes nearly all the security he enjoys to the protection of the law." "The disregard of an oath," he lamented, "and of truth in general among the natives is notorious; not less so is their readiness to gratify their malignant passions through the medium of vexatious litigation."[58] This gave to the legislator of colonial reform a responsibility far greater than would be the case in Europe simply because the stakes of moral improvement were greater. Unlike Europe, where the moral disposition was such that it did not require so many artificial constraints, in Ceylon the natives had at every turn to be met with devices and measures which constrained them against "immoral conduct."

> The truth is, that the administration of justice to natives is of far more importance than its administration to Europeans, because they are so much less disposed to do justice to each other voluntarily; and I know of no instrument so powerful for gradually inducing upon them habits of honesty and sincerity as a judicial establishment, by which fraud and falsehood may be exposed to the greatest possible risk of detection and punishment.[59]

A colonial difference, in Chatterjee's sense, is quite evidently at work here. But again, this is less significant than the fact that what the rationality of colonial power is doing is inscribing a new authoritative game of justice into the colonized space, one which the colonized could accept or resist, but to whose rules they would have to respond.

One site for inducing these effects on colonial conduct was the courtroom itself and particularly the jury system. A jury system had been introduced by Chief Justice Sir Alexander Johnston by the Charter of 1810. Cameron, who like most

Utilitarians was generally not well disposed toward juries (seeing them as cumbrous and wasteful),[60] felt that in the special case of Ceylon it was a useful, indeed indispensable, institution. "I attended nearly all the trials by jury which took place while I was in the island," he wrote, "and the impression on my mind is, that an institution in the nature of a jury is the best school in which the minds of the natives can be disciplined for the discharge of public duties." The jury was *exemplary* of a certain arrangement, the aim of which was to constrain the native's behavior in a certain direction. As with the school proper, crucial to the working of this technology was the overseeing "eye" of the European: the courtroom was to produce the effect of a panopticon. "The juror performs his functions under the eye of an European judge," Cameron continued, "and of the European and Indian public, and in circumstances which almost preclude the possibility of bribery or intimidation."[61] The point, in other words, was to establish a regulatory technique that would reach down to the very "motives" of the native and not only constrain or induce him to alter them but also encourage him to appreciate the alteration. Moreover, governmental rationality sought to organize things such that the native was made to work upon himself; he was now conceived as a productive agent. "In such a situation he has very little motive to do wrong, and he yet feels and learns to appreciate the consciousness of rectitude. The importance which he justly attaches to the office renders it agreeable to him; and he not only pays great attention to the proceedings, but for the most part takes an active part in them."[62]

In my view, then, the Colebrooke-Cameron Reforms ought to be inserted into an altogether different problematic about the modern than the one into which the modernization story has inserted it. If in that story the reforms mark a great leap forward in the march of rationality, progress, and freedom, in the story I want to tell they signpost the reconfiguration of colonial power – its redistribution and redeployment in relation to new targets, new forms of knowledge, and new technologies, and its production of new effects of order and subjectivity. Summing up the project of the reforms, G. C. Mendis, that consummate liberal-nationalist historian, remarked: "Thus both Colebrooke and Cameron believed that the bond between Britain and Ceylon could be maintained not by retaining British ascendancy in Government but by sharing power with the people, by giving them offices of trust, maintaining good relations between Europeans and Ceylonese and imparting justice equally to all both rich and poor."[63] However, what Mendis reads here as a democratization of power, as the generosity of a liberal British colonialism yielding a measure of autonomy to the natives, I would read rather as a *transformation* of power, as colonial power adopting a different strategy, working on and through different targets. On this view, the Colebrooke-Cameron Reforms are significant in that they displaced the old mercantile politics of territorial expansion and introduced into the colonial state a new politics – a politics in which power was now directed at the conditions of social life rather than the producers of social wealth, in which power was now to operate in such a way as to produce not so much extractive-effects on colonial bodies as governing-effects on colonial conduct. For what was at stake in the governmental redefinition and reordering of the colonial world was, to paraphrase Jeremy Bentham once more, to design institutions such that, following only their self-interest, natives would do what they ought.

To sum up, I have been trying to urge an approach to colonialism in which *Europe* is historicized in such a way as to bring into focus the differentia in the political rationalities through which its colonial projects were constructed. Europe, between the early modern sixteenth and the late modern nineteenth centuries, was an arena of profound alterations in the languages of the political – the concepts that it depended upon, the technologies that enabled it, the institutional sites through which it operated, the structures that guaranteed it, and the kind of subjectivities it required.[64] How these languages in turn altered the construction of the colonial project – that is, how colonial spaces were constructed as such and organized and inserted into this project as products of these changing rationalities – is still, I think, very poorly understood. Among these political rationalities, of course, the modern is crucial in large part because it remains, if in a tenuous and embattled way, our postcolonial present.

In the colonial world the problem of *modern* power turned on the politico-ethical project of producing subjects and governing their conduct. What this required was the concerted attempt to alter the political and social worlds of the colonized, an attempt to transform and redefine the very conditions of the desiring subject. The political problem of modern colonial power was therefore not merely to contain resistance and encourage accommodation but to seek to ensure that *both* could *only* be defined in relation to the categories and structures of modern political rationalities. This is what Charles Trevelyan urged when he wrote in the late 1830s (when liberalism was still aggressively optimistic) that whereas independence for India was inevitable it would come in one of two ways: reform or revolution. "The only means at our disposal for preventing [revolution] and securing [reform]," he said, "is to set the natives on a process of European improvement, to which they are already sufficiently inclined. They will then cease to desire and aim at independence *on the old Indian footing*."[65] If we are to grasp more adequately the lineaments of our postcolonial modernity, what we ought to try to map more precisely is the political rationality through which this old footing was systematically displaced by a new one such that the old would now only be imaginable along paths that belong to new, always-already transformed, sets of coordinates, concepts, and assumptions.

Notes

1 For one recent and interesting attempt to grapple with this problem, see Dipesh Chakrabarty, "Postcoloniality and the Artifice of History: Who Speaks for 'Indian'

Pasts?" *Representations* 37 (1992): 1–26. As will be evident from what follows, I do not entirely share his diagnosis of the problem of Europe or the solution he provides.

2   We all recall those stirring closing passages of Frantz Fanon's *The Wretched of the Earth* (New York: Penguin, 1967), p. 251, in which he exhorts us, "Leave this Europe where they are never done talking about Man, yet murder men everywhere they find them, at the corner of every one of their own streets, in all the corners of the globe." Part of the point I want to make is the obvious one that the politics of our critique of colonialist discourse cannot be the same as it was for Fanon.

3   One significant articulation of this argument is to be found in Ranajit Guha's celebrated essay, "Dominance without Hegemony and Its Historiography," in Ranajit Guha (ed.), *Subaltern Studies VI: Writings in South Asian History and Society* (Delhi: Oxford University Press, 1989), pp. 210–309.

4   See, in this regard, Nicholas Thomas's recent book, *Colonialism's Culture: Anthropology, Travel and Government* (Princeton: Princeton University Press, 1994). That Thomas and I share some concerns will be quite evident. He is concerned, as he says, with an "historicization of colonialism" (p. 19), with a more "nuanced understanding of the plurality of colonial endeavours" (p. 20). However, it seems to me that Thomas shares with many others – but *not* with me – that conceptual problematic in which the overriding concern is determining the nature of colonialism's *attitude* toward the colonized. My view, once again, is that we ought to give up this preoccupation.

5   Partha Chatterjee, "The Colonial State," in *The Nation and Its Fragments: Colonial and Postcolonial Histories* (Princeton: Princeton University Press, 1993), p. 14.

6   See, for example, Burton Stein, "State Formation and Economy Reconsidered," *Modern Asian Studies* 19, no. 3 (1985): 387–413; Frank Perlin, "State Formation Reconsidered," *Modern Asian Studies* 19, no. 3 (1985): 415–480; David Washbrook, "Progress and Problems: South Asian Economic and Social History, c. 1720–1860," *Modern Asian Studies* 22, no. 1 (1988): 57–96; Christopher Bayly, *Indian Society and the Making of the British Empire* (New York: Cambridge University Press, 1988); and idem, *Imperial Meridian: The British Empire and the World, 1780–1830* (London: Longman, 1989).

7   Vincent Harlow, of course, argued that this was the period in which there emerged a "new imperial system" or second British Empire. See his "The New Imperial System, 1783–1815," in J. Holland Rose, A. P. Newton, and E. A. Benians (eds.), *The Cambridge History of the British Empire*, vol. 2, *The Growth of the New Empire, 1783–1870* (Cambridge: Cambridge University Press, 1940).

8   Chatterjee, "The Colonial State," p. 32.

9   For a recent work that employs such a distinction between different political rationalities within the colonial period, see Timothy Mitchell, *Colonising Egypt* (New York: Cambridge University Press, 1988).

10 Chatterjee, "The Colonial State," p. 19.

11 Students of colonial plantation slavery in the Americas will perhaps be more keenly aware of the vicissitudes of "race" as a signifier of difference. See Thomas Gossett, *Race: The History of an Idea in America*, rev. ed. (New York: Schocken, 1987), though even here the concern is exclusively with the classificatory and representational side of the question. For a useful discussion of aspects of the transformation of the concept in the nineteenth century, see George W. Stocking,

Jr., *Race, Culture, and Evolution: Essays in the History of Anthropology* (Chicago: University of Chicago Press, 1968).

12 See, for example, Michael Ryan, "Assimilating New Worlds in the Sixteenth and Seventeenth Centuries," *Comparative Studies in Society and History* 23, no. 4 (1981): 519–538; Peter Hulme, *Colonial Encounters: Europe and the Native Caribbean, 1492–1797* (New York: Methuen, 1986); and Anthony Pagden, *European Encounters with the New World: From Renaissance to Romanticism* (New Haven: Yale University Press, 1993). For an interesting attempt to sketch the discontinuities in European discourses of the Other between the Renaissance and the emergence of modern professional anthropology, see Bernard McGrane, *Beyond Anthropology: Society and the Other* (New York: Columbia University Press, 1989).

13 I take this metaphor from J. C. Heesterman's "Was There an Indian Reaction? Western Expansion in Indian Perspective," in H. L. Wesseling (ed.), *Expansion and Reaction* (Leiden: Leiden University Press, 1978), p. 52. Also cited in John Breuilly, *Nationalism and the State* (Chicago: University of Chicago Press, 1982), p. 189.

14 Talal Asad, "Introduction," in *Genealogies of Religion: Discipline and Reasons of Power in Christianity and Islam* (Baltimore: Johns Hopkins University Press, 1993), pp. 23–24.

15 One might think, in this regard, of work such as Zygmunt Bauman's excellent *Legislators and Interpreters* (Ithaca: Cornell University Press, 1989).

16 See Talal Asad, "Conscripts of Western Civilisation," in Christine Gailey (ed.), *Dialectical Anthropology: Essays in Honor of Stanley Diamond*, vol. 1, *Civilization in Crisis* (Gainesville: University Press of Florida, 1992), p. 337.

17 Michel Foucault, *Discipline and Punish: The Birth of the Prison*, Alan Sheridan (trans.) (New York: Vintage, 1979).

18 Ernst Cassirer, *The Philosophy of the Enlightenment* (Princeton: Princeton University Press, 1951). Of course, in this sense, the Evangelicals were also but children of the Enlightenment. See Eric Stokes, *The English Utilitarians and India* (Delhi: Oxford University Press, 1989 [orig. 1959]), p. 33.

19 For a very acute discussion of this aspect of Burke's thought, see J. G. A. Pocock, "Burke and the Ancient Constitution: A Problem in the History of Ideas," in *Politics, Language, and Time: Essays on Political Thought and History* (Chicago: University of Chicago Press, 1989); and Elie Halévy, *The Growth of Philosophic Radicalism*, Mary Morris (trans.) (New York: Macmillan, 1928), pp. 155–181. And for a discussion of the importance of the kind of thinking represented by Burke's "traditionalism" for the colonial project in India, see Stokes, *The English Utilitarians*, pp. 8–25.

20 In England, in the second decade of the nineteenth century, when the movement for Parliamentary reform was gathering pace after the long period of war and political reaction, there emerged a distinction between "Radical Reformers" and "Moderate Reformers" – between "those who wished to alter the constitution in accordance with some grand general sweeping plan" and "those who were content with partial alterations, applicable to what they deemed particular grievances" (Halévy, *Philosophic Radicalism*, p. 261). More generally, see also Asa Briggs, *The Age of Improvement, 1783 to 1867* (London: Longman, 1979).

21 Zygmunt Bauman, "Modernity and Ambivalence," *Theory, Culture & Society* 7 (1990): 163.

22 For useful discussions of the concept of civil society, see John Keane, "Despotism and Democracy: The Origins and Development of the Distinction between Civil Society and the State, 1750–1850," in John Keane (ed.), *Civil Society and the State: New European Perspectives* (London: Verso, 1988); and Adam Seligman, *The Idea of Civil Society* (New York: Free Press, 1992).

23 Hannah Arendt, *The Human Condition* (Chicago: University of Chicago Press, 1958), pp. 38–58.

24 Jürgen Habermas, *The Structural Transformation of the Public Sphere*, Thomas Burger (trans.) (Cambridge, Mass.: MIT Press, 1989). This early work (first published in German in 1962) has recently begun to exercise an impressive influence on reexaminations of the Enlightenment and modernity. See, for example, Joan Landes, *Women and the Public Sphere in the Age of the French Revolution* (Ithaca: Cornell University Press, 1988); Roger Chartier, *The Cultural Origins of the French Revolution*, Lydia G. Cochrane (trans.) (Durham, NC: Duke University Press, 1991); and Mary Jacobs, *Living the Enlightenment: Freemasonry and Politics in Eighteenth-Century Europe* (New York: Oxford University Press, 1991).

25 For a discussion, see Craig Calhoun (ed.), *Habermas and the Public Sphere* (Cambridge, Mass.: MIT Press, 1992).

26 In some sense, Habermas's later work has constituted an attempt to formulate a theory of modernity that is less susceptible to this kind of criticism. See Jürgen Habermas, *The Theory of Communicative Action*, 2 vols. (Cambridge: Polity Press, 1991–92).

27 See Colin Gordon, "Governmental Rationality: An Introduction," and Graham Burchell, "Peculiar Interests: Civil Society and Governing 'The System of Natural Liberty,' " in Graham Burchell, Colin Gordon, and Peter Miller (eds.), *The Foucault Effect: Studies in Governmentality* (Chicago: University of Chicago Press, 1991).

28 For a discussion, see Didier Eribon, *Michel Foucault*, Betsy Wing (trans.) (Cambridge, Mass.: Harvard University Press, 1991); and James Miller, *The Passion of Michel Foucault* (London: HarperCollins, 1993).

29 See, for example, Michel Foucault, "*Omnes et Singulatim*: Towards a Criticism of Political Reason," *Tanner Lectures on Human Values* 2 (1981): 225–254; idem, "The Political Technology of Individuals," in Luther H. Martin, Huck Gutman, and Patrick H. Hutton (eds.), *Technologies of the Self: A Seminar with Michel Foucault* (Amherst: University of Massachussetts Press, 1988); and idem, "Governmentality," in *The Foucault Effect*.

30 See Foucault, "Governmentality," p. 103.

31 In a phrase, *omnes et singulatim*, all and each. See Foucault, "*Omnes et Singulatim*."

32 Foucault, "Governmentality," pp. 87–88.

33 See James Tully, "Governing Conduct," in his *An Approach to Political Philosophy: Locke in Contexts* (Cambridge: Cambridge University Press, 1993). Tully's thesis is that between the Reformation and the Enlightenment there emerges a new practice of governing conduct. "This mode of governance links together probabilistic and voluntaristic forms of knowledge with a range of techniques related to each other by a complex of references to juridical practices. Its aim is to reform conduct: to explain and then deconstruct settled ways of mental and physical behaviour, and to produce and then govern new forms of habitual conduct in belief and action. Finally, this way of subjection, of conducting the self and others, both posits and serves to bring about

a very specific form of subjectivity: a subject who is calculating and calculable, from the perspective of the probabilistic knowledge and practices; and the sovereign bearer of rights and duties, subject to and of law from the voluntaristic perspective. The whole ensemble of knowledge, techniques, habitual activity, and subjection I will provisionally call the juridical government" (p. 179).

34 See Gerhard Oestreich, *Neostoicism and the Early Modern State* (Cambridge: Cambridge University Press, 1982), especially chapters 2, 4, 9, and 15.

35 Foucault, "Governmentality," p. 95.

36 See Jeremy Bentham, *A Fragment on Government* (New York: Cambridge University Press, 1988 [orig. 1776]).

37 See Asad, "Conscripts of Western Civilisation," p. 336.

38 James Tully, "After the Macpherson Thesis," in *Approach to Political Philosophy*, p. 92.

39 Quoted in Stokes, *The English Utilitarians*, p. 43.

40 Ibid., p. 27, my emphasis.

41 Compare, in this regard, Mitchell, *Colonising Egypt*.

42 In more or less explicit terms, this is the case from the colonialist history of Sir James Emerson Tennent, *Ceylon*, vol. 2 (Colombo: Tisara Prakasakayo, 1977 [orig. 1859]), to the nationalist histories of G. C. Mendis, *Ceylon under the British* (Colombo: Colombo Apothecaries' Co., Ltd., 1944); Colvin R. de Silva, *Ceylon under the British Occupation, 1795–1832*, 2 vols. (Colombo: Colombo Apothecaries' Co., Ltd., 1941–42); and most recently, K. M. de Silva, *A History of Sri Lanka* (Berkeley: University of California Press, 1981).

43 For the circumstances that brought the Commission of Inquiry to Ceylon in 1829, see G. C. Mendis, Introduction to *The Colebrooke-Cameron Papers: Documents on British Colonial Policy in Ceylon, 1796–1833*, 2 vols., selected and edited by G. C. Mendis (London: Oxford University Press, 1956). See also Vijaya Samaraweera, "The Colebrooke-Cameron Reforms," *University of Ceylon History of Ceylon*, vol. 3 (Colombo: University of Ceylon Press, 1973). The papers were published in a period of great nationalist debate, indeed in a year – 1956 – of tremendous political significance for Sinhala Buddhist nationalism since it witnessed the electoral victory of the Mahajana Eksath Peramuna led by S. W. R. D. Bandaranaike's Sri Lanka Freedom Party.

44 *Colebrooke-Cameron Papers*, vol. 1, p. lxiv. For a discussion of Mendis, see K. M. de Silva, "History and Historians in Twentieth Century Sri Lanka – the G. C. Mendis Memorial Lecture," *Sri Lanka Journal of the Social Sciences* 1 (1978): 1–12. I am grateful, too, to Mrs. Sita Pieris, Mendis's daughter, for discussing some aspects of her father's career with me.

45 See "Instructions to the Commissioners of Inquiry," in *Colebrooke-Cameron Papers*, vol. 1, pp. 4–8.

46 Ibid., p. 56.

47 Ibid., p. 75.

48 Ibid.

49 For an important – because critical – discussion of the place of "public opinion" in the formation of liberal political theory, see Carl Schmitt, *The Crisis of Parliamentary Democracy*, Ellen Kennedy (trans.) (Cambridge, Mass.: MIT Press, 1988 [orig. 1923]).

50 See Denis Meuret, "A Political Genealogy of Political Economy," *Economy and Society* 17, no. 2 (1988): 227. For a more general discussion of Adam Smith in relation to the emerging science of the political in Edinburgh in the late eighteenth and early nineteenth centuries, see Donald Winch, "The System of the North: Dugald Stewart and His Pupils," in Stefan Collini, Donald Winch, and John Burrow (eds.), *That Noble Science of Politics: A Study in Nineteenth-Century Intellectual History* (Cambridge: Cambridge University Press, 1983).

51 Meuret, "Political Genealogy," p. 228.

52 Mendis, *Colebrooke-Cameron Papers*, vol. 1, p. 51.

53 For a discussion of this aspect of Bentham's thought in relation to Adam Smith, see Halévy, *Philosophic Radicalism*, pp. 89–120.

54 Quoted in Stokes, *The English Utilitarians*, p. 223. Sir Leslie Stephen was, of course, the first great memorializer of the Utilitarians. It is perhaps not altogether irrelevant to recall that this last Benthamite is in fact buried in Sri Lanka, to which he returned in 1875 at the age of eighty to take up the life of a planter. For some details see Mendis, *Colebrooke-Cameron Papers*, vol. 1, pp. xxxii–xxxiii n.

55 A curious – or, perhaps, not so curious – couple if one recalls both the rivalry and the kinship, the divergences as well as the convergences, between philosophic Whigs like Macaulay and philosophic Radicals like Cameron in the first half of the nineteenth century. The dispute between James Mill and Macaulay over the best approach to the "noble science of politics" is one of the most memorable and most instructive exchanges around emerging liberal conceptions of good government. On this relation in general, see Donald Winch, "The Cause of Good Government: Philosophic Whigs versus Philosophic Radicals," in *That Noble Science of Politics*.

56 Mendis, *Colebrooke-Cameron Papers*, vol. 1, p. 164.

57 Ibid., p. 165.

58 Ibid., p. 121.

59 Ibid., p. 136.

60 This institution, which was "the pride of English liberalism," the Utilitarians held in contempt. See Halévy, *Philosophic Radicalism*, pp. 256, 375, 400.

61 Mendis, *Colebrooke-Cameron Papers*, vol. 1, p. 146.

62 Ibid., pp. 146–147. It is well to note that Cameron's advocacy of the jury system also stemmed from considerations of the conduct of the European judges: "It is invaluable, I think, everywhere; but in our Indian possessions, it is . . . the only check and the only stimulus which can be applied to a judge placed in a situation remote from a European public, and necessarily almost insensible to the opinion of the native public, with whom he does not associate" (p. 168).

63 Ibid., p. xlii. See also G. C. Mendis, "The Evolution of a Ceylonese Nation – The Attainment of Independence in 1948 and the Conflicts That Arose from 1956," *Journal of the Royal Asiatic Society* (Ceylon Branch), n.s., 11 (1967): 1–22. I am grateful to Anoma Pieris for bringing this late lecture of her grandfather's to my attention.

64 See Anthony Pagden's edited volume, *The Languages of Political Theory in Early Modern Europe* (Cambridge: Cambridge University Press, 1987).

65 Quoted in Stokes, *The English Utilitarians*, p. 47. In Sri Lanka as in India, colonial liberalism would grow more authoritarian, more paternalistic, and more racist in the latter half of the nineteenth century. See de Silva, *History of Sri Lanka*, chapter 23.

2

Foucault in the Tropics:

Displacing the Panopticon

Peter Redfield

> *All my books . . . are, if you like, little toolboxes. If people want to open them, use a particular sentence, idea, or analysis, like a screwdriver or wrench, in order to short circuit, disqualify or break-up systems of power, including eventually the ones from which my books have issued . . . well, all the better!*
>
> Michel Foucault, 1975[1]

> *A name makes reading too easy.*
>
> Michel Foucault, 1980[2]

Testimonial

I first read Foucault in 1984, the year of his death. At Harvard such a reading could still feel like a subversive act; although widely present in bookstores and frequently referenced in oblique ways, Foucault's name did not feature in official course syllabi. His work (part of the heterogeneous assemblage of authors typed "post-modernist" by their opponents) circulated primarily among graduate students and junior faculty, those liminal enough to resent received wisdom and to embrace the promise of a different future. As an undergraduate one heard names, rumors of movements, all filtered through an atmosphere of institutional silence, one sufficiently disapproving to lend them a transgressive allure and hint at their potential significance. Prohibition bred curiosity, at least among those susceptible to it.

Foucault was particularly *not* taught in the Department of Anthropology, then a minor but resolute outpost of the British Commonwealth, and as such properly suspicious of things emanating from the wrong side of the Channel. Terms like structure and function hung ghostlike in the air, their influence acknowledged through their repeated repudiation. But it was in the context of an anthropology course that I followed my graduate student instructor's suggestion in response to a paper and sought out a copy of *Discipline and Punish*. The encounter was riveting: even now I recall that reading in terms of its feeling, the rare excitement of unexpected revelation. I must emphasize, however, that this thrill was not a purely intellectual affair, the sort of temptation derided in rhetorical dismissals of cleverness or novelty as fashion. I also felt a distinctly empirical resonance, an impression that this work addressed human experience in what was then the most immediate of habitats: a vast, complex educational institution dedicated to the production of certain types of individuals. *Discipline and Punish* offered a reconfigured understanding of its operation, interrogating assumptions of modern life in a manner that appeared at once skeptical, antidisciplinary, and rigorously incomplete. Simply put, it was not contained; by repositioning familiar elements amid the strange, the text opened less predictable possibilities of thinking about the problems of the present I identified around me. Most precisely, it put functionality itself into question, suggesting that the productive effects of a social form might not be bound to its successful realization. From this perspective Foucault's work recast the project of anthropology as it had been introduced to me, raising suspicions about the object and the institution of its study even as it participated in them. Read by someone young and peripheral at the most established of North American universities, *Discipline and Punish* could seem like a deeply practical book.

Introduction

In this essay, I will return to Foucault's work on the prison and consider it in relation to a historical form I later came to investigate, that of the penal colony, and its particular expression in French Guiana. Much has changed since the era of my first encounter with *Discipline and Punish*. The last few decades have witnessed its author's apotheosis in several sectors of the American academy, including cultural anthropology, and the emergence of interdisciplinary fields that feature frequent references to his writings, including colonial and postcolonial studies.[3] Yet as Ann Stoler noted in 1995, while Foucault's analytic framework has "saturated" work on empire, the engagement has generally remained one of applying given principles rather than one of sustained rereading (Stoler 1995: 1–2). The Foucault in circulation is frequently a digested entity, critical nutrients distilled and inert. While such may be the curse of any scholarly canonization, the memory of my formative encounter protests against it.[4] Returning to *Discipline and Punish* at a point when Foucault is a routine rather than marginal influence on the discipline of anthropology, my desire remains to read the text as a provocation, a point of departure, not a certain conclusion.

The task of this essay, then, will be to dislodge *Discipline and Punish* from its most familiar narrative boundaries. My immediate goal is to send elements of this text through an equatorial detour, exploring another lineage in the genealogy of the prison that Foucault forecloses. My larger goal in engaging in this exercise is to situate Foucault's work relative to an anthropology conscious of colonial perspective, that is to say an understanding shaped by a politics of space grounded in displacement and inequality. Like Stoler's (1995) rereading of *The History of Sexuality* in order to resituate colonial tensions about race at the center of emerging European norms of desire, here I seek to broaden the geographic horizon of *Discipline and Punish* in order to disrupt the spatial vision of modernity presented in it. Foucault's spatial vision notoriously floats over the West, and yet often implies universality, as in the introduction to *Discipline and Punish* where the author announces the justification of his project as a "history of the present" (Foucault 1979: 30–31). A now copious body of work on the legacy of imperial projects within the formation of European modernity suggests an altered frame: whatever it may be and wherever it may be found, "the history of the present" must derive from more than western Europe and the United States alone. The stakes here ultimately involve the representation of modernity and its "outside," the shifting frontier of time, space, and value made particularly visible in colonial regimes (Mitchell 2000).

For this project of rereading I will circle a prominent and influential moment in *Discipline and Punish*: Foucault's rediscovery of Jeremy Bentham's Panopticon. Well digested through frequent citation, the Panopticon presents a knot between conceptual levels at the center of *Discipline and Punish* as well as a spectacular image of disciplinary power. Yet it also, as it happens, offers a historical trail straight to the work's geographic edge and a contrasting form of punishment in a penal colony. The penal colony provides an ambiguous object with which to unsettle the narrative limits of Foucault's analysis and resituate key elements of his account. In particular I hope to resituate the Panopticon in such a way that its spectacular clarity does not overshadow a more heterogeneous field of modern discipline, or lead us to overlook Foucault's theme of productive failure within the emergence of modern institutions. From a colonial perspective, questions of power and geography are unavoidable, and the very categorizations deployed to distinguish present and past themselves historical. Indeed, the gap between dreams and practices may be especially telling in a colonial context where anxieties feed into expertise (Stoler 2002). Such is the case with failure and function, I want to suggest, particularly within a form of discipline that incorporated geographic distance directly into its operation and applied geographic limits into its calculation of relative success. Reading the French penal colony back through *Discipline and Punish* raises the specter of an ambiguous zone of failure at the edge of European modernity.

The Panopticon and the Penal Colony

As readers of *Discipline and Punish* know, Foucault found a key figure for his work in Jeremy Bentham's Panopticon, a set of plans for a new, rational prison based on a principle of visibility. This "simple idea of Architecture," as Bentham called it, sought to address a range of emerging social problems associated with crime and poverty by placing problem populations within a circular "inspection house" (Bentham 1962: 39). There they could be isolated in cells and exposed to continuous observation from a central tower, aware of their visibility and never certain of the eye of the inspector. In Foucault's reading, Bentham's "simple idea" locates a key mechanism of disciplinary formations of power and knowledge. The major effect of the Panopticon is to "induce in the inmate a state of conscious and permanent visibility that assures the automatic functioning of power" (Foucault 1979: 201). Here the deterrent presence of surveillance and guards becomes further refined into the deterrent possibility of their existence; ultimately in modern societies it is individuals who learn to guard themselves.

The Panopticon emerges from Foucault's text as a pure instrument of modern power, recognized by both Bentham and Foucault as the physical expression of a principle. It is at one and the same time a historical object, an element of theory, and a diagram for a machine. Not an artifact of analysis, nor necessarily unique, its selection as a paradigmatic example is nonetheless particularly interesting.[5] Amid Foucault's technically inflected vocabulary it remains one of the most elaborated and precisely defined examples of the instrumental edge of discourse. Moreover, the Panopticon makes its appearance near the center of *Discipline and Punish*, and implies a pivotal movement through the text's narrative time: the very ambition of the device reveals the scope of disciplinary power, shadowing the future with a heroic present rather than past. It thus is a very modern moment, in the sense of modernity as an attitude rather than an epoch (Foucault 1984: 39). It is also classically framed within a European context, featuring the powdered head and excited pen of a prominent English philosopher. Here, then, we find Foucault at an interpretive height, firmly centered in the West.

What fewer readers of *Discipline and Punish* may realize is that Bentham's dedication to the Panopticon extended beyond a single text. Indeed, the scheme grew into a central obsession of his life and the focus of over two decades of negotiation with the British government as he sought to have the structure built and himself compensated for it (Hume 1973, 1974; Semple 1993). Moreover, this "simple idea" did not emerge from the head of the philosopher alone, but rather derived from a project in the Russian Empire undertaken by his brother Samuel Bentham in the service of Prince Potemkin. As part of an effort to improve naval manufacturing on Potemkin's estate in Krichev, Samuel developed plans for an "inspection house," a structure that would, by its very structure, mediate problems of skill and discipline between imported English experts and local Russian peasants (Mitchell 1991: 35; Werrett 1999: 2).[6] The structure was never built, but Samuel's project inspired Jeremy, who had already been thinking about penal reform, and who made a trip to visit his brother in 1786.[7] Adopting (and acknowledging) his brother's plan, Jeremy removed its insight about visibility from the sweaty particularities of peasants and shipbuilding, and refined it into a universal principle, one applicable to prisons, poorhouses, schools, and hospitals, throughout Britain and the world. We will return to the significance of abstraction later.[8] For now the simple historical observation I wish to make is that the philosopher's Panopticon, reborn as a central motif in Foucault's reading, rests on situated sketches of the engineer's inspection house. Before the prison we find another problem: ropes and timbers, busy hands and foreign experts, state power and private interests, all to be ordered in the name of an expansionist policy and profit.[9] Thus the most clarifying image of disciplinary power has an antecedent in a modernizing endeavor at the margins of Europe, and in this sense a potentially colonial genealogy. Unlike some of the historical debates surrounding *Discipline and Punish*, this observation does not frame Foucault's interpretation in terms of affirmation or contradiction, but rather complicates it, unsettling the geographic parameters of the argument.[10] The "birth of the prison" is no longer an affair of western Europe and North America alone. Faintly, in the minor key of footnotes, a trace of modernizing, expanding Russia travels along.

Following Bentham's story a little more leads us even further away from metropolitan centers. During his long struggle with the British government, the philosopher opposed his plan to the practice of transportation and the establishment of a convict colony in New South Wales (Jackson 1987, 1988). Bentham took a rather dim view of colonies in general, and efforts to solve the crime problem through colonization struck him as misguided and duplicitous. The Australian penal colony not only represented an obstacle to the Panopticon, it also offended his general sense of principled economy and reason. As he was to express in disgust about the Australian venture:

> The ambiguous and indeterminate character of this establishment is a circumstance that may not have been of disservice to it in the way of defense against the attacks of reason. Ask if the Colony presents any prospect of paying its own expenses – oh, but it is an engine of punishment, to be substituted for the Hulks – Ask whether as an engine of punishment it is not an expensive one – oh, but it is a colony to boot, and a fifth quarter of the globe added to the British empire.[11]

The double logic supporting transportation, a shifting combination of empire and punishment, infuriated our utilitarian. Unlike his precise, universalizing inspection house, the penal colony remained inherently ambiguous, indeterminate, and inefficient. It was never only one thing.

Thus Bentham's historical Panopticon carries with it an interesting historical counterpart: the penal colony, an alternative solution to the social problems of immoral populations uncertainly justified by empire as much as any internal claim to efficacy. Along with elaborating his scheme, the philosopher expends ink on denouncing this rival, attacking it in the name of reason. Both these forms are European, and, at least in a historical sense, modern. But where the inspection house finds principle in architecture and proclaims itself as an enlightened break with the past, Australia's Botany Bay emerges as a more complex spatial reconfiguration, one derived from a plural algorithm that mixes the innovation in punishment with the geography of empire.

We will consider the particularities and possible implications of the penal colony form shortly. First, however, I want simply to recognize its historical significance relative to histories of punishment and emphasize its potential claim to modernity. Like confinement, the practice of exiling undesirable members of a population has a long and heterogeneous history. So too does the practice of forced labor, be it in a galley or a mine. And the combination of these two modes of punishment into the systematic transportation of people deemed guilty of common crimes to colonies emerged as a viable alternative to prisons and executions well before the end of Europe's eighteenth century. Nonetheless, the establishment of a convict colony in Australia marked a departure from earlier practices in terms of scale and administration.[12] In 1788, even as Jeremy Bentham returned from visiting his brother in Russia, the first fleet landed around the globe at Botany Bay. They were to be followed by many more, in an elaborate, evolving venture of penal colonization. Overall, some 160,000 convicts crossed the ocean before the final voyage in 1868, encountering not only a new land but also a new social order built around state-administered frontier labor (Hughes 1986). For all that the penitentiary system would eventually carry the day over transportation, in the short term Australia grew and Bentham's initial scheme met with failure. Furthermore, transportation would remain a viable penal option even after transportation to Australia ceased. In a case of particular interest to our discussion, the experiment in New South Wales inspired the planners of a French project. After several abortive ventures, the French established a penal colony in French Guiana in 1852, which remained operational in various iterations until the end of World War II. From a perspective located in the middle of the nineteenth century then, the penal colony could appear an active part of the future, not only a vestige of the past. Even as the penitentiary prison had begun to spread across continents (let alone schools, hospitals, and all the spatial configurations that Bentham had proposed to influence), the Panopticon was not the only machinery in sight.

The Penal Colony Form

The carceral network does not cast the unassimilable into a confused hell; there is no outside.

Foucault 1979: 301

What then to make of this alternate form, of a distinctively colonial mechanism of punishment? Foucault does not offer much help with placing the penal colony. *Discipline and Punish* recognizes in passing that transportation constituted an alternative to detention, but suggests that the British abandoned the practice (well before they did), calls the French case a "rigorous and distant form of imprisonment," and suggests it accomplished little in terms of colonization or economy (Foucault 1979: 272, 279).[13] But what might it have meant to have a "rigorous and distant form of imprisonment" located in an overseas extension of France and continuing until the mid-twentieth century? Is this colonial form simply the extension of the greater carceral system, an equivalent of the (Metropolitan) colony of Mettray (Foucault 1979: 293–296)? Or does geographic distance and location within empire have an effect on rigor relative to imprisonment? Following this margin of Foucault's thought back through its historical referent can further unearth the Panopticon's shadow twin. It will also carry us into the tropics, and a different scale of spatial alignment.

First I will quickly sketch the outlines of the substantive case.[14] While different French governments dreamed about and dabbled in deportation (before as well as after the Revolution of 1789), the closest parallel to Australia came into being under Louis Bonaparte, just after the short-lived Second Republic and the final abolition of slavery. France had long had a set of naval port prisons known as *bagnes*, descended from the practice of sentencing offenders to row in the galleys. These institutions demanded labor of their inmates, but under far less meticulous conditions than those of Bentham's project. Prisoners were generally held in communal cells under conditions that displayed few traces of Enlightenment reason.[15] Even as a number of colonial visionaries pined for a "French Botany Bay," penal reformers waged a campaign to close the *bagnes*. In the end both groups got their wish, and the *bagnes* were shifted overseas, most fatefully to French Guiana.[16] After a brief moment of official enthusiasm, death rates among convicts began to cast a pall over the project, and a Pacific outpost was established in New Caledonia in 1857, where it was hoped the climate would prove more conducive to European health. For a period between 1867 and 1887 French Guiana was reserved for prisoners of colonial origin. However, in the 1880s Freemasons and certain factions of the French government, seeking a harder line on crime and recidivism, helped popularize the image of New Caledonia as a "paradise" for its prisoners. After all, the death rate there was only 2 to 3 percent a year, less than a third of the Guiana statistic (Pierre 1982: 35).[17] Transportation to the Pacific ceased at the end of the nineteenth century, and convicts from all origins again returned to the Atlantic colony.

The operation distinguished several classes of *bagnards* within the *bagne*, each subject to different spatial controls and conditions of treatment in theory, and an even greater range of experience in practice. Those sentenced to hard labor for major offenses were usually placed in work camps, where the majority engaged in a variety of exhausting (but surprisingly unproductive) activities like logging and road-building, while keeping to timetable. Recidivist petty criminals lived in their own separate camps, as did the small number of political prisoners (most famously Alfred Dreyfus), who were not required to work.[18] Some prisoners were assigned as servants in or outside the penal establishment, while the most recalcitrant prisoners did time locked away in solitary punishment cells. The *bagne* also produced *libérés*, those who had served out their sentence but remained exiled in French Guiana, effectively sentenced to the most marginal forms of economic existence.

While conditions varied by period as well as classification and exact location amid the different establishments controlled by the penal administration, life in the *bagne* held little to recommend it. Disease was endemic, nutrition poor, violence common (both among prisoners and with the guards), and prospects bleak. Although escape remained a constant lure, it was also quite hazardous, requiring a lengthy journey through the forest or open sea. The *bagnards* languished, and many of them, perhaps half of the 70,000 total transported, died before completing their sentence.[19] In prison argot, the *bagne* was informally known as *la guillotine sèche*, the "dry guillotine." Despite a long history of attempts to reform it, the system remained in place until 1938, and then lingered on, its closure suspended, through a final episode of misery during World War II.

The sketch I have just given requires some amplification for analysis. First, we must note that it took time for this "dry guillotine" to take shape, and recall again that the French Guiana *bagne* grew partly out of a penal reform policy, the desire to close the old naval prisons and establish a better alternative. While we should not overestimate this will to reform, we should not underestimate it either. In the early years of the penal settlement, officials spent much time tracking the health and fortune of the convicts, and reporting their monthly statistics back to Paris.[20] When initial establishments on the mainland proved unhealthy, they tried other locations. When French Guiana as a whole seemed particularly deadly to European convicts, Paris shifted transportation of them to New Caledonia. Even in the later years, after that policy was reversed, after the camps for recidivists opened, and after the reputation of the enterprise grew to fit the name "Devil's Island," the French penal colony retained traces of reformist logic. However much sickness prevailed there was always an infirmary; however much the convicts lived in common each always had a carefully maintained file; however languidly demoralizing their punishment the camps always kept a timetable. Unlike the literal guillotine (also active in the colony), this instrument was never a matter of direct or efficient elimination.

Moreover, we must likewise note that this incarnation of the *bagne* grew partly out of a colonial policy, the desire to settle an undomesticated region of the empire where plantation slavery had failed. The dream of Botany Bay, of founding a tropical equivalent to Australia, floated not only through background studies to the project but into its early formation as well. The first arrivals were promised land (the governor announced that while they were working he would select "the most charming sites, the most fertile cantons"), in the expectation that once the establishment was up and running properly reformed criminals could become productive peasants.[21] A small number of women were sentenced to the colony, with the goal of encouraging convict marriages (imbued with the reformatory promise of domestic stability) and eventually a self-sustaining population. The experiment was not a success; while many did marry, many also died and few reproduced.[22] Nonetheless, traces of the colonial project survived, even after the transportation of women ceased and it was fairly clear that the *bagne* would never produce settler farmers. The labors assigned to convicts in the work camps generally conformed to those of settlement, sawing trees, building roads, and those engaged in more domestic pursuits such as gardening or cleaning helped maintain presence on the land. The results may have been materially disappointing – the road in particular crept along at a pitiful rate – and of dubious value to the greater colony of French Guiana as a whole. But the double logic that so infuriated Bentham is quite apparent throughout. Like Botany Bay, the French penal colony responded to both penal and colonial criteria of valuation. In this case, however, it "failed" on both accounts more dramatically than the Australian prototype, while lasting even longer.

There is also an additional anxiety of note, one less apparent in either Bentham's Panopticon or his concerns about Botany Bay. Across different periods, in different configurations, race was a constant issue within the *bagne*. While not all of the convicts came from European extraction, the majority did. At the same time, here the penal colony was inserted into an existing and recognized colonial social order, one that posited Europeans at its apex. Even before the enterprise began, the fact that French Guiana had been a part (however minor) of the greater Atlantic plantation complex gave planners pause. What, they wondered, would happen to the racial hierarchies of the plantation system if white convicts landed amid black slaves? Indeed, the small planter class was one of the obstacles frequently cited as a source of opposition to the project prior to abolition, attached as they were to the "nobility of the epidermis."[23] Race was also a technical category in the early phase of penal settlement. In keeping with environmental theories of the day, the administration allocated different food to prisoners of different racial categories, assigned them different tasks, and experimented with placing them in different locations to enhance survival. Europeans posed the greatest problem, as their constitutions were considered ill suited for life in the tropics, particularly when engaged in heavy labor. Despite efforts to "season" Europeans on the offshore islands (considered to be more salubrious) and to allocate the most burdensome tasks to colonial convicts, the administration failed to solve the problem of European mortality. Tensions over race continued throughout the later history of the enterprise, and provoked some of the international outrage over Devil's Island, where guards could have darker skin than prisoners.[24] In addition, the free civilian population surrounding the penal institution was largely composed of the descendents of former slaves. Thus within the restricted space of the *bagne*, the imperial order produced its own contradictory disruption. A minor inversion, but worthy of note: here the colonized could rule the colonizer.

What then to make of this alternate form, the penal colony, judging from its British and French materializations? Does the historical double of the Panopticon give us another pole from which to view the birth of the prison? It would be tempting to position the penal colony as an "anti-Panopticon," and certainly there is evidence to begin such an interpretation. Following Bentham, the Panopticon and penal colony become polar extremes, for where the former would perfect the architecture of internalization, the latter represents an extreme of externalization. One effects change within the individual through intensive surveillance, where the other alters the individual through geographical dislocation and a radical transformation of the environment. But in placing the penal colony in such a role against the Panopticon, we would not arrive at opposition in the sense of a single reversal, such as that found in a mirror, but rather a set of plural oppositions, some distinct, some overlapping. To illustrate the point let us consider three significant attributes of the penal colony: its spatial logic, the plural politics of visibility deployed within it, and its persistent ambiguity.

Like the Panopticon, the penal colony contains the kernel of a simple idea, likewise invested in spatial reconfiguration. In order to reorient the soul of the offender, why not reposition the body? Rather than the constant implied presence of the inspection house, here we have a spatial solution to crime that emphasizes removal and distance. Britain moved convicts from the rotting hulks of ships in the harbor to a new colony in the Antipodes, while France shifted them from port prisons to settlements within an existing colony in the tropics. In either case this removal incorporated a geographic geometry of empire beyond architecture. Where Bentham's device depended on precise alignments, once passed from Samuel to Jeremy it needed no particular ground. A prison in Pennsylvania, an asylum in Provence, either could be produced from a similar set of plans.[25] The concept of the penal colony, on the other hand, while discursively mobile, encountered translation problems in practice. The *bagne* moved more awkwardly overseas, and never quite succeeded in reproducing Botany Bay. For unlike the penitentiary, the penal colony requires location. Specificity of the site matters, since here it is the very place that is to enact the punishment and the reform, while simultaneously undergoing transformation. Thus French Guiana itself – soil, climate, flora, fauna, and myth – became unavoidable, since it would have to be domesticated for the redemptive logic to work.

The penal colony also involved principles of visibility and invisibility in its operation, if along less focused lines than Bentham's project. Rather than making the subjects of punishment internally visible in the name of moralization, the penal colony involved a more overt, if shadowy, display. By introducing a factor of distance into the equation of power, transportation displaced the spectacle of punishment before several audiences, while contributing to an ongoing imperial imagination of comparative place. Removed from their homeland, convicts remained actively on display to each other and to a colonial audience. For those in metropolitan France, the penal colony served as a hidden punishment, a distant if graphic terror, retaining elements of torture out of public view. For those in metropolitan nations outside France, the effect was equally distanced, while further removed; the punishment was not only hidden but also the product of another's justice. For those sent to French Guiana, however, the penal colony served directly as a public display, a constant reminder of the operations of justice. The convicts were not merely confined, but forced to labor on public works – hidden from France but not from its immediate colonial subjects. Official executions were performed by that once humane instrument, the guillotine, but before an audience of convicts, and by a fellow convict, far beyond the gates of Paris. Meanwhile the slow execution of the "dry guillotine" reminded the convicts that this punishment could only happen *here*, and not within metropolitan boundaries. And for those already living in French Guiana, the penal colony also served as a public spectacle, if one not aimed directly at them or of their making. Not only did the proximity of prison life to their own lives parade the power of justice before them in an immediate fashion, but the constant importation of prisoners for this apparatus of punishment emphasized the particularly colonial nature of this power. When all was said and done, French Guiana remained the destination of those deemed unworthy of France.

Most crucially of all, however, the penal colony appears to be a mixed form, and hence difficult to fix in a typology or simple opposition. As noted above, colonial transportation was simultaneously an innovation and the reconfiguration of an earlier system of punishment. Over time the project loses its claims to reform, and yet it never simply embraces repression. In some respects the penal colony appears like a partial anachronism, a reverse eddy in the flow of modern punishment. Transportation certainly had close ancestors in chain gangs, convict labor on public works, and the isolation of lepers, all practices that Foucault places in his earlier category of punishment. The prisoners were beaten and their fate was to some degree public. But the penal colony also displays traits of disciplinary control similar to the penitentiary. Every convict received a registration number and the administration maintained a dossier on each case. The prisoners were distanced and confined, effectively hidden from metropolitan France. Disciplinary infractions were primarily punished with isolation. The colony featured a variety of architectural forms in different settings, not only communal enclosures in prison camps on the mainland but also individual cells for special cases of insanity or incorrigibility on offshore islands. Different classes of prisoners were kept at different locations within the penal territories, and held under different conditions; as well as racial divisions, we find classifications by type of crime. Moreover, common convicts were sentenced to hard labor, while political prisoners were not required to work. On at least some level, the *bagne* was expected to rehabilitate its *bagnards*, and they to rehabilitate themselves. And yet they were also deported, and expected to spend their lives in a colony.

In short, the *bagne* was many things at once, always at a remove. Punishment, yes, but also colonial, and modern, in a shadowy and suspect way. Unlike the Panopticon, the penal colony never achieved the clarity of abstraction, remaining mired in the fantasies of empire and encumbered by the particularities of place. In this sense, we can see why it would not fit easily into the sharp contrasts of *Discipline and Punish*, or the chronological order of that text. Where Foucault focuses on a rupture within the history of Western responses to crime, the penal colony extends practices of the *ancien régime* into the greater carceral archipelago. Both elements of the dramatic opening of *Discipline and Punish* – executions and timetables – appear in the *bagne*. They are not separated by time, but rather conjoined awkwardly in a heterogeneous space and administered from a distance with local effects. Alongside the birth of the prison, we have the emergence of a colonial alternative, undeniably modern, and yet never purely modern. While the *bagne* shares some broad similarities to the agricultural settlement of Mettray, it lacked a settled agrarian landscape around it and was never devoted to the training of youth. Unlike the Mettray of Foucault's description, the penal colony was no model of training in education, religion, or hygiene, and produced no "penitentiary saint" who might regret a premature departure (Foucault 1979: 293). The dream of reform appeared there, but it mixed with other dreams and anxieties of empire. While not outside the carceral network, the *bagne* seems to at least mark a point on its frontier, a zone of confusion in which some could, and did, glimpse a form of hell for a different sort of modern soul. As the most famously incorrigible convict of the era told a journalist in the early 1920s: "I can no longer endure myself. The *bagne* has entered in me. I no longer am a man; I am a *bagne*.... A convict cannot have been a small child" (Londres 1975: 94).[26]

Displacement and Imperfect Technologies

Thus far in this essay I have followed the penal colony as a historical object, responding to Foucault's suggestive, offhand dismissal of the French *bagne* as a "rigorous and distant form of imprisonment," and suggesting instead that it represented an ambiguous colonial alternative to the Panopticon. The task now before us is to move this observation onto a more theoretical plane, and examine the possible significance of the existence of such a colonial alternative to the greater story of *Discipline and Punish*. What might be the effects of a space of ambiguity opposite Bentham's great architectural eye? What might the penal colony imply about the geography of modern power, or even the labor of anthropology? For assistance in this enterprise, I will first introduce elements of work by others who address aspects of Foucault's legacy in colonial contexts directly relevant to our topic.

In an article entitled "Panopticon in Poona: An Essay on Foucault and Colonialism," Martha Kaplan examines the decision of an early nineteenth-century British administrator named Elphinstone to build a prison modeled on the Panopticon in western India (Kaplan 1995). She sets herself two goals for this piece: first to situate the administrator's story relative to Foucault's reading of Bentham, and second to use the colonial context to query the historical frame of *Discipline and Punish*. "Thinking about Elphinstone and Foucault," she writes, "what might we learn about narratives of difference and historical trajectory?" (Kaplan 1995: 85). Kaplan's answer is that while we may indeed recognize panopticism within colonial rule in India, our real task is to recognize claims about temporal and civilizational difference as a powerful discourse of imagination, "a colonial project insistent on the creation of difference to establish power" (Kaplan 1995: 90). She notes that prior to British ascendancy and

Elphinstone's arrival, the Peshwa rulers in the region had developed detailed land and tax records, suggesting that panopticism may not have been a uniquely European innovation. Likewise she questions the modernity of Elphinstone's own vision, pointing out that the British themselves were prone to inefficiencies and addicted to spectacle. Finally, she finds evidence of the limits of power/ knowledge in Mahatma Gandhi's successful manipulation of the British Raj.[27] On the basis of these points, she advocates recognizing panopticism – and more generally modernity – as a plural possibility. Rather than Foucault's temporal orientation that defines the present against the past, we could define any system of rule against alternatives present in other cultural settings. The key mode of comparison would revolve around cultural difference, not time, and any history of the present could never claim singularity.[28]

While Kaplan's discussion ranges well away from prisons per se to a more general understanding of the possibilities of Benthamite visibility, it returns us to the question of the Panopticon itself relative to colonial contexts, and recognizes the stakes involved. If the birth of the prison described by *Discipline and Punish* indeed represents some sort of "history of the present" as Foucault famously intimated, then what to do with human difference? Are not present and past both heterogeneous domains? Would not any narrative built around a singular claim to modernity then ultimately prove a colonial project, reorienting other histories around a master metropole? In keeping with disciplinary tradition and anticolonial politics, Kaplan demands plurality along with particularity. This call to recognize difference and the dangers of temporal framing is an important caution, as discussions grounded in European history – particularly when undertaken by European intellectuals – slide easily into the universal mode.

But Kaplan's return to culture as both the source of human difference and the analytic frame within which to position it also opens other dangers. As we have seen, the original Panopticon was not simply an English (or even British) artifact, and the "Europe" it might represent only appears in transit.[29] Kaplan is surely correct in noting the significance of self-representation to imperial rule, but we should not ignore the *effects* of such representation, or simply dismiss its content. I suggest that it matters if European panopticists "envision and characterize their era of rule as an age of progress, science, and enlightenment" when other rulers have not (Kaplan 1995: 94). Actively embracing change within an extant system does not necessarily imply a particular "cultural" value or a universal human attribute; rather we might follow Foucault (1984: 39) in considering it a temporal ethos, a modernizing *attitude*. And actively seeking to expand a system into universal principles and institutions (whether successfully or not) implies a particular understanding of political possibility.

In arguing on behalf of cultural and historical particularity, Kaplan minimizes a key element of Bentham's particular inspection house: its insistent claims to a *mobile* form of instrumentality. Here the genealogy of the Panopticon itself proves useful, for it is the shift of vision between the Bentham brothers, glossed as Samuel's Russia and Jeremy's abstraction, that matters most. Once relocated to Britain the Panopticon became not only a doomed proposal but also the "simple idea" that justified it. In the name of this idea, Bentham would struggle against the rival project of Botany Bay, condemning its inefficiencies and ambiguous rationale. Yet this idea was also a principle of design, one associated with a specific, but very portable, set of plans.[30] The Panopticon not only suggested a different possibility for ordering life, it also provided a potential means to achieve it in a vast permutation of locations. We should not forget that Foucault (like many commentators on Bentham's project) refers to it repeatedly as a mechanism or machine. He insisted that we should not think of it as a dream building, but rather as "the diagram of a mechanism of power reduced to its ideal form." For once properly abstracted "it is in fact a figure of political technology that may and must be detached from any specific use" (Foucault 1979: 205). In repositioning the inspection house in a plural historical field, then, we will want to remember its instrumental ambition, and its ancestry in engineering along with philosophy. Whether placed in London or Poona, the design laid claim to both, and announced another possibility of their connection.

Here the work of David Scott provides another reference point with which to relocate Foucault in a colonial context. In chapter 1 of this volume, "Colonial Governmentality," Scott asks the question of what conceptual level to assign to Europe beyond geography as "an apparatus of dominant power-effects."[31] When dethroning that continent from its inherited status as the universal subject of history, he wants to avoid both the simple inversion of forgetting it and the generalization of positing a singular colonial condition, a danger he identifies with much postcolonial writing, including that of Chatterjee (1993). Instead he proposes to focus on what he calls the "*political rationalities* of colonial power," providing a closer accounting of the points of application of colonial rule and its constructed zone of functionality. Rather than ignoring Europe, such a project would transform it into a problem, and critically interrogate its varied extension through specific practices, modalities, and projects. Scott simultaneously seeks to recognize colonialism itself as a plural endeavor, and to retain the possibility of identifying a significant pattern within it: the emergence of a "modern" colonial state. Following Talal Asad (1992), he locates this modernity not in capitalism or the discourse of liberalism per se, but rather a shifting point of application of power to the body, and "the *conditions* in which that body is to live and define its life." Scott is particularly interested in what Foucault later called "governmentality," the art of rule that extends further than the maintenance of territory.[32] Beyond the immediate microscale of disciplinary techniques, government acts on a field of conditions, affecting the body indirectly. Its goal is to achieve an arrangement so that, as Scott alludes to Bentham's version of the concept, people following their own self-interest will "do as they ought." In a colonial context this translates into: "*the systematic redefinition and transformation of the terrain on which the life of the colonized was lived.*"

Scott goes on to analyze the particular case of British rule in Sri Lanka, and the emergence of an effort to alter the social world of the colonized in that setting in order to produce governable subjects. Here I want to focus on his suggestive use of the terms "terrain" and "conditions" in relation to an understanding of governmentality that explicitly acknowledges colonialism. Extending Foucault's sketch of the art of rule into the domain of empire, Scott's language implies the significance of *context* for the political rationality of what he calls the modern colonial state. This echoes points made earlier by Paul Rabinow (1989) about the significance of shifting concepts of milieu for urban planning in the French empire, where the question of the status of local particularities distinguishes different strains of modern plans. Setting, the alignment of things, a proper environment – these are essential concerns for a project of reaching and quietly administering bodies, and hence a crucial feature of any modernizing project. Just as reconfigurations were necessary in Europe for such a political rationality to take hold, so too were reconfigurations in the colonies; neither end of empire could be described as stable or a simple point of historical origin.

If we translate Scott's wording more literally into the enterprise of colonial settlement, away from the vast agrarian complexes of India and to the sparsely settled forest of the Guiana *bagne*, context incorporates obvious elements of nature amid the social order. Thus peering through the management perspective of governmentality, we can glimpse an ecological dimension of biopower, Foucault's general analysis of the incorporation of life into politics. For the population of a colony (particularly a settler colony) to survive as an appendage of a governing metropole, the landscape it occupies must, by definition, be habitable. Furthermore, to be governable (without significant alteration of a political rationality), this landscape must be recognizable as a territory, containing features appropriate for the application of power and the evaluation of its function. If bodies make up the target of power, they must be properly positioned and the conditions for reaching them established. Getting a Panopticon to work in any setting, in other words, involves a configuration of space more extensive than a simple application of architectural plans. It assumes a landscape of social and natural domestication.

Thinking of biopower in these ecological terms, we can now return to the penal colony to expand and complicate the point. Where would such a form stand relative to a political rationality of "colonial governmentality?" Let us again recall a few general facts of the French case. Initially, the removal of the *bagne* overseas claims some status as a reform policy. The administration demonstrates concern for the convict population, seeking to establish settlements conducive to survival. For a period European convicts are diverted to the Pacific, in the name of a racial understanding of health. For a different period women are also sent to the penal colony, and efforts made to encourage convict marriages in the hope of both domestication and reproduction. Clearly life is at issue in the *bagne*, and subject to a measure of governance; clearly bodies are targets within the exercise of power it employs. And yet these policies end in failure or reversal. Europeans are directed again to French Guiana, precisely in the name of its punitive death rates; the introduction of women does not produce stable families or a self-sustaining population. Death rates remain high and standards of health low, despite a more general domestication of the tropics (Curtin 1989; Anderson 1996). The *bagne*, and along with it French Guiana, acquires a new layer of sinister reputation. Rather than becoming a site where people "do as they ought" by virtue of following self-interest amid favorable conditions, the penal colony exemplifies a domain where people are not only controlled and punished through a variety of techniques, but also placed in conditions unfavorable to survival, let alone reform. Life is present but so too is death, in the shape of both the literal guillotine and its "dry," figurative cousin. The *bagne* lingers on, after an early period of experiments, after multiple calls for reform, after it is clear to all involved in its operation that the gap between the stated goals of behavior for its denizens and the conditions they inhabit is large.[33] Rather than governmentality we have something like its negative impression: a deployment of the possibility of government without its fulfillment. In this sense the French penal colony serves as an example of an alternative modernity constructed around *institutionalized failure*, a place where governmental norms are suggested but not applied.[34]

Reference to other exceptional biopolitical spaces amplifies this point about failure while clarifying a colonial dimension of the *bagne*. Writing about the politics of life and death within the Western tradition of sovereignty, Giorgio Agamben (1998: 168–171; 2000: 36–44) casts the concentration camp as the pure space where exception has become the rule. The penal colony shares some qualities with the concentration camp. Those in and outside it both identified it as an exceptional space, where norms did not apply. Further, it was not simply a killing machine devoted to execution, but rather a less coherent system whose byproduct was death. The key formula here was "to make survive" (Agamben 1999: 155), amid conditions which rendered survival a significant problem. The *bagne* also shares qualities of a contemporary Brazilian squatter settlement, described by João Biehl (2001: 131, 139) as a "zone of social abandonment" for those incapable of living with biopolitical norms yet included through their "waiting with death." Under a provision known as *doublage*, those convicts who survived their sentence of confinement faced a second sentence as a *libéré*, officially free yet forbidden to leave French Guiana and provided with no means of support. The fate of the *libéré* was certainly one of abandonment: an effectively empty return to citizenship under circumstances that continued to favor death. Yet the penal colony is also a historical artifact of European empire, one constructed around a colonial rather than national scale of difference. In such a context, I suggest, the effects of institutionalized failure play out differently, in that they adhere more closely to the particularities of milieu, and reflect the inherent impurity of always signifying a connection to another place.

Having earlier suggested that the penal colony is an ambiguous form as well as a historical alternative to Bentham's inspection house, I am now suggesting that this ambiguous form represents an *imperfect* mechanism, one built directly upon effects of displacement. By the term "imperfect," I mean not simply the everyday failings of any materialization to achieve the clarity of a diagram or rationale, but rather a deeper failing – the impossibility of maintaining an illusion of self-referential presence, of avoiding references to elsewhere. The penal colony depended on a marginal location and could never present itself – even in an abstracted form – as a universal center, only as an element of empire. In its French, tropical version it also produced an exceptional space, a site of colonial inversion and milieu of death within a wider field of rationality built on the management of life. The offset, destabilizing anti-Panopticon can also be cast as an offset, destabilizing domain of antigovernmentality. Here again the opposition is incomplete and the negative misleading. The administration of the *bagne* did not oppose itself in absolute terms to the *possibility* of governing any more than disciplining. Its rationale was full of bodies and allusions to their condition filled its documents. But these bodies were understood as repositioned entities, and their decline ascribed to the place they had come to occupy.

Recognizing a potential negative form of governmentality along with its limitations complicates our technical imagery of power, reintroducing variation in time and space. Such a move resonates with aspects of both Kaplan's and Scott's projects. On the one hand it disrupts the singular narrative of modernity implied in *Discipline and Punish* (if not in the culturally plural sense that Kaplan favors), on the other it disrupts the singular narrative of colonial difference and Europe (if in a slightly different direction than Scott suggests). The French penal colony, with its racial inversions and mixed disciplinary forms, does not suggest one history of the present emanating from Europe, nor only one colonial experience. But interpreting this extreme case in these terms also does one other thing of potential significance to a broader present: it emphasizes the possibility of *failure* within the given parameters of any project, and the potential for that failure to be reinscribed as a form of status identified with place. Management bears with it the possibility of mismanagement, large or small; a political rationality of modern power contains the possibility of inefficiency, breakdown, and endemic despair. While the penal colony was ultimately a secondary, lesser apparatus, and the French version produced nothing resembling a tropical Australia, it exemplifies a possible position within a greater array of modernizing projects: an environment of bad conditions, a space where norms are simultaneously asserted and violated. As analysis of international development inspired by Foucault suggests, such a position may be one produced in many modernization projects, conducted and maintained with a more singular sense of purpose than the penal colony (Ferguson 1990; Escobar 1995). Failure can also be internalized in the formation of subjects as well as international orders (Gupta 1998; Hansen and Stepputat 2001).[35] The very ambiguity of the *bagne*, then, may lead us back again to one of the starker insights of Foucault's analysis of the prison: power is rarely limited to stated function. The insight, however, is broadened and complicated. As well as considering political rationalities and their effects in a single temporal and geographic dimension, we would do well to consider their displacements, imperfections, and failures in multiple directions.

Foucault and Bentham, or the Problem of Theory

Through much of this essay I have drawn an implicit parallel between Foucault and Bentham, positioning both in relation to the Panopticon and their shared fascination with the clarity of the principle involved and the range of life it could affect. Yet a crucial distinction between their understandings of the inspection house remains. Where Bentham embraced the principle as a foundation for the dissemination of one kind of rational order, Foucault approached it with an attitude of perpetual suspicion. *Discipline and Punish* offers generalized observations, but not quite a general theory. It draws near enclosure and a claim to intellectual dominion, but stops just short, side-stepping and swerving. Consider again that elusive point in *Discipline and Punish* where Foucault provides the rationale for his project, describing it as a "history of the present." Attentive readers will notice that Foucault then ends the passage with a footnote, one restricting his project on the prison to the French case (Foucault 1979: 31, 309; 1975: 40).[36] No sooner is the sweeping rationale given than it is limited, and qualified with the most mundane of scholarly conventions appealing to evidence. Perhaps the challenge of that claim, then, lies not only in the particular framing of its problematic, but also the form of its announcement. Between a pronouncement and a footnote, different symptoms of the assertion of significance and the fragility of certainty, lies the possibility of an approach that both makes a problem broadly visible, insists strenuously on its importance, and yet refuses in the last instance to subsume the world into it. A space remains for response, the elaboration of other questions.

Where *Discipline and Punish* limits its geographic scope, narrows its methodological frame, and restricts its genealogy, it excludes even as it reveals. Thus Foucault's Panopticon mirrors Bentham's when it serves as a clarifying center of an epochal shift, while the more ambiguous penal colony drops away. Thus we might find ourselves caught, whether vaguely or precisely, in an eternal return to Europe. But as Gyan Prakash notes, "colonial modernity was never simply a 'tropicalization' of the Western form but its fundamental displacement, its essential violation" (Prakash 2000: 190). Following Foucault's footnote to the limits of his French case, we find the ambiguous form of the penal colony and a vision of modernity that includes not only the greater apparatus of normalization but also the shadow of its partial exceptions. There the theme of productive failure leads beyond direct critique of that apparatus to recognition of variations in the relative success of its application. Such variations, I suggest, together with the distance they create between sites of efficiency and sites of breakdown, might lead us to consider if modernity's most damaging other might not lie in its own possibilities of failure.[37]

For anthropology in particular, part of Foucault's crucial legacy must surely be the manner in which his work reopened modernity as a problem, refusing to accept its incessant official narration at face value, while at the same time refusing to reduce it to a cultural mirage or simply an epiphenomenon of capitalism. Yet no possible response to modern life could eliminate the deep tension of universalization implied within it. In an insightful recent essay, Timothy Mitchell (2000) returns to the problem of modernity and its colonial frame, arguing that the critical task remains one of disrupting the fundamental oppositions generated in the "performance" of the modern: oppositions between West and non-West and between representation and reality. "At issue, then," Mitchell writes, "is whether one can find a way to theorize the question of modernity that relocates it within a global context and, at the same time, enables that context to complicate, rather than simply reverse the narrative logic of modernization" (Mitchell 2000: 7). Our theoretical task, however, may lie even deeper within that awkward verb "theorize," including an effort to complicate knowledge at the point when it suggests imperial totality, and the rhetorical possibility of transcendence. Perhaps Foucault's more enduring provocation lies in an *attitude* toward theory, rather than in any particular position or statement. We should not forget that Foucault's repeated challenge to readers as well as himself was to use his work to dislodge self-certainty (Stoler 1995: 196; Foucault 1997c: 144; Rabinow 1997: xxxix). The stated goal was a continuing, critical project of self-interrogation, "the opposite of the attitude of conversion" (Foucault 1996: 461). In such a project, faith and continuity would be displayed not through ritual litany, but rather through questions and departures, the perpetual disorientation of serious engagement. For ours is a traveling present, its histories larger now, and growing ever more porous.

Notes

Acknowledgments. This work bears obvious genealogical debts accumulated at UC Berkeley. Beyond those, for various readings, discussion, and encouragement along this particular way I must thank Judy Farquhar, Diane Nelson, Rich Price, and Silvia Tomášková. Eduardo Restrepo lent some of his critical passion for Foucault to an earlier version of this essay, while both Ann Stoler and Jonathan Xavier Inda provided extensive and insightful comments for its final form.
1   The comment is from a 1975 interview with *Le Monde*, given just after the appearance of the French original of *Discipline and Punish* (Foucault 1994a: 720). Also quoted in Eribon (1991: 237), but here I am adopting John Johnston's more literal translation (Foucault 1996: 149). See also Macey (1993: xx) citing François Ewald on Foucault's attachment to the toolkit metaphor.
2   Foucault (1997b: 321) from a 1980 anonymous interview with *Le Monde*. "Le nom est une facilité" (Foucault 1994b: 104).
3   Surely there is no longer much doubt that Foucault can be cast as a "founder of discursivity" (his term for an author in the human sciences who establishes a productive orientation beyond specific claims), fulfilling the wager Paul Rabinow made decades

ago (Rabinow 1984: 26). However unwilling Foucault might have been to be defined – even by his own authorial categories – and however many qualifications we might have to bring to bear, the work of many readers and writers has turned that possibility into a social fact. While Foucault's positions have hardly met with universal approval, or even accurate paraphrase, his name appears regularly in bibliographies, syllabi, and the daylight of acknowledged thought. Indeed, part of his authorial presence in anthropology likely stems from the reception and contestation of his writing in colonial and postcolonial studies, not only as an effect of circulation, but also as a result of its unavoidable encounter with questions of difference within projects of modernity. Foucault now echoes through references to *Orientalism* (Said 1979), as well as other wide circuits of interdisciplinary scholarship addressing problematics of power and knowledge, of sexuality and governmentality. For a small sampling of work on colonial issues positioned in and around anthropology see the collections by Cooper and Stoler (1997) and Dirks (1992). Amid an earlier generation Cohn (1996) displays interesting resonance with Foucault's analytic.

4   Since my focus will be on an evolving reading through a particular text, I begin with this testimonial to stress from the outset that readings unfold within society, history, and the other abstractions of our analysis, and that any bookshelf displays traces of generation in addition to personality. The Foucault imagined here is indeed a transatlantic figure, altered through multiple translations of place and time between languages and institutions, but no less significant or authentic an entity because of it. Given a theme of colonialism and its historical inertia, I wish to start with a reminder that tensions of origin and descent also run through the academy, and to suggest that claims to knowledge should recognize transit and reinvention as well as source. For an interesting examination of the politics of theory translated over ground see Boyer (2001), whose title resonates with mine. Here, however, I am less concerned with questions of the political effects of academic theory and more concerned with colonial history in a more literal, rather warmer version of "the bush."

5   For discussion and clarification of the Panopticon's rhetorical role see Dreyfus and Rabinow (1983: 188–197).

6   Krichev was in the southern Mogilev province of White Russia, until 1772 a part of Poland and presently in Belarus (Christie 1993: 125, 130; Werrett 1999: 2). Mitchell (1991: 35, 185) follows Anderson (1956: 165–166) in recognizing the link from Jeremy to Samuel, but loosely assigns the Panopticon's origin to a general encounter between Europe and the Ottoman Empire, subsuming it to Russia's larger trajectory of modernization. As Kaplan (1995) confirms, however, he is quite correct in noting that India was a primary site of the construction of prisons following Bentham's general principles of design.

7   Bentham's interest in penal reform fits within a larger wave of British reformers, especially John Howard. Lest the complexity of genealogies be lost, it should be noted that Howard's views owed much to Dutch prisons, and other British reformers were aware of earlier experiments in France and elsewhere (Ignatieff 1978: 47–79).

8   In a provocative recent contribution to the *Journal of Bentham Studies*, Simon Werrett suggests that Samuel Bentham's problems stemmed less from problems of discipline among the peasants than among their unruly English supervisors (1999: 2–3). He also argues that Samuel's design reflects Russian absolutism based

on Byzantine theology and architecture (as opposed to Western Christianity), and thus the Bentham brothers' Panopticon represents not a new form of power but the decontextualization of an old one (1999: 8). While I do not find the latter point convincing as a refutation of Foucault's thesis (the decontextualized mobility of the Panopticon is surely "new" relative to the earlier formations of power he is describing, particularly when the guards are well trained), nonetheless his historical inquiry helpfully complicates Foucault's genealogy.

9   For more on issues related to shipbuilding on Potemkin's estate at Krichev see Werrett (1999) and Christie (1993, esp. 122–144 and 166–184). Given the theme of failure, we should also not forget that Samuel Bentham's scheme was never enacted, that Potemkin fell from power, and that Russia's southern expansion remained limited.

10 For a sampling of some of the debates about prisons in French historical circles see Perrot (1980), Petit (1984), and Petit et al. (1991). Garland (1990) offers an overview of punishment relative to social theory, Ignatieff (1978) an interesting, overlapping analysis of prisons, and Johnson (2000) a recent survey of prison architecture. Asad (1997) counters some misreadings and examines shifting understandings of pain within a larger historical frame.

11 Cited in Jackson (1987: 12). This is a draft passage apparently intended for his Finance Committee report; here I have altered his spelling of "defense" and "expenses" to conform with the conventions of my text. For further detail on Bentham's Panopticon scheme and his opposition to Australian transportation see Hume (1973, 1974) and Jackson (1987, 1988), in addition to Bentham (1962, 1977).

12 For some recent work on transportation in general see the electronic archive at the International Centre for Convict Studies (ICCS), iccs.arts.utas.edu.au/. For general orientation on Botany Bay in particular see Hughes (1986) and Shaw (1966).

13 "La seule alternative réellement envisagée a été la déportation que l'Angleterre avait abandonée dès le début du XIX siècle et que la France reprit sous le second Empire, mais plutôt comme une forme à la fois rigoureuse et lointaine d'emprisonnement" (Foucault 1975: 317). See also discussions in published interviews (Foucault 1980: 63–77, 146–165) and course outlines (Foucault 1997a: 17–37). Perrot (1980) includes studies of the Metropolitan (precolonial) *bagnes* in a collection of historical work responding to Foucault. In a discussion for a psychoanalysis journal, Foucault suggests that French relegation laws establishing the deportation of recidivist criminals to French Guiana and New Caledonia played a role in transforming Siberia from a site of simple exile to a site of labor camps. "In France we don't have a gulag, but we have ideas" (Foucault 1980: 224–225). The Siberian case presents an interesting parallel in a contrasting climate unfortunately beyond the scope of this essay; the circulation of penal ideas and practices (whether or not Foucault's off-the-cuff genealogy would withstand scrutiny), however, is one of my major concerns. Reading these texts with an eye toward the *bagne*, one gets the sense that Foucault was not particularly interested in French colonies beyond Algeria; French Guiana in particular comes across as *lointaine* [remote]. For more on the topic of comparison and circulation in definitions of colonial topics see Stoler (2001).

14 For more general background on the French Guiana *bagne* see Clair et al. (1990), Devèze (1965), and Pierre (1982), and for a discussion of its closure Donet-Vincent

(1992). Among English sources Miles (1988) provides a compact and vivid summary, Price (1998) an insightful biography of an unusual *bagnard*, and Wright (1983) a general history of nineteenth- and twentieth-century French penal practices. For more detailed historical exposition along the similar analytic lines as presented here see Redfield (2000). For background on French Guiana itself during this time period see Mam Lam Fouck (1987).

15 André Zysberg (1980: 165) opens his discussion of the Metropolitan *bagne* with a suggestive pairing between it and "anti-Panopticism." As we shall see, the later, colonial form of the *bagne* complicates the negative opposition further.

16 The selection of French Guiana as a site for this experiment was the product of considerable discussion. French Guiana emerged, as it had done repeatedly in earlier studies, as the most viable option as it was the right distance from Europe, relatively uninhabited, and – most crucially – under French control. The abolition of slavery removed a primary objection, rendering the small plantation economy of the existing colony obsolete. However, New Caledonia was of great interest to the committee in charge of the decision, and would eventually become the second French penal colony. See Redfield (2000: 56–66) and Forster (1996) for further background, also Bullard (2000) on the New Caledonian experience and the deportation of the remnants of the Paris Commune to that location.

17 Official death rates for the *bagne* in French Guiana fluctuated between 4.5 percent and 26 percent (Pierre 1982: 311–312). Overall, 10 percent can be taken as a rough average for the time period involved (Redfield 2000: 200).

18 For more on Dreyfus see Bredin (1986) for background and Menier (1977) for a specific discussion of his confinement on Devil's Island itself.

19 Pierre (1982: 311) reports official figures suggesting that out of the 48,537 who had arrived in French Guiana by 1921, 25,747 had expired, one way or another, while 7,636 had escaped or "disappeared," 5,194 had been paroled into the civilian population of the colony as *libérés*, and 3,896 had achieved repatriation to their land of origin.

20 E.g., as the Minister of the Navy and the Colonies responded to French Guiana's governor in December, 1854, "le chiffre de 26 décès pendant le mois de novembre est avec raison signalé par vous comme un grand progrès comparativement à la situation de l'année dernière, mais non comme constituant encore une proportion satisfaisante. Le nombre des malades donne lieu plus encore, à cette observation [the figure of 26 dead for the month of November is quite rightly pointed out by you as a significant improvement relative to the situation last year, but not yet constituting a satisfactory proportion. The number of sick lends still further support to this observation]," Letter 743, December 21, 1854. CAOM H bagne 14. As Prakash (2000: 219) notes in the Indian context, the use of statistics in such colonial documents is too widespread to easily single out.

21 "Vous allez descendre, travailler, préparer le terrain, élever des cases. Pendant ce temps-là, je parcourrai la colonie. Je choisirai, dans les sites les plus charmants, les cantons les plus fertiles; puis ces terres cultivées en commun seront partagées entre les plus méritants." The same governor sought to promote marriage between the convicts and prostitutes from Martinique; however his plans met with little success, and he was subsequently removed from office (Devèze 1965: 129; also Clair et al. 1990: 19). High turnover of officials was a factor in the administration of both the penal colony and French Guiana as a whole.

22 About 900 women arrived in French Guiana between 1858 and 1904. Another 1,000 or so would be sent to New Caledonia; the majority in each case sentenced under the recidivist laws of 1885 (Clair et al. 1990: 39). Mortality among them was remarkably high: 23–54 percent in New Caledonia, 44–69 percent in French Guiana. For a statistical breakdown see Krakovitch (1990: 283–295), Clair et al. (1990: 36–39), and Devèze (1965: 136), as well as the exhaustive early studies of Orgeas (1885).

23 "La caste blanche tient singulièrement à la noblesse de l'épiderme" (Ginouvier 1826). The same passage refers to a "bad joke" in circulation that suggested that convicts should be dyed black before embarkation.

24 The convict population usually ranged between 3,000 and 7,000, hovering around 20 percent of the total population of French Guiana. Despite the shipment of some 700 new arrivals per year, deaths and escapes kept the number of prisoners relatively constant. The average prisoner was metropolitan, French, nominally Catholic, partly educated, between 20 and 50 years of age, single, and from the lower end of the urban social order. However, this profile masks considerable variation, and the colonies were also well represented, with *bagnards* arriving from Algeria to Vietnam. Michel Pierre provides the breakdown of 63 percent European, 25 percent Arab, 7 percent black, and 5 percent Asian, but without specifying total figures (Pierre 1982: 41). A sample from 1907 shows 2,605 Europeans to 998 Arabs, 361 Africans, and 130 Indochinese (Le Clère 1973: 61). For further statistics see also Devèze (1965: 165–168), Krakovitch (1990: 260–261), and Pierre (1982: 307–315). The convicts were controlled by trustees and several hundred prison guards of mixed origin, including Corsicans, North Africans, and some Guyanais, as well as about six hundred troops, including a detachment of Senegalese. Herménégilde Tell, a Guyanais Créole, became director of the penal administration in 1919. For a sense of sensationalist accounts about Devil's Island, including Hollywood films, see Miles (1988). For a general discussion of race as a medical problem in imperial settings see Anderson (1996). For accounts of the penal colony by physicians with direct experience of it see Orgeas (1885) and Rousseau (1930).

25 To further complicate the opposition given here, it is worth noting that Bentham not only railed against the Australian penal colony, but also sought to have a Panopticon constructed in New South Wales (Hughes 1986: 123).

26 "Je ne puis plus me souffrir moi-même. Le bagne est entré en moi. Je ne suis plus un homme, je suis un bagne.... Un bagnard ne peut pas avoir été un petit enfant." The speaker is Roussenq, a figure legendary for defying the penal administration and spending an extraordinary amount of time in solitary punishment. He would eventually go on to write his own memoir called *L'Enfer du bagne* [*The Hell of the Penal Colony*] (Roussenq 1957). He was far from alone in this allusion: the titles of many accounts of the *bagne*, particularly in the twentieth century, conjure up images of damnation, while evincing colonial anxieties about the tropics and race. For examples and discussion see Redfield (2000: 76–108).

27 Kaplan maintains a rather restrictive interpretation of Foucault's understandings of power. Rather than proving an exception to power/knowledge, Gandhi's successful manipulation of visibility in anticolonial struggles would seem to confirm the point that power is attached to resistance as well as knowledge and that anyone could potentially occupy the Panopticon's central tower. See Faubion (2000).

28 Kaplan (1995: 94–95) recognizes this move as a return to a Boasian project of cultural comparison as an alternative to Foucault's temporal analytic. In Boas we find the old hope of detaching human difference from the inherent hierarchy of any evolutionary order, or, in Kaplan's context, of depriving the British Empire (and with it the West) of any monopoly on the present. In short, we have a central legacy of American anthropology.

29 For more on the historical imagination of geographic difference see Lewis and Wigen (1997).

30 As a diagram the Panopticon could be cast as an "immutable mobile" in the Latourian sense when passing from Samuel's first descriptions to Jeremy's elaborated calculations (Latour and Woolgar 1986). However, mutability in mobility is precisely what would seem most at issue in a colonial context. Here I simply want to insist on the significance of a transportable form; for an interesting discussion of mutability with a very different object see de Laet and Mol (2000).

31 An earlier version of the essay was published in the journal *Social Text*. See David Scott (1995).

32 Unlike sovereignty, government disposes of law tactically rather than directly, and deploys things as well as people (Foucault 1991: 93). The term "governmentality" has spawned a large body of writing; here I am less interested in it as a symptom of the liberal state and more interested in the way it permits a consideration of nonhumans and environments within human politics.

33 As alluded to above, the *bagne* produced a remarkable and long-lasting genre of exposé writing, both in the form of journalistic accounts and sensational memoirs (most famously Londres 1975 and Charrière 1970; see Miles 1988 and Redfield 2000 for additional examples). Here I am interested in emphasizing not only a difference between original intention and outcome, but also a shift in intentionality through time, one that readjusted the balance between action and inaction even as knowledge about the situation and the environment increased. While the later penal colony retained institutional elements of a concern for health (an infirmary, for example), many of the medical conditions reported could easily have been treated through better nutrition, sanitation, and medications available to French doctors elsewhere at the time. In addition to consistent descriptions of corruption and active abuse, we have the institutional preservation of what are – by public health standards of early twentieth-century tropical medicine – outdated norms. Like with the prison (Foucault 1979: 272), here we have the proclamation of failure together with maintenance, but particularized in place.

34 For more on alternative modernities see the *Public Culture* volume by that title (Gaonkar 2001). In his contribution, Charles Taylor opposes cultural and acultural variants of modernity, suggesting the image of a wave for the latter (2001: 182–183). Here I wish to leave cultural difference to one side, and simply highlight the complexity of fluid mechanics in the spread of institutional forms: backflows, swirls, eddies, and – in particular locations – stagnation. As Mitchell points out, such a representation itself depends on and hence reinforces the rhetorical frame of modernity; he rejects the coherence suggested by the term "alternative modernities," preferring to emphasize the "impossible unity" of both modernity and capitalism (Mitchell 2000: 24). Here I am less invested in contesting modernity as a term than in disrupting the implied functionality of theoretical language in general, and expanding the possibility of

"alternatives" into the central frame of modernity itself, including its technical dimensions. The multiple failings of colonial and postcolonial states could be another avenue for exploring what I am terming "imperfection" in comparing the materialized form of the French penal colony with Bentham's Panopticon. For a helpful review of recent literature on the topic see Hansen and Stepputat (2001).

35 This point acknowledges the significance of machines to projects of empire (e.g., Adas 1989 and Headrick 1981), but complicates the linear sense of function central to their presentation.

36 The note reads: "I shall study the birth of the prison only in the French penal system. Differences in historical developments and institutions would make a detailed comparative examination too burdensome and any attempt to describe the phenomenon as a whole too schematic" (Foucault 1979: 309). Foucault's writing varies considerably in its recognition of difference, occasionally cautioning about the limits of the analysis, often implying general relevance and usually floating in between. A more rigorous inventory and analysis of his geographic claims lies outside the scope of this essay. But in an interview with the French geography publication *Hérodote*, Foucault comments on the spatial framing of *Discipline and Punish*, acknowledging the ambiguity of his frame of reference between France and Europe (Foucault 1980: 67–68). He concludes: "There is indeed a task to be done of making the space in question precise, saying where a certain process stops, what are the limits beyond which something different happens – though this would have to be a collective undertaking" (1980: 68). As Ann Stoler notes in commenting on Foucault's response, this collective project has turned in a somewhat different direction than Foucault himself might have imagined, and yet resonates with his conception of critique as the art of "reflective insolence" (Stoler 1995: 208–209).

37 In deploying the term "failure" I do not mean to imply an essential state of being, but rather a particularly potent regime of valuation that figures into the *conditions* of action. Whether or not any of us have ever *been* modern (Latour 1993), some people (like Bentham) have certainly tried their best, with lasting effects.

References

Adas, Michael
  1989 Machines as the Measure of Men: Science, Technology and Ideologies of Western Dominance. Ithaca: Cornell University Press.
Agamben, Giorgio
  1998[1995] Homo Sacer: Sovereign Power and Bare Life. Stanford: Stanford University Press.
  1999 Remnants of Auschwitz: The Witness and the Archive. New York: Zone Books.
  2000[1996] Means Without End: Notes on Politics. Minneapolis: University of Minnesota Press.
Anderson, Matthew
  1956 Samuel Bentham in Russia, 1779–1791. American Slavic and East European Review 15(2): 157–172.

Anderson, Warwick
   1996   Disease, Race and Empire. Bulletin of the History of Medicine 70(1): 62–67.
Asad, Talal
   1992   Conscripts of Western Civilization. *In* Dialectical Anthropology, Essays in
      Honor of Stanley Diamond, vol. 1: Civilization in Crisis: Anthropological Perspec-
      tives. Christine Gailey, ed. Pp. 333–350. Gainesville: University of Florida Press.
   1997   On Torture, or Cruel, Inhuman and Degrading Treatment. *In* Social Suffering.
      Arthur Kleinman, Veena Das, and Margaret Lock, eds. Pp. 285–308. Berkeley:
      University of California Press.
Bentham, Jeremy
   1962[1787–1802]   Panopticon; or The Inspection-House, Panopticon vs. New South
      Wales, and A Plea for the Constitution. *In* The Works of Jeremy Bentham, vol. 4.
      John Browring, ed. Pp. 1–284. New York: Russell and Russell.
   1977[1787]   Le Panoptique. Paris: Pierre Belfond.
Biehl, João
   2001   Vita: Life in a Zone of Social Abandonment. Social Text 68: 131–149.
Boyer, Dominic
   2001   Foucault in the Bush: The Social Life of Post-Structuralist Theory in East
      Berlin's Prenzlauer Berg. Ethnos 66(2): 207–236.
Bredin, Jean-Denis
   1986[1983]   The Affair: The Case of Alfred Dreyfus. New York: George Braziller.
Bullard, Alice
   2000   Exile to Paradise: Savagery and Civilization in Paris and the South Pacific,
      1790–1900. Stanford: Stanford University Press.
Charrière, Henri
   1970[1969]   Papillon. Patrick O'Brian, trans. St. Albans: Panther Books.
Chatterjee, Partha
   1993   The Nation and Its Fragments: Colonial and Postcolonial Histories. Princeton:
      Princeton University Press.
Christie, Ian R.
   1993   The Benthams in Russia, 1780–1791. Oxford: Berg.
Clair, Silvie et al.
   1990   Terres de bagne. Exhibition catalogue. Aix-en-Provence: CAOM/AMAROM.
Cohn, Bernard S.
   1996   Colonialism and Its Forms of Knowledge: The British in India. Princeton:
      Princeton University Press.
Cooper, Frederick, and Ann Laura Stoler, eds.
   1997   Tensions of Empire: Colonial Cultures in a Bourgeois World. Berkeley: Univer-
      sity of California Press.
Curtin, Philip
   1989   Death by Migration: Europe's Encounter With the Tropical World in the
      Nineteenth Century. Cambridge: Cambridge University Press.
De Laet, Marianne, and Annemarie Mol
   2000   The Zimbabwe Bush Pump: Mechanics of a Fluid Technology. Social Studies of
      Science 30(2): 225–263.

Devèze, Michel, ed.
1965   Cayenne: Déportés et bagnards. Paris: Juillard.
Dirks, Nicholas B., ed.
1992   Colonialism and Culture. Ann Arbor: University of Michigan Press.
Donet-Vincent, Danielle
1992   La fin du bagne (1923–1953). Rennes: Editions Ouest-France.
Dreyfus, Hubert, and Paul Rabinow
1983   Michel Foucault: Beyond Structuralism and Hermeneutics. 2nd edition. Chicago: University of Chicago Press.
Eribon, Didier
1991[1989]   Michel Foucault. Betsy Wind, trans. Cambridge, MA: Harvard University Press.
Escobar, Arturo
1995   Encountering Development: The Making and Unmaking of the Third World. Princeton: Princeton University Press.
Faubion, James D.
2000   Introduction. *In* The Essential Works of Michel Foucault, 1954–1984, vol. 3: Power. James D. Faubion, ed. Pp. xi–xli. New York: New Press.
Ferguson, James
1990   The Antipolitics Machine: "Development," Depoliticization and Bureaucratic Power in Lesotho. Cambridge: Cambridge University Press.
Forster, Colin
1996   France and Botany Bay: The Lure of a Penal Colony. Melbourne: Melbourne University Press.
Foucault, Michel
1975   Surveiller et punir. Paris: Editions Gallimard.
1979[1975]   Discipline and Punish: The Birth of the Prison. New York: Vintage Books.
1980   Power/Knowledge: Selected Interviews and Other Writings, 1972–1977. Colin Gordon, ed. New York: Pantheon.
1984   What is Enlightenment? *In* The Foucault Reader. Paul Rabinow, ed. Pp. 32–50. New York: Pantheon.
1991[1978]   Governmentality. *In* The Foucault Effect: Studies in Governmentality. Graham Burchell, Colin Gordon, and Peter Miller, eds. Pp. 87–104. Chicago: University of Chicago Press.
1994a[1970–75]   Dits et écrits, 1954–1988, vol. 2. Daniel Defert and François Ewald, eds. Paris: Gallimard.
1994b[1980–88]   Dits et écrits, 1954–1988, vol. 4. Daniel Defert and François Ewald, eds. Paris: Gallimard.
1996   Foucault Live. New York: Semiotexte.
1997a   The Essential Works of Foucault, 1954–1984, vol. 1: Ethics: Subjectivity and Truth. Paul Rabinow, ed. New York: New Press.
1997b   The Masked Philosopher. *In* The Essential Works of Foucault, 1954–1984, vol. 1: Ethics: Subjectivity and Truth. Paul Rabinow, ed. Pp. 321–328. New York: New Press.
1997c   The Politics of Truth. New York: Semiotexte.

Gaonkar, Dilip Prarmeshwar, ed.
2001   Alternative Modernities. Durham, NC: Duke University Press.
Garland, David
1990   Punishment and Modern Society: A Study in Social Theory. Chicago: University of Chicago Press.
Ginouvier, T.
1826   Le Botany-Bay Français, ou colonisation des condamnées aux peines afflictives [*sic*] et infamants et des forçats libérés. Paris: Centre des Archives d'Outre-mer, H bagne 3.
Gupta, Akhil
1998   Postcolonial Developments: Agriculture in the Making of Modern India. Durham, NC: Duke University Press.
Hansen, Thomas Blom, and Finn Stepputat, eds.
2001   States of Imagination: Ethnographic Explorations of the Postcolonial State. Durham, NC: Duke University Press.
Headrick, Daniel R.
1981   The Tools of Empire: Technology and European Imperialism in the Nineteenth Century. New York: Oxford University Press.
Hughes, Robert
1986   The Fatal Shore. New York: Alfred A. Knopf.
Hume, L. J.
1973   Bentham's Panopticon: An Administrative History I. Historical Studies 15(61): 703–721.
1974   Bentham's Panopticon: An Administrative History II. Historical Studies 16(62): 36–54.
Ignatieff, Michael
1978   A Just Measure of Pain: The Penitentiary in the Industrial Revolution, 1750–1850. London: Penguin Books.
Jackson, R. V.
1987   Bentham vs. New South Wales: The Letters to Lord Pelham. University of London, Australian Studies Center, Working Paper Number 25.
1988   Luxury in Punishment: Jeremy Bentham on the Cost of the Convict Colony in New South Wales. Australian Historical Studies 23(90): 42–59.
Johnson, Norman
2000   Forms of Constraint: A History of Prison Architecture. Urbana: University of Illinois Press.
Kaplan, Martha
1995   Panopticon in Poona: An Essay on Foucault and Colonialism. Cultural Anthropology 10(1): 85–98.
Krakovitch, Odile
1990   Les femmes bagnardes. Paris: Oliver Orban.
Latour, Bruno
1993   We Have Never Been Modern. Cambridge, MA: Harvard University Press.
Latour, Bruno, and Steve Woolgar
1986[1979]   Laboratory Life: The Construction of Scientific Facts. 2nd edition. Princeton: Princeton University Press.

Le Clère, Marcel
    1973   La vie quotidienne dans les bagnes. Paris: Hachette.
Lewis, Martin, and Kären Wigen
    1997   The Myth of Continents: A Critique of Metageography. Berkeley: University of California Press.
Londres, Albert
    1975[1923–27]   L'homme qui s'evada/Au bagne. Paris: Union Générale d'Editions.
Macey, David
    1993   The Lives of Michel Foucault: A Biography. New York: Pantheon Books.
Mam Lam Fouck, Serge
    1987   Histoire de la société Guyanaise, Les années cruciales: 1848–1946. Paris: Editions Caribéennes.
Menier, Marie-Antoinette
    1977   La détention du Capitaine Dreyfus à l'île du Diable, d'après les archives de l'administration pénitentiaire. Revue française d'histoire d'outre-mer 64: 456–475.
Miles, Alexander
    1988   Devil's Island: Colony of the Damned. Berkeley: Ten Speed Press.
Mitchell, Timothy
    1991[1988]   Colonizing Egypt. Berkeley: University of California Press.
    2000   The Stage of Modernity. In Questions of Modernity. Timothy Mitchell, ed. Pp. 1–31. Minneapolis: University of Minnesota Press.
Orgeas, J.
    1885   Contribution à l'étude du non-cosmopolitisme de l'homme: La colonisation de la Guyane par la transportation: Étude historique et démographique. Paris: Octave Doin.
Perrot, Michelle, ed.
    1980   L'impossible prison: Recherches sur le système pénitentiaire au 19e siècle. Paris: Editions du Seuil.
Petit, Jacques, ed.
    1984   La prison, le bagne et l'histoire. Geneva: Librairie des Méridiens.
Petit, Jacques et al.
    1991   Histoire des galères, bagnes et prisons: XIIIe–XXe siècles: Introduction à l'histoire pénale de la France. Michelle Perrot, preface. Toulouse: Editions Privat.
Pierre, Michel
    1982   La terre de la grande punition: Histoire des bagnes de Guyane. Paris: Editions Ramsay.
Prakash, Gyan
    2000   Body Politic in Colonial India. In Questions of Modernity. Timothy Mitchell, ed. Pp. 189–222. Minneapolis: University of Minnesota Press.
Price, Richard
    1998   The Convict and the Colonel. Boston: Beacon Press.
Rabinow, Paul
    1984   Introduction. In The Foucault Reader. Paul Rabinow, ed. Pp. 3–29. New York: Pantheon Books.
    1989   French Modern: Norms and Forms of the Social Environment. Cambridge, MA: MIT Press.

1997   Introduction: The History of the Systems of Thought. *In* The Essential Works of Foucault, 1954–1984, vol. 1: Ethics: Subjectivity and Truth. Paul Rabinow, ed. Pp. xi–xlii. New York: New Press.

Redfield, Peter
  2000   Space in the Tropics: From Convicts to Rockets in French Guiana. Berkeley: University of California Press.

Rousseau, Louis
  1930   Un médecin au bagne. Paris: Editions Armand Fleury.

Roussenq, Paul
  1957[1934]   L'enfer du bagne: Souvenirs vécus inédits. Vichy: Pucheux.

Said, Edward
  1979   Orientalism. New York: Vintage Books.

Scott, David
  1995   Colonial Governmentality. Social Text 43: 191–220.

Semple, Janet
  1993   Bentham's Prison: A Study of the Panopticon Penitentiary. Oxford: Clarendon Press.

Shaw, A. G. L.
  1966   Convicts and the Colonies. London: Faber and Faber.

Stoler, Ann Laura
  1995   Race and the Education of Desire: Foucault's History of Sexuality and the Colonial Order of Things. Durham, NC: Duke University Press.
  2001   Tense and Tender Ties: The Politics of Comparison in North American History and (Post) Colonial Studies. Journal of American History 88(3): 829–865.
  2002   Developing Historical Negatives: Race and the (Modernist) Visions of a Colonial State. *In* From the Margins: Historical Anthropology and Its Futures. Brian Axel, ed. Pp. 156–185. Durham, NC: Duke University Press.

Taylor, Charles
  2001   Two Theories of Modernity. *In* Alternative Modernities. Dilip Parameshwar Gaonkar, ed. Pp. 172–196. Durham, NC: Duke University Press.

Werrett, Simon
  1999   Potemkin and the Panopticon: Samuel Bentham and the Architecture of Absolutism in Eighteenth Century Russia. Journal of Bentham Studies 2. Electronic document, www.ucl.ac.uk/Bentham-Project/journal/nlwerret.htm.

Wright, Gordon
  1983   Between the Guillotine and Liberty: Two Centuries of the Crime Problem in France. New York: Oxford University Press.

Zysberg, André
  1980   Politiques du bagne, 1820–1850. *In* L'impossible prison: Recherches sur le système pénitentiaire au 19ᵉ siècle. Michelle Perrot, ed. Pp. 165–205. Paris: Editions du Seuil.

Part II
Global Governance

3

Graduated Sovereignty in South-East Asia

Aihwa Ong

Globalization and State Action

Globalization has been taken to mean many things; our different concepts of globalization seem to color our understanding of the state. By now, claims that "the survival of the state" is threatened by globalization have been met by powerful counter-arguments (Evans, 1997; Ruggie 1998; Ong 1999). One cannot deny that economic globalization – in the relentless pursuit of market freedom – has brought about important changes in the state of "stateness." The fundamental question is what basic changes in the state, and in the analysis of the state, have been occasioned by global markets? For instance, it would be useful to understand how states in practice actually manage a range of transnational networks that variously integrate them into the global market and political community. If we look at the strategies of particular states in relation to economic neoliberalism, we will discover that smaller states have made institutional adjustments to meet the challenges of global forces, in the process refashioning state power vis-à-vis their populations and external institutions. Indeed, global markets have contributed to both the strengthening and the weakening of different activities of the state, and thus shaped its capacity to deal with global regulatory entities.

This essay seeks to explore the dynamic relations between global corporations and nonmarket entities on the one hand, and the actions of middle-range Asian states on the other. The rise of so-called new Asian tiger countries in South-East Asia has been accomplished by partially submitting to the demands of major corporations, and to global regulatory agencies like the United Nations. In the course of such interactions with global markets and transnational regulatory agencies, the governments have created new economic possibilities, social spaces and

Reprinted from Aihwa Ong, "Graduated Sovereignty in South-East Asia." *Theory, Culture & Society* 17, 4 (2000): 55–75.

political constellations, which in turn conditioned their further actions. The shifting relations between market, state, and society have resulted in an assemblage of governmental practices for treating populations in relation to global market forces. The experiences of these small, relatively open Asian states thus present an instructive case of how interactions with global forces have produced a variety of outcomes, leading to the state's flexible experimentations with different forms of sovereignty.

State Strategy and Graduated Sovereignty

Arguments about state power are often based on a restricted concept of sovereignty. I go beyond the conventional understanding of sovereignty as state power that is centralized and concentrated in the military appartus of the regime to ensure order and stability to safeguard the territorial integrity of the nation-state (Giddens 1987; Schmitt 1987). I maintain that we need to pay attention as well to other forms of state power like control, surveillance, and regulation vis-à-vis markets, populations, and external agencies. David Held has usefully distinguished between de jure sovereignty and de facto or practical sovereignty. He suggests that: "The often weak and debt-ridden economies of many third world countries leave them vulnerable and dependent on economic forces and relations over which they have little, if any, control" (1998: 32). But again, even less powerful states like Asian tigers, while vulnerable to the pressures of global markets, still have the capacity to manipulate global relations, and to adjust their relations with their society accordingly. An attempt to grasp sovereignty in practice requires an understanding of the different mechanisms of governance beyond the military and the legal powers. In his discussion of "the art of government," Foucault notes that modern sovereignty is no longer simply a "supreme power" over the population (1977, 1991). Thus, "there are several forms of government among which the prince's relation to his state is only one particular mode; while on the other hand, all these other kinds of government are internal to the state and society" (Foucault 1991: 91). Different modalities of state power coexist, and the distinctive modern forms are concerned with "governing" populations, individuals and oneself. In short:

> The art of government ... is essentially concerned with answering the question of how to introduce economy – that is to say, the correct manner of managing individuals, goods and wealth within the family ... and of making the family fortunes prosper – how to introduce this meticulous attention of the father towards his family into the management of the state. (Foucault 1991: 92)

State management of the population thus requires different modalities of government, based on mechanisms of calculation, surveillance, control, and regulation that set the terms and are constitutive of a domain of social existence. The different forms of regulation, of course, do not mean that states do not, now and again, here and there, resort to police and military action against their own people. This essay uses the model of graduated sovereignty to describe how certain states in South-East Asia have responded to global market forces with a particular mix of governing practices and military repression.

Manuel Castells calls the Asian tigers "developmental states" that base their legitimacy in their "ability to promote and sustain development, understanding by development the combination of steady high rates of economic growth and structural change in the productive system, both domestically and in its relationship to the international economy" (1998: 270–271). Others prefer the term "strong states" to stress the powerful bureaucracy, public enterprises, and state monopolies that have presided over capitalist development in South-East Asia (McVey 1992). And indeed, over the past two decades, Singapore, Malaysia, Thailand, and Indonesia have been strengthened by a great infusion of foreign direct investments, experiencing some of the highest rates of economic growth in history. Scholars, however, have not paid attention to the state strategies I call "postdevelopmental," referring to their basic goals of producing and governing middle classes and in forming links with global capital. While the typical state in the Association of South-East Asian Nations (ASEAN) continues to control a (diminishing) nationalized sector of its economy, an expanding multinational sector is dominated by global corporations. Elements of postdevelopmentalism can be found in Latin American countries (see for example O'Donnell 1993), but what is distinctive about Asian postdevelopmentalism is its claims of cultural unity and stability, combined with the selective adoption of neoliberal practices that have made South-East Asia more "bankable" in the eyes of global corporations. This penetration of global forces has affected the relations between state and society, also changing people's understanding of their investments in state power and the different possibilities of citizenship depending on one's relation to market forces.

Drawing on ethnographic research mainly from Malaysia and Indonesia, countries that, until the financial crisis in 1998, were respectively the new and aspiring Asian tigers, I will set out my notion of graduated sovereignty as a product of state–globalization interactions. There are two aspects to graduated sovereignty: (1) the differential state treatment of segments of the population in relation to market calculations, thus intensifying the fragmentation of citizenship already pre-formed by social distinctions of race, ethnicity, gender, class, and region; (2) the state–transnational network whereby some aspects of state power and authority are taken up by foreign corporations located in special economic zones. This system of graduated sovereignty has been temporarily upset by the financial firestorm of 1998, stimulating middle-class challenges to state authoritarianism, and state attempts to reterritorialize state power.

Differential Treatment of the Population

While others view the relationship between the state and its citizens strictly in terms of political power over legal subjects, I wish to discover the rationalities of government that variously regulate the forms of belonging (citizenship) and produce the condition of order and stability (sovereignty) in a polity. Foucault (1979) uses the term "biopower" to refer to a central concern of the modern liberal state in fostering of life, growth, and care of the population. Biopower, he argues, brings "life and its mechanisms into the realm of explicit calculations and made knowledge/power an agent of the transformation of human life" (Foucault 1979: 143; 1991).

The question is, what forms do biopolitical considerations take in Asian tiger countries, where reports of occasional political repression seem to overshadow our perception of different mechanisms of government? Robert Castel observes the emergence, in neoliberal states, of "differential modes of treatments of populations, which aim to maximize the returns on doing what is profitable and to marginalize the unprofitable" (1991: 294). Asian tiger states, which combine authoritarian and economic liberal features, are not neoliberal formations, but their insertion into the global economy has required selective adoption of such neoliberal norms for managing populations in relation to corporate requirements. Disciplinary technologies aimed at instilling self-discipline, productivity, and welfare (Foucault 1979) are integrated at the level of the state, and come to regulate society at large.[1] Furthermore, in countries such as Malaysia, Indonesia, and, to some extent, Thailand and Singapore, a "pastoral" logic defined particular objects of government, whereby certain segments of the population are given special treatment because of their race or ethnicity (Foucault 1981). Colonial divide-and-rule policies have continued in the state differentiation of citizens by ethnicity, gender, class, and nationality, thus producing and structuring society as a collection of ethno-racial entities. Such preexisting ethno-racializing schemes are now reinforced as well as crosscut by new ways of governing that differentially value populations according to market calculations. To remain globally competitive, the Asian tiger state makes different kinds of biopolitical investments in different subject populations, privileging one ethnicity over another, the male over the female, and the professional over the manual worker. Different sectors of the population are subjected to different technologies of regulation and nurturance, and in the process assigned different social fates.

Malaysia: The Biopolitics of Postdevelopmentalism

There are good reasons for using Malaysia as an illustrative example of a state that is developing a system of graduated sovereignty. Since its political independence from Great Britain in 1957, the country has favored the political rights of Malays on grounds of their status as an "indigenous" majority population and their general economic backwardness when compared with the ethnic Chinese and Indians who are descended from immigrant populations. But one can argue that from the early 1970s onward, a system of graduated sovereignty has come into effect as the government has put more investment in the biopolitical improvement of the Malays, or *bumiputra* ("princes of the soil," or original inhabitants), awarding them rights and benefits largely denied to the Chinese and Indian minorities. Special programs have awarded shares in state-held trusts, government contracts, business credit, scholarships, business licenses, university admissions, civil employment, and jobs in large firms to Malay subjects. This, in effect, has created the world's first affirmative action system tied exclusively to ethnicity. The pastoral power that has been employed on behalf of the Malays has unevenly favored the middle and upper classes, and Malays as a community enjoy more rights, benefits, and claims than non-Malays. Ethnic Chinese, a majority of whom are business operators, professionals, and urban workers, are disciplined especially in the realms of cultural expression and economic activities, while most ethnic Indians have remained plantation proletarians. Thus this system of ethnic-based governmentality has come to racialize class formation and naturalize racial differences in the country (Jomo 1988).

There are two aspects to Asian postdevelopmental strategy. On the one hand, there is the strengthening of nationalist concepts or ideologies about civilization, be it neo-Confucianism or the new Islam. On the other hand, there is the proliferation of state policies and practices through which different segments of the population relate or do not relate to global capitalism.

Globalization has induced new imagined communities that do not merely stress continuity, but also a resurgence of ancient traditions that go beyond past achievements to meet new challenges of modernity (Anderson 1991). In Malaysia, a burgeoning sense of economic power and cosmopolitanism has inspired narratives of an Asian renaissance (Anwar 1997) that harks back to precolonial centuries when Islam was the force that brought commerce and splendor to South-East Asian trading empires. The discourse claims that new era of vitality and autonomy has dawned because of the vibrant economic transformation of the region. To political leaders, the revival of the term "civilization" by Samuel Huntington (1996) seems to validate such nationalist claims of "enduring" Asian civilizations that can engender a modern sense of regionalism. Alongside the discourse of the new Islam, the secular Malaysian state gained control of Islamic law as an instrument of and a rationale for national growth that weds a religious re-flowering to an unswerving allegiance to the state. Islam should be used to turn Malaysia into a "model state," but what the politicians have in mind is not another Iran but rather a state in which a moderate and reasonable Islam helps to strengthen the state by working and meshing smoothly with global capitalism.

The new Islamic narrative is now infused with messages of economic development and entrepreneurialism. The prime minister, Mahathir Mohamad, has declared that "Islam wants its followers to be self-sufficient, independent, and progressive" (Khoo 1995: 165). During the decades when the government wanted to create a large Malay middle class and a Malay corporate elite, Mahathir had sought to demonstrate that "there is no reason why the Islamic faith, properly interpreted, cannot achieve spiritual well-being as well as material success for the Malays" (Khoo 1995: 179). A Malaysian scholar notes:

> The values listed in the Mid-Term Review of the Fourth Malaysia Plan were exactly the kinds of values to raise productivity at home, increase competitiveness abroad, and ensure political stability always. Among them were "better discipline, more self-reliance and striving for excellence" which together with "thriftiness" and "a more rational and scientific approach in over-coming problems" were "values which are progressive and consistent with the needs of a modernizing and industrializing plural society." (Khoo 1995: 181)

State favoritism toward middle-class and elite Malays seeks to make them competitive and enlightened Muslim professionals who can play the game of global capitalism. The Islamized norms of self-discipline in the production of the entrepreneurial and professional classes are buttressed by extensive affirmative action benefits in education, employment, and business activities. Young people are increasingly educated in Western universities through an economical twinning arrangement in which the first two years of a foreign curriculum are completed in Malaysia before students attend an American, Australian, or British university. A new class of superficially westernized Malay professionals now run the country according to American management principles, although there is substantial room left for increased efficiency and imagination. As in the United States, public universities are being downsized and corporatized, while the social sciences – for example anthropology – are being replaced by "social administration" studies. The outward symbols and forms of Malaysian urban elite culture are shaped more by Madison Avenue and Hollywood than by local culture. For instance, Kuala Lumpur has caught up with Singapore as a city of shopping malls: The American corporate presence in Kuala Lumpur is so pervasive that the city seems like an economic and cultural extension of California.

But the truly privileged are the "preferred Malays" (as they are called by the public) – the lucky, but not always talented, few who have been favored by the affirmative action policies and by the patronage of powerful politicians. As the subjects of Islamic corporate power, their distance from the suddenly passé Malay culture seems mirrored in the contrast between the old Moorish mosques and the Petronas twin towers that pierce the tropical sky. On a palm-fringed hillock stands the Kuala Lumpur Hilton, where attendants in white suits and batik sarongs rush forward to greet well-groomed Malay executives wielding cellular phones as they step out of limousines. But with regional economic integration, the horizons of new professionals have stretched beyond Malaysia. These new professionals are joining a segregated stratosphere – one created by the corporate networks, political parties, professional groupings, clubs and golf courses, think tanks and universities – that has increased cultural commonality among elite citizens of ASEAN countries while the gulf between them and ordinary Malays who work in factories and on the farms could not be wider. In addition to being the main beneficiaries of pastoral care, a few preferred Malays also have special access to political power that enables some to enjoy tax breaks and state bail-outs for their failing companies (Jomo 1998). The Malay elite thus enjoys both special state largesse and a corporate citizenship at a time of astonishing economic growth.

On the other hand, there are actual practices that regulate other sectors of the population who constitute the bulk of the workers that keep the economy flourishing. Two grades of cheap labor – bonded workers in factories, and migrant workers seeking even lower-paid jobs – are subjected to legal and social discipline, and to Foucauldian forms of surveillance and induced self-control. In the free trade zones, low-paid workers, a majority of whom are young Malay women, are frequently transported to distant workplaces where their bosses are often non-Muslim ethnic Chinese, Indian, or foreign managers. The state legally permits, but in practice limits, the activities of trade unions in these export-manufacturing zones, and policemen are quickly mobilized whenever workers engage in strikes. At the same time, state social policy benefiting the *bumiputra* ensures that the firms employ a majority of Malays in their workforce, and minimal wages and cost of living allowances to avoid charges of exploitation. The workers' freedom to pray during work hours also contributes to general norms that promote self-discipline and low levels of dissent (see Ong 1987).

The immigrant labor market – which draws workers from Indonesia, Bangladesh, the Philippines, and Burma – has grown in response to labor shortages in the plantation and construction industries. Almost one-third of the country's 8 million workers are immigrant workers. Despite or because of this dependence on foreign labor, which is even cheaper than home-grown female labor, the Malaysian state is especially strict in enforcing the time-limited contracts of employment and residence. Legal are immigrants employed in domestic service, construction, and plantations. They enjoy limited rights of employment, but they cannot apply for citizenship. There are no legal or social rights for illegals who slip into the country. While Muslim illegals may be more tolerated or better treated, and can often blend into the larger population by passing as Malays, non-Muslim workers, when exposed, are deported, with no rights of appeal. In the recent economic crisis, anti-immigrant sentiment has mounted, and ridding the country of illegal migrants is now considered a patriotic duty. The government selected female domestics from the Philippines as the first foreign workers to be expelled. But as the currency crisis worsens in Indonesia, tens of thousands of Indonesian workers have been sent home. Thailand has also expelled about 1 million workers from Burma and south Asia.

Another modality of governance is a mix of civilizing and disqualifying policies directed toward populations who are considered uncompetitive and who resist state efforts to make them more productive, in the eyes of the state. Official views of aboriginal peoples are highly ambivalent; they are a potential source for augmenting the Malay race and for attracting tourist dollars in theme parks. Administrators and developers also view aboriginal groups as backward and wasteful, however, and frequently as an obstacle to state projects and corporate development. Officials seek to lure the aborigines away from their nomadic life in the jungles and persuade them to become settlers. Although aboriginal groups are also technically *bumiputra* and, like the Malays, enjoy special affirmative-action rights, in practice they have access to these rights only if they abandon the aboriginal way of life and become absorbed into the larger Malay population by becoming agricultural producers. Jungle dwellers who resist the civilizing mission of schools, sedentary agriculture, markets, and Islam are left to their own devices in the midst of destruction caused by the encroaching logging companies. Generally, aboriginal groups in practice enjoy very limited protection vis-à-vis their territory, their livelihood, or their cultural identity. The Penan foragers of Sarawak have developed two different responses to territorial encroachment, each of which is shaped by a different sense of the Malaysian government's sovereignty. The Eastern Penan have actively blockaded logging activities and thus won international attention; whereas the Western Penan have acquiesced to logging as part of their acceptance of Malaysian rule (Brosius 1997). Either way, the risks to their survival as viable, self-reproducing cultural groups are enormous; in practice they are struggling mightily against encroachments that disqualify them from their nomadic way of life, and reclassify them as would-be Malays and their land as development projects. Thus, aboriginal groups in practice enjoy very limited protection vis-à-vis their territory, their livelihood, or their cultural identity. In O'Donnell's terms, such aboriginal populations, unprotected by rights and often exposed to violence, dwell in the "brown" areas of newly democratized countries (O'Donnell 1993: 1361). Irredentist and outlaw groups also dwell in the brown areas, and South-East Asia is riddled with such internal colonies of poverty and neglect. Frequently, the state seeks to evict rebel populations and open up their resource-rich areas to timber logging and the construction of golf courses and dams.

Graduated sovereignty then, as I have discussed it, refers to the differential treatment of populations – through schemes of biopolitical disciplining and pastoral care – that differently insert them into the processes of global capitalism. These gradations of governing may be in a continuum, but they overlap with pre-formed racial, religious, and gender hierarchies, and further fragment citizenship for people who are all, nominally speaking, citizens of the same country.

Indonesia: An Archipelagic Polity

While Malaysia has in times of crisis used the military against its own people, in Indonesia, military coercion is part of the everyday rule for large segments of the working population and the marginalized. Again, the considerations of profitability, resource extraction, and productivity influence state policies toward different segments of the population. There is no official policy of affirmative action in Indonesia, and the national motto of "unity in diversity" stresses the multicultural range of this nominally Muslim nation. Under Suharto's New Order regime (1965–98), the state implemented a military-industrial complex that over the past two decades transformed the nation into an industrializing, export-oriented economy. The New Order emerged out of the bloodbath of the mid-1960s, when over a million people were killed on suspicion of being communists. The new totalitarian state is based on two repressive apparatuses. First, a gulag prison system where thousands of educated political detainees were held in primitive conditions (Toer 1999). Second, the powerful military – at one time a 475,000-strong armed bureaucracy – has a "dual function" in military and civilian control. Its centralized power is concentrated in Jakarta and occupied places like East Timor and Aceh, but army personnel and apparatus are distributed in small cities, villages, and industrial zones throughout the archipelago of over 200 million people.

In the industrial zones located in Sumatra and Java, the army works hand in hand with factories to maintain social order among the 7 million labor force, many of them young women who had left rice-fields to assemble watches, clothing, shoes, toys, plastic goods, and furniture. They earn less than a living wage in factories operated by ethnic Chinese and Korean sub-contractors for brand-name companies such as Nike, Reebok, and The Gap. Up until 1994, women working 12-hour days sewing Gap outfits made less than US$2 a day, including overtime. That year, the Indonesian Prosperity Trade Union (SBSI), calculating that the average worker needed to earn at least US$2.50 a day, broke "the taboo on labor strikes" and called a national strike to protest against low wages (Goozner and Schmetzer 1994). After a long struggle, the government agreed to a minimum wage of US$2 a day, but this was unevenly enforced, coming into effect only in some urban factories. Indonesian factory women are still among the lowest paid in Asia, just slightly ahead of their counterparts in Vietnam and China. When I visited the area in mid-1996, workers claimed they needed at least US$5 a day to survive.

"Low-end" manufacturing work depends on gendered forms of labor control and harassment. Widespread surveillance and much of the daily control of female workers centers on their bodies, for instance, in the provision of food, in the granting or withholding of permission for menstrual leave, in the pressure for family planning, and in the physical confinement imposed during work hours. Examples of sexual harassment include timing visits to the toilet, and using the excuse of having to verify requests for menstrual leaves to conduct body searches. Workers are crammed into dormitories above or next to warehouses, thus creating firetraps. Managers punish the tardy by making them stand under the sun for hours, and are quick to fire those who demand basic survival wages (Emilia 1996; Ong 1997).

Not only are workers rarely protected by labor rights, they are in fact frequently harassed by the military. Whenever there is a strike, the army is deployed against the workers, no matter how peaceful they are (Wallace 1994). In my visit to the Tangerang zone, I noticed that military barracks are often adjacent to factory sites, and army personnel mingled freely with security guards outside the factory gates.[2] I was told that the army could reach any factory within 20 minutes of an outbreak of worker insurrection. Indonesians think it is normal for the army to keep industrial cities secure for factories, and factory bosses routinely make "donations" to local commanders to help meet their costs (Borsuk 1998). While most workers are denied the minimum wage and most basic social protection, they are constantly vulnerable to the state's repressive apparatus.

Despite the poor treatment of industrial workers, the state, in a policy that goes back to the colonial concept of Java-centrism, favors Javanese people over the more than 30 major ethnic groups in the archipelago, and the spread of Javanese from their overpopulated island has been a means for displacing pockets of local population and consolidating the empire. Among these are aboriginal peoples in jungle communities who fall into the official "tribal slot" (Li 2000) of "isolated peoples" (*orang terasing*), or those who are "backward" (*terbelakang*) or "left behind" (*tertinggal*). The state has not been content merely to define aboriginal peoples in simplified terms; it has sought progressively to erase, through different programs of arbitrary displacement, their very identity tied to ethnic territory. By introducing "efficient" extractive industries, state enterprises, the state has made inroads into aboriginal enclaves, opening them up for development. The ambiguous status of the tribal slot has allowed the state to resettle nomadic groups, or to encourage the resettlement of impoverished peasants from elsewhere under the transmigration project. For instance, tribal groups in Irian Jaya have lost their land to the American mining company Freeport Copper, which has since leveled two mountains and is planning to open more mines in the highlands. The displaced Amungme people have not been compensated nor employed, and local authorities represented by the company import Javanese to staff their mining town (Lewis 1994: 223–231).

In West Kalimantan (Borneo), migrant Madurese have claimed land rights against the indigenous Dayaks by appealing to the nationalist concept of citizenship and the primacy of entrepreneurialism extolled by the government (Peluso and Harwell 1998). The Dayaks are also fighting a larger battle against timber companies that are grabbing their lands. Security forces tied to timber concessions are routinely used to destroy Dayak crops and jungle resources, to enforce land theft and torture people into accepting "compensation" for land taken to develop plantations. The Dayaks, in defense of their territorially based identity and in accordance with customary law (*adat*), have launched attacks on Madurese migrants and timber estate developers (Sinapan 1997). These clashes have produced killing fields in the jungles; the bloodshed has gained renewed ferocity in the aftermath of the financial crisis in late 1998.

At the other end of the spectrum, state corporatism favors a tiny elite that controls corporations monopolizing the distribution of food and fuel, and protecting agricultural products from foreign interests. Such monopolies have allowed the Suharto family to amass vast fortunes through their links with members of the military and the wealthy Chinese who bankrolled them. Besides producing and reproducing a tiny political economic elite, state corporatism helps to contain the centripetal forces – class, religion, ethnicity, island – that threaten to pull state and society apart.

State corporatism also involves awarding timber concessions in outlying areas to military generals, who run practically autonomous fiefdoms. Provincial governors, military officers, and business tycoons have begun to avoid the dictates of Jakarta, and develop separate trading relations with foreign traders and enterprises. In Irian Jaya, large areas of the Pancak Jaya–Grasberg mountain complex are under the control of the Freeport Indonesia mining company, which controls authorities like the Tembagapura Community Development Project. In East Kalimantan, former Suharto crony Mohammed Bob Hasan controls huge concessions and has engaged in extensive forest-clearing in the name of "sustainable development" for plywood production. The nation's environment minister, who had been unable to get Jakarta to act to stop the forest burning, called Kalimantan "part of a nation without government, like parts of America in the 19th century."[3]

Such military dominance of the provinces has intensified separatist movements. South-East Asia is riddled by "internal colonies": the East Timorese and Acehnese in Indonesia, Dayaks in Malaysia and Indonesia, the Moros in the Philippines, Shans and Karens in Burma, and the Patani Malays in Thailand (Aditjondro 1996). For decades, Indonesia has amassed troops in Aceh and in East Timor (since the 1975 invasion). George J. Aditjondro (1996), notes that because "all ASEAN governments have their own 'East Timors' in their backyard," ASEAN has become "a conspiracy of repressive regimes, busy protecting each other's behinds." Criticisms of human rights violations in these colonies by citizens and sympathetic outsiders are immediately suppressed by the state.[4] Such outlaw groups are usually treated with overwhelming coercion (as was the case in East Timor), but in other situations, state support is simply withdrawn, so that a kind of low-grade struggle continues to fester amidst poverty and neglect (Patani in Thailand). State brutality against its outlawed citizens is highly influenced by market interests. Frequently, the state seeks to rid the territory of rebel populations, and open the resource-rich areas they occupied to timber logging, building petroleum pipelines or dams.

Graduated sovereignty, as I have discussed it so far in Malaysia and Indonesia, refers to the differential treatment of populations according to ethno-racial differences, and the dictates of development programs. Segments of the population are differently disciplined and given differential privileges and protections, in relation to their varying participation in globalized market activities. These gradations of governing – disciplinary, pastoral, civilizing/disqualifying policies, or military occupation and de facto autonomous domains – may be in a continuum, but their effects are to fragment citizenship for subjects who are all, nominally speaking, citizens of the same country. The elites are showered with every economic, social, and political benefit, while others are abandoned and deprived of sustenance to survive. As has been indicated, such variegated citizenship is of course greatly reinforced when the state reorganizes national space into new economic zones that promote international trade and investments.

State–Transnational Production Networks

The other dimension of graduated sovereignty, which overlaps with and reinforces the ethno-racial discriminations of populations, is the rise of production and technological zones which have required certain legal compromises in national sovereignty. In the interest of national competitiveness, the middle-range economies of South-East Asia have used two mechanisms for attracting foreign investments and technology transfers. These are, first, linking up with corporations that have regionalized production networks; and, second, the state promotion of technological parks with the aim of attracting international technologies, expertise, and investments. In both cases, governments have become flexible in their management of sovereignty, so that different production sites vary in their mix of legal protections, controls, and repressive regimes. Citizens in zones that are differently articulated to global production and financial circuits are subjected to different kinds of surveillance, and in practice enjoy different sets of civil, political, and economic rights.

Since the liberalization of foreign relations regulations in the late 1980s, the massive influx of mainly East Asian investments created regionalized production networks in South-East Asia. Building on preexisting corporate alliances, these inter-firm networks are hierarchized, with Japanese firms providing the latest technological knowledge and skills, Taiwanese and Korean companies the management and the goods, and local South-East Asian firms the labor (Bernard and Ravenhill 1995). In recent years, a variety of Western companies and local firms have participated in these production networks as well. Such corporate patterning of investments, production, and trade flows among contiguous localities of three or more countries thus carves out "natural economic territories" called growth triangles (GTs) or sub-regional economic zones (Jordan and Khanna 1995). Growth triangles are determined by an "economic geometry," in which location, the accessibility of cheap labor, the possibility of exploitation of complementary resources, and the proximity of a regional hub such as Singapore enhance the competitive advantage of the region in the global economy. So far, three GTs have formed by linking contiguous parts of neighboring countries. The country configurations are Indonesia–Malaysia–Singapore (Sijori); Indonesia–Malaysia–Thailand; and Brunei–Indonesia–Malaysia–Philippines. Sijori is a massive industrial park astride the Riau archipelago that draws on complementary labor and technical resources of the three countries to enhance investment opportunities. From the Singaporean perspective, this growth triangle allows

Singapore to retain command/control functions at home, while moving "low-end" jobs offshore. It takes advantage of cheap Indonesian labor, and it also ameliorates tensions over the presence of too many guest-workers within the city-state. Sijori thus represents a zone of low-cost production in which Singaporean capital and expertise can be used for training and managing regional workers. It represents the low end of a system of zones in which the city-state is the site of continuously upgrading human capital (Macleod and McGee 1996). The South-East Asian state finds itself playing a subordinate role as facilitator of investments, and provider of infrastructure and cheap labor to global capital. Such "extended metropolitan regions" are thus the result of refining the time-space coordinates of flexible production techniques (Harvey 1989) that have large implications for the redesigning of national sovereignty.

What is the political architecture of such cross-border zones? We can try to tease out the legal and political compromises whereby the state temporarily cedes control of these zones, and the subjects within them, to quasi-state authorities. First, providing the location for growth triangles means that the participating state must be flexible in its relation with foreign capital, in a way that goes beyond giving the usual incentives of on-site infrastructure, tax breaks, and special export allowances. In Malaysia, participating firms negotiate on a case-by-case basis with the national industrial development authority. For instance, there is the implicit arrangement whereby union activities are suppressed, or corporate disciplining is allowed to curb worker activism.

What kinds of "conducive regulatory environment" and labor discipline prevail under corporate management? Both state and corporate authorities cooperate in determining the rules of inclusion and exclusion, and the rights and privileges of workers from different countries. The Sijori triangle, for instance, has a graded system of labor and material conditions in each of the triangle's nodes: in Singapore, one finds skilled labor and sophisticated business and control services; in Johore (Malaysia), skilled and semi-skilled labor, recreation, and land; and in Batam and Riau (Indonesia), "low-cost, controlled" labor and some natural amenities (beaches) (Macleod and McGee 1996: 443).

The GT logic has also reengineered gender relations across national lines. Different grades of workers are drawn from different countries. Tens of thousands of young Indonesian women are employed, alongside their semi-skilled Malaysian counterparts, in industries set up by some 8,000 global companies. They are all supervised by male technicians and managers from Singapore. The integration of different tiers of labor markets can only limit the capacity of workers at the bottom, who are in an ambiguous, liminal order, to appeal to their own govern-ment for protection. Each participating state is no longer interested in securing uniform regulatory authority over all their citizens outside or within these zones.

Second, the thinning of state power at these border zones is compensated for by the thickening of the regulatory functions of quasi-state authorities that set the legal and social forms of control. Through the differential deployment of state power, populations in different zones are variously subjected to political control and to social regulation by state and nonstate agencies. More research needs to be done to discover what kinds of inter-governmental compromises are negotiated with corporate power. The Batam Authority (controlling the Indonesian part of the Sijori triangle), for instance, offers "fewer regulations" regarding land titles, various building permits, the number of expatriates to work at the enterprises, "and exemptions from the licensing requirements of the regional government authorities."[5] This means that the Batam authority is autonomous of even the regional government and can enter into contractual relations with foreign capital. The chairman of the agency left no doubt as to its main function: "Social stability will be a key factor in attracting foreign investors."[6] The administration of the GT is so efficiently regulated that the May 1998 riots in Jakarta and subsequent disturbances in the rest of Indonesia have not disrupted workers in Sijori. The Batam factories and ports operated like clockwork and there have been no street demonstrations calling for reforms (*reformasi*).

While the cross-border growth zones are the product of corporate networks, the Malaysian state has set aside its own technological center as a site for the nurturing of a superprivileged elite. As Asian tigers are losing investments to China, states have begun to seek a way to attract foreign investments. Malaysia, following the examples of Taiwan and Singapore, is building a technological park to promote local research and development, and to link up with the transnational technological "research and development" community. The grandly named Multimedia Super Corridor (MSC) is projected to become a "springboard to serve the regional and world markets for multimedia products and services."[7] The corridor, which will link Kuala Lumpur to a new technological research center and a new international airport, dovetails with the policy of favoring corporate Malays, since they appear to be its main local beneficiaries. Malaysia already has a Silicon Valley in Penang, but it is dominated by ethnic Chinese technical and professional personnel employed in foreign electronic industries.

The MSC can be seen as a zone for experimenting with a daring kind of Islamic governmentality. Special cyber-laws, policies, and practices are being drafted to encourage investment in a new kind of Malay subject who will be fully at home in a multimedia world. Bill Gates, of Microsoft, and other high-technology industry executives from the United States and Japan have been persuaded to commit themselves to building enterprises in the zone. Affirmative-action employment policies will be suspended to free up the flow of capital, talent, and information that will ultimately favor the Malay corporate elite. Visas will be readily issued to foreigners known as "knowledge workers," who represent "the best minds." Students will be trained in "smart" (high-tech) schools and a new university. For these privileged few, there will be no censorship of the Internet. New practices include residents having access to distance-learning technology, to telemedical services, and to an electronic-wired government. The MSC is thus a project that involves an enormous state investment, and is intended to breed and nurture a new kind of Malay computer-literate culture. The official explanation for the MSC is that

it is a "test-bed" to experiment safely with "modernization without undermining
... traditional values" (Wysocki 1997: 10); in reality it will be a superprivileged
zone where the Malay elite plugs into the world of high-technology industry.

The galaxy of differentiated zones is thus unevenly integrated into the
structures of state power and global capital. Technology zones and growth
triangles are plugged tightly into globalization processes, while aboriginal and
ethnic-minority reserves are often disarticulated from national and regional
centers of power. In short, the structural logic of globalization has not resulted
in the solidification of differences among civilizations (Huntington 1996), but
rather in the proliferation of differentiated sovereignty within and across borders.
The moral regulation of the state both homogenizes and individualizes its subjects, so that while unifying images and forms of Asian values emphasize uniformity, there is differentiation between normal and deviant subjects, and the
social categories of ethnic minorities, jungle dwellers, and illegals make them less
legitimate, and give them little moral claim on the political order. Such differential policies toward citizens are reinforced when segments of the population are
differently linked to global circuits of production, competitiveness, and exchange.

Sovereignty after the Asian Financial Crisis

The series of devaluations of Asian currencies in late 1997 plunged South-East
Asian states into a crisis of sovereignty. The very strategy of graduated sovereignty
that embeds society in global production and financial markets can be their
undoing, exposing them to disruptive economic forces. Asian states have
responded in two interesting ways: Indonesia (like Thailand) submitted to the
economic prescriptions of the IMF, while Malaysia resisted, instead reimposing its
territorial state sovereignty.

The so-called Asian financial crisis was viewed by the international press as
the outcome of reckless borrowing and lending, the building of mega-projects,
and the lack of market controls in the tiger economies. Western observers tend
to see the problem as one caused exclusively by crony capitalism or "lack of
transparency" in economic practice. What is needed, they argue, is a heavy
dose of neoliberal rules of global market efficiency imposed mainly through the
IMF on third world politicians. Asian observers point to the fact that global
companies and bankers have been happy to work with these same problems for
decades, and global institutions like the World Bank have lauded the capitalist takeoff in Asia (World Bank 1993: 9; 1994). Politicians like Malaysia's Mahathir, who
has been criticized for crony capitalism, preferred to blame international financiers
like George Soros, whom he demonized as anti-Asia, and "anti-poor countries":

> We are told that we must open up, that trade and commerce must be totally free.
> Free, for whom? For rogue speculators. For anarchists wishing to destroy weak

countries in their crusade for open societies, to force us to submit to the dictatorship of international manipulators. We want to embrace borderlessness but we still need to protect ourselves from self-serving rogues and international brigandage.[8]

Indeed, while Asian economies are guilty of economic irrationality in their practices, very little attention has been paid to irrational financial markets that have made integration into the global economy the source for both strengthening and weakening of the state. Gradually, as the financial crisis unfolded across a number of major countries, more observers admitted that the crisis was fueled by speculations in hot money and market panics that engendered massive outflows. Clearly worrying were not only the effects of unstable markets on emerging states, but also the moral hazards that may require the IMF and advanced states to bail out bad loans by profligate investors.[9] In any case, it is difficult, if not impossible, to distinguish between explosive growth and speculative bubbles, and debate continues about the causes of the crash.

The different responses of Malaysia and Indonesia to interventions by global monetary authorities reflect not only the relative strength of their respective economies, but also which parts of the state are losing or resisting control vis-à-vis global regulatory agencies. The IMF represents the strategic aspect of "disciplinary neoliberalism" (Gill 1995) whereby emerging states are subjected to rules that intensify their subordination to global market forces. As a result of the disastrous devaluation of the *rupiah*, Indonesia has suffered a major reversal, with more than half its population living at or below the poverty level. The central bank is now more open to being inhabited by the global monetary agenda. The Indonesian response has been to submit to IMF prescriptions, after some initial resistance. B. J. Habibie replaced Suharto, but the state led by a "family and friends cabinet" is essentially the same apparatus, with a much shrunken economic and military base, and diminished store of legitimacy. While the IMF prescriptions are necessary to improve banking practices and curtail corruption in high places, industrializing countries are now subjected to the same rules of benefiting global capitalist interests. For instance, fire-sales have allowed foreign corporate take-overs of more local companies, especially in Indonesia and Thailand, thus further undermining national sovereignty.

In contrast to Indonesia, more healthy industrializing countries have responded to the financial crisis by strengthening the hand of the state against capital flows. The Hong Kong government (a special autonomous region of China), in an unprecedented move, has intervened to protect the property sector from foreign speculators. Chile has added a penalty for the precipitous withdrawal of foreign investments. In Malaysia, Mahathir has imposed even more rigid controls on capital flows, challenging the truism that markets must have total freedom. In a partial recovery of national power vis-à-vis global capital, Mahathir has resisted the global agendas of financial traders, banks, and corporations, which he calls "Anglo-Saxon capitalism." He put the government back in control of the inter-state zone of financial dealings and currency trading. While Mahathir was in turn demonized in the Western press, he was merely following a logical suggestion by American economist Paul Krugman: in times of financial crisis, capital controls allow middle-range countries a temporary breathing space to stabilize their economies. These industrializing states have been caught between pursuing capital while seeking to protect society.[10] They (and in a different way, Russia) have challenged the credibility of the IMF. Western economists now see that the very irrationality attributed exclusively to crony capitalism has been magnified by an on-line global oligarchy driving much of the developing world into recession. The IMF and other global regulatory agencies are calling for a new "architecture" of new rules to control the workings of global financial markets. Unfortunately, Western observers often conflate subordination to the "dictatorship" of global markets (Attali 1997) with the spread of democracy, so that any state that stands up to neoliberal disciplining is framed as necessarily anti-human rights.

It is also unfortunate that the Mahathir regime plays into this construction, combining his anti-IMF stance with greater repression at home. Mahathir had his former deputy prime minister Anwar Ibrahim arrested for being an aficionado of the IMF (but officially charging him for corruption and violating anti-buggery laws, a British colonial detail now resurrected for political expediency). The government continues to prop up local companies that engage in risky investments, and has not ended connections with favored developers (Jomo 1998). Thus while Malaysia reasserted state power vis-à-vis global markets, he continues the practice of preferential treatment for the corporate elite.

But it was the arrest and sentencing of Anwar that stirred the middle classes from their general inaction. Hundreds of young professionals took to the streets, like their Indonesian brethren, calling for the kind of *reformasi* that had removed Suharto from power.[11] The evolving role of the middle classes may hold the seeds of a transformation in the logic of graduated sovereignty. They have been produced and nurtured by the late-developing state, and have a weak and ambivalent role in relation to state power. In western Europe, the bourgeois revolution gave birth to the liberal tradition which, over the course of decades of struggle, set limits on state power and enshrined individual autonomy as a human right. In South-East Asian countries, the middle classes are weak, most having been recently produced by the industrializing regimes in the space of two decades (Robison and Goodman 1996), compared to more than a hundred years of bourgeois development in the West. There is no home-grown tradition of political liberalism, and it is only under recent conditions of relative economic affluence that the new middle classes are beginning to fight for human rights against the state which has enabled their own emergence. Ironically, the financial crisis has opened up the space for the middle classes to fight even more vigorously for human rights reforms, because the state has suddenly become more repressive against members of the middle classes and the elite circles, as well as the marginalized segments of the population.

The final question, then, is how these middle-range and small industrializing states have evolved in relation to the constantly changing web of relations with international capital and affiliated agencies. As industrializing states become more vulnerable to neoliberal globalization, to what extent are they being reconstituted and disciplined through the "structural adjustments" imposed by global agencies, and their peripheries reconstituted and governed by quasi-governmental-corporate authorities? The broader point seems to be that the overall market-oriented agenda can mean lots of different things. The model of graduated sovereignty shows that it is not so much a question of the market versus the state, but that market society at our particular moment in history means that there are certain areas in which the state is very strong and its protections very significant, and certain areas where it is near-absent, because these zones must be flexible vis-à-vis markets, or they are structurally irrelevant.

In less powerful regions of the world, we find that the nature of state sovereignty must be rethought as a set of coexisting strategies of government within a single national space. There is discipline in the Foucauldian sense, there is labor discipline in the old sense; there are zones of corporatist power and zones of special production; there are "brown" spots of neglect and heavily militarized sites of insurgency. What we see, then, is a system of dispersed sovereignty, a model of galactic governance that has premodern roots in South-East Asian trading empires (Tambiah 1977; Reid 1988), and is now finely adjusted to the different "allocative mechanisms" of global capitalism in relation to the assets of particular populations and sites (Stroper 1995). Graduated sovereignty is the result of a flexible set of state strategies that are not congruent with the national space itself, but are attuned to the workings of global markets.

Notes

Acknowledgment. Thanks to Stephen J. Collier for comments on an earlier draft of the essay.

1   Compared to, say, advanced neoliberal democracies like the United States and Britain, where a panoply of private agencies has become much more important for the production of normativity, whereby individuals are encouraged to become rational, calculative, self-managing subjects (see Rose 1996).

2   In 1993, a young worker at a watch factory in Surabaya was abducted, gang-raped, and murdered for leading a strike to demand that a US$0.25 meal allowance be added to the US$0.84 daily wage. The murder provoked a national outcry, which led to the arrests of some people. There was widespread belief that the military was implicated. See Ong (1997: 125).

3   Reuters, "Minister: Fires Out of Control in Indonesia" (April 14, 1998).

4   For instance, pro-democracy activists in Malaysia who demonstrate against Indonesia's occupation of East Timor have been suppressed by the Malaysian government, which uses the excuse that such activities damage state-level relations within the region. Protests in Malaysia, Thailand, and the Philippines against the admission of the Burmese regime into ASEAN are barely reported in local media.

5 www.stat-usa.gov, Globus & NTDB, "Region 3: Asia and the Pacific Rim: International Business Practices," USDOC, International Trade Administration (downloaded April 28, 1999).
6 *Far Eastern Economic Review* (*FEER*), "Advertisement: Batam: Bigger and Better" (January 28, 1999: 32–33).
7 *New Straits Times*, "Conduit to Fully Tap Creativity" (July 30, 1997: 6).
8 *New Straits Times*, "Currency Speculators Out to Undermine Asian Economies" (July 25, 1997: 29).
9 *The Economist*, "Towards a New Financial System: The Perils of Global Capital" (April 11, 1998: 53).
10 In *The Great Transformation*, Karl Polanyi (1957) maintains that in the unruly conditions produced by global markets in the 1930s, new forms of state arose to assert social control over apparently natural laws of economic forces.
11 As I write (August 1999), East Timor, after a brutal punishment from militia forces mobilized by the Indonesian military, has gained freedom from Jakarta. Other potential breakaway provinces include Aceh and West Irian.

References

Aditjondro, George J.
  1996 All in the Name of an ASEAN Solidarity. Sydney Morning Herald November 14.
Anderson, Benedict
  1991 Imagined Communities, 2nd edition. London: Verso.
Anwar Ibrahim
  1997 The Asian Renaissance. Kuala Lumpur: Times Publications.
Attali, Jacques
  1997 The Crash of Western Civilization: The Limits of the Market and of Democracy. Foreign Policy 107(summer): 54–64.
Bernard, Mitchell, and John Ravenhill
  1995 The Pursuit of Competitiveness in East Asia: The Regionalization of Production and its Consequences. *In* American Competitiveness, East Asia, and the World Economy: International Political Economy Yearbook, Vol. 8. D. P. Rapkin, ed. Boulder, CO: Lynne Rienner.
Borsuk, Richard
  1998 Fear of Unrest Grows in Indonesian City. Wall Street Journal February 20: A12.
Brosius, Peter
  1997 Prior Transcripts, Divergent Paths: Resistance and Acquiescence to Logging in Sarawak, East Malaysia. Comparative Studies in Society and History 39: 468–510.
Castel, Robert
  1991 From Dangerousness to Risk. *In* The Foucault Effect: Studies in Govermentality. Graham Burchell, Colin Gordon, and Peter Miller, eds. Pp. 281–298. Chicago: University of Chicago Press.
Castells, Manuel
  1998 End of the Millennium. Vol. 3 of The Information Age: Economy, Society, and Culture. Oxford: Blackwell.

Emilia, Stevie
 1996 Fired Female Worker Fights for Better Labor Conditions. Jakarta Post August 25.
Evans, Peter
 1997 The Eclipse of the State? Reflection on Stateness in an Era of Globalization. World Politics 50(October): 67–87.
Foucault, Michel
 1977 Power/Knowledge: Selected Interviews and Other Writings, 1972–1977. New York: Vintage.
 1979 The History of Sexuality, Vol. 1. New York: Vintage.
 1981 Omnes et Singulatim. *In* The Tanner Lectures on Human Values, II. Sterling M. McMurrin, ed. Salt Lake City: University of Utah Press.
 1991 Governmentality. *In* The Foucault Effect: Studies in Governmentality. Graham Burchell, Colin Gordon, and Peter Miller, eds. Pp. 87–104. Chicago: University of Chicago Press.
Giddens, Anthony
 1987 The Nation-State and Violence. Vol. 2 of A Contemporary Critique of Historical Materialism. Berkeley: University of California Press.
Gill, Stephen
 1995 Globalization, Market Civilization, and Disciplinary Neoliberalism. Millennium: Journal of International Studies 24(3): 399–423.
Goozner, Merril, and Uli Schmetzer
 1994 Asian Workers Fighting Back: Low Wages, Terrible Working Conditions Foster Strikes. Chicago Tribune November 7.
Harvey, David
 1989 The Condition of Postmodernity. Oxford: Blackwell.
Held, David
 1998 Democracy: From City-States to a Cosmopolitan Order? *In* Prospects for Democracy: North, South, East, West. David Held, ed. Stanford: Stanford University Press.
Huntington, Samuel
 1996 The Clash of Civilizations. New York: Simon and Schuster.
Jomo, K. S.
 1988 A Question of Class: Capital, the State, and Uneven Development in Malaya. New York: Monthly Review Press.
 1998 Malaysia Props Up its Crony Capitalists. Asian Wall Street Journal December 21.
Jordan, Amos A., and Jane Khanna
 1995 Economic Interdependence and Challenges to the Nation-State: The Emergence of Natural Economic Territories in the Asia-Pacific. Journal of International Affairs 48(2): 433–462.
Khoo Boo Teik
 1995 Paradoxes of Mahathirism. Kuala Lumpur: Oxford University Press.
Lewis, Norman
 1994 An Empire of the East: Travels in Indonesia. New York: Henry Holt.
Li, Tania Murray
 2000 Articulating Indigenous Identity in Indonesia: Resource Politics and the Tribal Slot. Comparative Studies in Society and History 42(1): 149–179.

Macleod, Scott, and T. G. McGee
    1996 The Singapore-Johore-Riau Growth Triangle: An Emerging Extended Metro-
        politan Region. *In* Emerging World Cities in the Asia Pacific. Fu-chen Lo and Yue-
        man Yeung, eds. Tokyo: United Nations University Press.

McVey, Ruth
    1992 The Materialization of the Southeast Asian Entrepreneur. *In* Southeast Asian
        Capitalists. Ruth McVey, ed. Pp. 3–34. Ithaca: Southeast Asia Program, Cornell
        University.

O'Donnell, Guilermo
    1993 On the State, Democratization and Some Conceptual Problems: A Latin Ameri-
        can View with Glances at Some Postcommunist Countries. World Development
        21(8): 1355–1369.

Ong, Aihwa
    1987 Spirits of Resistance and Capitalist Discipline: Factory Women in Malaysia.
        Albany: State University of New York Press.
    1997 Strategic Sisterhood or Sisters in Solidarity? Questions of Communitarianism
        and Citizenship in Asia. Indiana Journal of Global Legal Studies 4(1): 107–135.
    1999 Flexible Citizenship: The Cultural Logics of Transnationality. Durham, NC:
        Duke University Press.

Peluso, Nancy, and Emily Harwell
    1998 Land Filled with Tears: Territory and the Cultural Politics of Headhunting in
        Indonesian Borneo. Paper presented at Berkeley, Autumn.

Polanyi, Karl
    1957 The Great Transformation: The Political and Economic Origins of Our Time.
        Boston: Beacon Press.

Reid, Anthony
    1988 The Land Below the Winds. Vol. 1 of Southeast Asia in an Age of Commerce,
        1450–1680. New Haven: Yale University Press.

Robison, Richard, and David S. G. Goodman
    1996 The New Rich in Asia: Economic Development, Social Status, and Political
        Consciousness. *In* The New Rich in Asia. Richard Robison and David S. Goodman,
        eds. London: Routledge.

Rose, Nikolas
    1996 Governing Advanced Liberal Democracies. *In* Foucault and Political Reason:
        Liberalism, Neo-Liberalism, and Rationalities of Government. Andrew Barry, Thomas
        Osbourne, and Nikolas Rose, eds. Pp. 37–64. Chicago: University of Chicago Press.

Ruggie, John
    1998 Constructing the World Polity. London: Routledge.

Schmitt, Carl
    1987 Political Theory: Four Chapters on the Concept of Sovereignty. George
        Schwab, trans. Cambridge, MA: MIT Press.

Sinapan, Samydorai
    1997 The Killing Fields of West Kalimantan. Human Rights Solidarity (Hong Kong)
        7(2): 5–7, 29.

Stroper, Michael
    1995 The Resurgence of Regional Economies, Ten Years Later. European Urban &
        Regional Studies 2(3): 191–221.

Tambiah, Stanley
  1977   The Galactic Polity: The Structure of Traditional Kingdoms in Southeast Asia. Annals of the New York Academy of Sciences 293: 69–97.
Toer, Pramoedya Ananta
  1999   The Mute's Soliloquy: A Memoir. New York: Hyperion.
Wallace, Charles
  1994   Relief Elusive for Asia's Labor Pains. Los Angeles Times December 13.
World Bank
  1993   Sustaining Rapid Development in East Asia and the Pacific. Washington, DC: World Bank.
  1994   Indonesia: Sustaining Development. Washington, DC: World Bank.
Wysocki, Bernard, Jr.
  1997   Malaysia is Gambling on a Costly Plunge into a Cyber Future. Wall Street Journal June 10: A10.

4

Spatializing States:

Toward an Ethnography of Neoliberal Governmentality

James Ferguson and Akhil Gupta

Recent years have seen a new level of anthropological concern with the modern state. In part, the new interest in the state arises from a recognition of the central role that states play in shaping "local communities" that have historically consti- tuted the objects of anthropological inquiry; in part, it reflects a new determin- ation to bring an ethnographic gaze to bear on the cultural practices of states themselves. An important theme running through the new literature has been that states are not simply functional bureaucratic apparatuses, but powerful sites of symbolic and cultural production that are themselves always culturally repre- sented and understood in particular ways. It is here that it becomes possible to speak of states, and not only nations (Anderson 1991), as "imagined" – that is, as constructed entities that are conceptualized and made socially effective through particular imaginative and symbolic devices that require study (Bayart 1993; Bernal 1997; Cohn 1996; Comaroff 1998; Coronil 1997; Corrigan and Sayer 1985; cf. Fallers 1971; Geertz 1980; Joseph and Nugent 1994; Nugent 1997; Scott 1998; Taussig 1996).

In this essay, our contribution to this literature is twofold. First, we argue that discussions of the imagination of the state have not attended adequately to the ways in which states are spatialized.[1] How is it that people come to experience the state as an entity with certain spatial characteristics and properties? Through what images, metaphors, and representational practices does the state come to be understood as a concrete, overarching, spatially encompassing reality? Through specific sets of metaphors and practices, states represent themselves as reified entities with particular *spatial* properties (specifically, what we will describe as properties of "vertical encompassment").[2] By doing so, they help to secure their legitimacy, to naturalize their authority, and to represent themselves as

Reprinted from James Ferguson and Akhil Gupta, "Spatializing States: Toward an Ethnography of Neoliberal Governmentality." *American Ethnologist* 29(4): 981–1002. Copyright © 2002, American Anthropological Association.

superior to, and encompassing of, other institutions and centers of power. We refer to the operation of these metaphors and practices as "the spatialization of the state." In the first part of this essay, we identify some key methods through which states achieve this spatialization and seek to show, via an ethnographic example, that mundane bureaucratic state practices are integral to such achievements.

In the second part of the essay, we build on this discussion by showing its relevance to the question of globalization. We argue that an increasingly transnational political economy today poses new challenges to familiar forms of state spatialization. After developing a concept of transnational governmentality, we discuss the relation between weak African states and an emerging network of international organizations and transnational nongovernmental organizations (NGOs), and show how these developments confound conventional understandings of state spatiality. We suggest that attention to the changing forms of state spatialization might enrich the anthropology of the state and clarify certain aspects of the contemporary politics of globalization.

Part One: The Spatialized State

Conceptual Issues

Two images come together in popular and academic discourses on the state: those of *verticality* and *encompassment*. *Verticality* refers to the central and pervasive idea of the state as an institution somehow "above" civil society, community, and family. Thus, state planning is inherently "top down" and state actions are efforts to manipulate and plan "from above," while "the grassroots" contrasts with the state precisely in that it is "below," closer to the ground, more authentic, and more "rooted." The second image is that of *encompassment*: Here the state (conceptually fused with the nation) is located within an ever-widening series of circles that begins with family and local community and ends with the system of nation-states.[3] This is a profoundly consequential understanding of scale, one in which the locality is encompassed by the region, the region by the nation-state, and the nation-state by the international community.[4] These two metaphors work together to produce a taken-for-granted spatial and scalar image of a state that both sits above and contains its localities, regions, and communities.

Such images of state vertical encompassment are evident, for instance, in scholarly discussions of so-called state–society relations, a topic that has dominated recent discussions of the state in political science and political theory. The idea of "civil society" has been embraced both by neoliberal advocates of structural adjustment in Africa and India and, for different reasons, by many of their strongest critics (cf. Ferguson in press). But whatever else might be said about the opposition between state and civil society, it is evident that it normally brings with it a quite specific, if often unacknowledged, image of vertical encompassment, one in which the state sits somehow "above" an "on the ground" entity called "society."[5] The state, of course, has long been conceived in the West, through an unacknowledged "transcoding" of the body politic with the organismic human body (Stallybrass and White 1986), as possessing such "higher" functions as reason, control, and regulation, as against the irrationality, passions, and uncontrollable appetites of the lower regions of society.[6] It is therefore unsurprising that where Western political theory has opposed civil society to the state, it has often been as a kind of buffer between the low and the high, an imagined middle zone of contact or mediation between the citizen, the family, or the community, on the one hand, and the state, on the other.[7] For Hegel (to take one foundational instance), the state was literally "mind objectified" (1942: 156), and civil society precisely the intermediary between the foundational natural particularity of the family and the ideal universality of the state. The state was therefore "higher" than civil society (ethically as well as politically) and also encompassed it.[8]

Few scholars today, of course, would endorse Hegel's conception of the state bureaucracy as the embodiment of society's highest collective ideals, and feminist criticism has long since laid bare the maneuvers through which the separation of a public, political "society" from a private, personal "family" naturalized patriarchal domination (e.g., Ferguson 1984; Pateman 1988; Rosaldo 1980; Yanagisako and Collier 1987). But the old topographic metaphor that allowed civil society to appear as a zone of mediation between an "up there" state and an "on the ground" community continues to be omnipresent and surprisingly resistant to critical scrutiny. Participants in recent debates on the public sphere (e.g., Calhoun 1992) and civil society (Chatterjee 1990; Cohen and Arato 1992; Harbeson et al. 1994; Taylor 1990) advance diverse political and theoretical positions; but they largely share a commonsense topography within which the object of their theorizing lies in some sense "between" the state and the communities, interest groups, and lifeworlds that states must govern.

An imagined topography of stacked, vertical levels also structures many taken-for-granted images of political struggle, which are readily imagined as coming "from below," as "grounded" in rooted and authentic lives, experiences, and communities. The state itself, meanwhile, can be imagined as reaching down into communities, intervening, in a "top down" manner, to manipulate or plan society. Civil society, in this vertical topography, appears as the middle latitude, the zone of contact between the "up there" state and the "on the ground" people, snug in their communities. Whether this contact zone is conceived as the domain of pressure groups and pluralist politics (as in liberal political theory) or of class struggle in a war of position (as in Gramscian Marxism), the vertical topography of power has been an enormously consequential one.

Picturing the state's relation to society through the image of vertical encompassment fuses in a single, powerful image a number of analytically distinct propositions. Is the state's encompassing height a matter of superior rank in a political hierarchy? Of spatial scale? Abstraction? Generality of knowledge and interest? Distance from nature? The confusion engendered by bundling these distinct propositions together is in fact productive, in the Foucauldian sense, in that it constructs a commonsense state that simply *is* "up there" somewhere, operating at a "higher level." The point is not that this picture of the "up there" state is false (still less that there is no such thing as political hierarchy, generality of interest, etc.), but that it is constructed; the task is not to denounce a false ideology, but to draw attention to the social and imaginative processes through which state verticality is made effective and authoritative.

Images of state vertical encompassment are influential not only because of their impact on how scholars, journalists, officials, activists, and citizens imagine and inhabit states, but because they come to be embedded in the routinized practices of state bureaucracies. The metaphors through which states are imagined are important, and scholarship in this area has recently made great strides.[9] But the understanding of the social practices through which these images are made effective and are experienced is less developed. This relative inattention to state practices seems peculiar, because states in fact invest a good deal of effort in developing procedures and practices to ensure that they are imagined in some ways rather than others (Scott 1998). They seem to recognize that a host of mundane rituals and procedures are required to animate and naturalize metaphors if states are to succeed in being imagined as both higher than, and encompassing of, society.

The importance of the mundane rituals and routines of state spatialization is easily recognized where the regulation and surveillance of the borders of nation-states is concerned. But the policing of the border is intimately tied to the policing of Main Street in that they are acts that represent the repressive power of the state as both extensive with the territorial boundaries of the nation and intensively permeating every square inch of that territory, respectively.[10] There is more to state spatialization, though, than policing or repression. State benevolence, no less than coercion, must also make its spatial rounds, as is clear, for instance, in the ritual tours of US presidents who drop from the sky in helicopters to dispense aid in the wake of natural disasters.

Although such spectacular examples make convenient illustrations, it may be more important to look at the less dramatic, multiple, mundane domains of bureaucratic practice by which states reproduce spatial orders and scalar hierarchies.[11] Any attempt to understand state spatialization, therefore, must simultaneously attend to theoretical understandings and bureaucratic embodiment. The force of metaphors of verticality and encompassment results both from the fact that they are embedded in the everyday practices of state institutions and from the fact that the routine operation of state institutions *produces* spatial and scalar hierarchies.

In the section that follows, we explore this relation between spatial and statist orders by showing how they produce each other.[12] Because state practices are coimplicated with spatial orders and metaphors, an analysis of the imaginary of the state must include not only explicit discursive representations of the state, but also implicit, unmarked, signifying practices. These mundane practices often slip below the threshold of discursivity but profoundly alter how bodies are oriented, how lives are lived, and how subjects are formed. Such a practice-oriented conception calls for an ethnographic approach. We do not attempt to provide a full ethnographic treatment here because this essay is principally concerned to identify a research program rather than to present the results of one. But it may be helpful to provide a brief illustration of how an ethnographic view of mundane state practices can illuminate the mechanics of state spatialization.

Rituals and Representations of the Spatialization of State Power in India

The Government of India in 1975 launched the Integrated Child Development Services program (ICDS), popularly known as the Anganwadi Program, soon after the formulation of the National Policy for Children. It was spurred by awareness that India exhibited some of the world's highest rates of infant mortality, morbidity, and malnutrition, and extremely high rates of maternal mortality during birth. The goal of the Anganwadi Program was to provide a package of well-integrated services consisting of supplementary nutrition for pregnant women and young children as well as education, immunizations, and preventive medicine for poor and lower-caste children. The Anganwadi Program well illustrates the concern with the welfare of the population that Foucault identifies as the central aspect of "governmentality" in the modern world.[13]

The structure of command of the ICDS bureaucracy at the District level followed a typical pyramid shape. The District Program Officer (DPO) headed the office. Reporting to him were the two Child Development Project Officers (CDPOs) who headed the programs at the Block level.[14] The CDPOs supervised an office consisting of clerical staff and a driver, and also supervised the four Supervisors (*Mukhya Sevikas*) who, in turn, looked after the 86 Anganwadi Workers and an equal number of Helpers in the Block.[15] The pyramid-shaped hierarchy of the program was made visible to its employees through standard bureaucratic representational devices like organizational charts.[16] But, more importantly, hierarchy was realized through a panoply of practices of spatial encompassment, some examples of which are given below.

The Anganwadi Program operated through Anganwadis or Centers, run by a Worker and her Helper from 9:00 a.m. to 1:00 p.m., six days of the week. Running the Center involved taking care of as many as 45 children, teaching them, cooking food for their midday meal, supervising their medical care, and maintaining the records. In Mandi, the Block from which these data have been collected, all the Helpers, Anganwadi Workers, and Supervisors as well as the CDPO were women; the rest of the office staff were men.[17]

Exploring this project in the context of an analysis of state spatiality immediately gives rise to several questions: How was the ICDS program spatialized? By what procedures and techniques of bureaucratic rationality did state verticality and encompassment become real and tangible? How were certain people and populations fixed in place, made "local," whereas others higher up could be seen to be more mobile, more encompassing? Village-level state workers, in particular, represented an interesting paradox. On the one hand, their presence in the village made it more difficult to sustain the image of the state standing *above* civil society and the family; on the other hand, as marginal members of the state apparatus, they provided a concrete example to other villagers of the verticality and encompassment of the state. Anganwadi Workers, perhaps even more than other villagers, experienced the state as an organization "above them" that was concerned primarily with surveillance and regulation, even as they themselves served as agents of that surveillance.

In order to contextualize the ethnographic examples that follow, we will begin with a short description of the ICDS office in Mandi.[18] When first looking for the ICDS office, the ethnographer (Gupta) walked right past it because the directions given had been keyed to a blue UNICEF jeep that served as the unofficial mascot for the program. He could not locate the office because the jeep was missing, and unlike other government offices that displayed large signs, there was no outward indication that an office existed in that building. It was a nondescript space, consisting of a small driveway barely large enough for a vehicle, and a narrow flight of stairs to one side. The stairs led to a terrace, opening up to three rooms, the furthest of which belonged to the dynamic and articulate CDPO of Mandi Block, Asha Agarwal. Sitting behind a fairly large desk in a sparsely furnished and decorated room, she had a buzzer on her desk, which she pressed whenever she needed to get the attention of the peon.

By doing fieldwork in the ICDS office, it was possible to see how encompassment came to be actually instantiated in the everyday practices of the program. The most important mechanism was that of the surprise inspection. Anganwadi Workers were positioned at the bottom of a bureaucratic hierarchy in which the ritual of surveillance and regulation as an instrument of control was central. They were subject to surprise inspections by a host of visiting superior officers. One of the officers' primary concerns was to monitor the degree to which the Anganwadi Workers collected data, especially information about women and children who were the targets of the ICDS program. In this sense, the object of the officers' surveillance was the surveillance exercised by the Anganwadi Worker on "their" populations. The logic of this kind of recursive regulation cannot be explained in functional terms because most of this activity was irrelevant to the needs of the state. Rather, what such rituals of surveillance actually accomplished was to *represent* and to *embody* state hierarchy and encompassment.

It was possible to accompany Asha Agarwal on a couple of inspections. She had carefully planned the itinerary to include Anganwadi centers that had records of good performance. But the fact that these were surprise visits meant that they could not serve as unproblematic public relations exercises. The first trip was on a cold and overcast day in February 1992, soon after the office had received a fresh disbursement of funds for purchasing gasoline for the jeep.

The first village was Kalanda. There were two Anganwadis in Kalanda that had been operating since 1985, when the ICDS project began in Mandi Block. The village was most unusual for the well-maintained quality of its inner roads and the complete absence of sewage water and garbage on the streets. Many men in the village were masons, returnees from the Gulf, who had volunteered their labor to lay the roads and the drains.

The first inspection was of an Anganwadi housed in a dark room that served as the storage area for a farm family. A huge pile of lentils occupied half the room, completely covering one wall and a sizeable proportion of the floor space. The local Anganwadi Worker, a pleasant and energetic woman, quickly sent the Helper to round up additional children to add to the 14 who were already there. Asha asked the children to count and to recite the alphabet, which they did with practiced ease. One child in particular, who was a little older than the rest, had written down numbers all the way to 100 on his slate and had also memorized all the poems and songs that the children had been taught. During the visit, a number of children came in, looking washed and scrubbed. Asha told me that the teacher only had a high school degree, but seemed to be doing a good job with the children. She scolded the Anganwadi Worker for not removing the charts, which functioned as teaching aids, from the wall where the lentils had been piled. "It is your job to look after the charts," she told her. "When you knew that the crop was going to be stored there, why didn't you remove the charts beforehand?" After inspecting the Attendance Registers and writing a brief report in the Inspection Register, which noted when the inspection took place, how many children were there, and what the children had demonstrated, Asha indicated that it was time to leave the Center and move on to the second one.

The second Center in Kalanda operated on the porch of a house. But the Anganwadi Worker was nowhere to be seen. There was only a handful of very young children present. The Helper claimed not to know the whereabouts of the Anganwadi Worker. Asha and the Supervisor attempted to coax some of the children to stand and recite the number table or to identify objects on an alphabet chart. None of them complied. It was hard to tell whether this was out of fear of the visitors or because of their unfamiliarity with the task. Asha left a note in the Inspection Register demanding that the Anganwadi Worker produce an explanation within 24 hours as to why she was missing from her station. Just as Asha's party was headed back to the jeep, the Anganwadi Worker arrived. She apologized profusely and blamed her delay on the fact that the bus she was traveling on had broken down. Asha chastized her in no uncertain terms. Even if her bus had broken down, she said, this was no excuse for reaching the Center at 11:15 a.m. instead of 9:00 a.m. The Anganwadi Worker lamented her fate, saying that it was her bad luck that the one day when she started late was the day when Asha happened to visit. Asha noted wryly how much better the Center that was operated by the woman who was only "high school pass" seemed compared to the second one, despite the fact that the second Anganwadi Worker had a

Master's degree. She appeared surprised at this because, in the past, she had found that the better-educated teacher had done a very good job.

One of the chief functions of Anganwadi Workers, and by far their most time-consuming activity, consisted of documenting and generating statistics. A plethora of registers recorded different aspects of the Anganwadi's functioning: For example, an *Attendance Register* noted such things as how many children were in a Center each day, and who they were – their names, fathers' names, and castes. A *Nutrition Register* recorded how much food and fuel was consumed; a third register was used to record the birth dates of each child born in the village, its parents' names, ages, and castes. Similar records were kept of all deaths. The name, age, and caste of each pregnant woman and a record of the outcome of the pregnancy were recorded in another register. A *Travel Log* maintained a record of when and why an Anganwadi Worker was missing from a Center. An *Inspection Register* was maintained in which Supervisors, the CDPO, and other visitors recorded their impressions about the functioning of the Anganwadi. Registers were devices for self-monitoring – technologies of self-discipline that were simultaneously portfolios for recording the effectiveness of the care of the population, on the one hand, and for enabling the surveillance and control of the Workers, on the other.[19]

Surprise inspections and registers were two devices by which verticality and encompassment were practiced. It was not only that superior officers at "higher" levels traveled in jeeps, thereby establishing their control over the geographical space of the block, district, and state (whatever their jurisdiction happened to be), it was also that they traveled in order to conduct inspections, to discipline, reward, encourage, and punish. Registers helped them do just that because registers enabled them to check their observations against what had been noted. For example, Asha complained that Workers who ran Anganwadi Centers in their homes often brought in additional children when they saw the dust of the approaching jeep in the distance. Thus, by the time the CDPO actually reached the Center, there were many children there even if the Anganwadi had not been operating; however, she managed to catch the Worker's "deception" in such cases by checking the names of the children present against the names (if any) entered in the Attendance Register. The CDPO's ability to swoop down on the space of the Anganwadi Worker was thus mediated by the semiotic of dust, a smoke signal delivered by that very device – the jeep – that enabled her to suddenly enter the professional space of the local Anganwadi Worker.

The surprise inspection was a ritual of control that established and demonstrated hierarchy, but the mode of conducting the inspection, the sudden swooping "down" into the geographical space of the Anganwadi Worker, was a demonstration of the inequality of spaces. Anganwadi Workers went to the main ICDS office at a prescribed time each month; their ability to enter the space of the superior officer was limited and circumscribed, a sharp contrast to the surprise inspection. The ability to transgress space (the prerogative of "higher" officers) was also a device of encompassment, as it was their position in the vertical hierarchy that gave officers the privilege of a particular kind of spatial mobility, a mobility whose function and goal was to regulate and discipline.

The conjunction of hierarchy with ever-wider circuits of movement finds a different kind of expression in the system of transfers, which are a major aspect of the lives of state employees in India. Government servants are supposed to be transferred every three years; in practice, this period is even shorter. What is interesting for the purposes of thinking about the spatialization of the state is the circumference of what Benedict Anderson (1991) has called "bureaucratic pilgrimages." The "higher up" officials are, the broader the geographical range of their peregrinations, and the more encompassing their optics on the domain of state activity and its relation to what is merely "local." Once again, we find verticality and encompassment to be intimately tied to one another.

One of the chief mechanisms by which officials "higher up" in the bureaucracy came to embody the higher reaches of the state (with its connotation of greater vision; a better sense of the general good; and national, as opposed to local, interest) was by positioning "lower-level" workers, "local" politicians, and "local" villagers as people who belonged to, and articulated the interests of, particular communities, with limited generalizability across geographical areas, or across class and caste divisions. How did such localization work in practice? By what mechanisms were certain people fixed in space as local people with local concerns while others came to be seen, and to see themselves, as concerned with "larger" issues that traversed geographical and political space? Some concrete examples of localization in the ICDS program might help to make this dynamic visible.

By its very etymology – the word *angan* means "courtyard," the space in north Indian village homes where women spend most of their time – the Anganwadi program emphasized its relation to a confined, encircled, and domestic space. Contrary to the image conjured by this association, Anganwadi Centers were in fact usually run in public spaces, either porches of homes or, when available, in community centers. It was one of the expectations of the ICDS that these spaces for the Anganwadis would be donated by the community. Thus, there was no provision for rents in the ICDS budget. Apart from reducing the cost of administering the program, such a requirement was intended to provide the community with a stake in the operation of the Anganwadis and was, most likely, influenced by the design of international and bilateral agencies such as UNICEF, USAID, and DANIDA (Danish International Development Assistance). According to development orthodoxy, one of the lessons learned from the high failure rate of development projects in the past is that they lacked participation by the local community. Hence, ICDS had a "slot" for community participation, in the form of the provision of space. This created a great deal of difficulty for Anganwadi Workers and was one of their chief complaints, as free space was scarce and often reclaimed for wedding parties and storage of the harvest.

Is it surprising that the agents of localization were precisely those entities – the Indian state and multilateral aid agencies – that claim for themselves geographies and interests that are national and universal? The program thus worked to create a structural and spatial location for the Anganwadi Worker as an official who was marked by her ties to locality and particularity. Localization of the Anganwadi Worker is precisely what enabled those overarching institutions to disavow the particular, and to claim to represent the "greater" good for the "larger" dominion of the nation and the world.

Part Two: Transnational Governmentality – Contemporary Challenges to State Spatialization

Governmentality and the Global

In the previous section, we showed some of the means through which a state may be able to create, through mundane and unmarked practices, a powerful impression of vertical encompassment of the "local." But such efforts by states to establish their superior spatial claims to authority do not go uncontested. This is especially true at a time when new forms of transnational connection are increasingly enabling "local" actors to challenge the state's well-established claims to encompassment and vertical superiority in unexpected ways, as a host of worldly and well-connected "grassroots" organizations today demonstrate. If state officials can always be counted on to invoke the national interest in ways that seek to encompass (and thereby devalue) the local, canny "grassroots" operators may trump the national ace with appeals to "world opinion" and e-mail links to the international headquarters of such formidably encompassing agents of surveillance as Amnesty International, Africa Watch, or World Vision International. The extent to which states are successful in establishing their claims to encompass the local is therefore not preordained, but is a contingent outcome of specific sociopolitical processes. And, as the precarious situation of many states in Africa today makes especially clear, the state has no automatic right to success in claiming the vertical heights of sovereignty.

In thinking about the relation between states and a range of contemporary supranational and transnational organizations that significantly overlap their traditional functions, we have found it useful to develop an idea of *transnational governmentality*, borrowing and extending the idea of "governmentality" first introduced by Michel Foucault (1991). Foucault draws attention to all the processes by which the conduct of a population is governed: by institutions and agencies, including the state; by discourses, norms, and identities; and by self-regulation, techniques for the disciplining and care of the self. Political economy as knowledge and apparatuses of security as technical means have operated on the population as a target to constitute governmentality as the dominant mode of power since the eighteenth century (Foucault 1991: 102). Governmentality is concerned most of all with "the conduct of conduct" (Dean 1999: 10), that is, with the myriad ways in which human conduct is directed by calculated means. Foucault was interested in mechanisms of government that are found within state institutions and outside them, mechanisms that in fact cut across domains that we would regard as separate: the state, civil society, the family, down to the intimate details of what we regard as personal life. Governmentality does not name a negative relationship of power, one characterized entirely by discipline and regulation; rather, the emphasis is on its productive dimension.

More recently, scholars working in this tradition have sought to refine the analysis of governmentality to deal with the shift from the Keynesian welfare state toward so-called free-market policies in Western democracies. Although this move to neoliberalism has often been understood (and variously celebrated or lamented, depending on one's politics) as a "retreat" or "rolling back" of the state, Barry et al. stress that it has, rather, entailed a transfer of the operations of government (in Foucault's extended sense) to nonstate entities, via "the fabrica-tion of techniques that can produce a degree of 'autonomization' of entities of government from the state" (1996: 11–12). The logic of the market has been extended to the operation of state functions, so that even the traditionally core institutions of government, such as post offices, schools, and police, are, if not actually privatized, at least run according to an "enterprise model" (Burchell 1996). Meanwhile, the social and regulatory operations of the state are increas-ingly "de-statized," and taken over by a proliferation of "quasi-autonomous non-governmental organizations" (Rose 1996: 56).[20] But this is not a matter of less government, as the usual ideological formulations would have it. Rather, it indicates a new modality of government, which works by creating mechanisms that work "all by themselves" to bring about governmental results through the devolution of risk onto the "enterprise" or the individual (now construed as the entrepreneur of his or her own "firm") and the "responsibilization" of subjects who are increasingly "empowered" to discipline themselves (see Barry et al. 1996; Burchell 1996; cf. Burchell et al. 1991; O'Malley 1998; Rose 1996; Rose and Miller 1992).

Such extensions of the Foucauldian concept of governmentality to neoliberal-ism are undoubtedly illuminating and suggestive. But they remain strikingly Eurocentric, and closely tied to the idea of the territorially sovereign nation-state as the domain for the operation of government.[21] We propose to extend the discussion of governmentality to modes of government that are being set up on a global scale. These include not only new strategies of discipline and regulation, exemplified by the WTO and the structural adjustment programs implemented by the IMF, but also transnational alliances forged by activists and grassroots organ-izations and the proliferation of voluntary organizations supported by complex networks of international and transnational funding and personnel. The outsour-cing of the functions of the state to NGOs and other ostensibly nonstate agencies, we argue, is a key feature, not only of the operation of national states, but of an emerging system of transnational governmentality.

The increasing salience of such processes ought to bring into question the taken-for-granted spatial and scalar frames of sovereign states. But instead of spurring a wholesale rethinking of spatial and scalar images, what we find is that received notions of verticality and encompassment have been stretched – often improbably – to adapt to the new realities. Thus, institutions of global governance such as the IMF and the WTO are commonly seen as being simply "above" national states, much as states were discussed vis-à-vis the grassroots. Similarly, the "global" is often spoken of as if it were simply a superordinate scalar level that encompasses nation-states just as nation-states were conceptualized to encompass regions, towns, and villages.

Struggles between agencies that are attempting to foster global government and their critics have made headlines first in Seattle in November and December 1999, then in Washington, DC, in April 2000, and, more recently (September 2000), in Prague. One of the most interesting aspects of these protests, as well as of the documentary coverage and commentary about them, is the difficulty experienced by participants and observers alike in articulating the role of the national state vis-à-vis "global" agreements and "grassroots" protests. Are the institutions that promote globalization, such as the World Bank, the IMF, and the WTO, making policy decisions that affect the lives of people all over the world without the normal mechanisms of democratic accountability, as the protestors charge? Or are these international bodies merely facilitating efforts at "good governance" proposed and enforced by national governments, as they counter? Observers and commentators struggle to make sense of this situation. Journalists note that the protestors consist of seemingly unrelated groups that are protesting for very different causes and reasons; moreover, many of the "grassroots groups" opposing globalization are themselves arguably leading examples of it: well-organized transnational organizations with offices or affiliations spread out across the world, coordinating their demonstrations over the Internet, and even in real-time (during the events) by cellular phones and walkie-talkies.

The confusion evident in the understandings both of important agencies of globalization and of the activist groups that oppose them (as well as those who report on them and study them) is at least in part about how states are spatialized and what relations exist between space and government. Processes of globalization have disturbed the familiar metaphors and practices of vertical encompassment (still taken for granted by the participants in debates on globalization, including journalists and academics), and the new landscape that is emerging can be understood only through a rethinking of questions of space and scale. To accomplish such a rethinking, it will be necessary to question both common-sense assumptions about the verticality of states and many received ideas of "community," "grassroots," and the "local," laden as they are with nostalgia and the aura of authenticity.[22]

In making this move, we find it useful to turn from our Indian ethnographic example, in which a relatively strong state succeeds in spatializing itself in familiar ways, to a macrological overview of Africa, where many contemporary states are, in significant ways, no longer able to exercise the powers normally associated with a sovereign nation-state, or even (in a few cases) to function at all as states in any conventional sense of the term. Such undoubtedly extreme cases will help us to decenter the state and to foreground new forms of transnational governmentality that we suggest are not unique to Africa, even if they are especially visible and important there. It should be noted that our aim is not to make a comparison between Africa and India. Rather, the discussion of the precarious situation of African states aptly illustrates one part of our argument (about the rising salience of transnational governmentality), just as the Indian material usefully illustrates another part of the argument (about the way that states secure their authority and legitimacy through unmarked spatial practices that create effects of vertical encompassment).[23]

Beyond Vertical Encompassment: Transnational Governmentality in Africa

Contemporary scholars of African politics continue to rely on images of vertically encompassing states, even as the empirical situations being described are becoming ever less amenable to being captured in such terms. It is clear enough that there exists a range of phenomena in contemporary Africa that cannot be understood in the old "nation-building" optic that saw postcolonial African politics as a battle between a modernizing state and primordial ethnic groups. But the dominant response to this evident fact has been a recourse to the idea of "civil society" to encompass a disparate hodgepodge of social groups and institutions that have in common only that they exist in some way outside of or beyond the state (for a critical review, see Comaroff and Comaroff 1999: 1–43). Definitions of "civil society" in the state and society literature are usually broad and vague, but in practice, writers move quite quickly from definitional generalities to a much more specific vision that is restricted almost entirely to small, grassroots, voluntary organizations. This narrow usage leaves some rather important and obvious phenomena out of the picture. One is never quite sure: Is the Anglo-American Corporation of South Africa part of this "civil society"? Is John Garang's army in Sudan part of it? Is Oxfam? What about ethnic movements that are not so much opposed to or prior to modern states, but (as recent scholars show) produced by them (see, e.g., Vail 1991; Wilmsen and McAllister 1996)? And what of international mission organizations – arguably as important a part of the African scene today as ever, but strangely relegated to the colonial past in much Africanist scholarship? Such things fit uncomfortably in the "state" versus "civil society" grid, and indeed cannot even be coherently labeled as "local," "national," or "international" phenomena. Instead, each of these examples, like much else of interest in contemporary Africa, both embodies a significant local dynamic, and is indisputably a product and expression of powerful national, regional, and global forces.

The state, meanwhile, when apprehended empirically and ethnographically, starts itself to look suspiciously like "civil society." This can be literally so, as when government officials moonlight by using their educational and institutional capital to start (and gain resources through) their own "grassroots" organizations. (As a Zambian informant put it, "An NGO? Oh, that's just a bureaucrat with his own letterhead.") More profoundly, as Timothy Mitchell has argued, the very conception of "the state" as a set of reified and disembodied structures is an *effect* of state practices themselves (1991). Instead of opposing the state to something called "society," then, we need to view states as themselves composed of bundles of social practices, every bit as local in their materiality and social situatedness as any other (Gupta 1995).

To break away from the conventional division into vertical analytic levels of state and society here is to go beyond the range of questions that such a division imposes (how do states rule, what relations exist – or ought to exist – between state and society, how can civil society obtain room to maneuver from the state, and so forth), and open up for view some of the transnational relations that we suggest are crucial for understanding both the putative "top" of the vertical picture (the state) and the "bottom" ("grassroots" voluntary organizations).

The State

If, as some neoliberal theorists of state and society suggest, domination is rooted in state power, then rolling back the power of the state naturally leads to greater freedom, and ultimately to "democratization." But the argument is revealed to be fallacious if one observes that, in Africa and elsewhere, domination has long been exercised by entities other than the state. Zambia, to take an example, was originally colonized (just a little over a hundred years ago) not by any government, but by the British South Africa Company, a private multinational corporation directed by Cecil Rhodes. Equipped with its own army, and acting under the terms of a British "concession," it was this private corporation that conquered and "pacified" the territory, setting up the system of private ownership and race privilege that became the colonial system. Today, Zambia (like most other African nations) continues to be ruled, in significant part, by transnational organizations that are not in themselves governments, but work together with powerful First World states within a global system of nation-states that Frederick Cooper has characterized as "internationalized imperialism."[24]

Perhaps most familiarly, international agencies such as the IMF and World Bank, together with allied banks and First World governments, today often directly impose policies on African states. The name for this process in recent years has been "structural adjustment," and it has been made possible by both the general fiscal weakness of African states and the more specific squeeze created by the debt crisis. The new assertiveness of the IMF has been, with some justification, likened to a process of "recolonization," implying serious erosion of the sovereignty of African states (e.g., Saul 1993). It should be noted that direct impositions of policy by banks and international agencies have involved not only such broad, macroeconomic interventions as setting currency exchange rates, but also fairly detailed requirements for curtailing social spending, restructuring state bureaucracies, and so on. Rather significant and specific aspects of state policy, in other words, are, for many African countries, being directly formulated in places like New York, London, Brussels, and Washington.

As critics have pointed out, such "governance" of African economies from afar represents a kind of transfer of economic sovereignty away from African states and into the hands of the IMF. Yet, because it is African governments that remain nominally in charge, it is easy to see that they are the first to receive the blame when structural adjustment policies begin to bite. At that point, democratic elections (another "adjustment" being pressed by international donors) provide a means whereby one government can be replaced by another; but because the successor government will be locked in the same financial vice-grip as its predecessor, actual policies are unlikely to change. (Indeed, the IMF and its associated capital cartel can swiftly bring any government that tries to assert itself to its knees, as the Zambian case illustrates vividly.) In this way, policies that are in fact made and imposed by wholly unelected and unaccountable international bankers may be presented as democratically chosen by popular assent. In this way, "democratization" ironically serves to simulate popular legitimacy for policies that are in fact made in a way that is less democratic than ever (cf. Ferguson 1995).

"The Grassroots"

Civil society often appears in African Studies nowadays as a bustle of grassroots, democratic local organizations. As Jane Guyer has put it, what this ignores is "the obvious: That civil society is made up of international organizations" (1994: 223). For, indeed, the local voluntary organizations in Africa, so beloved of civil society theorists, very often, on inspection, turn out to be integrally linked with national and transnational-level entities. One might think, for instance, of the myriad South African community groups that are bankrolled by USAID or European church groups (Mayekiso 1996; Mindry 1998); or of the profusion of local Christian development NGOs in Zimbabwe, which may be conceived equally well as the most local, grassroots expressions of civil society, or as parts of the vast international bureaucratic organizations that organize and sustain them (Bornstein 2001). When such organizations begin to take over the most basic functions and powers of the state, as they very significantly did, for instance, in Mozambique (Hanlon 1991), it becomes only too clear that NGOs are not as "NG" as they might wish us to believe. Indeed, the World Bank baldly refers to what they call BONGOs (bank-organized NGOs) and even GONGOs (government-organized NGOs).

That these voluntary organizations come as much from "above" (international organizations) as from "below" (local communities) is an extremely significant fact about so-called civil society in contemporary Africa. For at the same time that international organizations (through structural adjustment) are eroding the power of African states (and usurping their economic sovereignty), they are busy making end runs around these states and directly sponsoring their own programs and interventions via NGOs in a wide range of areas. The role played by NGOs in helping Western development agencies to get around uncooperative national governments sheds a good deal of light on the current disdain for the state and celebration of civil society that one finds in both the academic and the development literature right now.

But challengers to African states today are not only to be found in international organizations and NGOs. In the wake of what is widely agreed to be a certain collapse or retreat of the nation-state all across the continent, we find forms of power and authority springing up everywhere that have not been well described or analyzed to date. These are usually described as "subnational," and usually conceived either as essentially ethnic (the old primordialist view), or alternatively (and more hopefully) as manifestations of a newly resurgent civil society, long suppressed by a heavy-handed state. Yet, can we really assume that the new political forms that challenge the hegemony of African nation-states are necessarily well conceived as "local," "grass-roots," "civil," or even "subnational"?

Guerrilla insurrections, for instance, not famous for their civility, are often not strictly local or subnational, either – armed and funded, as they often are, from abroad. Consider Savimbi's União Nacional para a Independência Total de Angola (UNITA) movement in Angola: long aided by the CIA, originally trained by the Chinese government, with years of military and logistic support from apartheid South Africa, and funding from sources that range from the international diamond trade to donations from US church groups. Is this a subnational organization? A phenomenon of an emerging civil society? Or consider the highly organized transnational forms of criminality that so often exist in such a symbiotic partnership with the state that we may even come to speak, as Bayart et al. have recently suggested (1999), of "the criminalization of the state" in many parts of Africa. Can such developments be grasped within the state–society or local–global polarities? What about transnational Christian organizations like World Vision International, which play an enormous role in many parts of contemporary Africa, organizing local affairs and building and operating schools and clinics where states have failed to do so (Bornstein 2001)? Are such giant, transnational organizations to be conceptualized as "local"? What of humanitarian organizations such as Oxfam, Cooperative for Assistance and Relief Everywhere (CARE), or Doctors Without Borders, which perform statelike functions all across Africa?

Such organizations are not states, but are unquestionably statelike in some respects. Yet they are not well described as subnational, national, or even supranational. They ignore the nation-building logic of the old developmentalist state, which sought to link its citizens into a universalistic national grid (cf. Scott 1998) and instead build on the rapid, deterritorialized point-to-point forms of connection (and disconnection) that are central to both the new communications technologies and the new, neoliberal practices of capital mobility (Ferguson 1999, 2002). Local and global at the same time, such entities are transnational – even, in some ways, anational; they cannot be located within the familiar vertical division of analytic levels presented above. Not coincidentally, these organizations and movements that fall outside of the received scheme of analytic levels are also conspicuously understudied – indeed, they have until recently been largely invisible in theoretical scholarship on African politics, tending to be relegated instead to "applied," problem-oriented studies.

In all of these cases, we are dealing with political entities that may be better conceptualized not as "below" the state, but as integral parts of a transnational apparatus of governmentality. This apparatus does not replace the older system of nation-states (which is – let us be clear – not about to disappear), but overlays and coexists with it. In this optic, it might make sense to think of the new organizations that have sprung up in recent years not as challengers pressing up against the state from below but as horizontal contemporaries of the organs of the state – sometimes rivals; sometimes servants; sometimes watchdogs; sometimes parasites; but in every case operating on the same level, and in the same global space.

The implication is not simply that it is important to study NGOs and other transnational nonstate organizations, or even to trace their interrelations and zones of contact with the state. Rather, the implication is that it is necessary to treat state and non-state governmentality within a common frame, without making unwarranted assumptions about their spatial reach, vertical height, or relation to the local. Taking the verticality and encompassment of states not as a taken-for-granted fact, but as a precarious achievement, it becomes possible to pose the question of the spatiality of contemporary practices of government as an ethnographic problem.

Conclusion: Toward an Ethnography of Neoliberal Governmentality

Studying the relationship between states, space, and scale opens up an enormous empirical and ethnographic project, one that has not been systematically pursued in anthropological analysis. In this essay, we have drawn attention to two central features of state spatialization, *verticality* and *encompassment*. These images of space and scale are not "mere" metaphors. What gives verticality and encompassment their efficacy as commonsensical features of states is their embeddedness in a host of mundane bureaucratic practices, as the examples from the ICDS program in India demonstrate. Instead of understanding space as a preexisting container and scale as a natural feature of the world in which states operate, we have argued that states themselves *produce* spatial and scalar hierarchies. In fact, the production of these hierarchies is not incidental but central to the functioning of states; they are the raison d'être of states (and perhaps their raison d'état). It might be worth rereading the ethnographic record to reinterpret the data concerning how state claims to verticality and encompassment have been legitimized and substantiated in everyday life in a multiplicity of empirical situations around the world (although the data might well be too thin in many cases to carry out such a project).

Although the spatial and scalar *ideologies* of states have always been open to critique, the new practices associated with neoliberal globalization have opened up opportunities for a deeper questioning. In a global order where the organization of capitalism coexisted more easily with the hegemony of nation-states, statist projects of verticality and encompassment seemed "natural" and were usually easily incorporated into the everyday routines of social life. However, the conflicts engendered by neoliberal globalization have brought the disjuncture between spatial and scalar orders into the open, revealing the profoundly transnational character of both the "state" and the "local," and drawing attention to crucial mechanisms of governmentality that take place outside of, and alongside, the nation-state. Claims of verticality that have historically been monopolized by the state (claims of superior spatial scope, supremacy in a hierarchy of power, and greater generality of interest and moral purpose) are being challenged and undermined by a transnationalized "local" that fuses the grassroots and the global in ways that make a hash of the vertical topography of power on which the legitimation of nation-states has so long depended. For increasingly, state claims of encompassment are met and countered by globally networked and globally imaged organizations and movements – manifestations of "the local" that may claim (in their capacity as ecological "guardians of the planet," indigenous protectors of "the lungs of the earth," or participants in a universal struggle for human rights) a wider rather than narrower spatial and moral purview than that of the merely national state.

We do not mean to suggest that such transnationalized local actors always win their fights, or that national states have become incapable of exercising their authority over localities. Neither do we intend to imply that states' new difficulties in spatializing their authority are likely to usher in a new era of enlightenment and greater public good. (On the contrary, the diminishment of state authority is as likely to undermine the position of subaltern groups as it is to enhance it, as the recent political history of much of Africa in particular shows.) That state claims to vertical encompassment are today increasingly precarious does not mean that they no longer exist; as we have shown, vertical encompassment continues to be powerfully institutionalized and instantiated in daily practices. If the nature of these institutions and the sites of this instantiation are being transformed, it is precisely to these transformations that we must attend in our empirical investigations.

What is necessary, then, is not simply more or better study of "state–society interactions" – to put matters in this way would be to assume the very opposition that calls for interrogation. Rather, the need is for an ethnography of encompassment, an approach that would take as its central problem the understanding of processes through which governmentality (by state and nonstate actors) is both legitimated and undermined by reference to claims of superior spatial reach and vertical height. Indeed, focusing on governmentality calls into question the very distinction insisted on by the term *nongovernmental organization*, emphasizing instead the similarities of technologies of government across domains.

An ethnography of the spatiality of governmentality has to confront several problems. First, as originally formulated by Foucault (1991), "governmentality" as a form of power exercised over populations assumes the frame of the nation-state. Extending this concept to account for neoliberal globalization forces us to reformulate the spatial and scalar assumptions of governmentality.[25] For example, we cannot just think of transnational governmentality as a form of global government, a suprastate that is superimposed on various nation-states much as the European Union is on its member governments. Institutions of global governance are not simply replicating on a bigger scale the functions and tasks of the nation-state, as both proponents and opponents of transnational governmentality often assume. Verticality and encompassment continue to be produced, but not in the same way by the same institutions or groups. Globalized "grassroots" groups and nongovernmental organizations are good examples of how scales have collapsed into each other. Neil Smith has attempted to understand this phenomenon of the "active social and political connectedness of apparently different scales" (1992: 66) by referring to such activities in terms of "jumping scales." John Ruggie (1993) has attempted to understand the reconfiguration of territorial sovereignty in the world system as forming an "unbundled space" where nation and state are not homologous in their control and regulation of territory. Other forms of spatial and scalar production are clearly imposing themselves on state spatiality and territoriality (Brenner 1997; Storper 1997; Swyngedouw 1997). At the same time, different institutions and organizations, including nation-states and metastates like the European Union, are attempting to reinstate verticality and encompassment in territories that are not necessarily contiguous, or united in cultural, political, and economic spheres. The ethnographic challenge facing us today with neoliberal globalization is to understand the spatiality of all forms of government, some of which may be embedded in the daily practices of nation-states while others may crosscut or superimpose themselves on the territorial jurisdiction of nation-states.

Such an approach might open up a much richer set of questions about the meaning of transnationalism than have been asked up to now. It is not a question of whether a globalizing political economy is rendering nation-states weak and irrelevant, as some have suggested, or whether states remain the crucial building blocks of the global system, as others have countered. For the central effect of the new forms of transnational governmentality is not so much to make states weak (or strong), as to reconfigure states' abilities to spatialize their authority and to stake their claims to superior generality and universality. Recognizing this process might open up a new line of inquiry into the study of governmentality in the contemporary world.

Notes

Acknowledgments: We wish to thank Rozita Dimova for research assistance. When this essay was revised, Akhil Gupta was a Fellow at the National Humanities Center and James Ferguson was a Fellow at the Center for Advanced Studies in the Behavioral Sciences. We gratefully acknowledge the support of both those institutions.

1 There is a long and rich tradition of studies by geographers and social theorists on the social construction of space under conditions of modernity and postmodernity. Building on an old, if often undervalued, tradition of spatial thinking within Marxism (esp. the seminal work of Henri Lefebvre [1991]), social geographers like David Harvey (1985a, 1985b, 1990) and Doreen Massey (1984, 1994) have shown how changing forms of capitalist production have structured urban spaces and the social experiences that unfold within them. Meanwhile, theorists of globalization, such as Saskia Sassen, have shown how state practices of regulation (from immigration control to financial regulations) intersect with transnational flows of capital to generate highly differentiated national and subnational economic zones within an increasingly global economic space (1991, 1996, 1998). But although such contributions help to show how states may act to construct social and economic space and to shape the way that places are built, experienced, and inhabited, they do not deal with the related but distinct question that concerns us here: How are states themselves spatialized?

   We have also benefited greatly from a recent body of work in anthropology that seeks to understand ethnographically the spatial consequences of state policies (see, e.g., Bernal 1997; Darian-Smith 1999; Grant 1995; Herzfeld 1991; Merry 2001; and Verdery 1996). It is this literature that has enabled us to pursue our own, slightly different, question of how the state itself is spatialized.

2 Ann Anagnost presents a wonderful example of this phenomenon in her discussion of splendid China (1997: 161–175).

3 A different kind of critique of this position has been advanced by Marilyn Strathern (1995), who argues that just because anthropology appears to route its knowledge through persons, it does not follow that the person constitutes an elementary scale of social organization. Maurer (1998) offers an example of how spatial and statist projects converge when encompassment is realized through incorporation.

4 That spatial encompassment is often imagined in terms of such neatly nested circles does not imply that regions, localities, or communities really do fit so neatly within the "higher" levels that supposedly encompass them – indeed, a range of phenomena from borderlands to transnational communities in practice confound this image. Part two develops the implications of this observation.

5 The concept of "civil society" clearly grows out of a specific, European history; like Chatterjee (1990), we emphasize the historical and cultural particularity of the concept, even as we are concerned with its operational universalization as part of the standard package of institutional and ideological forms that have come to be as widely distributed as the modern state itself. But it is not simply the category, "civil society," that requires to be seen in its cultural particularity, but a larger imaginary topography through which the state and society are visualized in relation with each other.

6 Verdery makes a very interesting connection between the nation and the body (1996: 63).

7   Not all theorists have made such an opposition; indeed, the earliest writers on civil society (e.g., Locke) saw "civil society" as synonymous with "political society" (see Taylor 1990: 105).

8   On the history of the concept of civil society, see Burchell 1991; Chatterjee 1990; Comaroff and Comaroff 1999; and Seligman 1992.

9   See especially such contributions as Bayart's (1993) discussion of "eating" as a metaphor of state power in Africa and Mbembe's (1992) analysis of how the imagery of the vulgar and the grotesque in the popular culture of Cameroon comes to invest the symbols of state power. The ways that the spatial metaphors of vertical encompassment that we discuss here may coexist with other metaphors for picturing states are a rich ground for future investigation. Other important contributions to a lively recent discussion on the state in postcolonial Africa include Bayart et al. 1999; Chabal and Daloz 1999; Mamdani 1996; and Werbner and Ranger 1996.

10 One particularly clear example of such policing is provided by the treatment received by Mexican laborers in the United States at the hands of the INS and the police, which demonstrates quite clearly that the border is not just a line that one crosses into a zone of safety but a zone of exclusion that permeates the interior of the territory of the nation-state (see, for instance, Chavez 1998). Heyman (1998) goes even further in making an explicit connection between control of the US–Mexico border and foreign wars such as Vietnam through the trope of illegality.

11 The term *order* is here used both in its directive intent as well as in its organizing connotations.

12 The point is neither to reduce one to the other nor to claim some kind of privileged relationship, as compared to, say, the relationship of space to capital.

13 See the discussion on pp. 114–15.

14 The Block is the smallest administrative unit in India, comprising approximately one hundred villages.

15 The number of Anganwadi Workers and Helpers varied from one Block to another, depending on population to be served and the funds allocated to the program.

16 The pyramidal structure of the bureaucracy followed a classic, Fordist pattern of industrial organization. Unlike the bureaucracies of late-capitalist firms or of other post-Fordist organizations, there was no hint of a flat organizational structure or decentralized decision-making.

17 Following anthropological convention, the name "Mandi," as well as the names of the people and villages below, are pseudonyms.

18 The following text is based on fieldwork observations conducted by Akhil Gupta.

19 Although we have here chosen to focus on the surveillance of the Anganwadi Worker rather than the welfare of the population, our point about state verticality and encompassment could equally have been demonstrated by focusing on the "positive" aspects of governmentality.

20 A good example is provided by the privatization of prisons: Increasingly, private companies have taken over the job of constructing and operating prisons for the state. Once an "enterprise model" becomes dominant, there is little reason for many state functions to be performed by state institutions.

21 It is striking, for instance, that Rose (1996: 53) characterizes "advanced liberalism" as a set of strategies that "can be observed in national contexts from Finland to Australia" – without any discussion of the vast range of national contexts (most of the

world, it would seem) to which his account does not apply. Nor is there any consideration of the relations between the breakdown of notions of welfare at the national level and those of development at the international or of the ways that the proliferation of "quasi-autonomous NGOs" might be linked to changes in the role and function of the nation-state within a global system.

22 Recently, a great many anthropologists have been concerned to problematize the traditional anthropological notion of the "local" (although usually without relating this notion to the question of state spatialization). For reasons of space, we will not review this literature here, but only refer the reader to our extensive discussion of this issue in Gupta and Ferguson 1997.

23 No doubt it is the empirical differences between the situation of the state in the two regional contexts that accounts for why each best illustrates a different part of our argument (broadly, the relative strength of the Indian state versus the institutional and financial weakness of so many African ones), but it is not our purpose to explore those differences systematically here.

24 We borrow this evocative term from remarks made by Cooper (1993). It should be noted, however, that we are here connecting the term to larger claims about transnational governmentality that Cooper may not have intended in his own use of the term.

25 Sally Merry (2001) has developed the idea of "spatial governmentality" to draw attention to forms of governmentality that seek to regulate people indirectly through the control and regulation of space.

References

Anagnost, Ann
    1997   National Past Times: Narrative, Representation, and Power in Modern China. Durham, NC: Duke University Press.
Anderson, Benedict R.
    1991   Imagined Communities: Reflections on the Origin and Spread of Nationalism. 2nd edition. New York: Verso.
Bayart, Jean-François
    1993[1989]   The State in Africa: The Politics of the Belly. New York: Longman.
Bayart, Jean-François, Stephen Ellis, and Béatrice Hibou, eds.
    1999   The Criminalization of the State in Africa. Bloomington: Indiana University Press.
Barry, Andrew, Thomas Osborne, and Nikolas Rose, eds.
    1996   Foucault and Political Reason: Liberalism, Neo-Liberalism and Rationalities of Government. Chicago: University of Chicago Press.
Bernal, Victoria
    1997   Colonial Moral Economy and the Discipline of Development: The Gezira Scheme. Cultural Anthropology 12(4): 447–479.

Bornstein, Erica
2001 The Good Life: Religious NGOs and the Moral Politics of Economic Development in Zimbabwe. PhD dissertation, Program in Social Relations, University of California at Irvine.

Brenner, Neil
1997 Global, Fragmented, Hierarchical: Henri Lefebvre's Geographies of Globalization. Public Culture 10(1): 135–167.

Burchell, Graham
1991 Peculiar Interests: Civil Society and Governing "The System of Natural Liberty." *In* The Foucault Effect: Studies in Governmentality. Graham Burchell, Colin Gordon, and Peter Miller, eds. Pp. 119–150. Chicago: University of Chicago Press.
1996 Liberal Government and Techniques of the Self. *In* Foucault and Political Reason: Liberalism, Neo-liberalism and Rationalities of Government. Andrew Barry, Thomas Osborne, and Nikolas Rose, eds. Pp. 19–36. Chicago: University of Chicago Press.

Burchell, Graham, Colin Gordon, and Peter Miller, eds.
1991 The Foucault Effect: Studies in Governmentality. Chicago: University of Chicago Press.

Calhoun, Craig, ed.
1992 Habermas and the Public Sphere. Cambridge, MA: MIT Press.

Chabal, Patrick, and Jean-Pascal Daloz
1999 Africa Works: Disorder as Political Instrument. Bloomington: Indiana University Press.

Chatterjee, Partha
1990 A Response to Taylor's "Modes of Civil Society." Public Culture 3(1): 119–132.

Chavez, Leo R.
1998 Shadowed Lives: Undocumented Immigrants in American Society. Fort Worth: Harcourt Brace College Publishers.

Cohen, Jean L., and Andrew Arato
1992 Civil Society and Political Theory. Cambridge, MA: MIT Press.

Cohn, Bernard S.
1996 Colonialism and Its Forms of Knowledge. Princeton: Princeton University Press.

Comaroff, John L.
1998 Reflections on the Colonial State, in South Africa and Elsewhere: Factions, Fragments, Facts and Fictions. Social Identities 4(3): 321–361.

Comaroff, John L., and Jean Comaroff, eds.
1999 Civil Society and the Political Imagination in Africa. Chicago: University of Chicago Press.

Cooper, Frederick
1993 Historicizing Development. Workshop. Emory University, Atlanta, December.

Coronil, Fernando
1997 The Magical State: Nature, Money, and Modernity in Venezuela. Chicago: University of Chicago Press.

Corrigan, Philip, and Derek Sayer
1985 The Great Arch: English State Formation as Cultural Revolution. New York: Blackwell.

Darian-Smith, Eve
  1999 Bridging Divides: The Channel Tunnel and English Legal Identity in the New Europe. Berkeley: University of California Press.
Dean, Mitchell
  1999 Governmentality: Power and Rule in Modern Society. Thousand Oaks, CA: Sage Publications.
Fallers, Lloyd A.
  1971 The Social Anthropology of the Nation-State. Chicago: Aldine.
Ferguson, James
  1995 From African Socialism to Scientific Capitalism: Reflections on the Legitimation Crisis in IMF-Ruled Africa. *In* Debating Development Discourse: Popular and Institutionalist Perspectives. David Moore and Gerald Schmitz, eds. Pp. 129–148. New York: St. Martin's Press.
  1999 Expectations of Modernity: Myths and Meanings of Urban Life on the Zambian Copperbelt. Berkeley: University of California Press.
  2002 Global Disconnect: Abjection and the Aftermath of Modernism. *In* The Anthropology of Globalization. Jonathan Xavier Inda and Renato Rosaldo, eds. Pp. 136–153. New York: Blackwell.
  In press Transnational Topographies of Power: Beyond "the State" and "Civil Society" in the Study of African Politics. *In* The Forces of Globalization. Gabriele Schwab, ed. New York: Columbia University Press.
Ferguson, Kathy E.
  1984 The Feminist Case Against Bureaucracy. Philadelphia: University of Pennsylvania Press.
Foucault, Michel
  1991 Governmentality. *In* The Foucault Effect: Studies in Governmentality. Graham Burchell, Colin Gordon, and Peter Miller, eds. Pp. 87–104. Chicago: University of Chicago Press.
Geertz, Clifford
  1980 Negara: The Theatre State in Nineteenth-Century Bali. Princeton: Princeton University Press.
Grant, Bruce
  1995 In the Soviet House of Culture: A Century of Perestroikas. Princeton: Princeton University Press.
Gupta, Akhil
  1995 Blurred Boundaries: The Discourse of Corruption, the Culture of Politics, and the Imagined State. American Ethnologist 22(2): 375–402.
Gupta, Akhil, and James Ferguson, eds.
  1997 Culture, Power, Place: Explorations in Critical Anthropology. Durham, NC: Duke University Press.
Guyer, Jane
  1994 The Spatial Dimensions of Civil Society in Africa: An Anthropologist Looks at Nigeria. *In* Civil Society and the State in Africa. John W. Harbeson, Donald Rothchild, and Naomi Chazan, eds. Pp. 215–230. Boulder: Lynne Rienner Publishers.
Hanlon, Joseph
  1991 Mozambique: Who Calls the Shots? Bloomington: Indiana University Press.

Harbeson, John W., Donald Rothchild, and Naomi Chazan, eds.
  1994   Civil Society and the State in Africa. Boulder: Lynne Rienner Publishers.
Harvey, David
  1985a   Consciousness and the Urban Experience: Studies in the History and Theory
    of Capitalist Urbanization. Baltimore: Johns Hopkins University Press.
  1985b   The Urbanization of Capital: Studies in the History and Theory of Capitalist
    Urbanization. Baltimore: Johns Hopkins University Press.
  1990   The Condition of Postmodernity: An Enquiry into the Origins of Cultural
    Change. Cambridge, MA: Blackwell.
Hegel, Georg Wilhelm Friedrich
  1942[1821]   Philosophy of Right. Thomas Malcolm Knox, trans. Oxford: Clarendon
    Press
Herzfeld, Michael
  1991   A Place of History: Social and Monumental Time in a Cretan Town. Princeton:
    Princeton University Press.
Heyman, Josiah McC.
  1998   State Escalation of Force: A Vietnam/US–Mexico Border Analogy. *In* State and
    Illegal Practices. J. M. Heyman, ed. Pp. 285–314. Oxford: Berg.
Joseph, Gilbert M., and Daniel Nugent, eds.
  1994   Everyday Forms of State Formation: Revolution and the Negotiation of Rule in
    Modern Mexico. Durham, NC: Duke University Press.
Lefebvre, Henri
  1991   The Production of Space. Cambridge, MA: Blackwell.
Mamdani, Mahmood
  1996   Citizen and Subject: Contemporary Africa and the Legacy of Late Colonialism.
    Princeton: Princeton University Press.
Massey, Doreen
  1984   Spatial Divisions of Labour: Social Structures and the Geography of Production.
    London: Macmillan.
  1994   Space, Place and Gender. Cambridge: Polity.
Maurer, Bill
  1998   Recharting the Caribbean: Land, Law, and Citizenship in the British Virgin
    Islands. Ann Arbor: University of Michigan Press.
Mayekiso, Mzwanele
  1996   Township Politics: Civic Struggles for a New South Africa. New York: Monthly
    Review Press.
Mbembe, Achille
  1992   The Banality of Power and the Aesthetics of Vulgarity in the Postcolony. Public
    Culture 4(2): 1–30.
Merry, Sally Engle
  2001   Spatial Governmentality and the New Urban Social Order: Controlling Gender
    Violence Through Law. American Anthropologist 103(1): 16–29.
Mindry, Deborah
  1998   "Good Women": Philanthropy, Power, and the Politics of Femininity in Con-
    temporary South Africa. PhD dissertation, Program in Social Relations, University of
    California at Irvine.

Mitchell, Timothy
1991   The Limits of the State: Beyond Statist Approaches and Their Critics. American
        Political Science Review 85(1): 77–96.
Nugent, David
1997   Modernity at the Edge of Empire: State, Individual, and Nation in the Northern
        Peruvian Andes, 1885–1935. Stanford: Stanford University Press.
O'Malley, Pat
1998   Indigenous Governance. *In* Governing Australia: Studies in Contemporary
        Rationalities of Government. Mitchell Dean and Barry Hindess, eds. Pp. 156–172.
        Cambridge: Cambridge University Press.
Pateman, Carole
1988   The Sexual Contract. Stanford: Stanford University Press.
Rosaldo, Michelle Z.
1980   The Use and Abuse of Anthropology: Reflections on Feminism and Cross-
        Cultural Understanding. Signs: Journal of Women in Culture and Society 5(3):
        389–417.
Rose, Nikolas
1996   Governing "Advanced" Liberal Democracies. *In* Foucault and Political Reason:
        Liberalism, Neo-liberalism and Rationalities of Government. Andrew Barry, Thomas
        Osborne, and Nikolas Rose, eds. Pp. 37–64. Chicago: University of Chicago Press.
Rose, Nikolas, and Peter Miller
1992   Political Power beyond the State: Problematics of Government. British Journal
        of Sociology 43(2): 172–205.
Ruggie, John
1993   Territoriality and Beyond: Problematizing Modernity in International Rela-
        tions. International Organization 47(1): 139–174.
Sassen, Saskia
1991   The Global City: New York, London, Tokyo. Princeton: Princeton University
        Press.
1996   Losing Control? Sovereignty in an Age of Globalization. New York: Columbia
        University Press.
1998   Globalization and Its Discontents: Essays on the New Mobility of People and
        Money. New York: New Press.
Saul, John S.
1993   Recolonization and Resistance: Southern Africa in the 1990s. Trenton: Africa
        World Press.
Scott, James C.
1998   Seeing Like a State: How Certain Schemes to Improve the Human Condition
        Have Failed. New Haven: Yale University Press.
Seligman, Adam B.
1992   The Idea of Civil Society. Princeton: Princeton University Press.
Smith, Neil
1992   Contours of a Spatialized Politics: Homeless Vehicles and the Production of
        Geographical Scale. Social Text 33: 54–81.
Stallybrass, Peter, and Allon White
1986   The Politics and Poetics of Transgression. Ithaca: Cornell University Press.

Storper, Michael
    1997   Territories, Flows, and Hierarchies in the Global Economy. *In* Spaces of Glob-
        alization: Reasserting the Power of the Local. Kevin R. Cox, ed. Pp. 19–44. New
        York: Guilford Press.
Strathern, Marilyn
    1995   The Relation: Issues in Complexity and Scale. Cambridge: Prickly Pear Press.
Swyngedouw, Erik
    1997   Neither Global Nor Local: "Glocalization" and the Politics of Scale. *In* Spaces
        of Globalization: Reasserting the Power of the Local. Kevin R. Cox, ed. Pp. 137–
        166. New York: Guilford Press.
Taussig, Michael
    1996   The Magic of the State. New York: Routledge.
Taylor, Charles
    1990   Modes of Civil Society. Public Culture 3(1): 95–118.
Vail, Leroy, ed.
    1991   The Creation of Tribalism in Southern Africa. Berkeley: University of California
        Press.
Verdery, Katherine
    1996   What Was Socialism, and What Comes Next? Princeton: Princeton University
        Press.
Werbner, Richard, and Terence Ranger, eds.
    1996   Postcolonial Identities in Africa. Atlantic Highlands, NJ: Zed Books.
Wilmsen, Edwin N., and Patrick McAllister, eds.
    1996   The Politics of Difference: Ethnic Premises in a World of Power. Chicago:
        University of Chicago Press.
Yanagisako, Sylvia J., and Jane F. Collier
    1987   Toward a Unified Analysis of Gender and Kinship. *In* Gender and Kinship:
        Essays Toward a Unified Analysis. Jane F. Collier and Sylvia J. Yanagisako, eds. Pp
        14–50. Stanford: Stanford University Press.

Part III
Technico Sciences

5

Performing Criminal Anthropology:

Science, Popular Wisdom, and the Body

David G. Horn

Anthropology needs numbers.

Cesare Lombroso, 1889

Introduction

A number of studies over the past 20 years, many in conversation with the work of Michel Foucault, have focused on the invention of "the criminal" in the late nineteenth century – on the technologies of discipline and government that constituted the criminal and his body as objects of medical knowledge and sites of social prophylaxis (Foucault 1994a; Leps 1992; Mucchielli 1994; Pasquino 1980; Sekula 1986; Villa 1985). This chapter focuses, in a complementary fashion, on the invention of the criminal anthropologist – on the fashioning of a new kind of scientific expert, qualified to read the deviant body and to diagnose social dangers. In fact, as I have argued elsewhere (Horn 2005b), it might be more apt to speak of the *co*-production of criminals and scientists. Criminal anthropology's claims to the status of science – and thus its ambitions to govern the social – were, on one hand, dependent on the presence of bodies that lent themselves to a discriminating quantification: in the laboratory, the prison, the university lecture hall, and the courtroom the expert would be required to point with some measure of confidence to bodies that were marked off from the normal, that seemed to announce their difference and their dangerousness. At the same time, the facticity of "the criminal body" was dependent on the authority of anthropologists such as Cesare Lombroso, who in publications and in testimony before juries had to struggle to contain the variability of real bodies' surfaces and structures, to overcome criminals' multiple forms of resistance to scrutiny, and especially to disqualify competing knowledge claims. I want here to foreground the contingency and the fragility of this scientific authority, notwithstanding the pervasive medicalization of the social domain. By focusing on the performance of criminal anthropology in the laboratory and the court-room, I want to explore the complex negotiations between science and common wisdom – including folk discourses of dangerousness and responsibility – that criminologists were obliged to undertake.

This essay is part of a larger project of mine to trace, following a variety of genealogical threads, the history of our turning to the body as a locus and kind of evidence. I wish to make visible the cultural and historical specificity of the very idea that bodies can testify (or be made to testify) to legal and scientific truths. The project is focused on nineteenth-century Europe, and Italy in particular – a site of emergence of a family of discourses and techniques intended to qualify and quantify bodies: legal medicine, forensic psychiatry, and criminal anthropol-ogy. In each proto-discipline, though with some important differences, the body was made an index of the interior states and dispositions of suspected individuals, a sign of the evolutionary status of groups, and a more or less reliable indicator of present and future dangers to society. Bodies were measured, palpated, shocked, sketched, photographed, and displayed in order that judges, penologists, educa-tors, and social planners might be guided in the identification and treatment of individuals, and in the development of appropriate measures of social hygiene.

In Italy, criminal anthropology positioned itself as a "modern" science, claim-ing links not only to the evolutionary theories of Giovanni Canestrini and Charles Darwin but also to the emergence of the science of statistics, to the discovery of "social facts," and to the identification of the national population as an appro-priate object of scientific knowledge and government. Each contributed in the nineteenth century to the reconfiguration of crime as a social and scientific problem: a patterned and predictable, if undesirable, consequence of social life, rather than the sum total of individual acts threatening the sovereignty of law or the king. Crime became a "risk" that forensic experts proposed to know and manage through detailed knowledge of social laws and exegesis of the criminal body.

Lombroso's "positive school" of criminology was distinguished, at least in its own mythology, from its predecessor and rival, the "classical school," by a shift of objects from the crime to the criminal (Ferri 1968: 60). As Pasquale Pasquino (1980: 19–20) has put it, the classical school had operated around the triangle of law, criminal act, and punishment. The juridical problem was to adjust penalties to offenses; the individual to be punished was interesting only insofar as his or her identity and legal responsibility (the capacity of free will) were at issue. The positive school socialized crime, and centered instead on the two main poles of the criminal and society. On the one hand, anthropologists expressed a new concern with statistical regularities. They complained that the classical school had not been able to explain (and indeed had never thought to explain) why there were 3,000 murders every year in Italy, and not 300 or 300,000 (Ferri 1968: 72). On the other hand, anthropologists argued it was necessary to take account of the social dangerousness of individual offenders. They proposed replacing the classical school's typology of *crimes*, which Enrico Ferri termed a "juridical anatomy" of deeds (1968: 71), with a typology of *criminals* and an anatomy of deviant and dangerous bodies grounded in scientific measurements. In this way, they sought to break classical theory's link between an individual's responsibility and state practices of punishment. As Lombroso's collaborator Raffaele Garofalo argued, the social dangerousness of an individual might, in fact, be greatest when his or her legal responsibility was least (Lombroso et al. 1886: 197). Indeed, for the first time, one could be a criminal (that is, a danger to society) without having committed a crime (Fletcher 1891: 210), something that had been literally unthinkable for the classical school. The introduction of the notion of "dangerousness," Foucault has observed, meant that the individual would be engaged not at the level of his acts but "at the level of his virtualities" (Foucault 1994b: 593).

This "social" construction of the problem of criminality also implied a new regime of judicial and governmental practices that obeyed a double logic of diagnosis and prevention. Anthropologists called for the elimination of juries, who would not be competent to weigh medical evidence or calculate social risks, and charged judges with making minute "anthropological" investigations (Lombroso et al. 1886: 197).[1] The anthropological problem, as Garofalo put it, was to determine "in what manner and to what degree it is necessary for the health of society to limit the rights of delinquents" (Lombroso et al. 1886: 201). Specific crimes figured merely as "indications" of dangerousness (Lombroso et al. 1886: 198). Remedies and penalties, meanwhile, were supposed to give way to practices of surveillance, preventive detention, and parole, and to proposals for making talented criminals "serviceable to civilization" (Lombroso-Ferrero 1972: 212–216). Vagabonds, Lombroso suggested, might be used to colonize wild and unhealthy regions; murderers might perform surgery or serve in the military; and swindlers might pursue police work or journalism (Lombroso 1968: 447). In the end, the Italian anthropologists demanded nothing less than "an exit from the law – a veritable de-penalization of crime" (Foucault 1994b: 457).

At the same time, this emergent scientific discourse was engaged in an effort to define its relationship to other existing understandings of the body.[2] If attention to criminals and their bodies promised to displace a "metaphysical" focus on criminal acts and the problem of will, criminal anthropology also felt the need to mark its distance, particularly through practices of quantification, from alternative knowledges of embodied dangerousness. Ironically, criminologists (and especially Lombroso) often relied precisely on these other knowledges to buttress and make intelligible their own claims. Thus, Lombroso at times drew on the discourses of physiognomy and phrenology, which had purported to find signs of interior intellectual and moral states on the body's surfaces, particularly at the level of the head and the face.[3] And though he insisted on the modernity of criminal anthropology, Lombroso was also not above calling on "the ancients," and in particular Homer and Avicenna, to say there was nothing new about his criminological claims (Lombroso et al. 1886: 42).

Popular Culture and Proverbial Wisdom

More broadly, knowledge of deviant bodies was not presumed to be exclusive to anthropologists. Artists, writers, the "lower classes," and even children, according to Lombroso, were aware of and could reproduce in paintings and poems the contours of criminal physiognomy (Lombroso et al. 1886: 11; Lombroso-Ferrero 1972: 48–51), and the various editions of *L'uomo delinquente* are choked with examples drawn from Italian popular culture. If the knowledge physiognomists and artists had of criminals might plausibly have been gained through experiment and experience, Lombroso was convinced also that modern humans had an instinctive understanding of the criminal type. What some might have called an "intuitive sense" was for Lombroso more likely the result of a vaguely Lamarckian evolutionary process, a "phenomenon inherited from the epoch in which the weak, although fearing the violence of the wicked, were becoming a majority." Impressions of evildoers, he reasoned, had been transmitted from fathers to sons, eventually becoming a kind of "unconscious knowledge." The process was similar, he suggested, to what happened to domesticated birds: "born and raised in our houses, they are nevertheless frightened in their cages by the eagle and the predatory hawk who fly past in the distance, and whose image tormented their grandfathers and great-grandfathers" (1896, vol. 1: 311).[4]

This "involuntary but universal consciousness" of a special physiognomy of criminals had led, in Lombroso's view, to phrases such as "face of a thief" and the "look of a murderer" (1896, vol. 1: 311–312). Indeed, an entire proverbial wisdom had developed, in Italy and elsewhere, which Lombroso proposed to use as a further support for the conclusions of criminologists. But in an article on "crime in popular consciousness," Lombroso was obliged to position himself carefully. On one hand, he wished to disqualify the "strange accusation" made by opponents of the positivist school that "its conclusions are at odds with popular convictions" (1890a: 26). But at the same time he acknowledged a difficulty faced by any knowledge that wished to count as "science": "to overcome prejudices and preconceptions that are nothing other than a way of judging things according to one's own habits and those of one's ancestors." Equally damning, in other words, would be the charge that criminal anthropology had simply borrowed its conclusions from the sayings of the folk.

Here, Lombroso wished principally to suggest that the evidence in support of anthropological claims was so extensive and overwhelming that it had even found its way into the "barely illuminated consciousness of the public; thus it leaves its traces in proverbs, in folksongs and in those verses composed by authors who have, as in a polished mirror, reflected the ideas of the folk" (1890a: 26).[5] For example, the "altogether distinctive physiognomy of the born criminal" was intuited in the Roman saying "There is nothing worse under the sky than a scanty beard and a colorless face" [*Poca barba e niun colore, sotto il ciel non vi ha peggiore*]. Venetian proverbs taught that one should "Greet from afar the red-haired man and the bearded woman" [*Omo rosso o femina barbuta da lontan xe mejo la saluta*] and warned "Beware the woman with a man's voice" [*Vardete de la donna che gha ose de omo*] (1890a: 26).[6]

At times, acknowledged Lombroso, proverbs went further than even the most daring anthropologists had been willing to venture, as when they spoke "with a singular accord" of "the wicked tendencies of the man with a turned up nose" (1890a: 28). On the other hand, the "irresistibility of the impulse of the passions when excited and violent" was well expressed by the saying "*La mano tira – il diavolo porta.*" And proverbs recognized, better than Lombroso's jurist critics, the recidivist nature of the true delinquent, independent of his or her economic circumstances, and the atavism of the born criminal (1890a: 28–29).

On this last point, Lombroso could rely on the support of Giuseppe Pitrè (1841–1916), the most prominent folklorist in Italy and the editor of the *Archivio per lo studio delle tradizioni popolari*.[7] Writing about atavism and folklore, Pitrè found that the concept of the inheritance of vices and virtues was "diffuse, indeed rooted in the folk. Rarely is the daughter of a bad woman honest, the son of a madman sane" (Pitrè 1969: 147). The experience of the people had resulted in the formulation of a "series of maxims" that, Pitrè suggested, could be a resource for the criminologist who wished to take account of folk ways of thought. Sicilians, for example, had observed that "the children of wolves are born with the canine tooth" [*Li figghi di lu lupu nàscinu cu lu scagghiuni*] (1969: 148).[8] Lombroso, however, choosing his words carefully, avoided the idea of folklore as a "resource" for the production of scientific knowledge. It was enough (rhetorically) to silence his "metaphysical" critics – and to show that it was *they* who were at odds with common sense – by finding that the ideas of the anthropological school were "not merely echoed by, but ... in complete accord with the popular imagination" (1890a: 33).

An example of this kind of negotiation with common wisdom is provided by the anthropological discussions of left-handedness. Left-handedness in Italy, as elsewhere, had been linked linguistically and culturally with danger, dishonesty, and fraud. This was due not only to the plural connotations of the word "left" [*sinistra*], but also to the multiple valences of "left-sidedness" [*mancinismo*], the root *manco* signaling at once the left side of the body and a lack or absence. As Lombroso explained, there were a small number of people who worked more agilely "*a manca*," the so-called "*mancini*" (Lombroso 1884). These were, he and fellow criminologists argued, more commonly to be found among children, women, savages, and in ancient times – sure signs of the atavistic nature of mancinism.

For prison physician Carmelo Andronico, the pathological nature of left-handedness was well established. In contrast to the "nobility of right-handedness" – which had been confirmed by the Bible, Aristotle, and Avicenna, among others – left-handedness presented itself as an "anomaly." It was most prevalent, Andronico remarked, among savage peoples: "among Papuans in New Guinea, among the inhabitants of the islands of Pelew, where the men pierce their left ears; among the blacks of Sennaar and Dongola, who wear the leather purse in which they keep coins and tobacco on their left arms" (Andronico 1884: 481).[9] Lombroso cited as further evidence of the link between left-handedness and atavism the fact that women button their shirts from the "opposite side" (1884: 128).

Lombroso proposed to build upon this common wisdom by exploring the relations of left-sidedness and criminality. The raw numbers appeared to be telling enough: mancinism had a frequency of 4 percent in normal men, 5.8 percent in normal women, 13 percent in male criminals, and 22 percent in female criminals. The mentally ill, by contrast, had roughly the same frequency of mancinism as normal women and men (1884: 126). However, the presence of a single atavistic feature in an individual, Lombroso reminded his readers, did not mean his or her entire organism was in a state of arrested development or inferiority. Mancinism was by itself but a "musical note," which could only signal criminality or madness when taken together with other notes (1884: 130).

Lombroso and his contemporaries associated left-sidedness with brain laterali-zation – "Everyone recognizes that mancinism . . . depends on the prevalence of the right hemisphere over the left" (Lombroso 1883: 445) – and relied also on research proposing to explain such asymmetries as due to inherited differences in blood supply (asymmetry of branches of the aorta) to the right and left brains.[10] As Lombroso summed it up, "while the honest person would think with the left brain, the criminal thinks with the right" (1883: 446). Lombroso would also undertake what he called a "bit of physiological police work," testing the sensitiv-ity to touch and pain of the right and left sides of subjects' bodies. By investigating friends, colleagues, and members of the working classes, as well as criminals, Lombroso was able to uncover a pervasive "sensory mancinism" – that is, a greater sensitivity on the left – that was much more frequent (26 percent) than mancinism in healthy people, and most frequent among lunatics (Lombroso 1884: 126).[11]

Finally, Lombroso reported that criminals almost always exhibited mancinism while walking. A study by a certain Peracchia had found that among normal men strides with the right leg averaged 65 centimeters, while those with the left averaged 63; by contrast, among criminals the averages were 70.6 on the right and 72 on the left. In addition, the "angle of deviation" of the left foot was, among criminals, greater than that of the right foot, while the lateral displace-ment was greater on the right. The longer strides of criminals were, Lombroso reasoned, a sign of their greater "robustness" (see Horn 2005a), but the marked and inverted "lateralism" of their walk testified to their incomplete evolution. Indeed, a deviant stride offered itself as a "differential characteristic," making it possible to distinguish among thieves, murderers, and rapists – among the last, for example, the strides were small with only modest mancinism (Lombroso 1896, vol. 1: 407).

Again, argued Lombroso, this was something his countrymen already and instinctively knew, even at the level of their bodies. So when, in another experi-ment, a normal individual was told under hypnosis that he was a brigand, he unconsciously modified his walk to resemble that of a criminal. The lateral displacement of the stride extended on the right and declined on the left, the angle of deviation of the foot increased on the left and decreased on the right, and the stride grew in length by 11.6 centimeters on the right and 22.5 on the left (1896, vol. 1: 407).[12] Taken together, the results of laboratory experiments and anatomical measurements both extended and reconfirmed proverbial wisdom: "when the people, whether on the basis of their own observations or on the basis of figures of speech, are suspicious of the left-handed man, they have exaggerated and generalized a fact that is fundamentally true." Remarkably, the folk – and particularly the inhabitants of Emilia and Lombardy – had most closely associated left-handedness with the swindler, that variety of criminal in which experiments revealed "the highest quota (33 percent) of *mancini*" (1883: 447).

Reading Bodies: The Child, the Savage, and the Scientist

If, to some extent, knowledge of criminal anatomy was instinctive, it was only logical to expect that it would also guide the reading practices of individuals. Lombroso pointed to the frequent cases on record of honest persons, "extraneous to the world of crime," who had escaped certain death by recognizing, in a "sinister glance," the intentions of an assailant (1896, vol. 1: 311). Lombroso recounted that even his mother, who had lived "cut off from the world" and thus could not have gained any knowledge of men, twice guessed the criminal character of young men whom no one had suspected previously, but who revealed themselves to be wicked many years later (1896, vol. 1: 310). Similarly, a 16-year-old noble girl who, according to Lombroso, had never left her ancestral manor and had no experience of life, refused to speak with a villager named Francesconi, treating him like a villain even though others in town acclaimed him. "If he is not an assassin," she correctly predicted, "he will become one." Although Lombroso himself found nothing in the man's photograph to signal his future ferocity, the girl had seen it "in his eyes" (1896, vol. 1: 311).

The reading practices of the lay public could, indeed, be put to the test. Lombroso reported an experiment in which he had presented 200 photographs of young men to three physicians, asking them which in their opinion presented the "criminal type." All had agreed on a single individual. Next, Lombroso had shown the photographs to a 12-year-old girl; her judgment had been "perfectly in agreement with the others" (Lombroso et al. 1886: 7). Lombroso was pleased to point out that the man identified by all four as a typical criminal had at the time of the identification committed no illegal acts. Later, however, having risen to a high position, he had "cruelly betrayed" those who had helped him to succeed. Thus, while he might not have been a criminal "juridically" when he was photographed, he was one "anthropologically" (Lombroso et al. 1886: 7).

Lombroso often chose to rely on children, women, and even non-Western "primitives" as test subjects. On one occasion he solicited the help of a teacher who presented "20 portraits of thieves and 20 of great men" – we are told nothing further about the nature of these images – to 32 schoolgirls; 80 percent of the children were able to recognize "the first as wicked, evil and deceitful people" (Lombroso 1896, vol. 1: 311). The "courtesy" of physician Cesare Nerazzini, the author of several books on Ethiopia, allowed Lombroso to perform an even more "curious" experiment (1890b: 247). The doctor had brought with him from Abyssinia a Somali servant named Mohamed Ismail, a "young man of lively intelligence," who in a conversation with Lombroso boasted of his ability to identify by sight the "rogues" of his native land. Ismail made his identifications by attending to the movements of the major blood vessels of the neck. He went on to say he could also identify Italy's criminals, no matter how they were dressed, simply by looking at their faces: "They have necktie, but I look inside eye, nose, ears, and know bad man right away." Lombroso showed Ismail a series of images, including photographs, of "great men," ordinary men, and criminals, while Nerazzini recorded the Somali's judgments. Lombroso reports that the visitor correctly identified 148 of 162 images, declaring Michelangelo, for example, to be "good, serious, and big-brained." Lombroso delighted in contrasting the "savage's" ability to see with the stubborn blindness of his opponents (both the classical school and the French sociologists): "Oh, poor academic," he mused, "that a poor, savage Somali manages to correct your weakly supported assertions, and to serve as your teacher." When not led astray, the mind of a savage was "worth more than that of the most cultivated man who is trapped in old and new beliefs" (1890b: 248).

But if folk typologies and the reading practices of children and savages served to reinforce the findings of the criminologists, and to defend them against charges of an "exaggerated somaticism" (Morselli 1888), they also have risked calling into question the privileged position of the anthropological observers, or (as some critics charged) the scientific status of their theories (Lombroso et al. 1886: 11). Jurist Aristide Gabelli, for example, accused Lombroso and his colleagues of an unscientific reliance on common wisdom. Like Lavater before them, argued Gabelli, criminal anthropologists were content to try to clarify and give order to those "popular instincts" that allow people, in their everyday lives, to pronounce a man a "gentleman" or a "rogue" on the basis of his appearance alone (Gabelli 1885: 580). On one hand, Gabelli protested, such judgments were often wrong or impossible to make, and he invited his readers to repeat on the street an "anthropological" experiment he had often performed in the courtroom: "While we might be able quickly to recognize bricklayers, coal-sellers, and chimneysweeps, we would however confuse the lawyer with the doctor, and the shopkeeper with the clerk, not to mention the honest ones with those who are not" (1885: 581). On the other hand, Gabelli complained that science should combat rather than affirm the "human vanity" that forms a foundation of popular knowledges. Otherwise, he concluded, we would have "as many sciences as there are curiosities, desires, dreams, [and] prejudices among the masses" (1885: 581).

Lombroso, in turn, attacked Gabelli for concluding, on the basis of a single article, that criminal anthropology took its cues from the wisdom of the folk, "which – it is true – often errs" (Lombroso et al. 1886: 11). "We have never dreamed," Lombroso protested, "of turning to the folk for our conclusions." As proof, Lombroso cited the many elements of folk wisdom science had been *unable* to confirm. In the end, he said proverbial wisdom was cited only to show conclusions were not as far from "popular consciousness" as some people had claimed (Lombroso 1890a). For Lombroso and his colleagues, the anthropologist was to be distinguished from the observant and instinctive folk by his specialized techniques for measuring and reading the body: by a corporeal literacy that made possible both an exegesis and a diagnosis. The anthropologist did not offer fortune-telling or prophecy, as the masses and critics believed, but a "reading." The criminal's body was a "palimpsest in reverse," made more easily legible because the anthropologist did not limit himself to the face, but also included "calligraphy, gestures, sensibility" (Lombroso et al. 1886: 8).

The gaze of the criminologist could be shown, for example, to be more practiced. Antonio Marro invoked his experience as a physician attached to the judiciary prison of Turin to disqualify the amateur diagnoses of prison visitors: "People generally think they recognize the murderer or the assassin in the most striking physiognomies – protruding brows, a full and shaggy beard, and a surly gaze." For the expert, however, who had learned not to be deceived by appearances, an accused's steady, "glacial" gaze was far more significant than one that "spit flames and fury" (Marro 1885: 94). Still, Marro found he could not do without the rhetorical support of popular wisdom: "As the proverb says, still waters run deep, and the most bloodthirsty beasts are often hidden behind a hairless and pale face."

Lombroso cited examples of novelists who had given fictional criminals a too-frightening appearance, and complained physiognomists such as Casper had committed the opposite error, imagining no difference between delinquents and normal men. The point, claimed Lombroso, was not that the appearance of criminals was always *threatening*, but that it was "entirely *particular*"; indeed, it was "almost unique for each form of delinquency" (Lombroso 1889: 230). Thus, thieves were characterized by "a notable mobility of the face and hands," small eyes, and a thin beard, while arsonists displayed "feminine characteristics." However, as a *science* forensic medicine could not content itself with these "generic and isolated descriptions." The anthropology of the criminal body, argued Lombroso, "needs *numbers*" (1889: 239, emphasis added).

Stephen Jay Gould has identified the "allure of numbers" as an element of a faith that swept through the human sciences in the second half of the nineteenth century (1981: 73–74).[13] Despite this, there was always a danger that the data published by anthropologists could be seen as gratuitous quantification,[14] and some criminological readings remained avowedly qualitative – we might even say aesthetic. But there is another sense in which it is misleading to suggest that "numbers" alone distinguished criminal anthropology from alternative and popular knowledges. In fact, what differentiated the scientist from the popular reader of faces was the ability to enter prisons, asylums, schools, and orphanages to perform tests; the authority to enlist "volunteers" from the populations of "normal" women and men; the access to instruments that were expensive and often difficult to manipulate; and the means to disseminate results (journals, conferences, university lecture halls, and, of course, the witness stand). On one hand, we need to keep in view the power relations that enabled physicians and biological scientists to move freely in nonpublic spaces, to require subjects to remove their clothes, to probe and manipulate the body, and even to inflict pain (Horn 2005b). On the other hand, we need to explore the roles played by tools, techniques, manuals, and other elements of *practice* in the elaboration and consolidation of a criminological science.[15] In so doing, I hope to call attention to the performative qualities of the new anthropology – to the acts of manipulating instruments, tabulating measurements, and testifying about numbers that aimed at elevating the work of criminologists above the level of popular wisdom, and at the same time sought to create a new kind of scientific "common sense." What I have in mind, though I do not undertake it in these pages, is to attend to the varied and messy kinds of work (manual, theoretical, interpretive, rhetorical) that was required to go from the manufacture, say, of a Zwaardesmaker double olfactometer in Geneva, to its manipulation in a cramped prison cell in Turin, to the transcription of olfactory thresholds in a pre-printed form, to testimony on the witness stand about the sensory atavism of a criminal defendant – testimony meant both to speak to the particular circumstances of the defendant and to affirm the competence of the scientific criminologist, and him alone, to recognize social dangers.

Making Numbers: Bodies and Tools

Historian Renzo Villa, piecing together accounts from the local press, tells the story of a tour of the city of Turin led by Lombroso during the sixth international congress of criminal anthropology in 1906. Lombroso guided a delegation of male and female visitors to a variety of sites of production of criminological knowledge, ending in the local prison. While touring the cells, reports Villa, Lombroso and his party came upon a boy who displayed "certain physical particularities that could be catalogued as degenerative stigmata." Lombroso did not hesitate, after the women were excused, to have the boy undressed, with the goal of searching his naked body for other signs of the criminal type (Villa 1985: 31). For the next hour, delegates to the congress watched Lombroso examine other "sad specimens" collected by the head guard: a shoemaker convicted of sexual molestation, a recidivist thief, and particularly a second thief whose body was covered with tattoos. As Villa reports, the "clinical" examination of these subjects included a cataloging of surface anomalies and pathologies, measurement and palpation of the body, interrogations, even a diagnosis of the subject's handwriting (1985: 32).

The ability of the criminal anthropologist to command the presence of the criminal body, to compel it to be undressed, to be measured, even to yield to painful manipulations, was in many ways an example of the broader relations of power that characterized the practice of medicine – particularly in prisons – at the beginning of the twentieth century (Sim 1990). But if in 1906 the prison could be said to constitute the laboratory of the criminologist (Villa 1985: 33), only a few years earlier Lombroso had been greeted with indifference or hostility in similar spaces, and had had considerable difficulty gaining access to the bodies of criminals.

Biographer Luigi Ferrio reports that Lombroso received an "icy reception" in Turin in 1876; when he went there to assume a chair in legal medicine, Lombroso was obliged to set up a laboratory at his own expense, and found prisons and asylums locked their doors to him (1962: 20–21).[16] Lombroso's daughter Gina explains that her father first obtained clients for his psychiatric practice by putting a handwritten sign on his door offering free consultations – the reputation of the doctor, "contested" at the university, was well established among the populace, his daughter reports (Lombroso-Ferrero 1915: 197). The patients who came in turn allowed him to teach a course on psychiatry at the university that he had been denied on the excuse that he had no patients to present. It was, however, decidedly more difficult to study the "living criminal." Criminals did not present themselves at the door of Lombroso's laboratory, even when they were offered cash. Lombroso therefore enlisted his assistant Giovanni Cabria, by trade a bookbinder and lithographer, to go out and find criminals and bring them back to the lab. In a few months, Lombroso-Ferrero reports, Cabria became a "veritable bloodhound for criminals." He searched the arcades and taverns, and when he had found a potential client, convinced him of the need to visit the lab, negotiated a price, and walked him to the lab (Lombroso-Ferrero 1915: 198). Cabria also was responsible for collecting hundreds of skulls unearthed by the urban renovation of Turin, which destroyed the cemeteries of criminals, soldiers, Jews, and monks, furnishing valuable material for a comparative anthropology (Bulferetti 1975: 256–257).

Many of Lombroso's later collaborators would be directors of asylums, hospitals, and orphanages, and could therefore rely on captive populations for observation, measurement, and experimentation. But even many of these also needed to recruit others, and in particular those normal or healthy women and men who served as points of comparison. Although it is clear that there was a somewhat regular supply of ordinary citizens willing to give their bodies over, even to embarrassing and uncomfortable experiments, we learn little about their recruitment, class positions, or level of education. At times, criminologists – like others working in experimental medicine or physiology – were obliged to rely on their own bodies to construct norms for the healthy body (see Horn 2005).

There were other limits to the power of the physician to read the body. For example, Lombroso complained in his study of criminal women and prostitutes about his inability to use pictures of Italian women because of a prohibition in his own country against measuring, studying, or photographing criminals once they had been convicted; instead, he was obliged to reproduce images of Russian and French prostitutes collected by Pauline Tarnowsky. The same prohibition had required Lombroso in *L'uomo delinquente* to rely on photographs from the German prison *Album*, the *National Police Gazette* (New York), and the *Illustrated Police News* (Boston) (Lombroso 1896, vol. 1: 221).[17] "As long as there is a presumption of innocence," remarked a sarcastic Lombroso, "as long as [criminals] are only indicted or accused, you can defame them in any way you like and give them maximum publicity.... But when they are recognized once and for all as rogues, when they are locked up forever in prison – oh, then they become sacred. Woe to those who touch them. Woe to those who study them." What is more, these limits on the power of social experts contrasted with the rules governing the training of physicians: "Consumptive patients [and] pregnant women may be manipulated, even to their hurt, by students for the good of science, but rogues – God help us!" (Lombroso and Ferrero 1915: 195).

The access of criminologists to the dead bodies of criminals was, for a time, also restricted. As we saw, scientists could be forced to scavenge for the crania of criminals, or to rely on the generosity of family members for the skeletal remains of normal people or "geniuses." It was not until 1883 that an accord between the Ministries of the Interior and Public Education allowed university professors to perform autopsies on criminals who died while in the prison infirmary (Sciamanna 1884). Ezio Sciamanna, who prepared a guide for anatomical and anthropological research on the cadavers of convicts, noted that such research could result in the compilation of statistics that would help scientists to address two important social problems: the links between criminal acts and states of health and disease, and the physical consequences of incarceration. The autopsies Sciamanna proposed involved a variety of anthropometrical measurements, and a section on "special investigations" recommended that doctors keep parts of the brain and head, and that tattooed skin be cut and preserved (1884: 243).

Augusto Tamburini, the director of the Manicomio di Reggio d'Emilia, and Giulio Benelli, employed by the Casa di Custodia in Reggio, later campaigned to have the same kind of research undertaken on all living prisoners. In an open letter to the inspector of prisons, Martino Beltrani-Scalia, Tamburini argued that material that was "too precious" and in great supply was being lost to science. "The careful and conscientious study of the entire criminal population enclosed therein, conducted without prejudice and with precision and uniformity of method, would certainly furnish, in a few years, an immense amount of material that would serve to solve a great many problems pertaining to penal and criminal disciplines" (Tamburini and Benelli 1885: 136). Tamburini proposed creating a manual for the anthropological study of living inmates, similar to that developed by Sciamanna for autopsies. Each establishment would be furnished with a low-cost craniometer and a dynamometer. As Benelli noted, the first edition of Lombroso's *L'uomo delinquente* had summarized results from 830 criminals; the third edition 3,839. "But this number must grow further," wrote Benelli, calling for uniform studies on 100,000 criminals (Tamburini and Benelli 1885: 137). Yet Lombroso would lament ten years later that there were no provisions in Italy for even routine judicial anthropometry. One of his "dearest disciples," Luigi Anfosso, had invented an instrument he called the "tachianthropometer," which allowed a series of measurements of the body to be made rapidly (Lombroso dubbed the device an "anthropometric guillotine"), but "after much negotiation" the Italian government had not accepted it (Lombroso 1895: 47).

Anthropometry and physiological experiments were, in obvious ways, dependent on the availability not only of docile subjects (and dead bodies), but also on an appropriate selection of reliable instruments. The coherence and authority of criminology would come to depend on scientists' ability to contain a potentially limitless proliferation of measurements, and to deploy those instruments that promised to demonstrate systematic and significant difference between pathological and normal bodies. Lombroso, in his handbook for forensic experts, suggested that a well-appointed laboratory would include the Anfosso tachianthropometer, Broca's auricular goniometer, Sieweking's esthesiometer, a Eulenberg baristesiometer, a Nothnagel thermesthesiometer, a Zwaardesmaker olfactometer, a Regnier-Mathieu dynamometer, a Mosso ergograph, and a modified campimeter, as well as a more mundane selection of compasses, measuring tapes, eye charts, magnets, and odoriferous substances (Lombroso 1905: 490–544).[18] We might well ask how this bewildering array of instruments came to be found in medical laboratories, a question that might lead us to the conditions of the instruments' design, manufacture, and international circulation. But the selection of instruments (why each of these, and not others?) also tells us something about which measurements could and could not count as significant at particular moments in the history of criminology, and about how the body was imagined and mapped *through* tools. In a sense, each instrument produced the body anew, giving rise to an index, a threshold, or a capacity that could not have mattered previously.[19] Of course, the rhetoric of anatomical and physiological measurement tended to deny the constructed nature of what was measured, instead relying on (and reproducing) the illusion that indices were *features of bodies*, simply to be found on its surfaces and structures.

Though there clearly was a vigorous circulation of devices across the boundaries of discipline and nation, it is difficult to reconstruct this traffic from anthropological journals and conference proceedings.[20] It is striking, for example, that there was no space provided for a display of tools at the first international congress of criminal anthropology in 1886; Severi and Lombroso complained of the absence of anthropometrical instruments (with the exception of a single example of a Regier's graphical craniometer), arguing such an exhibit could have been of "greatest importance" and given rise to "productive comparisons" (Severi and Lombroso 1886: 27).[21] The occasional laments of criminologists are indeed often as revealing as the announcements made of new or improved instruments. Many devices were, to judge by the published reports, very difficult to use properly. Giuseppe Sergi admitted that he struggled to manipulate a Benedikt craniophore – a device for holding and orienting skulls in order to make craniometric measurements – even though he had had it demonstrated by its inventor during a visit to Vienna. Use of the device remained "a long and difficult operation for those who do not have experience with instruments of precision" (Sergi 1893: 143–145). Other researchers worried about the consistency of measurements made by a rapidly growing range of competing instruments. Carlo Gaudenzi, in an article devoted to the clinometer – a device to measure angles of the head – complained of the proliferation of "goniometric" instruments. The development of the field of craniometry required so many different single devices that there was, in addition to a concern about time and money, a danger of multiplying possible errors. These errors were not avoided, Gaudenzi warned, by graphical instruments such as craniographs and cephalographs because these provided no direct measurements. The central problem was to choose a consistent point of orientation for subsequent measurements, and he offered as a solution a device that allowed more than three dozen measurements to be taken on a skull or the head of a living person (Gaudenzi 1891).[22] Paolo Mantegazza also worried in print about the errors and inconsistencies introduced by scientists, especially in comparative work: while all anthropologists measured the cranium, they used different methods and instruments to collect their observations. In order for these measurements to "have the same value" and serve as bases for comparison, it was necessary that each procedure be "diligently described" in the text (1871: 61).

A number of devices sought to overcome both the sloppiness of scientists and the requirement of an accompanying narrative by calculating indices themselves; for example, Lombroso described an index-craniograph as "automatically giving" an index as a relation of two cranial diameters (1896, vol. 3: 648).[23] Such devices, in fact, appeared to read or record indices directly from the body and in an unmediated way; in a sense, it was the criminal body itself that produced the index, telling the story of its own dangerousness. Ironically, the scientist, who was elsewhere so insistent on his special ability to read the body, was in the act of collecting an index made to withdraw from view.

This tension was particularly marked for graphical instruments, that array of devices (cardiographs, ergographs, pneumographs, mylographs) that produced inscriptions from the criminal and the normal body, and that promised to overcome the limits and fallibility of the human senses.[24] As Robert Frank observes, while some instruments (for example, the microscope) sharpened or extended a perception or sense, others such as the sphygmograph "took a human sense that was imprecise, variable, fleeting and translated it into the movement of an instrument." They "made possible the rearrangement of sense experience into some new format" (Frank 1988: 213). If the graphical method sought, on one hand, to overcome the deficiencies and vagaries of the observer's senses, it also promised to overcome the inadequacies of spoken language. It yielded a record ostensibly unaffected by the prejudices of the observer and that could speak across language barriers, circulating freely – in texts and in lecture halls – and with a particular rhetorical force (Brain 2002: 156; Latour 1987). The recorded traces were at times characterized as the language of science, at others as the language of the phenomena themselves, or of *life* itself. The fantasy, as Robert Brain puts it, was one in which "automatic recording instruments would generate a vast heterotopic space of inscription that would push out speech altogether and replace it with mechanized forms of thinking and communication" (2002: 156).

If the body of the scientist (marked by its sensory weaknesses and the imprecision of its utterances) receded into the background, the body of the experimental subject was at the same time foregrounded and given a new agency. Whether the brain "wrote" or the pulse was "armed with a pen" (Frank 1988: 212), the body was imagined to tell its own truth, and to give itself away. This notion of bodies testifying – of intimate truths made objective and public – characterized much of the writing associated with tracing devices, and would take on particular meanings in relation to criminality, where the hiding of the intimate posed particular social dangers (Horn n.d.).

The Expert Witness

Of course, for anthropometrical measurements and physiological graphs to have the *effects* desired by criminologists, it was necessary that they leave the confines of the laboratory or the scholarly journal. Quantifying measures and the diagnoses they enabled were supposed to matter, above all, in the decisions of judges and juries. In 1879 Lombroso had imagined that the introduction of the experimental method to legal medicine would effect a radical transformation. In the past, judges and juries might have smiled when alienists spoke of an accused's "degree of imputability," of variations in "free will," or of "transitory madness." But experimental phreniatry would "put an end to all of this." In place of the "inconclusive formulations and imprecise abstractions" of experts who failed even to use their senses, the new science would substitute "a few arid facts, but facts nevertheless: the weight of the body; the condition of the skin and hair; measurements of the cranium; evaluations of temperature, urine, muscular force, sensibility, writing and pronunciation" (Lombroso 1962: 83).

In practice, however, the authority of the new criminological experts, and of the medical and social facts they deployed, was frequently compromised. As Garofalo complained, judges and legislators persisted in "abstracting the crime from the criminal," and were therefore reluctant to reform codes of criminal procedure. This meant that the unfolding of expert testimony occurred under conditions ill suited to the pursuit of scientific truths: experts did not have adequate time to prepare, to construct family histories, or to conduct experiments on the body, all of which made it difficult to reach reliable conclusions (Garofalo 1891: 577). But the performance of expertise in the courtroom was also problematic: "The experts, wishing to show off their science, vie with one another in a Greek technical language that the jury cannot begin to comprehend." The result of the hastily arranged "scientific jousting tournament" was that jurors became bored and confused – overwhelmed by divergent opinions they ended by having none of their own (1891: 577).

Indeed, the very continued presence of the jury in the Italian courtroom testified to the failures of procedural reform, to an inability practically to "exit from the law." But the jury's presence was also, I wish to suggest, an embarrassing reminder of the proximity of folk and medical discourses, and threatened to collapse the spaces of medical authority. Juries, as Lombroso put it, did not simply represent the folk, but "an armed and powerful folk" (1962: 84). For Antonio Raffaele, the persistence of the jury meant not only that justice was "compromised," but that the dignity of the medical profession was routinely "offended." The physician "feels a justifiable resentment when he sees jurors, who are ignorant of science, choose not to trust in his judgment but arrogate unto themselves the right to examine what they cannot comprehend" (Raffaele 1877: 73–74). And as Patrizia Guarnieri has shown, criminological theories, for all their reliance on folk wisdom, ran up against the common sense of juries when they suggested criminals should not be held responsible for their crimes (1986: 129). Jurors, complained Lombroso, were "blind in acquitting and even more so in convicting"; they "followed their hearts rather than the findings of science, and pursued a social vendetta" (1962: 84). The situation was, in any event, far removed from one in which, as Raffaele envisioned, "both judges and juries [would] be obliged to accept, without reservation, the judgments of men who occupy themselves exclusively with research and scientific laws" (1877: 74).

One sign of the crisis in medical authority in the courtroom was the publication in 1905 of Lombroso's *La perizia psichiatrico-legale*, a manual for expert witnesses. The text reflects in its organization and contents a renewed tension between the scientific and the commonsensical. Designed for the educated layman (and thus implying that almost anyone can become a forensic expert), it sought at the same time to shore up the wall dividing science from other cultural practices. It did this by constructing forensic expertise as a form of *practice* or *discipline* – with its own tools, procedures, conventions, and specialized vocabulary.

The first part of the volume consists of a series of summarized case studies provided by various criminologists and alienists, many of which conclude in a perfunctory but triumphant declaration: "a clear case of irresponsibility" or "a true cretin." These examples of "classic expert testimony" were marshaled both to "confirm with secure documents the theories advanced in *L'uomo delinquente*," and "to guide the hand of the forensic neophyte" (1905: viii). The second part, devoted to expert-witness methodology, was intended to "meet the needs of those who complain they cannot follow these [earlier] studies because they lack . . . a familiarity with specialized techniques." Lombroso proposed to teach readers "the few maneuvers necessary for anthropometric and psycho-physical measurements and research, and [to] show how to apply these to expert testimony and to scientific investigations" (1905: x). Finally, the text included a glossary of the most important terms in scientific criminology – terms whose meanings might otherwise remain elusive.

In his discussion of expert practices, Lombroso advised that the work of the forensic expert ought properly to resemble scientific research: "both aim at the accumulation of objective proofs," and should therefore confine themselves to a somatic and psychological study of the accused (1905: 486). However, cautioned the author, the authority of science in the courtroom was far from assured: "since judges and, even more so, members of the jury are not scientists, and are instead for the most part averse to science, they would become fed up by an excess of subtle scientific analyses and would not be able to follow the witness; they might indeed arrive at a contrary verdict out of spite or boredom" (1905: 487). Thus, in the case of ordinary expert reports, Lombroso recommended that witnesses restrict their research and testimony. After a brief exposition of the case, he advised, experts should report the weight and height of the accused, then move quickly to the general anthropological characteristics. He further suggested that witnesses have before them one of the forms developed by Tamburini and Benelli, or by Carrara and Strassmann, "which in a few lines group together the most necessary investi-gations and determine the order in which one should proceed." The expert's final tasks were to link the anthropological characteristics to the acts in question, and to provide a synthesis that will "illuminate" the judge (1905: 487).

While *La perizia* was intended to help consolidate the achievements of the positive school of criminology, readers today must be struck by the fragility of this enterprise. This text made it clear how easy it was for things to unravel – an expert might fail adequately to complete a questionnaire or might provide too much detail; a jury might scoff at the evidence when it was presented. And the assump-tion that was implicit in this manual – that anyone with the right tools, tech-niques, and rhetoric could become a forensic expert – may actually have worked to undermine the specificity and authority of the scientific.

The Italian criminological project has, in recent years, been evaluated in rela-tion to a struggle between the scientific (or the pseudo-scientific) and the juridical. And while criminal anthropology is often judged to have been quickly disqualified, and to have had few durable effects, Foucault's genealogy of "dan-gerousness" makes it clear that "certain of its most fundamental theses, which were also the most extravagant in relation to traditional law, gradually became anchored in penal thought and practice" (1994a: 459). Of course, as Foucault has pointed out, this was not because of the "truth value" of anthropological claims, but instead because of changes in *civil* law – around the notions of accidents, risk, and responsibility – that made possible new articulations of legal codes and human sciences (1994a: 459–460). But I want to suggest that as we explore the genealogy of the body-as-evidence we attend not only to the struggle between science and law, but also to medicine's confrontation with another stubborn force, a popular culture that was at once the condition of possibility of a medicalizing, somaticizing discourse of crime, and for a time set limits to the authority of physicians to decide the facts of the matter, to treat deviant individuals, and to elaborate solutions to social problems.

Notes

Acknowledgments: An earlier version of this chapter was presented to the conference on "Michel Foucault et la médecine" organized by the Centre Michel Foucault and held in Caen in 1999. I am grateful to Philippe Artières, Luc Berlivet, Frédéric Chauvaud, Daniel Defert, Jan Goldstein, Jonathan Inda, Jean-François Laé, Peter Redfield, and Francisco Vásquez García for their comments on previous drafts.

1 In the eyes of Enrico Ferri, judges needed to have "sufficient knowledge, not of Roman or civil law, but of psychology, anthropology, and psychiatry" (1968: 36).

2 Compare Patrizia Guarnieri's discussion of asylum doctors' efforts to distance themselves from popular and previous medical understandings of madness (Guarnieri 1986: 136).

3 See Sekula (1986: 11–12) and Stafford (1991: 84–129). While the focus on the head was in some ways "common-sensical" and continuous with popular practices of reading faces, Sekula suggests it also worked to "legitimate on organic grounds the dominion of intellectual over manual labor" (1986: 12).

4 Lombroso offered a similar explanation for the gestures that accompanied prayer, movements that had been inherited from barbarous times in which they signaled submission and saved the lives of defeated combatants.

5 On proverbs also see Balladoro (1897) and Castelli (1890).

6 Also see Lombroso-Ferrero (1972: 50). Lombroso does not comment on the fact that many of these sayings are examples of gender transgression.

7 Pitrè and Lombroso had, however, a pointed exchange in *Rivista Europea* about the songs and poems written by criminals and prisoners. See Lombroso (1876a, 1876b) and Pitrè (1876). Pitrè, a specialist on southern Italian songs, objected to Lombroso's transcriptions and interpretations of Sicilian passages, as well as his claim that criminal songs were confined to the south.

8 Michele Pasquarelli (1896) also invoked Pitrè to argue that modern psychiatry, in its "somatomania," takes its cues from popular wisdom.

9 Also see Ottolenghi (1889). Lombroso pointed out that Polemon's (88–145) writings on physiognomy had anticipated his claims about the left-handedness of criminals (Lombroso et al. 1886: 42).

10 See, for example, Faralli (1872). On the (failed) attempt to link left-sidedness with blood pressure asymmetries, see Lombroso and Audenino (1901).

11 Also see Horn (2005a).

12 In a similar experiment, Lombroso suggested to a hypnotized young boy "of honest habits" that he was the brigand La-Gala; the boy in this case reproduced the handwriting typical of criminals, abandoning his own "refined" and "feminine" hand in favor of "crude" letters (1896, vol. 1: 564).

13   On the authority of numbers and practices of quantification also see Porter (1995) and, for Italy, Patriarca (1996: 238–239).

14   For example, in a scathing review of Lombroso's *Pensiero e meteore*, a volume that argued for a causal connection between climate and criminal dangerousness, anthropologist Paolo Mantegazza argued that the volume merely had the *appearance* of science: "the numbers and figures figure as a contrivance, not as a basis for arguments and conclusions" (1879: 326).

15   For insightful discussions of the history of anthropometrical instruments and techniques in Italy see Barsanti et al. (1986).

16   For a description of the Turin laboratory see Lombroso-Ferrero (1915: 195–198).

17   Lombroso observed that the difficulties were doubled in the case of female offenders and prostitutes: "We might have offended the sense of shame of these chaste virgins" (Lombroso and Ferrero 1915: 195).

18   Also see Galton (1885).

19   On the relations between the refinement of instrumentation, the construction of models, and the evolution of conceptual frameworks see Lenoir (1986).

20   See the appendices to Lombroso (1896, vol. 3).

21   Evidently, no one had thought to invite instrument makers from Italy or abroad.

22   Also see Mariani and Prati (1902).

23   Also see Belloni (1902). Belloni's index-compass automatically calculated the cephalic index.

24   On the graphical method in the physiological sciences see Frank (1988), Dror (1998), and Brain (2002).

References

Andronico, Carmelo
  1884   Il mancinismo in rapporto alla delinquenza. Archivio di Psichiatria, Scienze Penali ed Antropologia Criminale [hereafter Archivio] 5: 480–482.
Balladoro, A.
  1897   L'antropologia criminale nei proverbi veneti. Archivio 18: 157–162.
Barsanti, Giulio, Simonetta Gori-Savellini, Patrizia Guarnieri, and Claudio Pogliano, eds.
  1986   Misura d'uomo: Strumenti, teorie e pratiche dell'antropometria e della psicologia sperimentale tra '800 e '900. Florence: Istituto e Museo di Storia della Scienza.
Belloni, Cesare
  1902   Il compasso indice. Archivio 23: 133–138.
Brain, Robert
  2002   Representation on the Line: Graphic Recording Instruments and Scientific Modernism. *In* From Energy to Information: Representation in Science and Technology, Art, and Literature. Bruce Clarke and Linda Darymple Henderson, eds. Pp. 155–177. Stanford: Stanford University Press.
Bulferetti, Luigi
  1975   Cesare Lombroso. Turin: UTET.
Castelli, A.
  1890   Delitti e pene nei proverbi. Archivio 11: 558–559.

Dror, Otniel E.
   1998   Creating the Emotional Body: Confusion, Possibilities, and Knowledge. *In* An Emotional History of the United States. Peter Stearns and Jan Lewis, eds. Pp. 173–194. New York: New York University Press.
Faralli, Giovanni
   1872   Sulla preeminenza del lato destro del corpo: Studii del Dott. Ogle, del Dott. Savory, e del Prof. Iacini Filipo. Archivio per l'Antropologia e la Etnologia 2: 67–75.
Ferri, Enrico
   1968[1901]   The Positive School of Criminology: Three Lectures by Enrico Ferri. Stanley E. Grupp, ed. Pittsburgh: University of Pittsburgh Press.
Ferrio, Luigi
   1962   La vita di Cesare Lombroso. *In* Antologia Lombrosiana. Pp. 7–38. Pavia: Società Editrice Pavese.
Fletcher, Robert
   1891   The New School of Criminal Anthropology. American Anthropologist 4(3): 201–236.
Foucault, Michel
   1994a   L'évolution de la notion d'"individu dangereux" dans la psychiatrie légale du XIXe siècle. *In* Dits et écrits, vol. 3. Pp. 443–464. Paris: Gallimard.
   1994b   La vérité et les formes juridiques. *In* Dits et écrits, vol. 2. Pp. 538–646. Paris: Gallimard.
Frank, Robert G.
   1988   The Tell-Tale Heart: Physiological Instruments, Graphic Methods, and Clinical Hopes 1854–1914. *In* The Investigative Enterprise: Experimental Physiology in Nineteenth-Century Medicine. William Coleman and Frederic L. Holmes, eds. Pp. 211–290. Berkeley: University of California Press.
Gabelli, Aristide
   1885   La nuova scuola di diritto penale in Italia. Nuova Antologia 82: 569–600.
Galton, Francis
   1885   On the Anthropometric Laboratory at the Late International Health Exhibition. Journal of the Anthropological Institute of Great Britain and Ireland 14: 205–221.
Garofalo, Raffaele
   1891   Le perizie psichiatriche. La Scuola Positiva 1: 577–582.
Gaudenzi, Carlo
   1891   Un nuovo strumento per le misure angolari del capo. Archivio 12: 305–322.
Gould, Stephen Jay
   1981   The Mismeasure of Man. New York: Norton.
Guarnieri, Patrizia
   1986   Misurare le diversità. *In* Misura d'uomo: Strumenti, teorie e pratiche dell'antropometria e della psicologia sperimentale tra '800 e '900. Giulio Barsanti, Simonetta Gori-Savellini, Patrizia Guarnieri, and Claudio Pogliano, eds. Pp. 120–169. Florence: Istituto e Museo di Storia della Scienza.
Horn, David G.
   2005a Blood Will Tell: The Vascular System and Criminal Dangerousness. In Body Parts: Critical Explorations in Corporeality. Christopher E. Forth and Ivan Crozier, eds. Pp. 17–47. Lanham: Lexington Books.

2005b   Making Criminologists: Tools, Techniques, and the Production of Scientific Authority. *In* Criminals and Their Scientists: The History of Criminology in International Perspective. Richard Wetzell and Peter Becker, eds. Ch. 14. Cambridge: Cambridge University Press.

Latour, Bruno
1987   Science in Action: How to Follow Scientists and Engineers through Society. Cambridge, MA: Harvard University Press.

Lenoir, Timothy
1986   Models and Instruments in the Development of Electrophysiology, 1845–1912. Historical Studies in the Physical and Biological Sciences 17: 1–54.

Leps, Marie-Christine
1992   Apprehending the Criminal: The Production of Deviance in Nineteenth-Century Discourse. Durham, NC: Duke University Press.

Lombroso, Cesare
1876a   La poesia ed il crimine. Rivista Europea 7(1): 475–490.

1876b   Sui canti carcerari e criminali in Italia: Lettera al Prof. G. Pitrè. Rivista Europea 7(3): 155–160.

1883   Il mancinismo sensorio ed il tato nei delinquenti e nei pazzi. Archivio 4: 441–447.

1884   Il mancinismo. Rivista di Discipline Carcerarie 14: 126–130.

1889   L'uomo delinquente. 4th edition. 2 vols. Turin: Bocca.

1890a   Il delitto nella coscienza popolare. *In* Pazzi ed anomali: Saggi. 2nd edition. Pp. 26–34. Citta di Castello: S. Lapi.

1890b   Un esperimento nuovo sulla fisionomia criminale. *In* Pazzi ed anomali: Saggi. 2nd edition. Pp. 246–248. Citta di Castello: S. Lapi.

1895   Criminal Anthropology: Its Origins and Application. The Forum 20: 33–49.

1896   L'uomo delinquente, in rapporto all'antropologia, alla giurisprudenza ed alle discipline carcerarie. 5th edition. 3 vols. Turin: Bocca.

1905   La perizia psichiatrico-legale coi metodi per eseguirla e la casuistica penale classificata antropologicamente. Turin: Bocca.

1962[1879]   Prolusione al corso di medicina legale. *In* Antologia lombrosiana. Pp. 79–85. Pavia: Società Editrice Pavese.

1968[1911]   Crime: Its Causes and Remedies. Henry Horton, trans. Montclair, NJ: Patterson Smith.

Lombroso, Cesare, and Edoardo Audenino
1901   Contribution à l'étude de l'asymétrie de pression du sang chez les épileptiques, les prostituées et les criminels. Congrès internationale d'anthropologie criminelle: Compte rendu des travaux de la cinquième session tenue à Amsterdam du 9 au 14 septembre 1901. Pp. 282–285. Amsterdam: J. H. De Bussy.

Lombroso, Cesare, and Guglielmo Ferrero
1915   La donna delinquente, la prostituta, e la donna normale. 3rd edition. Turin: Bocca.

Lombroso, Cesare, Enrico Ferri, Raffaele Garofalo, and Giulio Fioretti
1886   Polemica in difesa della scuola criminale positiva. Bologna: Zanichelli.

Lombroso-Ferrero, Gina
1915   Cesare Lombroso: Storia della vita e delle opere. Turin: Bocca.

1972[1911]   Criminal Man, According to the Classification of Cesare Lombroso. Montclair, NJ: Patterson Smith.

Mantegazza, Paolo
   1871   Una nota sull'indice cefalospinale. Archivio per l'Antropologia e la Etnologia 1: 59–62.
   1879   Untitled [Review of Cesare Lombroso, *Pensiere e meteore*]. Archivio per l'Antropologia e la Etnologia 9: 326.
Mariani A., and G. Prati
   1902   Nuovo goniometro per misurare l'angolo facciale, il prognatismo e tutti gli altri elementi del triangolo facciale. Archivio 23: 43–48.
Marro, Antonio
   1885   I carcerati: studio psicologico del vero. Turin: Roux e Favale.
Morselli, Enrico
   1888   Dalla storia della fisiognonomia. Archivio 9: 103–104.
Mucchielli, Laurent, ed.
   1994   Histoire de la criminologie française. Paris: L'Harmattan.
Ottolenghi, Salvatore
   1889   Il mancinismo anatomico nei criminali. Archivio 10: 332–338.
Pasquarelli, Michele
   1896   Il folk-lore nell'antropologia criminale. Archivio 17: 507–518.
Pasquino, Pasquale
   1980   Criminology: The Birth of a Special Savoir. I&C 7: 17–32.
Patriarca, Silvana
   1996   Numbers and Nationhood: Writing Statistics in Nineteenth-Century Italy. Cambridge: Cambridge University Press.
Pitrè, Giuseppe
   1876   Sui canti popolari italiani di carcere [letter to the editor, Angelo De Gubernatis]. Rivista Europea 7(2): 320–326.
   1969[1896]   Medicina popolare siciliana. Bologna: Forni.
Porter, Theodore
   1995   Trust in Numbers: The Pursuit of Objectivity in Science and Public Life. Princeton: Princeton University Press.
Raffaele, Antonio
   1877   Della dignità del medico nelle questioni di giustizia e delle relative riforme all'attuale legislazione. Rivista di Freniatria Sperimentale 3: 73–111.
Sciamanna, Ezio
   1884   Guida nelle recerche anatomiche e antropologiche sui cadaveri dei condannati. Rivista di Discipline Carcerarie 14: 234–271.
Sekula, Allan
   1986   The Body and the Archive. October 39: 3–64.
Sergi, Giuseppe
   1893   Craniforo di Benedikt. Archivio 14: 143–145.
Severi A., and Cesare Lombroso
   1886   Prima esposizione internationale d'antropologia criminale a Roma. Archivio 7: 19–28.
Sim, Joe
   1990   Medical Power in Prisons: The Prison Medical Service in England 1774–1989. Philadelphia: Open University Press.

Stafford, Barbara Maria
1991   Body Criticism: Imaging the Unseen in Enlightenment Art and Medicine. Cambridge, MA: MIT Press.
Tamburini, Augusto, and Giulio Benelli
1885   L'antropologia nelle carceri. Rivista di Discipline Carcerarie 15(4): 136–147.
Villa, Renzo
1985   Il deviante e i suoi segni: Lombroso e la nascita dell'antropologia criminale. Milan: Franco Angeli.

6

Science and Citizenship under Postsocialism

Adriana Petryna

Introduction

This essay explores science as a political technique and the place of scientific knowledge in the dynamics of a postsocialist transition by taking the management of the aftermath of the Chernobyl nuclear catastrophe as a case in point. I begin with a brief exploration of three ways of conceiving of science as political technique: science as repression, science as a forging of a cosmopolitan ethos, and science as a way of rooting people in political regimes. Variations on these approaches informed the management of Chernobyl during the Soviet period and in the post-Soviet period of nation-state building, and this Soviet and post-Soviet management has significantly shaped the experiential, legal, and biological aspects of the disaster's aftermath. While, for example, in the Soviet period of the disaster's management 31 people were said to have died, during the post-Soviet management of the disaster, more than 3.5 million people in Ukraine alone claim to be suffering from the disaster's effects. The web of scientific, political, and social interests behind this stark numerical contrast is explored here. In mapping environmental contamination, measuring individual and population-wide exposures, and arbitrating claims of illness, the biological effects of Chernobyl became inseparable from the political interventions that were meant to contain them. Scientifically informed policies recast the aftermath as a complex political and technical experience in which administrators and affected people alike negotiated the scale of the aftermath, forms of remediation and compensation, and claims to social equity and human rights. These processes had their own bureaucratic and legal contours and exemplify how science supports a field of political and moral agency through which the dynamics of postsocialist state-building, democratization, and citizenship can be understood.

Reprinted from Adriana Petryna, "Science and Citizenship under Postsocialism." *Social Research* 70, 2 (2003): 551–578.

Aftermath

In writing the troubled history of genetics, German scientist Benno Muller-Hill observes that in the twentieth century, "the rise of genetics was characterized by a gigantic process of repression" (Muller-Hill cited in Nelkin and Tancredi 1989). This model of science as repression was most catastrophically exemplified by the Nazi deployment of biology as its program of scientific racism became the very foundation of the Nazi state (*Staatsraison*; see Proctor 1988: 45). In his chilling condemnation of the prewar German scientific community that legitimated Nazi racial theories, historian of science Robert Proctor wrote that for many German scientists and politicians, Nazism was treated as an "applied biology" (Proctor 1988: 7). Soviet dissident scientists who suffered from Soviet state repression claimed a different purpose for science: as a guarantor of freedom and as the human right to engage in the pursuit of knowledge, uncontaminated by political interference. Such claims to freedom from state repression through science were reinforced by the idea that scientists have the natural right to physical mobility and an independence from authorities because of their membership in a particular vocational order: science. This cosmopolitan community claimed to be distinct from cultural politics and national claims of origin. The extent to which dissident scientists were actually free of the exigencies of inhospitable, indeed life-threatening, times and places is captured well in Andrei Sakharov's recollection of himself observing columns of political prisoners being brutally marched to work at Azamas 16 (an atomic weapons research establishment run by the ruthless head of the Soviet secret police, Lavrenti Beria). At the same time, he sat at his desk developing the Tokamak model of controlled nuclear fusion (Graham 1998: 69).

A second model of science to be gleaned from the Soviet experience is not disconnected from the preceding model and is what I will call nativist. Trofim Lysenko epitomizes this Soviet nativist model of science widely regarded as false and as drastically retarding social and technical progress. In the 1930s, when the agricultural revolution based in modern genetics in the West was under way, Lysenko spearheaded what many observers considered to be a "catastrophe of Soviet biology" (Graham 1993: 4). Denying the existence of the gene, Lysenko promoted methods of accelerating crop growth and yields through vernalization, a labor-intensive process whereby the flowering of plants (particularly wheat) can be induced or accelerated by exposure to an extended period of near-freezing temperatures. Lysenkoism rejected a motorized image of agriculture in which human labor mattered less. Rather, the aim of this proletarian science was to break down the division between the theoretical and the applied in science (Roll-Hansen 1985: 272), and to convince each peasant of his or her individual capacity to participate in the experimental optimization of nature in the field – in this case the phasic development of plants.

This nativist model of science undercuts the positivism of science and marks a pertinent shift in knowledge: from one that is accessible to only a few, to one that provides more people with a stake in its epistemological rules (Kohler 2001). Lysenko's methods were unsupported by convincing empirical evidence and ultimately failed. Yet as historian of Soviet science Loren Graham has argued, Lysenkoism, as catastrophic as it was scientifically, had "psychological value" for a society experiencing acute grain shortages and undergoing deep agricultural crisis and the forced collectivization of the first five-year plan. According to Graham, "The fact that Lysenko was simultaneously denying the existence of the gene, that he was discarding all of modern genetics, meant less to these people than the fact that he was actually getting [Soviet] peasants to work in the field and that crops were being harvested" (1998: 21). Not freed by science, but not necessarily repressed, peasants who participated in the Lysenkoist project enrolled in the great Soviet experiment through which each could find his or her place and value in emergent labor regimes and collectives. Agriculture was not merely a neutral instrument used for the increase of food stocks, but became a means of cultivating "human resources" for a new type of governance, a critical point that I will come back to at the end of this essay. This was in addition to the fact that in the name of Lysenkoism, hundreds of biologists and other scientists were arrested and put to death in the Soviet Union and in China.

The truth or falsity of scientific claims is not what is most at stake in the political and social embodiment of Lysenkoism. In this case, the most ostensibly cosmopolitan of enterprises – science – seeps into the realm of everyday human affairs and becomes integral to the creation of populations and labor and production regimes. Scientific knowledge not only is ideological, but also enframes life as both living process and as practical political technique. With Lysenkoism, science is recast as a domain of applied ethical activity. Scientific know-how is brought in line with some form of political know-how: what one knows and how one knows it can determine how well one is positioned to survive the uncertainties of a dramatic political change.

Lysenko-like views and practices, as I discovered in the course of my historical and ethnographic work, framed the Soviet management of the Chernobyl catastrophe as well as the actions of postsocialist citizens who were desperate to claim disability status and compensations from a post-Soviet state. For example, Soviet administrators who were keen to cover up the scale of the disaster's effects used scientific measures as a means of ordering perceptions, limiting liability, and heightening social controls. From 1986 to 1989, they had established a high 35 rem (a unit of absorbed dose and spread over an individual's lifetime) as the threshold of allowable radiation dose intakes.[1] This politically defined threshold, much lower than the one set by international standards for human populations, restricted the scope of resettlement actions. Within the so-called Zone of Exclusion, an area 30 kilometers in diameter circumscribing the disaster site, administrators simultaneously withheld meteorological information and set occupational standards of radiological exposure artificially high. As a result, thousands of clean-up workers were exposed to dangerous and lethal doses. Technical laxity fit well with this process as well as with the way the Soviet administrators attempted to adjust a general population to a postcatastrophic environment. For example, a follow-up report from a Soviet–American bioscientific cooperation stated that "external measurements were unavailable at the time of the accident; they were either not designed for these levels of radiation or were destroyed or lost as a consequence of circumstances associated with this accident" (Baranov et al. 1989: 205).[2]

An international community of scientists (affiliated with the International Atomic Energy Agency [IAEA]) helped craft representations that minimized the scope of the disaster, or at least, of making the point that it was impossible to know the scope with any precision. The Soviet policymakers relied on crude maps in claiming that the plume somehow magically had not extended beyond the limits of the Zone of Exclusion. These claims were initially validated by international experts in an August 1986 meeting, four months after the disaster. But just *days* after the disaster, their international colleagues at several major scientific research institutions were able to track the contaminated plume for a distance and, based on meterological conditions, could estimate concentrations of radioactive contamination at any point in time down a computer-generated trajectory. One scientist doing this work from Livermore, California, told me that his computer programs "weren't ready" for what they had found:

> We typically operated within a two-hundred by two-hundred-kilometer area. This area had been sufficient to model prior releases such as the one at Three Mile Island and American and Chinese nuclear weapons tests. Our first calculations were on a two-hundred-kilometer square grid. We did the imaging near the Chernobyl plant, but the grid was so saturated, I mean, you couldn't even make sense of it because every place had these enormously high values – *they filled the whole grid, in every direction*.... Our codes were not prepared for an event of this magnitude.

Knowledge about the disaster and its scale at the international scientific cooperative level became grossly disconnected from knowledge at the domestic level. In internationalizing the problem of radiation protection, international experts and Soviet administrators redefined the scope of the problem in empirically unconvincing terms. As this internationalization of science progressed, the real physical management of contamination at the accident site was "internalized" to the domestic sphere of Soviet state control and its traditional modus operandi. Limited maps justified limited forms of radiation monitoring and resettlement actions. Large doses received by at least 200,000 workers between 1986 and 1987 were inadequately documented. According to one biochemist, many of the clean-up workers "received 6–8 times the lethal dose of radiation" (at 400 rem, bone marrow failure sets in). "They are alive. They know that they didn't die. But they don't know how they survived." One directive released by the Soviet Health Ministry at the height of the scientific cooperation told medical examiners in the zone to "classify workers who have received a maximum dose as having 'vegeto-vascular dystonia,' " which is a kind of panic disorder, or a novel psychosocial disorder called "radiophobia." These categories were used to filter out the majority of disability claims.[3] In such a politically engineered technical universe, key ethical questions about the immediate and long-term biological effects of high- and low-dose radiation exposure, particularly among clean-up workers, were evaded.

Tinkering with available knowledge and technical constructions of strategic nonknowledge became crucial to the establishment of authoritative knowledge. The initial scientific and medical assessments of the disaster's extent and biological impact, the delay in making public announcement, the selective measurement of individual and population-wide exposures, and the limitations on state remediation activities shaped Chernobyl as a *tekhnohenna katastrofa* (a technogenic catastrophe), in the words of many of my scientific and state informants. A series of informational omissions, technical choices, and semi-empirical models and approximations, along with international scientific assistance, produced a picture of a circumscribed biological reality. Combined, these practices initially produced an image of a known, circumscribed, and manageable biological reality. Later, these biological effects were seen as political products. Technical unknowns were refashioned in the post-Soviet period as part of a democratizing strategy that state and citizen alike could deploy.

Science as Political Technique

Along with the profound changes that accompanied the collapse of the Soviet Union, Chernobyl epitomized anxious moments when rigid controls over knowledge broke down – when relations between social organization and the state on the basis of some normed experience of truth dissolved – and when new populations, state–science regimes, and citizens were delimited anew. Science with its politics of imprecision, knowledge, and ignorance became a key tool both controlling people in this altered environment and enabling them to continue to live in the face of the immediate losses of primary securities such as employment and social welfare. The more abstract political discourses on human rights were realized on a biological level. In the post-Soviet period, as will be shown later, a large and largely impoverished segment of the population learned to negotiate the terms of its economic and social inclusion using the very constituent matter of life. One is faced with a massive experimental reality, the vicious circle of the world of experiment (Arendt 1958) through which science comes to constitute the practical conditions in which one lives and the studied and careful awareness on the part of citizenry of the conditions they embody in terms of political membership and as living beings.

With Chernobyl, science left the domain of the experiment and became central to authorizing democratic institutions and regulating the terms in which individuals are included in the public realm of citizenship (Arendt 1958: 299, 324).

Michel Foucault's famous framing of biopower, or that which "brought life and its mechanisms into the realm of...calculation and made knowledge-power an agent of transformation of human life" has also become a tool in understanding the dynamics of knowledge/power as formative of controlling experiences in modern life (1980b: 143).[4] Biopolitics operates at two levels: in the human body as a site of normalization and discipline, and in the population – understood as the body of the species, that is, regulated by science and welfare. Western states (inasmuch as their formation was bound up with capitalism), argued Foucault, are founded on an incessant, almost predatory drive to locate citizens and their attributes on a mesh of known categories. Knowability, utility, and profitability are linked.

But to describe the micro-instantiated panoptical and numerical impositions of mid-nineteenth-century France that he described, Foucault, almost paradoxically, projects a positivism in the workings of scientific facts. Statistics are said to seize the individual body in its actions and self-understandings, thus increasing the state's knowledge of people, as do calculations of life expectancy and measures of labor utility. This picture shows the state as an efficient machine for the production of power, yet it does not entirely capture the contingent and even ironic aspects of knowledge as they afford the translation into or shift in political capacity. Consider the anarchic words of Alfred North Whitehead on this very point: "Heaven knows what seeming nonsense may not to-morrow be demonstrated truth" (Whitehead, cited in Arendt 1958: 291). What is to count as knowledge in structuring relations between states and their subjects, what claims to human nature are being made, and what moral and cultural agents are being suggested in the nexus of science and the state: these are what inform political technique.[5]

Historians of science Shapin and Schaffer provide a detailed supplement to understanding the enfolding of state forms and scientific forms, and the ethical terms in which certain groups come to be players in this field. Their book, *Leviathan and the Air-Pump: Hobbes, Boyle, and the Experimental Life* (1985), is a historical and sociological interpretation that illustrates the contingencies of the rise of science in early modern England and more generally, of how modern science and the state developed simultaneously, using the other for legitimacy and support. The authors reframe the notion of experiment and use this reframing as a central support to their rich ethnographic description. The traditional notion of experiment as involving "singular, well-defined instances embedded in the elaboration of theories" (Rheinberger 1995: 109) is considered to assume far too much of a god's eye authority. Rather, the authors are more interested in the uncertainty of the experimental process in terms of the knowledge and social and political forms it incorporates and can produce (see also Hacking 1999). The experiment becomes a historical and social field in itself, connected to the production of morally and politically valid publics (or communities of "valid witnesses"). More important, it serves as a window into the state–science nexus and does not presume any fixed or constant relationship between certainty and truth.

Political organizations like states can be viewed as experimental realizations, no longer machines of fact accumulation, but open systems that can be generative of new aggregate conditions and unanticipated resources. Not more pure knowability, but awareness of the practical conditions in which one lives marks the possibilities of order and citizenry. When the cultural peculiarities of the state–science interchange are introduced, potentially, the assumption under which the Foucauldian paradigm operates disappears. Thus a different map of a postsocialist field, for example, with specific physical, experiential, political, economic, and spatial dimensions appears.

This experimental framing of states and polities, which is not empirically known in advance, finds considerable resonance with recent anthropological literature on postsocialist and market transitions (Verdery 1996; Humphrey 1999; Grant 1995) that has rejected predictive models that treat movement toward free market and democracy as inevitable. The challenge has been to account for continuities between socialist and postsocialist societies, as well as to develop methods of understanding processes and relations of power at the global level that are reworked nationally and "shift the rules of the game, the parameters of action within which actors pursue their daily routines and practices" (Burawoy and Verdery 1999: 2). In this sense, not only have the empirical boundaries of the state shifted or been removed (Trouillot 2001: 126; Warren 2002; Ferguson and Gupta 2002), but so have the contents and methods of how to be a citizen (Greenhouse 2003; Biehl 2002; Petryna 2002a). We have come a long way from the traditional concept of citizenship that images citizens as bearers of natural and legal rights that are (and must be) protected as a matter of birthright and, thus, legally protected. Today, there is nothing obvious or natural as to who may or may not belong or who may or may not be protected as a citizen. Indeed, in many new states, protection as a key domestic function – be it in the form of police security or public health – is being privatized, outsourced, "racketed," or simply disappearing (Comaroff and Comaroff 2002; Caldeira 2002; Humphrey 1999; Volkov 2002; Petryna 2002b). In Brazil, for example, the state's life-protecting functions have turned into life-taking violence, intended for certain parts of the population.[6] In Ukraine, the dire economic starting conditions in which the Soviet republics turned nation-states declared independence have accelerated division and competition among social groups for protection (that is, social welfare). The demand for protection and the politics of its rationing became even more acute in the face of an overwhelming biological threat. My contribution to this field of inquiry focuses on how political and technical interventions limited the scope of crisis (and its knowability), and on the scientific, ethical, and legal circumstances of citizenship that ensued in a state where populations are basically no longer protected. The search for protection conveys the "human engineering, not to mention violence, chaos, and despair [and] hidden costs of establishing nation-states" (Burawoy and Verdery 1999: 10). In this context, the very idea of citizenship is charged with the superadded burden of survival. Protection is a legal right no longer self-evidently emanating from the state, but whose existence is at least partially assured by citizens' everyday exercise of their democratic capacities to identify, balance, or neutralize opposing forces that give or take life.

Let me provide a roadmap of my inquiry into this vexed environment (that is, the specific ethnographic sites and methods) and the challenges of developing an ethnographic sensibility. In the process, I suggest some of the empirical processes through which citizens come to identify with new states.

Between 1992 and 1997, I worked among resettled families and radiation-exposed workers, carried out archival research in the country's Health Ministry and Parliamentary Commissions on Human Rights; I also conducted interviews with key scientific and political players in both Kiev and Moscow, comparing scientific standards informing risk and safety in the Soviet and post-Soviet administrations in the aftermath. I became scientifically literate – inquiring into the circulation and assimilation of scientific knowledge at national, international, and local levels and explored their tensions. For example, persistent claims by international experts that the health effects of the disaster were limited were not supported by laboratory scientists working at United States government laboratories. At a United States government laboratory, I learned some of the radiobiological techniques for assessing the impact of radiation at the cell and DNA level. As one laboratory scientist told me, the difference between this manipulable animal environment and population-wide exposures to low-dose radiation remains a "black box." Although causal links between high doses of radiation and human biological effects have been well established, the same cannot be said for continuous human exposure to low doses. These sciences themselves are marked by an ambiguity of how to measure, interpret, and intervene in radiation exposures. In the absence of agreed-upon standards, a distinct post-socialist arena was in the making. Conflicts over the scope of injury inflicted by this disaster and how to model it continued to influence policy, social mobilizations, and not least the very course of illness in the affected population with which I worked.

In the process, I learned just how staked such disputes over the truthful scope of injury, technical knowledge, research, and resources were in the evolving political and economic arenas. The country inherited the actual power plant when it declared independence. Ukraine's government immediately defined new and ambitious safety measures. This meant stabilizing the deteriorating shelter, following new norms of workers' safety, limiting future contamination, and closing the last remaining working units of the Chernobyl plant. The implementation of this new management had also become a key asset in Ukraine's foreign policy. In response to these efforts, European countries and the United States promised Ukraine further technical assistance, loans, and potential trading partnerships. All this legitimately opened a new political site in which money, influence, and corruption loomed in the already powerful energy sector.

Who would be protected (biologically, economically, politically, socially) in this post-Chernobyl world? When? On what terms? And for how long? These were some of the questions that preoccupied me as well as my informants in this unmarked, unfixed, and transforming field. What are the empirical means by which citizens come to identify with new states? Capturing my anthropological attention was the rapid growth of a new part of the citizenry claiming radiation exposure and receiving access to some form of welfare protection – a group totaling 7 percent of the total population. Belarus, where 23 percent of the territory is considered contaminated – three times more than Ukraine – had contained a number of claimants, as had Russia. Dr. Angelina Guskova, who oversaw the Russian compensation system in Moscow and was responsible for the airlifting and care of the approximately 500 suspected acute accident victims, felt the Ukrainians were inflating their numbers of exposed people, that their so-called invalids "didn't want to recover." She related the illnesses of this group to personality problems and to a "struggle for power and material resources related to the disaster."

When I asked Dr. Angelina Ceanu, a neurophysiologist and physician to Chernobyl victims in Kyiv, for a reaction to her former colleague's indictment, she said, "It is inconceivable that an organism of any kind is passive to its own destruction." Ceanu was not being philosophical; she was quoting the Soviet botanist and radiobiologist V. L. Komarov, who observed in one of his experiments in the 1950s that sleeping rats, without prodding, wake when exposed to minute doses of ionizing radiation.[7] From these examples you can start to see how lack of agreement over scientific models (animal vs. human; psychometric vs. biological; laboratory vs. field-based), different funding priorities, and different moral stances toward the unknown health effects of the disaster were not simply at odds with each other (or waiting to be assessed for their suitability or nonsuitability). Their confrontation and juxtaposition engendered a new social environment or better, a political economy of radiation illness. Developing alongside this economy was yet another social phenomenon. It was the boom of civic organizations called *Fondy* or Funds that administered international charity and the compensation claims of the zone workers. Also, since these more than 500 Funds are tax exempt, they have sparked a large informal economy based on imports (of a variety of goods, including pharmaceuticals, cars, foodstuffs, and so on).

In this political economy of Chernobyl-related illnesses, it was common knowledge that a person classified as "disabled" was far better compensated than a mere "sufferer." Built into the system was the possibility of sequentially transforming oneself from a sufferer to a disabled person. For both groups, it made little sense to drop out of the system since the state provided no better alternative to this form of social protection. The sufferer's position, and the work required to keep that position, constituted an investment for life. Those outside the Chernobyl system of sufferers knew they had even less of a chance of getting decent social protections from the state. In this context, scientific knowledge became a crucial medium of negotiating individual and family survival. The effectiveness of relating one's dose exposures to radiation-related symptoms and experiences and work histories in the zone determined the position one could occupy in the hierarchy of sufferers, and the extent to which one could wield capital that could further guarantee state protections. Rural workers, industrial workers, professionals, intelligentsia – laborers of unequal status under state socialism – became part of a novel national collectivity of Chernobyl sufferers transcending class and educational and employment categories.[8] The state established a Chernobyl welfare system and health services sector as autonomous subdivisions of the state's social welfare services and public health ministry. Pensions and free medical care, among other services, were authorized for a large group of sufferers.[9]

"Here, the worst is to be healthy," said one clinician working at a state-sponsored radiation research clinic. Her words suggest that in a moment of political and economic crisis, individuals gave greater importance to the material benefits of social organization around illness than to their rights and responsibilities to be "healthy" citizens. Socialist societies tried to guarantee universal access to a minimum standard of living. A system of social protections included state-provided education, health, pension benefits, and basic food subsidies, which lowered living costs. What was the Soviet health sector is now either severely curtailed in its services or is being privatized, leaving significant sectors of the population's health unaddressed. The clinician's wry observation suggested that being "healthy" today means being left alone, abandoned by the state, and without social supports. Under such conditions, what were once states of health are now states of illness. "Illness" provided some measure of protection against the vagaries of joblessness and social disorientation. People were converting themselves from Soviet citizens into (biological) citizens in their efforts to maintain a tie with the state and to avoid abandonment.

The key site of my study became the Radiation Research Center, also known as Klinika, which had been established by the Soviets in 1986. The center monitors patients and conducts research, especially on low-dose radiation exposure. It houses the central Medical-Labor Committee (Ekspertiza), a group of scientists, clinicians, and administrators who authorize the so-called Chernobyl "tie" – a legal document affirming the connection between certain illnesses and radiation exposure and entitling the bearer to social protection in the form of pensions, health care, and even education benefits for children. This package of benefits is much higher than average pensions and is therefore very desirable.[10] I observed interactions between physicians, nurses, and patients, routinely sat in meetings related to compensation claims, and examined current research, particularly in the Division of Nervous Pathologies. This choice of division was intentional. Medical-labor committee members had indicated that over 60 percent of all disability claims were channeled through neurological wards. In addition to talking to scientists, health workers, and administrators, I also documented the course of illnesses, diagnosis, and progress in securing disability status among male and female patients. A substantial part of my work involved following the activities of five of the clinic's male patients and their wives and children. I was interested in how the insertion of men into this political economy of illness was dramatically changing their roles as breadwinners and father figures as well as their mental health. I focused on their altered sense of *lichnost'*, a Russian concept of person-hood expressing one's commitment to work and to the labor collective (Khar-khordin 1999); in the kinds of reasoning married couples used to construct radiation illness as a plausible means of subsistence; and in the techniques they used to have their illnesses count within the rational-technical domain in which their life was being addressed.

Biology and State Identity

What is traceable in the Chernobyl aftermath is not just how an understanding of vulnerability is technically mediated and shaped, but the process by which the state as a protective shell falls apart, and how it was subsequently carved up as two worlds with two distinct populations: those who are protected and those who are not. These worlds were supported by scientific and legal apparatuses and political rationalities and their existence was conveyed to me repeatedly. One former worker who was forcibly recruited to work six months at the Chernobyl disaster site and who worked without protective gear, lamented, "the [Soviet] state took my life away."[11] He also felt entirely abandoned by and insecure in the new state in which he lived. He initially refused to participate in the informal system that would allow him access to some state benefits; he perceived "thieves and dishon-orable people" as having more legal status than himself. The choice to profit from his illness was also demeaning. Over time, he lived as if forced to inhabit a landmass cut adrift: "I detest being on this side of the world." His strategies of getting over to the other side involved a careful blend of illegality, networking, and scientific know-how, since he also learned to use his damaged biology to negotiate the terms of his political membership and survival in the new Ukrainian democracy and transition to the market.

For biology to be linked with state identity is not new. Clifford Geertz (1963), for example, defined the problem of the relationship between biology and iden-tity in terms of sentiment. He treated ethnobiological categories along with the " 'givens' of place, tongue, blood, looks, and way-of-life to shape an individual's notion of who, at bottom, he is" (1963: 128) as the starting materials with which to consider how citizens would come to identify with new states following the massive decolonization after World War II. In defining a method and an investi-gative field around the "modern sense of political community," Geertz encour-aged anthropologists and other scholars to explore the "unreflective sense of collective selfhood in the steadily broadening political process of the national state" (1963: 128). Yet there was nothing obvious about how this steady broad-ening would take place, and how people would come to specify themselves within the political process. The innovativeness of new states, according to Geertz, was related to how leaders would institutionally administer primordial sentiments. Primordiality was like the DNA of emergent states – a cultural order of nature that, if decoded properly, would turn the potential unruliness of clans, kinships, and tribalisms into a logic of exponential power for the state. He proposed the uncovering of a specific cultural and institutional logic as the material of large-scale comparative reflection on new states. Geertz was interested in the experimental quality of these undertakings, as well as in identifying successful experiments. He wanted to find ways of anticipating the dynamics of interaction between natural human orders and "alien civil orders" of national emancipation imposed by the nation-state form, especially if and when its promises of bringing dignity and human rights to the colonially oppressed failed to be realized.

More than a decade earlier, Hannah Arendt reported on the political experiments of states, but from a different historical vantage point. In a key essay, Arendt reflects on the "horrifying unfinished business" left behind by the deaths of Hitler and Stalin, and explicates the political and scientific contexts that enframe orders of citizenship. She states that at the birth of the nation-state, large numbers of people are outside of it and are in an extralegal status. They are "human being[s] in general – without a profession, without a citizenship, without an opinion, without a deed by which to identify or specify himself – *and* different in general, representing nothing but his own absolutely unique individuality which, deprived of expression within and action upon a common world, loses all significance" (1994: 302). The stateless inhabit a constitutive outside for which no law is available to them. Their condition is marked by a "calamity of experience" vis-à-vis a nation-state that works like a fiction. Arendt shows how, in attempting to regain a legal identity and a social tie, even if through criminality (1994: 286), the actions of the stateless are capitalized upon by state and trans-state entities such as the police in terms of fortifying their own bureaucratic and legal mechanisms. Her analysis points to a way of specifying existing experiments in postsocialist strategies of state building: how populations become enrolled as human resources in the creation of new states, and the role of legality and extralegality as citizens struggle to forge an existence for themselves in arenas where life, ostensibly, can no longer be protected.

Ukraine constituted itself as a state around an indistinct outsider group. Its separate and unaccounted for existence was constituted by Soviet interventions. Severely limiting the size of populations considered to be at risk, state scientific policies made these populations politically superfluous. The assignment of these populations outside of state forms of accountability opened the way to a new politics of protection and accountability, now staked in a technically and politically constituted Chernobyl unknown. In a resolution entitled "The Concept of Inhabitation" (1991), Ukrainian deputies declared their entire national territory "a zone of ecological calamity." The Soviet administration was denounced for its "willful disregard of the safety of populations living and working around and in the contaminated zones," and as an "act of genocide." It made the task of collecting systematic knowledge and the identification of exposed populations a top priority. Obtaining "positive identification of an exposed individual would be a difficult task because knowledge of doses received by the general Ukrainian population immediately after the blast was lacking. The reconstruction of this dose is critical." A system for registering exposed territories and populations was introduced. By the fall of 1991, any person who might have been exposed to low doses of irradiation by being present in the exclusion and contaminated zones for short or prolonged periods was likely to undergo clinical monitoring, to put his or her name and medical history in a national registry of sufferers, and to claim his or her entitlement to compensations, including preferential and free medical care and examinations at specialized radiation centers and special Chernobyl hospital wings. Cities, territories, and villages were designated as "protected" by the new state.

As new forms of governance and public domains are being engendered in postsocialism, the political terms of Chernobyl-related biologies were redefined. Bioscientific knowledge became a crucial medium in state-building processes. For example, law-makers lowered the Soviet threshold dose from 35 rem to 7 rem, comparable to what an average American would be exposed to in his or her lifetime. They expanded territories considered contaminated. In addition to expanding territories considered unsafe, the state's social welfare system expanded to accommodate the large influx of newly designated Chernobyl sufferers. This rapid expansion defined Western prescriptions for a smooth neoliberal transition – prescriptions that mandated a decrease in the social expenditures of the state. Sufferers, scientists, civil servants, and policymakers became knowing participants in the logic of this transition. Statistics from the Ukrainian Ministry of Health indicate the sharp increases in 1991 of zone workers, resettled persons, and inhabitants of contaminated territories registering their disability and the annual patterns of enrollment of this new population the state committed itself to care for. As was noted earlier, compared with the 31 who suffered under the Soviet model, by 1996 Ukrainian officials had now tallied, according to their scientific measures, that it was now 3.5 million of their citizens who had suffered.

The political response to Chernobyl's rational-technical legacy combined humanism with strategies of governance and state building; and market strategies with forms of economic and political corruption. Such interrelated processes generated new kinds of formal and informal social networks and economies that have allowed some segments of the population to survive on and benefit from politically guaranteed subsidies. They constituted a moral microcosm of the paradoxes of an emerging democracy founded on ethical principles of justice, benevolence, and human rights. If these Chernobyl laws engendered new and demonstrably democratic forms of civic organizing and opportunities for non-governmental action, they also became one of the state's most notorious instruments of corruption through which *blat*, for example (a Soviet term denoting the informal and unofficial practice of lending access to state privileges and protections), could flourish (Ledeneva 1998). One had to become an outlaw first in order to return to society.

An example of how this relationship between legality and illegality worked in the everyday: Symon Lavrov, the country's most distinguished expert on scientific matters related to the disaster, was well known in international science spheres for his development of computerized fallout models and calculation of population-wide doses in the post-Soviet period. But he told me that "when a crying mother comes to my laboratory and asks me, Professor Lavrov, 'tell me what's wrong with my child?' I assign her a dose and say nothing more. I double it, as much as I can." The scientist's gift of a higher dose increased the probability that the mother would be able to obtain social protection because she had a potentially sick child. The mother and the scientist were two of the many figures whose work I documented. They illustrated how government and scientific interventions not only contributed to a lack of resolution to the Chernobyl aftermath, but were also entangled with and to some extent created new social tensions, inequalities, and informal regimes. Given such dynamics, Lavrov conveyed what I believed to be his own vision of the aftermath's scale: "We have learned that tragedy is not defined by the numbers who have died," and suggested that the truth of Chernobyl was much more somber than what numbers can tell. Indeed, his own mode of work placed limits on what he and others could legitimately aim for in the quest for truth.[12]

Converging here are aspects of the three ways of conceiving of science as political technique and how truth figures in each. In response to Soviet tactics, the immediate postindependence discourse in Ukraine centered on the recovery of truth; Ukrainians justified their failure to know in terms of a state repression. In the cosmopolitan model, truth was liberated and a science in the promotion of human rights was asserted. As the realities of the harsh market conditions entered everyday life, this model of organizing suffering and promoting rights quickly gave way to a different kind of scientific negotiation that had to do with the remaking of post-Soviet populations. A paralegal realm was introduced in which some found themselves inside and some found themselves outside of the truth and indeed, outside of the law. Informal economies of knowledge, differential medical access, a continuum of diagnoses, and other resources related to risk were mobilized and began to function as institutions in parallel with the state's official legal social protection system. These new resources functioned more like advances of credit, insuring social protections in the uncertain future for people whose temporal horizons were limited.

In this context, the mother in the above example could give her child a dose, a probability of sickness, and through this a guarantee of social protection from the state on the basis of her child's supposedly injured biology. What she could give – perhaps the most valuable gift she could give – is a particular biological knowledge, a history of exposure, and a legal category of sufferer. The child's "exposure" and the knowledge that would make that exposure an empirical fact were not something to be repressed or denied (as had been tried in the Soviet model) but rather something to be turned into a resource and then parceled out.

The play of probability in relation to radiation-related disease became a central resource for local scientific research, making clear once again how problems of knowledge are also problems of social order. In my fieldwork in a state radiation research clinic, I could see how this tinkering with probability was being projected back into nature, so to speak, through an intricate local science. Young neuro-psychiatrists made the best of the inescapability of their circumstances (they could not get visas to leave the country) as they integrated international medical taxonomies into Soviet forms and developed classifications of mental and nervous disorders that in expert literatures were considered far too low to make any significant biological contribution. For example, they engaged in a project aimed at detecting cases of mental retardation in children exposed in utero in the first year after the disaster. In the case of one such child, a limping 9-year-old boy, researchers and parents worked together to reconstruct the child's disorder to show it had a radiation origin. Even though the boy's radiation dose was low, he was given the status of "sufferer" mainly because of his mother's occu-pation-related exposure (she was an emergency doctor who elected to work in the zone until late in her pregnancy), and also because a PET scan did reveal a cerebral lesion that was never hypothesized as being related to anything else other than radiation (it could have been birth trauma). Just as a human research cohort was being made, so was a destiny – a destiny that the parents were intent on passing to this child. As researchers and citizens relied on probabilistic characters of knowledge and technologies, they gained political recognition and access to some form of welfare entitlement, now made more accessible by a new biological status.

Biological Citizenship

In the Ukraine–Chernobyl nexus, collective efforts are not so much aimed at securing political rights as they are at guaranteeing a probability of economic survival through an injured biology. The collective exploitation of probable harm resulted in a dynamic application of state power that, in turn, became a venue of claims making and an expanding state, with an equally expanding domain of informal economics where diagnoses, symptoms, and medical access were traded and protections were brokered or bought. To the extent that knowledge became public property, biology became a resource in a multidimensional sense – versatile material through which the state protectorate could be made to appear, and a means through which citizens could be safely situated as state-protected human subjects. I began to think about these official and unofficial practices and inter-actions collectively as a kind of a "biological citizenship," a massive demand for but selective access to a form of welfare based on such medical, scientific, and legal criteria. Citizens (acutely aware of the new structures of exclusion in the nation-state) consciously manipulated those elements in their lives (measures, numbers, symptoms) that could connect to a broader technical and political history of error, mismanagement, and risk, and that could afford them a probability of economic entitlement – at least in the short term.

This concept may appear to be emphasizing the agency of persons in a transitional state. In fact, it shows how limited their agency is when reflecting on the changed nature of citizenship in postsocialist spheres. The theme of citizenship is particularly important here not only because of its traditional role in framing life chances of individuals by increasing their welfare and health-care access – services formally guaranteed by permanent employment in socialist enterprises. The very idea of citizenship is now charged with the superadded burden of survival. This process represents a shift, perhaps a reversal, in the underlying principles of a classical citizenship inasmuch as those principles cannot guarantee the basic biological existence of populations that precedes political life. Though this may seem like an obvious point, it is also a devastating one. The level of competition for scarce resources, the uncertain nature of entitlements, hierarchies of entitlement, the vagaries of law, the legal and illegal means of obtaining legal personhood, and illness as a form of work: all these realities are embedded in the phrase "biological citizenship." It is a collective and individual survival strategy representing a complex interface of social institutions and the intense vulnerabilities of populations exposed to the determinations of international political economy; it is also part of a larger story of democratization and new structures of governance in the postsocialist states and of the violence that inheres in the formation of new biological groups.

Tracking these formations, one can look back and ask about the workings of the state and economy in this region. What is observed is a state that is highly selective in terms of the populations it addresses, with commitments that are never backed by the stability of law, and beset by corruption. Perhaps what we learn about most is what anthropologist João Biehl calls "life determinations" (2002), and these are more enduring than ideologies of the state or of science – how citizens are recruited into new cooperative regimes in scientific research and international and local forms of (human subjects) protection – and the places and values they find for themselves. At stake is not so much the moral relationship governing state and individual subjects, although this is still central, but the collectivities that are empirically in the making and that ethnography can chart and critique, particularly in relation to how people live with the new experimental investments that draw value from them. These lived dynamics, I suggest, are part of the new materials of large-scale comparative and anticipatory reflection on citizens in new postsocialist states.

Notes

1 An individual's lifetime is understood as a standard 70-year span.
2 The initial Soviet report to the IAEA in August 1986 stated that "environmental monitoring devices or individual radiation meters or badges, were of limited value at Chernobyl" (USSR State Committee 1986).

3   In my interviews I heard instances of workers mimicking symptoms of ARS [acute radiation sickness] (vomiting, for example). This shows the level of desperation on the part of some of these workers to receive permission to leave the zone.

4   The nuclear era represented biopower's culmination. "If nuclear energy is the modern capacity to expose populations to unprecedented kinds of risk and potential death, it is also the underside of the power to generate life through the biological administration of individuals and populations" (Foucault 1980b: 137).

5   Foucault referenced Lysenkoism as a starting point for reflection on power and knowledge in Western psychiatry and criminality and delinquency. He stressed the sham nature and ideological function of the phenomenon, and missed some of its nativizing aspect. See "Truth and Power" in Foucault (1980b).

6   Katharina Bodirsky, précis, Anthropology of the State, Graduate Faculty of Political and Social Science, New School University, April 10, 2003. I thank members of my graduate seminar on the anthropology of the state for their engagement with many of the issues here.

7   Komarov's life tells of the close interactions between politics of protection and particular biological visions. In the 1930s, V. L. Komarov was a well-known botanist with Lamarckian views. Komarov positively appraised Lysenko's work for its holistic approach, and criticized the genotype/phenotype split in genetics (Roll-Hansen 1985: 275). Decades later, as Lysenkoism became more entrenched, he protected genetics against Lysenkoist assaults (radiation biology provided shelter for geneticists).

8   Research in Russia shows that social organizing in response to economic pressures also transcends class and educational and employment categories. See Ahl (1999: 175).

9   To enter the system, sufferers were required to show proof of dose. Acceptable forms included (1) proof of residency in one of the four zones; (2) a dose of irradiation exceeding the allowable threshold norms; (3) a dose value deduced from work routes, meteorological measurements, or chromosomal aberration counts; (4) documentation of a period of work in the zones; (5) documented degree of loss of labor capacity based on medical records; or (6) a court appearance in the company of witnesses testifying to the claimant's presence in the zones.

10 As of 2000, the state paid an average of $12 per month for social insurance. The poverty line was approximately $27 a month. Monthly pension benefits for those disabled by the Chernobyl accident average between $54 and $90 per month, depending on degree of disability. A "sufferer," a person who does not have disability status but who has the status of having suffered from the Chernobyl accident, received $20 per month on average.

11 This worker drove bags of lead oxide, sand, and gravel right up to the reactor; the bags were airlifted and dumped over the burning reactor by men in helicopters (many of whom died soon after their work). He does not know how much radiation he absorbed. Over time, his symptoms progressed. His medical records indicated that he experienced chronic headaches, that he lost his short-term memory, exhibited "anti-social behavior," developed a speech disorder, and that he experienced seizures and impotence, among many other symptoms.

12 On tragic modes of employment see Hayden White's *Metahistory: The Historical Imagination in Nineteenth-Century Europe* (1973: 9).

References

Ahl, Richard
   1999   Society and Transition in Post-Soviet Russia. Communist and Post-Communist Studies 32(2): 175–182.
Arendt, Hannah
   1994[1951]   The Decline of the Nation-State and the End of the Rights of Man. *In* The Origins of Totalitarianism. Pp. 267–304. New York: Harvest Books.
   1958   The Human Condition. Chicago: University of Chicago Press.
Baranov, A., et al.
   1989   Bone Marrow Transplantation after the Chernobyl Nuclear Accident. New England Journal of Medicine 321(4): 205–212.
Biehl, João
   2002   Biotechnology and the New Politics of Life and Death in Brazil: The AIDS Model. Princeton Journal of Bioethics 5(Spring): 59–74.
Burawoy, Michael, and Katherine Verdery, eds.
   1999   Uncertain Transition: Ethnographies of Change in the Postsocialist World. Lanham, MD.: Rowman and Littlefield.
Caldeira, Teresa
   2002   The Paradox of Police Violence in Democratic Brazil. Ethnography 3(3): 235–264.
Comaroff, Jean, and John Comaroff
   2002   Criminal Obsessions: Imagining Order after Apartheid. Lecture, New School University.
Ferguson, James, and Akhil Gupta
   2002   Spatializing States: Toward an Ethnography of Neoliberal Governmentality. American Ethnologist 29(4): 981–1002. Reprinted as Chapter 4 in this volume.
Foucault, Michel
   1980a   The History of Sexuality. Vol. 1. Robert Hurley, trans. New York: Vintage Books.
   1980b   Truth and Power. *In* Power/Knowledge: Selected Interviews and Other Writings, 1972–1977. Colin Gordon, ed. and trans. New York: Pantheon.
Geertz, Clifford
   1963   The Integrative Revolution: Primordial Sentiments and Civil Politics in the New States. *In* Old Societies and New States. Clifford Geertz, ed. Pp. 105–157. New York: Free Press.
Graham, Loren R.
   1993   Science, Philosophy, and Human Behavior in the Soviet Union. New York: Columbia University Press.
   1998   What Have We Learned about Science and Technology from the Russian Experience? Stanford: Stanford University Press.
Grant, Bruce
   1995   In the Soviet House of Culture: A Century of Perestroikas. Princeton: Princeton University Press.
Greenhouse, Carol
   2003   States of Discourse: Questions and Challenges for the Ethnography of Law. Lecture. Dept. of Anthropology Seminar Series. New School University, April 2.

Hacking, Ian
  1999   Making Up People. *In* Science Studies Reader. Mario Biagoli, ed. New York: Routledge.
Heyman, Josiah, ed.
  1999   States and Illegal Practices. Oxford and New York: Berg.
Humphrey, Caroline
  1999   Russian Protection Rackets and the Appropriation of Law and Order. *In* States and Illegal Practices. Josiah Heyman, ed. Pp. 285–314. Oxford and New York: Berg.
Kharkhordin, Oleg
  1999   The Collective and the Individual in Russia: A Study of Practices. Berkeley: University of California Press.
Kohler, Robert
  2001   The Particularity of Biology in the Field. Manuscript Presented at Princeton Workshop in the History of Science, "Model Systems, Cases, and Exemplary Narratives." Princeton University.
Ledeneva, Alena
  1998   Russia's Economy of Favours: Blat, Networking, and Informal Exchange. Cambridge: Cambridge University Press.
Nelkin, Dorothy, and Laurence Tancredi
  1989   Dangerous Diagnostics: The Social Power of Biological Information. New York: Basic Books.
Petryna, Adriana
  2002a   Life Exposed: Biological Citizens after Chernobyl. Princeton: Princeton University Press.
  2002b   The Human Subjects Research Industry. Manuscript. W. H. R. Rivers Workshop, "Global Pharmaceuticals: Ethics, Markets, Practice." Harvard University.
Proctor, Robert
  1988   Racial Hygiene: Medicine under the Nazis. Cambridge, MA: Harvard University Press.
Rheinberger, Hans-Jorg
  1995   From Experimental Systems to Cultures of Experimentation. *In* Concepts, Theories, and Rationality in the Biological Sciences. G. Wolters, J. Lennox, and P. McLaughlin, eds. Pp. 107–122. Pittsburgh: University of Pittsburgh Press.
Roll-Hansen, Nils
  1985   A New Perspective on Lysenko? Annals of Science 42(3): 261–279.
Shapin, Steven, and Simon Schaffer
  1985   Leviathan and the Air-Pump: Hobbes, Boyle, and the Experimental Life. Princeton: Princeton University Press.
Trouillot, Michel-Rolph
  2001   The Anthropology of the State in the Age of Globalization. Current Anthropology 42(1): 125–139.
USSR State Committee on the Utilization of Atomic Energy
  1986   The Accident at Chernobyl Nuclear Power Plant and Its Consequences. Information compiled for the IAEA Experts' Meeting, August 25–9, 1986, Vienna. Working Document for the Post-Accident Review Meeting.

Verdery, Katherine
  1996   What Was Socialism, and What Comes Next? Princeton: Princeton University Press.
Volkov, Vadim
  2002   Violent Entrepreneurs: The Use of Force in the Making of Russian Capitalism. Ithaca: Cornell University Press.
Warren, Kay
  2002   Toward an Anthropology of Fragments, Instabilities, and Incomplete Transitions. *In* Ethnography in Unstable Places. Carol J. Greenhouse, Elizabeth Mertz, and Kay B. Warren, eds. Durham NC: Duke University Press.
White, Hayden
  1973   Metahistory: The Historical Imagination in Nineteenth-Century Europe. Baltimore: Johns Hopkins University Press.

Part IV
Biosocial Subjects

7

Artificiality and Enlightenment:

From Sociobiology to Biosociality

Paul Rabinow

Michel Foucault identified a distinctively modern form of power, "bio-technico-power." Biopower, he writes, designates "what brought life and its mechanism into the realm of explicit calculations and made knowledge-power an agent of transformation of human life." Historically, practices and discourses of biopower have clustered around two distinct poles: the "anatomo-politics of the human body," the anchor point and target of disciplinary technologies, on the one hand; and a regulatory pole centered on population with a panoply of strategies concentrating on knowledge, control, and welfare.[1] Today, I believe the two poles of the body and the population are being rearticulated into what could be called a postdisciplinary, if still modern, rationality.

In the annex to his book on Michel Foucault – entitled *On the Death of Man and the Superman* – Gilles Deleuze presents a schema of three *force-forms*, to use his jargon, which are roughly equivalent to Michel Foucault's three *epistemes*. In the classical form, infinity and perfection are the forces shaping beings; beings have a form toward which they strive and the task of science is to represent correctly the table of those forms in an encyclopedic fashion. In the modern form, finitude establishes a field of life, labor, and language within which Man appears as a distinctive being, who is both the subject and object of his own understanding, which is never complete because of its very structure. Finally, today in the present, a field of the *surhomme*, or "afterman," in which finitude, as empiricity, gives way to a play of forces and forms Deleuze labels *fini-illimité*.[2] In this new constellation beings have neither a perfected form nor an essential opacity. The best example of this "unlimited-finite" is DNA: an infinity of beings can and has arisen from the four bases out of which DNA is constituted. François Jacob, the Nobel prize-winning biologist, makes a similar point when he

Reprinted from Paul Rabinow, "Artificiality and Enlightenment: From Sociobiology to Biosociality," in Mario Biagioli (ed.), *The Science Studies Reader*. New York: Routledge, 1999, pp. 407–416.

writes: "a limited amount of genetic information in the germ line, produces an enormous number of protein structures in the soma...nature operates to create diversity by endlessly combining bits and pieces."[3] Whether Deleuze has seized the significance of Jacob's facts remains an open question. Still, we must be intrigued when something as cryptic as Rimbaud's formula that "the man of the future will be filled (*chargé*) with animals" takes on a perfectly material meaning, as we shall see when we turn to the concept of model organism in the new genetics.[4]

Deleuze convincingly claims that Foucault lost his wager that it would be language of the anthropological triad – life, labor, language – that would open the way for a new *episteme*, washing the figure of Man away like a wave crashing over a drawing in the sand. Foucault himself acknowledged that his prediction had been wrong when, a decade after the publication of *The Order of Things*, he mocked the "relentless theorization of writing, not as the dawning of the new age but as the death rattle of an old one."[5] Deleuze's claim is not that language is irrelevant but rather that the new epochal practices are emerging in the domains of labor and life. Again, whether Deleuze has correctly grasped the significance of these new practices remains to be seen; regardless, they are clearly important. It seems prudent to approach these terms heuristically, taking them singly and as a series of bonded base pairs – labor and life, life and language, language and labor – to see where they lead.

My research strategy focuses on the practices of life as the most potent present site of new knowledges and powers. One logical place to begin an examination of these changes is the American Human Genome Initiative (sponsored by the National Institutes of Health and the Department of Energy) whose mandate is to produce a map of our DNA. The Initiative is very much a technoscience project in two senses. Like most modern science, it is deeply imbricated with technological advances in the most literal way, in this case the confidence that qualitatively more rapid, accurate, and efficient machinery will be invented if the money is made available. The second sense of technological is the more important and interesting one: the object to be known – the human genome – will be known in such a way that it can be changed. This dimension is thoroughly modern, one could even say that it instantiates the definition of modern rationality. Representing and intervening, knowledge and power, understanding and reform, are built in, from the start, as simultaneous goals and means.

My ethnographic question is: How will our social and ethical practices change as this project advances? I intend to approach this question on a number of levels and in a variety of sites. First, there is the initiative itself. Second, there are adjacent enterprises and institutions in which and through which new understandings, new practices, and new technologies of life and labor will certainly be articulated: prime among them the biotechnology industry. Finally, the emergence of bioethics and environmental ethics lodged in a number of different institutions will bear scrutiny as potential reform loci.

The Human Genome Initiative

What is the Human Genome Initiative? A genome is "the entire complement of genetic material in the set of chromosomes of a particular organism."[6] DNA is composed of four bases, which bond into two kinds of pairs wound in the famous double helix. The current estimate is that we have about 3 billion base pairs in our DNA; the mouse has about the same number, while corn or salamanders have more than 30 times as many base pairs in their DNA as we do. No one knows why. Most of the DNA has no known function. It is currently held, not without a certain uneasiness, that 90 percent of human DNA is "junk." The renowned Cambridge molecular biologist Sydney Brenner makes a helpful distinction between "junk" and "garbage." Garbage is something used up and worthless, which one throws away; junk, though, is something one stores for some unspecified future use. It seems highly unlikely that 90 percent of our DNA is evolutionarily irrelevant, but what its precise relevance could be remains unknown.

Our genes, therefore, constitute the remaining 10 percent of the DNA. What are genes? They are segments of the DNA that code for proteins. Genes apparently vary in size from about 10,000 base pairs up to 2 million base pairs. Genes, or at any rate most human genes known today (1 percent of the presumed total), are not simply spatial units in the sense of a continuous sequence of base pairs; rather, they are regions of DNA made up of spans called *exons*, interspersed by regions called *introns*. When a gene is activated (and little is known about this process) the segment of DNA is transcribed to a type of RNA. The introns are spliced out, and the exons are joined together to form messenger RNA. This segment is then translated to code for a protein.

We don't know how many genes we have. It is estimated that *Homo sapiens* has between fifty and one hundred thousand genes – a rather large margin of error. We also don't know where most of these genes are; neither which chromosome they are found on nor where they are located on that chromosome. The initiative is designed to change all this: literally to map our genes. This poses two obvious questions: What is a map? And who is the "Our" in "our" genes?

For the first question, then: at present there are three different kinds of maps (linkage, physical, and sequence). Linkage maps are the most familiar to us from the Mendelian genetics we learned in high school. They are based on extensive studies of family genealogies (the Mormon historical archives provide the most complete historical documentation and the French have a similar project) and show how linked traits are inherited. Linkage maps show which genes are reinherited and roughly where they are on the chromosomes. This provides a helpful first step for identifying the probable location of disease genes in gross terms, but it is only a first step. In the hunt for the cystic fibrosis gene, for example, linkage maps narrowed down the area to be explored before other types of mapping completed the task.

There are several types of physical maps: "a physical map is a representation of the location of identifiable landmarks on the DNA." The discovery of restriction enzymes provided a major advance in mapping capabilities. These proteins serve to cut DNA into chunks at specific sites. The chunk of DNA can then be cloned and its makeup chemically analyzed and then reconstructed in its original order in the genome. These maps are physical in the literal sense that one has a chunk of DNA and one identifies the gene's location on it; these have been assembled into "libraries." The problem is to locate these physical chunks on a larger chromosomal map. Cloning techniques involving bacteria were used for a number of years but new techniques, such as in situ hybridization techniques, are replacing the more time-consuming cloning techniques.

Polymerase Chain Reaction reduces the need for cloning and physical libraries. It is necessary to clone segments of DNA in order to get enough identical copies to analyze but this multiplication can now be done more rapidly and efficiently by having the DNA do the work itself, as follows. First, one constructs a small piece of DNA, perhaps 20 base pairs long, called a *primer*, or oligonucleotide, which is then commercially made to specification. The raw material from which one takes the base pairs (to be assembled like Lego blocks) is either salmon sperm or the biomass left over from fermentation processes. A particularly rich source are the by-products of soy sauce (hence the Japanese have an edge in this market). This DNA is refined into single bases, or nucleosides, and recombined according to the desired specifications at a cost of about one dollar per coupling in a DNA synthesizer. The nucleosides could all be made synthetically, but it is currently cheaper given the small quantities needed – most primers are about 20 bases long – to stick to salmon sperm and soy sauce biomass. The current world production of DNA for a year is perhaps several grams but as demand grows there will be a growing market for the oligonucleotides, custom-made strips of DNA. As Gerald Zon, a biochemist at Applied Biosystems, Inc., put it, the company's dream is to be the world's supplier of synthetic DNA.[7]

Two primers are targeted to attach themselves to the DNA at specific sites called STSs or sequence-tagged sites. These primers then simply "instruct" the single strand of DNA to reproduce itself without having to be inserted into another organism; this is the polymerase chain reaction. So, instead of having physically to clone a gene, one can simply tell one's friends in Osaka or Omaha which primers to build and where to apply them, and they can do the job themselves (eventually including the DNA preparation, which will be automated). The major advantage of the PCR-STS technique is that it yields information that can be described as information in a data base: no access to the biological materials that led to the definition or mapping of an STS is required by a scientist wishing to assay a DNA sample for its presence. The computer would tell any laboratory where to look and which primer to construct, and within 24 hours one would have the bit of DNA one is interested in. These segments could then be sequenced by laboratories anywhere in the world and entered into a data base. Such developments have opened the door to what promises to be a common language for physical mapping of the human genome. Sequencing means actually identifying the series of base pairs on the physical map. There is ongoing controversy about whether it is necessary to have the complete sequence of the genome (after all, there are vast regions of junk whose role is currently unknown), the complete set of genes (what most genes do is unknown) or merely the sequence of "expressed" genes (i.e., those genes whose protein products are known). While there are formidable technological problems involved in all this, and formidable technological solutions appearing with the predicted rapidity, the principles and the goal are clear enough.

Still, even when the whole human genome is mapped and even when it is sequenced, we will know nothing about how it works. We will have a kind of structure without function. Much more work remains to be done, and currently is being done, on the hard scientific problems: protein structure, emergent levels of complexity, and the rest. Remember, the entire genetic makeup of human beings is found in most of our cells, but how a cell becomes and remains a brain cell instead of a toe cell is not known. What we will have a decade from now is the material sequence of the *fini-illimité*, a sequence map of 3 billion base pairs and between fifty and one hundred thousand genes.

As to the second question: Whose genome is it? Obviously not everyone has exactly the same genes or junk DNA for that matter, if we did we would presumably be identical (and probably extinct). There was some debate early on in the project as to exactly whose genome was being mapped; there was a half-serious proposal to have a very rich individual finance the analysis of his own genome. The problem is now shelved, literally in the clone libraries. The collective standard consists of different physical pieces mapped at centers around the world. Given the way genes are currently located on chromosomes, i.e., linkage maps, the easiest genome to map and sequence would necessarily be composed of the largest number of abnormal genes. In other words, the pathological would be the path to the norm.

Interestingly, all of the sequenced genes need not come from human beings. Genomes of other organisms are also being mapped. Several of these organisms, about which a great deal is already known, have been designated as model systems. Many genes work in the same way, regardless of in which living being they are found. Thus, in principle, wherever we find a specific protein we can know what DNA sequence produced it. This "genetic code" has not changed during evolution and therefore many genes of simpler organisms are basically the same as human genes. Since, for ethical reasons, many simpler organisms are easier to study, much of what we know about human genetics derives from model genetic systems like yeast and mice. Fruit flies have proved to be an extremely useful model system. Comparisons with even simpler organisms are useful in the identification of genes encoding proteins essential to life. The elaboration of protein sequences and their differences has led to new classifications and a new understanding of evolutionary relationships and processes. An Office of Technology Assessment report laconically asserts the utility of comparisons of human and mouse DNA sequences for the "identification of genes unique to higher organisms because mice genes are more homologous to human genes than are the genes of any other well characterized organism."[8] Hence, today, Rimbaud's premonition of future men "filled with animals" can be made to seem perfectly sound.

From Stigma to Risk: Normal Handicaps

My educated guess is that the new genetics will prove to be a greater force for reshaping society and life than was the revolution in physics, because it will be embedded throughout the social fabric at the microlevel by a variety of biopolitical practices and discourses. The new genetics will carry with it its own distinctive promises and dangers. Previous eugenics projects have been modern social projects cast in biological metaphors. Sociobiology, as Marshall Sahlins and so many others have shown, is a social project: from liberal philanthropic interventions designated to moralize and discipline the poor and degenerate; to *Rassenhygien* and its social extirpations; to entrepreneurial sociobiology – the construction of society has been at stake.[9]

In the future, the new genetics will cease to be a biological metaphor for modern society and will become instead a circulation network of identity terms and restriction loci, around which and through which a truly new type of autoproduction will emerge, which I call *biosociality*. If sociobiology is culture constructed on the basis of a metaphor of nature, then in biosociality, nature will be modeled on culture understood as practice. Nature will be known and remade through technique and will finally become artificial, just as culture becomes natural. Were such a project to be brought to fruition, it would stand as the basis for overcoming the nature/culture split.

A crucial step in overcoming of the nature/culture split will be the dissolution of the category of "the social." By "society" I don't mean some naturalized universal which is found everywhere and studied by sociologists and anthropologists simply because it is an object waiting to be described: rather, I mean something more specific. In *French Modern: Norms and Forms of the Social Environment*, I argue that if our definition is something like Raymond Williams's usage in the first edition of his book of modern commonplaces, *Keywords*, that is, the whole way of life of a people (open to empirical analysis and planned change), then society and the social sciences are the ground plan for modernity.[10]

We can see the beginnings of the dissolution of modernist society happening in recent transformations of the concept of risk. Robert Castel, in his 1981 book *La gestion des risques*, presents a grid of analysis whose insights extend far beyond his specific concerns with psychiatry, shedding particular light on current trends in the biosciences. Castel's book is an interrogation of postdisciplinary society, which he characterizes thus: first, a mutation of social technologies that minimizes direct therapeutic intervention, supplanted by an increasing emphasis on a preventive administrative management of populations at risk; and second, the promotion of working on oneself in a continuous fashion so as to produce an efficient and adaptable subject. These trends lead away from holistic approaches to the subject or social contextualism and move instead toward an instrumentalized approach to both environment and individual as a sum of diverse factors amenable to analysis by specialists. The most salient aspect of this trend for the present discussion is an increasing institutional gap between diagnostics and therapeutics. Although this gap is not a new one, to be sure, the potential for its widening nonetheless poses a new range of social, ethical, and cultural problems, which will become more prominent as biosociality progresses.

Modern prevention is above all the tracking down of risks. Risk is not a result of specific dangers posed by the immediate presence of a person or a group but rather the composition of impersonal "factors" which make a risk probable. Prevention, then, is surveillance not of the individual but of likely occurrences of diseases, anomalies, deviant behavior to be minimized, and healthy behavior to be maximized. We are partially moving away from the older face-to-face surveillance of individuals and groups known to be dangerous or ill (for disciplinary or therapeutic purposes), toward projecting risk factors that deconstruct and reconstruct the individual or group subject. This new mode anticipates possible loci of dangerous irruptions, through the identification of sites statistically locatable in relation to norms and means. Through the use of computers, individuals sharing certain traits or sets of traits can be grouped together in a way that not only decontextualizes them from their social environment but also is nonsubjective in a double sense: it is objectively arrived at and does not apply to a subject in anything like the older sense of the word (that is the suffering, meaningfully situated, integrator of social, historical, and bodily experiences). Castel names this trend "the technocratic administration of differences." The target is not a person but a population at risk. As an AIDS group in France put it: it is not who one is but what one does that puts you at risk. One's practices are not totalizing, although they may be mortal.

Although epidemiological social tracking methods were first implemented comprehensively in the tuberculosis campaign, they came to their contemporary maturity elsewhere. The distinction that Castel underscores as symptomatic of this change is that between disease and handicap.[11] A handicap, according to a French government report authored by the highly respected technocrat François Bloch-Lainé, is "any physical, mental or situational condition which produces a weakness or trouble in relation to what is considered normal; normal is defined as the mean of capacities and chances of most individuals in the same society."[12] The concept of handicap was first used officially in England during World War II as a means of evaluating the available workforce in a way that included as many people as possible. Handicaps were deficits to be compensated for socially, psychologically, and spatially, not illnesses to be treated: orthopedics not therapeutics. "The concept of handicap naturalizes the subject's history as well as assimilating expected performance levels at a particular historical moment to a naturalized normality."[13] True, this particular individual is blind or deaf or mute or short or tall or paralyzed, but can he or she operate the lathe, answer the telephone, guard the door? If not what can we do to him or her, to the work or to the environment, that would make this possible? Performance is a relative term. Practices make the person; or rather, they don't; they just make practitioners.

There is a large historical step indeed from the rich web of social and personal significations Western culture inscribed in tuberculosis to the inclusive grid of the welfare state, which has yet to inspire much poetry or yield a celebrated *Bildungs-roman*. It has, however, increased life expectancy and produced millions of documents, many of them inscribed in silicon. The objectivism of social factors is now giving way to a new genetics and the beginnings of a redefinition and eventual operationalization of nature.

In a chapter entitled "What Is (Going) To Be Done?" in his book *Proceed with Caution: Predicting Genetic Risks in the Recombinant DNA Era*, Neil A. Holtz-man documents the ways that genetic screening will be used in the coming years when its scope and sensitivity is increased dramatically by such technological advances as Polymerase Chain Reaction which will reduce cost, time, and resist-ance. There are already tests for such conditions as sickle-cell anemia, and diag-nostics for cystic fibrosis and Alzheimer's are on the horizon. These diseases are among the estimated four thousand single-gene disorders. There is a much larger number of diseases, disorders, and discomforts that are polygenetic. Genetic testing will soon be moving into areas in which pre-symptomatic testing will be at a premium. Thus, Holtzman suggests that once a test is available for identifying a "susceptibility-conferring genotype" for breast cancer, earlier and more fre-quent mammograms would be recommended or even required (for insurance purposes). He adds, "monitoring those with genetic predispositions to insulin-dependent diabetes mellitus, colorectal cancer, neurofibromatosis, retinoblas-toma, or Wilms tumor for the purpose of detecting early manifestations of the disease might prove beneficial. Discovering those with genetic predispositions could be accomplished either by population-wide screening or, less completely, by testing families in which disease has already occurred."[14] This remark involves a large number of issues, but the only one I will underline here is the likely formation of new group and individual identities and practices arising out of these new truths. There already are, for example, neurofibromatosis groups who meet to share their experiences, lobby for their disease, educate their children, redo their home environment, and so on. That is what I mean by biosociality. I am not discussing some hypothetical gene for aggression or altruism. Rather it is not hard to imagine groups formed around the chromosome 17, locus 16,256, site 654,376 allele variant with a guanine substitution. Such groups will have medical specialists, laboratories, narratives, traditions, and a heavy panoply of pastoral keepers to help them experience, share, intervene, and "understand" their fate.

Fate it will be. It will carry with it no depth. It makes absolutely no sense to seek the meaning of the lack of a guanine base because it has no meaning. One's relation to one's father or mother is not shrouded in the depths of discourse here, the relationship is material even when it is environmental: Did your father smoke?

Did your mother take DES? Rest assured they didn't know what they were doing. It follows that other forms of pastoral care will become more prominent in order to overcome the handicap and to prepare for the risks. These therapies for the normal will be diverse, ranging from behavior modifications, to stress management, to interactional therapies of all sorts.[15] We might even see a return of tragedy in postmodernist form, although we will likely not simply rail against the gods, but rather be driven to overcome our fates through more technoscience.

Labor and Life

The emergence of modern food, that is, food industrially processed to emphasize uniformity and commoditized as part of an internationalization of world agriculture and distribution, can be dated to the 1870–1914 period. Industrial sugar refining and flour milling for the production of white bread was one of the first examples of a constructed consumer need linked to advertising, transportation expansion, a host of processing and preservation techniques, as well as incidentally the rise of modernism in architecture (for example, Buffalo's silos and Minneapolis' grain elevators, as Reyner Banham has shown in his *Concrete Atlantis*).[16] With these changes agricultural products were on their way to becoming merely an input factor in the production of food, and food was on its way to becoming a "heterogeneous commodity endowed with distinctive properties imparted by processing techniques, product differentiation, and merchandising."[17] These processes accelerated during World War I, which here, as in so many other domains, provided the laboratory conditions for inventing, testing, and improving food products on a truly mass scale. Millions of people became accustomed to transformed natural products like evaporated milk as well as new foods like margarine, in which an industrially transformed product substituted for a processed "rural" product, vegetable fats instead of butter. Using methods developed in the textile industry, it was now possible not only to produce foods at industrial levels not constrained by the "natural rhythms" or inherent biological qualities (even if people had bred for these), but even to get people to buy and eat them.

The cultural reaction against foods classified as "artificial" or "processed" was spearheaded in the years between the wars by a variety of lifestyle reformist groups, satirized by George Orwell. Ecological and environmental campaigns, conducted on a national scale by the Nazis with their characteristic vigor, agitated for a return to natural foods (especially whole grain bread), the outlaw of vivisection, the ban of smoking in public places, and the exploration of the effects of environmental toxins on the human genetic material and so on. Hitler, after all, did not smoke or drink and was a vegetarian.[18] As we have seen in recent decades, not only have the demand for wholesome foods and the obsession with health and environmentalism not meant a return to "traditional" products and processes (although the image of tradition is successfully marketed), few would advocate a return to the real thing with its infected water supplies, low yield, and the like, but it has even accelerated, and will continue to accelerate, the improvement, the enculturization of nature drawing on tradition as a resource to be selectively improved.

Once nature began to be systematically modified to meet industrial and consumer norms – a development perhaps embodied best by the perfect tomato, the right shape, color, size, bred not to break or rot on the way to market, missing only the distinctive taste that dismayed some and pleased others – it could be redescribed and remade to suit other biopolitical specifications, like "nutrition." The value of food is now cast not only in terms of how much it imitates whole natural food in freshness and look but in terms of the health value of its component constitutents – vitamins, cholesterol, fiber, salt, and so on. For the first time we have a market in which processed, balanced foods, whose ingredients are chosen in accordance with nutritional or health criteria, can be presented as an alternative superior to nature. Cows are being bred for lower cholesterol, canola for an oil with unsaturated fats.

Bernardo Sorj and his coauthors, in their *From Farming to Biotechnology,* claim once the basic biological requirements of subsistence are met, the natural content of food paradoxically becomes an obstacle to consumption. Once this cultural redefinition and industrial organization are accepted, then nature, whether as land, space, or biological reproduction, no longer poses a binding constraint to the capitalist transformation of the production process and the social division of labor because the "the rural labor process is now not so much machine-paced as governed by the capacity of industrial capitals to modify the more fundamental rhythms of biological time."[19] This process leads to increased control over all aspects of the food production process and efforts to make it an industry like any other. New biotechnological techniques working toward the industrial control of plant biology increase the direct manipulation of the nutritional and functional properties of crops, accelerating the trends toward rationalization and the vertical integration of production and marketing required for efficiency. Biotechnological advances like nitrogen fixing or the herbicide resistance of newly engineered plant (and eventually animal) species diminish the importance of land quality and the physico-chemical environment as determinants of yields and productivity.

Calgene, a leading California agro-biotech company based in Davis, is proud of its genetically engineered PGI Tomato seeds whose fruit, their 1989 annual report boasted, is superior to a nonengineered control group. Calgene's engineering is no ordinary engineering though, even by biotech standards; their tomatoes employ an "antisense" technique considered to be one of the cutting-edge achievements in the pharmaceutical and therapeutic fields. Antisense involves disrupting the genetic message of a gene by interfering with either the synthesis of messenger RNA or its expression, that is before its instructions to make a protein are carried out. While the concept is simple, developing techniques refined and specific enough to achieve the desired results is not. Field trials, according to the annual report, "verified the ability of Calgene's antisense (AS-1) gene to reduce fruit rotting while increasing total solid content, viscosity and consistency." The gene significantly reduces the expression of an enzyme that causes the breakdown of pectin in fruit cell walls and thereby decreases the shelf life. "This new technology provides a natural alternative to artificial processing, which means that the tomatoes delivered to consumers in the future promise to be closer to homegrown in firmness, color and taste."[20] It looks good, it travels well, and it may soon taste like what those who have still eaten traditional tomatoes think they should taste like.

Traditional tastes pose a challenge, not a threat to technoscience; the more one specifies what is missing from the new product the more the civilizing process proceeds. Tomatoes aren't what they used to be? But you don't like bugs either? Let's see what can be done. A company in Menlo Park is perfecting a bioengineered vanillin, one of the most complex of smells and tastes. Scientists are approaching museums armed with the PCR technique, which enables them to take a small piece of DNA and amplify it millions of times. This recovered DNA could then, at least in principle, be reintroduced into contemporary products. If eighteenth-century tomatoes are your fancy, there is no reason a priori why one day a boutique biotech company aiming at the Berkeley or Cambridge market couldn't produce one that is consistently pesticide resistant, transportable, and delicious for you – and those just like you. In sum, the new knowledges have already begun to modify labor practices and life processes in what Enlightenment botanists called nature's second kingdom.[21]

A Challenge

François Dagognet, a prolific French philosopher of the sciences, identifies a residual naturalism as the main obstacle to the full exploration and exploitation of life's potentials. He traces the roots of "naturalism" to the Greeks who held that the artisan or artist imitates that which is – nature. Although man works on nature, he doesn't change it ontologically because human productions never contain an internal principle of generation. From the Greeks to the present, a variety of naturalisms have held to the following axioms: (1) the artificial is never as good as the natural; (2) generation furnishes the proof of life (life is autoproduction); (3) homeostasis (autoregulation) is the golden rule.[22] Contemporary normative judgments continue to affirm the insecurity of human works, the risks linked to artificiality, and the certitude that the initial situation – the Golden Pond or the Sierras – was always incomparably better.

Dagognet argues that nature has not been natural, in the sense of being pure and untouched by human works, for millennia. More provocatively, he asserts that nature's malleability offers an "invitation" to the artificial. Nature is a blind *bricoleur*, an elementary logic of combinations, yielding an infinity of potential differences. These differences are not prefigured by final causes and there is no latent perfection seeking homeostasis. If the word "nature" is to retain a meaning, it must signify an uninhibited polyphenomenality of display. Once understood in this way, the only natural thing for man to do would be to facilitate, encourage, accelerate its unfurling: thematic variation, not rigor mortis. Dagognet challenges us in a consummately modern fashion: "either we go toward a sort of veneration before the immensity of 'that which is' or one accepts the possibility of manipulation." As with nature, so too, it seems, with culture?

Notes

1 Michel Foucault, *The History of Sexuality, Vol. I: An Introduction* (New York: Pantheon Books, 1978), p. 139. Special thanks to Vincent Sarich, Jenny Gumperz, Frank Rothchild, Guy Micco, Hubert Dreyfus, Thomas White.
2 Gilles Deleuze, *Foucault* (Paris: Editions de Minuit, 1986), p. 140.
3 François Jacob, *The Possible and the Actual* (New York: Pantheon Books, 1982), p. 39.
4 Deleuze, *Foucault, "L'homme de l'avenir est chargé des animaux,"* p. 141.
5 Michel Foucault, "Truth and Power," p. 127.
6 *Mapping Our Genes, Genome Projects: How Big, How Fast?* (Washington, DC: Office of Technology Assessment, 1988), p. 21.
7 Interview with the author, March 19, 1990.
8 *Mapping*, p. 68.
9 Marshall Sahlins, *The Use and Abuse of Biology: An Anthropological Critique of Sociobiology* (Ann Arbor: University of Michigan Press, 1976). Robert N. Proctor, *Racial Hygiene, Medicine Under the Nazis* (Cambridge, MA: Harvard University Press, 1988). Daniel J. Kevles, *In the Name of Eugenics, Genetics and the Uses of Human Heredity* (Berkeley: University of California Press, 1985). Benno Muller-Hill, *Murderous Science: Elimination by Scientific Selection of Jews, Gypsies, and Others, Germany 1933–45* (Oxford: Oxford University Press, 1988).
10 Paul Rabinow, *French Modern: Norms and Forms of the Social Environment* (Chicago: University of Chicago Press, 1995 [orig. 1989]).
11 Robert Castel, *La gestion des risques, de l'anti-psychiatrie à l'après-psychanalyse* (Paris: Editions de Minuit, 1981).
12 François Bloch-Lainé, *Etude du problème général de l'inadaptation des personnes handicapées* (Documentation française, 1969), p. 111, cited in Castel, *La gestion*, p. 117.
13 Ibid., p. 122.
14 Neil A. Holtzman, *Proceed with Caution: Predicting Genetic Risks in the Recombinant DNA Era* (Baltimore and London: Johns Hopkins University Press, 1989), pp. 235–236.
15 Robert Castel, *Advanced Psychiatric Society* (Berkeley: University of California Press, 1986).

16 Reyner Banham, *A Concrete Atlantis: U.S. Industrial Building and European Modern Architecture 1900–1925* (Cambridge, MA: MIT Press, 1986).

17 David Goodman, Bernardo Sorj, and John Wilkinson, *From Farming to Biotechnology: A Theory of Agro-Industrial Development* (Oxford: Blackwell, 1987), p. 60.

18 Proctor, *Racial Hygiene*, ch. 8, "The 'Organic Vision' of Nazi Racial Science."

19 *From Farming to Biotechnology*, p. 47.

20 *Planning for the Future* (Calgene 1989 Annual Report), p. 14.

21 François Delaporte, *Nature's Second Kingdom* (Cambridge, MA: MIT Press, 1982 [orig. 1979]).

22 François Dagognet, *La maitrise du vivant* (Paris: Hachette, 1988), p. 41.

8

Flexible Eugenics:

Technologies of the Self in the Age of Genetics

Karen-Sue Taussig, Rayna Rapp, and Deborah Heath

In other words, our essence is ours to choose, depending on how we direct our selves with all our baggage, DNA included.

David Barash, *"DNA and Destiny,"* 1998

In 1994, John Wasmuth and his laboratory colleagues published an account of the discovery of FGFR3, the gene for achondroplasia – the most common form of heritable dwarfism – in the journal *Cell* (Shiang et al. 1994). Hailed soon after in the *Scientist* as the article most frequently cited during 1995, Wasmuth's publication revealed that 98 percent of those affected with achondroplasia have an identical mutation in the molecule FGFR3, a receptor for what is called a growth factor.[1] Among other things, the discovery opened the possibility for prenatal screening for this condition. During the many years of work that led to the publication of Wasmuth's article, molecules, scientists, and technicians were drawn into engagements not only with one another but also with patients, physicians, and genetic counselors. Genetic knowledge emerged, in this case as in others, as a coproduction of clinical diagnosis and treatment regimes as well as the molecular technologies and other research practices that constitute laboratory life. Patient populations contributed to laboratory and clinical knowledge through their tissue samples in countless experimental and diagnostic contexts, and through what the historian M. Susan Lindee (2003) describes as the emotional knowledge that families living with genetically different members accumulate.

The long-term work on dwarfism and related skeletal dysplasias depended on the collection of research samples from individuals from all over the

Reprinted from Karen-Sue Taussig, Rayna Rapp, and Deborah Heath, "Flexible Eugenics: Technologies of the Self in the Age of Genetics," in Alan H. Goodman, Deborah Heath, and M. Susan Lindee (eds.), *Genetic Nature/Culture: Anthropology and Science beyond the Two-Culture Divide*. Berkeley: University of California Press, 2003, pp. 58–76.

world affected by these conditions. The samples were held in a tissue registry established to bank research materials. This story, too, had its fair share of competition and collaboration, not only in the search for a "dwarfism gene" but also in the quest for the gene for Huntington's disease,[2] on which Wasmuth had previously worked, and which, as it turned out, lies on the same chromosome as FGFR3. Indeed, the successful search for the Huntington's gene figures prominently in the mobilization of scientific and popular support for initiating the Human Genome Project, but that is another story. The multilayered discovery processes we recount here are instances of science-as-usual at the beginning of the twenty-first century.

One year after Wasmuth published his article, Clair Francomano, chief of medical genetics at the National Human Genome Research Institute at the National Institutes of Health, attended the national convention of the Little People of America (LPA), the US national organization for people of short stature. Dr. Francomano is a long-standing researcher and health service provider for people with heritable dwarfism and a member of the LPA Medical Advisory Board. As she tells her story, "The first thing I saw when I came to this convention last year [after the discovery of the gene was publicized] was one of the people wearing that 'Endangered Species' T-shirt.[3] It really made a very big impact on me. And I really worry about it. I worry about what we're doing and about how it's going to be used and what it means to the people here" (Francomano 1997, personal communication).

Dr. Francomano's response was to chair several workshops for LPA members on the Human Genome Project. There, she explained genetic technologies and programs, listening attentively to the fears and hopes of short-statured people. She also expressed her own aspirations concerning the possibilities opened up by genetic research, and her dismay that new discoveries might be eugenically deployed. Her aspirations centered on gene therapy for specific ailments – such as ear and breathing problems, back pain, and skeletal problems – associated with dwarfism. In addition, Dr. Francomano collaborated in designing a membership-wide survey for the LPA on attitudes toward prenatal testing. Like Dr. Francomano and the officers of the LPA, we also want to know what Little People – a term widely used among people with dwarfing conditions to refer to themselves – in all their biomedical and political diversity want and do not want from this emergent genetic technology. We consider such desires to be part of science-as-usual in this history of the rapidly transforming present.

In this essay, we examine forms of embodiment and subjectivity emerging from relations between biomedical experts and lay health advocates in an era when genetic explanations, and desires for genetic improvement, appear to be proliferating throughout US public culture. We address both biomedical technologies, like limb-lengthening surgery and prenatal diagnosis, and social technologies, like the organization of self-help groups such as the Little People of America. Our analysis of genetic and eugenic thinking in action underscores what Foucault (1988) calls "technologies of the self," the practices by which subjects constitute themselves, and work to improve themselves, while living within institutional frameworks of power. The expansive salience of genetic narratives and practices across a broad range of social groups in the United States today shapes embodied understandings of selfhood in historically specific ways. Those living with heritable dwarfism, and the researchers associated with them, are no less subject to these social and historical processes than the general population is: increasingly, we all live inside a world saturated by genetic discourses. Yet the consequences of dwelling inside these geneticized perspectives and practices are highly differentiated.

Born with bodies that historically have been stigmatized, dwarfs were among the first people in the United States to form an organization of social solidarity based on phenotypical difference.[4] The LPA, founded in 1957, became one of the first US health advocacy groups to cooperate with biomedical and, especially, genetic researchers. This biosocial coalition between those born with a stigmatized difference and researchers and medical service providers was at once a site of productive resistance to widespread social prejudice and a domain of normalization. More recently Paul Rabinow (1996) has used the term *biosociality* to describe the conscription into a new identity politics as people come to align themselves in terms of genetic narratives and practices. This is something that Little People (LPs) began experimenting with as a social form decades before recombinant technology called into play new social forms.

By elaborating the diverse strategies through which dwarfs deploy technologies of the self, or an "ethics of self-care," we are able to illustrate the types of agency by which individuals "can resist the normalizing effects of modern power" (Bevir 1999: 78). In the contemporary United States, LPA members act within a society marked by a long-standing attachment to ideologies of individualism and free choice, which are increasingly imbricated with the intensified commodification and market orientation of the recent neoliberal era. LPs, along with the rest of us, are obliged to be free and are presented with an array of technically mediated choices and with varied discourses of perfectibility: we all live within dominant ideologies of power (Althusser 1971) – in this case, the idea of both choosing and perfecting oneself.[5] There is a convergence, or constitutive tension, between genetic normalization and an individualism that increasingly engages biotechnology – *biotechnological individualism*. From this tension, what we call *flexible eugenics* arises: long-standing biases against atypical bodies meet both the perils and the possibilities that spring from genetic technologies.

We have learned about the genetics of dwarfing conditions and the advocacy of the LPA through our collaborative ethnographic project on new knowledge production in the field of genetics.[6] In order to understand how scientists, clinician-physicians, and members of lay health organizations perform their daily work, we constituted ourselves as a mobile research team. In addition to ourselves, we worked with three graduate research assistants – Erin Koch, Barbara Ley, and Michael Montoya. During the project, we lived on two coasts and were attached to five institutions; much of our communication took place over the Internet, a common enough situation among the genetic knowledge producers we were tracking, but an uncommon way for cultural anthropologists to conduct research. Our traveling methodology followed genetic stakeholders in and out of their various milieus, from national meetings of health advocacy groups to basic research laboratories, and from interviews with clinicians to encounters with families living with heritable conditions like achondroplasia. Like Dr. Franco-mano and the members of the LPA, our team is concerned about the ways in which molecular discoveries may reinforce eugenic thinking and practices. And like many members of the constituencies among whom we conducted fieldwork, we also recognize the complex interplay that makes it difficult to distinguish the gifts from the iatrogenic poisons of contemporary medical genetics.

A discourse of benefits and burdens, perils and possibilities, and danger and opportunity now surrounds contemporary discussions of genetic technologies and their presumed power to rock the foundations of nature (Paul 1995; Strathern 1992). The attribution of social upheaval to scientific advancement is, of course, not new: interwoven fears and hopes have long been attached to biomedical attempts to "play God" with nature, as the history of nineteenth-century surgery or twentieth-century reproductive medicine bears out. Here and throughout our collective work, we hope to tease out imbrications of the old and the new, the innovations and constraints through which public enthusiasm and dis-ease regularly collide. On this unstable terrain, other powerful cultural discourses surrounding notions of the mastery and perfectibility of nature – including human nature, biology, and molecular genetics – intersect one another with complex and often contradictory effects.

While eugenic thinking has a long and tenacious history in Western societies, we want to be attentive to the specificities of the present moment. Under the shadow of the Human Genome Project and the rise of the biotechnology indus-tries, a heterogeneous array of actors has been drawn into a worldview in which human diversity is increasingly ascribed to genetic causality.[7] In many ways, this perspective builds on older versions of biological reductionism in which barely concealed, barely secularized Protestant notions of predestination identified a social elite by its alleged physical, mental, and social superiority. At the same time that contemporary medical geneticists powerfully distance themselves from prior notions of biological superiority and inferiority, they relocate the interven-tion of authority and explanations of the body to the molecular level. We have all benefited from previous forms of scientific reductionism and medicalization, as well as suffered their social consequences selectively.

Yet in the popular imagination, as Abby Lippman (1991) points out, the con-nection between the perceived heritability of complex social traits like intelligence or criminality and the assumed explanation at the level of individually carried DNA underlies powerful beliefs in both genetic determinism and the importance of new biotechnologies of genetic improvement. Thus we see the persistence of eugenic thinking in the United States today, where many people across a broad spectrum of social groups consider the genome to be the site at which the human future must or can be negotiated. For us, this expanding genetic worldview among all constituencies, including research scientists, clinicians, lay support groups, and more general populations, is constituted dialectically: on the one hand, an ever-increasing number of actors and practices are conscripted into a world defined genetically, in which reductive determinism looms large. On the other hand, democratic possibilities open up as genetic discourses and practices come to occupy multiple locations and to conscript a wider range of actors. Some of those actors may use their new and multiple locations to contest a too-easy determinism or to develop interventions – molecular and otherwise – that they consider choice-enhancing. They may well be viewed as a vanguard in the politics of biosociality, a vanguard from which the rest of us have much to learn. Those who have a consequential stake in this story have taught us to appreciate and track this dialectic in practice, as illustrated in the following narratives drawn from our observations at the LPA national conventions in 1997, 1998, and 1999.

Agency, Normalization, and Contested Identities

The LPA offers not only a site for biomedical research but also a self-affirming social environment. Most members bear a diagnosis of one of the many heritable dwarfing conditions, and the organization brings them together in a well-elaborated example of biosociality. Genetic enrollment includes conscription into a new identity politics as people come to align themselves with categories increasingly refashioned through emergent genetic discourses and practices. In our era, contemporary social life is rapidly being rescripted in terms of genetic narratives and practices (Taussig et al. 1999). But some aspects of biosociality build on forms of medicalization that predate molecular genetics, providing other embodied foundations for individual recruitment to group identity.[8] Indeed, although the LPA initially was founded as a support organization for all people of short stature, and its membership requirement is based on height rather than medical diagnosis, the LPA has long been interpolated into the milieu of medical genetics. At the same time, not all those born with heritable dwarfism accept the body politics that have emerged from the LPA's hard-fought advocacy.

One site at which we witness the tensions embedded in contemporary genetic and eugenic thinking in action is the meetings of the medical advisory boards that virtually all lay health groups organize. These advisory groups help members communicate with researchers and biomedical service providers who are experts in their particular (and often rare) conditions. For example, the Medical Advisory Board of the LPA comprises both members of the organization and medical professionals who serve at the invitation of its officers. Since its inception in 1957, the LPA has maintained a strong grassroots orientation. While there is a tradition of cooperative medical research conducted within the LPA membership, the organization's leadership has asserted conscious control over researchers' permissions and protocols. Engagements between medical professionals and membership are carefully negotiated, as is the membership's access to the results of that research. When we interviewed one senior LPA member, for example, he stressed that the organization insists that researchers cooperate with each other, sharing blood and tissue samples that are already banked, avoiding oversampling. He told us a joke about LPA members who have become polka-dotted from the numerous skin biopsies they have provided to researchers over the years. Specific medical interventions are sharply debated and contested in ongoing and negotiated relations.

During our most recent visit to the Medical Advisory Board, a longtime physician member of the board reported on his recent trip to Spain. There, he had visited a surgeon who has been doing limb-lengthening surgeries on dwarfs for 20 years, a procedure that many dwarfs find controversial. The physician presented a video of a young American woman who had gained 12 inches in height through multiple surgeries. The ten-minute video documents a testimonial speech she gave at a fund-raiser for a genetics medical center. The opening image – a life-size blowup of the young woman before the surgeries, standing at 3 feet 10 inches – is followed by her dramatic appearance onstage on crutches (a result of her last operation). She gives a polished and thoughtful speech about how limb lengthening was not merely cosmetic. It gave her not only 12 inches in height but also the experience of being wheelchair-bound for two years, providing enforced tolerance for a range of disabilities. The woman tells her audience, "It's a better life and I'm happier. I'm more independent and confident. Many inner changes took place. I learned that the change was everything I ever wanted." She was 15 when she reached her decision to have the surgery. Hers is a narrative of challenge, perfectibility, and growth. Reactions on the Medical Advisory Board immediately challenged the young woman's narrative.

During the video screening, the room buzzed with sotto voce comments; as the video ended, the room fell silent. The first to speak was a doctor who raised issues about insurance coverage and the competence of certain surgeons to perform such a complicated task. The first LP to speak asked, "Did she have any involvement with the LPA?" to which the presenting doctor answered, "Yes." The LP continued, "I find it surprising, when you can come here and see at least five hundred successful adults; most would say – if asked the question 'Would you change it' – they'd say 'No.' Here in America, accessibility is a minor issue [that is, for LPs in the United States when compared to Spain]. I like to keep an open mind, but I think it's easier to adapt the environment than to adapt the person." Doctors and LPs rapidly entered the fray. One of each deemed the video's life-size blowup offensive. As the physician put it, "The video itself presents a cardboard cutout of an LP as undesirable and unattractive, in contrast to the whole person who is a foot taller than before."

Dissent broke out among the physicians, including practicing orthopedic surgeons who do not perform limb lengthening. One said, "I have devoted my life to treating the medical symptoms [of dwarfism], and I could never bring myself to lengthen limbs, because I find it abhorrent. I cannot stretch them out for social acceptance. It's more abhorrent to me than prenatal diagnosis." His denunciation highlights the perceived continuities between orthopedic and genetic interventions in the presumed foundational and moral rectitude of "nature" and "natural" variation. It also highlights diverse responses among researchers and clinicians, many of whom express complex critiques anchored in worldviews ranging from religion to political economy and civil rights.

The presenting doctor replied that in a society which promotes breast enlargement, rhinoplasty, and liposuction, dwarfs, too, deserve their right to aesthetic free choice in the medical marketplace. Yet even as he defended the practice, he also stressed that the operation should not be done before adolescence, when the patient and not the parents (who are most often of average stature) can consent to the procedure. Furthermore, he thought most people should not have the operation. He pointed out that, over the past decade, he and his colleagues had performed only 13 surgeries. One of the elders of the LPA responded, "This is good information to have, and ... it would be good to make it widely available, because it counters the widespread impression that the clinicians carrying out limb lengthening had created a surgical 'production line.' " Another LP, who works in a clinical setting, offered a final word:

> It's an attitude thing. I look at this as an enhancement, not a correction. But I don't need a correction. I'm OK. Most LPs, especially in this organization, look upon this as, you're telling me something's wrong. I'll make that choice. But I worry about calls from [average-statured] parents with new [dwarf] babies. I get phone calls every day from parents who aren't worried by [serious medical conditions associated with dwarfism, e.g.,] decompression, sleep apnea, with two-week-, four-week-, two-month-old kids, but they want to know about limb lengthening.[9] We'll all benefit from bringing this information out in the open.

Despite their different subject positions, the LPA officers and the physicians all inhabit a world in which the benefits of individual access to information and tropes of free marketplace choice predominate. A controversial surgical orthopedic intervention into body morphology shows how both its supporters and detractors invoke free choice in presenting their views on variations of biotechnological individualism. Indeed, the LPs, the members of the Medical Advisory Board, and we ourselves are no less citizens of what the legal historian Lawrence Friedman (1990) has so usefully labeled the "republic of choice." Limb lengthening proposes to change the individual's recognizable phenotype without intervention into the underlying genotype, a kind of aesthetic and highly technical mastery of normalization. Those who choose the surgery, demonstrating the agency of choice in the biomedical marketplace, elude the judgment of prescriptive "natural" dwarfism inherent negatively in the form of social prejudice and positively in the biosociality of the LPA. Notions of mastery and perfectibility extend well beyond the contemporary United States, of course. But they have been given an upgrade and brought into the realm of science and technology within the rubric loosely identified as modernity, in which individual embodied choices reveal an attachment to the pursuit of progress and perfectibility (Berman 1982). What C. B. Macpherson classically labeled "possessive individualism" (1962) is here linked to identities, the realm of the body, and indeed, genetics.

What we are describing here as flexible eugenics thus involves technologies of the self through choosing and improving one's biological assets.[10] The desire to choose one's self in terms of technological interventions into the individual body incorporates both old and new aspects, from the distant promise of gene therapy to low-tech or routinized technologies such as cosmetic surgery.[11] Such instances signal a shift, one that Emily Martin, inspired by Michel Foucault, identifies as a move away from the powerful external interventions that produced the "docile bodies" so essential to the success of an earlier era of capitalism. Now, with postwar neoliberalism and its expanding emphasis on commodification and marketability, we see the emergence of "flexible bodies" (Martin 1994) obliged to be free, constrained by the tyranny of choice. In this marketplace of biomedical free choice, technology and technique become objects of desire invested with diverse meanings that surely vary for producers and consumers, for research scientists, clinicians, and individual patients, all of whom may imagine their relationship to choice and perfectibility quite differently.[12]

With advances in molecular biology, through which genes are becoming alienable and the modification of specific genes and bodies imagined more and more as an individual choice, biotechnological interventions in the service of individual perfectibility become the objects of desire. Deploying both social and biomedical "technologies of the self" enables people to modify, and imagine modifying, what is seen as natural, while our collective and individual stakes in what counts as natural are continuously renegotiated (Franklin 1997; Ragoné 1994; Strathern 1992). That is, in a world increasingly marked by flexible eugenics, self-realization can become attached to genetic characteristics, increasingly understood as susceptible to improvement and choice. Thus, long-standing discourses on individualism and choice are now filtered through newer interventions that include the molecular or genetic, as well as older and constantly escalating ones provided by pharmacology and surgery, all in the service of sculpting flexible bodies. It is this flexibility of the individual body as an object of biotechnological choice and desire that then intersects innovations in eugenic thought and practice.

Love, Death, and Biotechnical Reproduction

How might the discourses of biotechnological individualism observed in action at the LPA highlight some social values while obscuring others? This question is richly woven through myriad discussions of love, marriage, family formation, and children, objects of desire prominent in many of the LPA workshops and informal conversations in which we participated. These, of course, involve relations across the generations and are therefore not only aesthetic but also eugenic in the classic sense of the term. For example, discussions concerning aspirations for and cele-brations of dwarf children were common throughout the LPA. We also noted a particular emphasis on the value of dwarfs having babies. Thus an affirmation of the value of dwarf children struck us as a sign of resistant biosociality: although dwarfs conventionally have been despised and labeled as imperfect, kinship with and by dwarfs across the generations here has been given an elevated significance, an affirmation of diffuse and enduring identity in the face of the widespread discrimination LPs often face in the larger world.

In a workshop for new parents that was packed with family members of both average and short stature, for example, all participants introduced themselves by saying where they were from and what type of dwarfing condition their child had. Many new parents of average stature were seeking support as they dealt with the shock of having a dwarf child. Other average- and short-statured parents were there to lend such support. An achondroplastic dwarf introduced himself and his wife as expecting a child and said, "And we hope it's a dwarf!" The audience responded to this comment with loud applause.

Two of us attended a workshop on women's health chaired by two female high-risk obstetrician-geneticists. In an audience of 20 short-statured women and two average-statured anthropologists, the first comment offered came from Kather-ine,[13] who shot her hand up, saying, "I'll start. I'm four months pregnant...." She was interrupted instantly with enthusiastic applause and murmurs of delight from everyone, including the two physicians in the room. Then Katherine asked about her childbirth options, and a long discussion, framed in extremely positive and supportive tones, ensued about the logistics of childbirth for women of short stature. Doctors and audience were united in viewing pregnancy and childbirth as highly desirable, both looking to biomedical technology to offer progress in obtaining safer and less complicated reproductive outcomes.

Katherine, like many pregnant American women, was concerned about how soon she would be able to hold her newborn child. Her physician had told her that because of prior adhesions in her lumbar area (a common problem associated with dwarfism), her only option for childbirth was a cesarean section under general anesthesia. Women with dwarfing conditions virtually always have cesar-ean sections, because the shape of the pelvis does not allow for passage of a baby's head. In the United States, cesarean sections typically are done with a spinal block rather than general anesthesia. One of the physicians explained that a spinal block was complicated in cases of people with spinal differences: it "is a really controversial issue.... Anesthesiologists are really afraid of...[spinal] abnormal-ities, and with good reason. It's really uncharted territory.... If your anesthesiol-ogist is most comfortable doing general [anesthesia],...then you're going to have a good outcome; and putting a needle in your back is risky after adhesions, so I wouldn't take the risk." Katherine then asked, "What about the short stature makes it dangerous?" The response from one of the doctors highlights the fact that what are often considered routine medical procedures may be linked to conceptions of standardized bodies. She explained:

When they're doing regional anesthetic, whether it's spinal or epidural, what they need to get is either a catheter or a needle into that little space – and what is the space like, is there a space? Sometimes in LPs there is no space.... They [the doctors] have to have landmarks. They're doing this blindly.... If they push on your back ... they're looking for landmarks and they're saying, "There's a landmark." ... If you have an alteration in your landmark, they have nowhere to start.

The conversation continued, with the physicians focusing on childbirth protocols for women of short stature, members of the audience chiming in with their own experiences, and Katherine trying to figure out how she could ensure that she would hold her child as quickly as possible after delivery.

The encounter between physicians and women with dwarfing conditions underscores three salient points. First, at this meeting the issue was not whether LP women should have children, but the physical logistics of pregnancy and delivery. We imagine that this discussion is a new one: it is unlikely that 20 years ago there even existed high-risk obstetrician-geneticists who would universally support LP women having pregnancies, and dwarfs' aspirations to reproduce were more highly stigmatized. Second, the concern about obstetrics brings to light the challenges of applying standardized medical techniques to people with nonstandard bodies. The familiar waltz between the normal and the pathological reveals the hidden costs of standardization (Canguilhem 1989; Starr 1991). Finally, the encounter illustrates that the different subject positions of the participants shape their concerns about reproduction. The physicians are caught up in the practical matters of applying standardized medicine to people with spinal differences: their agency is best expressed through continuous enhancement of the expertise that will make pregnancies safer.[14] But Katherine, whose questions about anesthesia prompted the discussion of obstetric procedures, is caught up in issues of love and kinship. She wants to know about medical feasibility because she is concerned with maternal–infant bonding after surgery.

The complications of pregnancy and delivery, made even more difficult by the physical challenges of certain forms of dwarfism, may prove too daunting for some short-statured women. Such concerns may be part of the reason there is an active adoption network coordinated by the LPA. The national LPA newsletter, *LPA Today*, says, "The purpose of this service is to find a loving home for every dwarf child.... By outreaching to adoption agencies, doctors, hospitals and geneticists and others, we are able to locate available dwarf children for adoptions, and perspective [*sic*] parents who are interested in adopting. The LPA adoption service is not limited to the dwarf community. Average size parents are more than welcome."[15] At the three sessions on adoption at the LPA meetings we attended, flexible eugenics was the norm. Two sessions provided information to people seeking to adopt dwarf children, while the third presented an opportunity for people to discuss their experiences with adoption. All the sessions were attended by both short- and average-statured people interested in, or having experience with, adopting dwarf children, and all offered positive models of self-help.

In each of these sessions, questions arose about the scarcity of American dwarf children available for adoption. The coordinator of the adoption program responded to such questions by telling people they should expect to adopt foreign children. She then explained how she handles the rare American dwarf child who becomes available for adoption. Underlining the predominance of foreign children in the adoption network, the adoption page of the LPA newsletter lists children from India, Bulgaria, and Colombia as available for adoption,[16] and a long article describes a short-statured couple's trip to Russia to adopt a dwarf child there (Dagit 1998: 8).

During the several discussions of the scarcity of American children available for adoption that we witnessed, invariably someone expressed hope that parents in the United States were choosing to keep their dwarf children and not opting to terminate pregnancies after a prenatal diagnosis of a dwarfing condition. This discourse about dwarfism, adoption, and abortion after prenatal diagnosis reveals participants' awareness and imagination of the future in light of recent and expected scientific discoveries and their application in medical practice. Here, heightened consciousness of individual choice and biotechnological futurism converge.

As we have described, many short- and average-statured people we encountered at the LPA celebrate dwarf children but are well aware of the potential for eugenic practices to emerge from the discovery of the genes causing different forms of dwarfism. Although the gene for achondroplasia is known, and prenatal testing is therefore available, it is not routinely tested for today. The condition is simply too rare for widespread prenatal screening to be conducted expressly to detect it. Rather, prenatal diagnosis usually is made as a by-product of routine ultrasound testing sometime during the third trimester, making pregnancy termination illegal and, therefore, unlikely.

As both clinicians and many people affected by genetic abnormalities are aware, however, scientists have developed high throughput biochips with the potential to dramatically change prenatal diagnosis as we know it. Already on the market, these microarrays use silicon chips etched to receive multiple, minute samples of DNA, which may then be rapidly screened using automated computer technology.[17] Instead of testing for a few of the more common genetic conditions, such as Down's syndrome, or a condition specific to the family of a particular couple, as is now usual, the biochip technology will soon provide the means to offer rapid and relatively cheap diagnosis of a wide range of genetic conditions. Achondroplasia is regularly mentioned as one condition for which prenatal DNA chip screenings should and would become generally available. Once again, both the power of biotechnological individualism and the quite understandable fears of a marketplace-driven flexible eugenics are evident in LPA discussions of the chip.

The prospect of a highly efficient diagnostic chip also underscores the significance of speed in contemporary imaginings of the future (Rifkin 1987; Virilio 1986). The cage of late capitalism is a silicon cage and the tempo with which it is associated increases the velocity of industrial machinery (Weber 1958) to that of the nanosecond tempo of computer technology. The changes suggested by such near-futuristic technologies are deeply unsettling. Yet we stress that, at the present moment, virtually all of us already live "inside" scientific and rapid technological innovation, culturally speaking. Many social groups, from the Catholic Church to some highly creative and respected feminist scholars (e.g., Hubbard 1990; Hubbard and Wald 1993; Rothman 1990, 1998) call for resistance to our inscription into new reproductive technologies like prenatal diagnosis, labeling these technologies perversions of nature and repressive aspects of capitalism. We contend that the issues involved are more complicated. There are enabling as well as constraining aspects to genetic knowledge and its associated technologies (Giddens 1984: 177).

This is a position we have come to appreciate ethnographically, through our work with the LPA. The point is nowhere more clear than in the fraught politics of prenatal diagnosis. Historically, and even now, LP couples may have opted for adoption because of the double dominant effect when two people with genetically caused dwarfing conditions reproduce together. Achondroplasia is dominantly inherited in a simple Mendelian fashion. Thus two people with achondroplasia have a 25 percent chance of producing a child with that condition, a 25 percent chance that the two nonachondroplastic genes will combine to produce an average-statured child, and a 25 percent chance (considered very high by genetic counseling standards) of producing a child with what is known as double dominance, an inevitably fatal condition. Prenatal testing allows LP couples to learn whether their fetus has this double dominant condition and to make a choice about whether or not to terminate the pregnancy rather than deliver a dying baby.

The issue of double dominance was raised during the LPA session on reproductive health. One woman asked whether the physicians knew the consequences of double dominance in cases of partners who are both short statured but have different dwarfing conditions. Another woman explained that her husband had achondroplasia and she had spondyloepiphyseal dysplasia (SED, another type of dwarfism); they had five children with the double dominant condition, all of whom had died. In response to the question about the effects of hybrid double dominance, one of the physicians offered the observation that almost nothing was known. She then gestured toward the speaker saying, "We have the best evidence [of the consequences] right here." The doctor's evocation of "evidence" tempts us to imagine the complex imbrications between *Laboratory Life*,[18] where animal models are developed for rare conditions that cannot be investigated through human breeding experiments, and the data real people unexpectedly produce for scientists in the course of living their lives as bearers of both rare conditions and children. Here, too, we see flexible eugenics at work.

Physicians at the LPA session stressed the importance of having a definitive diagnosis for one's own dwarfing condition in advance of becoming pregnant. One told a story about a pregnant couple who thought they were both achondroplastic dwarfs, but lo and behold they weren't. One was and one wasn't, and we didn't know what the other had and no way of finding out, . . . so the pregnancy was on the line. . . . If you were in a situation . . . where you had SED and you were pregnant and your partner had achondroplasia, and your concern was that you would have a double dominant, then you might want to have amniocentesis for a prenatal test. Some people would choose to end the pregnancy and other people would not do that, [but] they would have to know the prenatal diagnosis early in the pregnancy. . . . But if you become pregnant [without knowing your own diagnoses], that all becomes either not possible or extremely difficult.

The idea of choice is powerfully present in this discussion. Here, physicians encourage genetic tests so their dwarf patients can make individual choices about their own reproduction.[19]

The story of double dominance illustrates how a controversial technology involving reproductive choice and eugenic abortion holds different meanings when used inside and outside a particular community. Within the LPA there are widespread fears that the general public will use testing to eliminate dwarf fetuses, not to prevent the birth of dying infants, as dwarfs themselves may choose to do. Indeed, in discussing her aspirations for gene therapy with us, Dr. Clair Franco-mano was very clear that she believed the only appropriate use of prenatal diagnosis was to avoid the birth of a child with the double dominant condition. The value of choice also underlies the apocryphal stories we have heard repeatedly about dwarf couples using prenatal testing to prevent the birth of children of average stature.[20]

We use the term *flexible eugenics* to underscore the sort of productive and problematic contradictions outlined above. These examples illustrate the complexities of living in a market-driven society that places a premium on individual choice and, at the same time, largely embraces the emergent standards posed by genetic normalization. But as our analysis demonstrates, the idea of a specifically eugenic relation to one's individual genes does not play out in a simple fashion. The people we have met through the LPA are highly attuned to the perils of eugenic thinking; many of them alternately resist and counterappropriate the push to perfectibility as specifically biological or biomedical. Yet like the rest of us, they may desire individual improvement or perfectibility in other ways that are deeply consonant with shared aspects of our cultural milieu.

Pessimism of the Intellect, Optimism of the Will

Genetic counseling and the kind of advice we see circulating at the LPA provide arenas in which both flexible eugenics and resistance to it may become operationalized. At the LPA meetings, one of our team who has conducted long-term fieldwork among genetic counselors met an unusual genetic counselor. As a person with osteogenesis imperfecta (brittle bone syndrome), the genetic counselor told the story of both her struggles and the support she had received in becoming a genetic counselor with great reflexivity. Some doctors did not want an obviously disabled person confined to a wheelchair to counsel pregnant women about conditions that might include her own. Others immediately defended her right as a professional to work with *all* clients, not merely the ones who could handle what they presumed to be the visual impact of her condition. Volatile mixes of paternalism, affirmative action, and eugenic and feminist thinking swirl through the personal life and professional experiences of this young woman. In response, she has resolved to specialize as a genetic counselor in reproductive issues affecting people with disabilities. She is surely well positioned to hear the aspirations, fears, and consequences that molecular genetic technologies invoke as they are played out in the lives of those whose stake in their outcome is most direct. Yet in less obvious ways, we all have a stake in this unfinished story.

Flying home from the LPA meetings in Los Angeles, we chatted with a flight attendant whose family, as it turned out, lives in the suburb where the LPA meetings had just been held. When she heard the reason for our journey, she immediately commented that her town was buzzing: her mother and her mother's friends had all noted the presence of Little People at the many malls and restaurants where tourists and locals might mingle. They found the LPs "cute" or "interesting." She, however, had gotten into a fight over the dwarfs with her best friend from high school. The friend had exclaimed, "I just saw the most disgusting thing: two dwarfs, a couple, with a baby carriage and a baby dwarf. Why would people like that want to reproduce?" The flight attendant said to us, "I told her they probably want to have babies just like you and me; everyone wants to have babies, why not them? I bet their lives aren't so bad. You've got [facial] neuralgia, I bet your life is tougher than theirs is." Our airborne informant continued for some minutes to express her shock and indignation at her friend's bad attitude.

Reframing the problem, if we engage an understanding of the impact of contemporary American genetic thinking and practices empirically, both flexible eugenic thinking and resistance to it are everywhere, permeating outward from the researchers, clinicians, and affected people to the suburban residents, service personnel, and sympathetic anthropologists who encounter them in daily life. We are all rapidly being interpolated into the world of genetic discourse, where resonances, clashes, and negotiations among interested parties occur at increasing velocity. While all historical moments are, by definition, transitional, we live in particularly fraught times insofar as an understanding of a shift in scientific and social thought surrounding genetics is concerned. At the risk of abusing a Gramscian truism, we note that a working knowledge of the political history of eugenics gives us reason for pessimism of the intellect, but an ethnographic perspective on the openness of these encounters and practices may give some cause for optimism of the will.

Notes

1 The FGFR3 mutation is a genetic rarity in which all cases of achondroplasia are caused by the same mutation. The general rule is that different mutations within a given gene lead to the same disorder. For instance, virtually every family affected with Marfan syndrome (Heath 1998a, b), also a focus of our ongoing research, has a distinctive mutation in the gene for the connective tissue molecule fibrillin.

2 A dominantly inherited, fatal neurological disorder that has played an important role in the development of the Human Genome Project and in recent discoveries in molecular biology.

3 At the annual LPA meetings, a number of T-shirts are available for purchase at the expo. One such T-shirt in 1998 was a takeoff on the Tommy Hilfiger logo with the words "Tommy Dwarfiger." Another looked like a university T-shirt, with the text "Dwarf U." One of the more popular T-shirts in the last few years has been one with the text "Dwarf, Endangered Species" on the front.

4 Representations of dwarfs wishing ill to people of average stature resonate with a discriminatory apparatus that dwarfs face which is deeply rooted in popular culture and folklore and evident in stories like "Rumplestiltskin" and in movies like *Freaks* and, more recently, the Austin Powers movies (for the masses) and the *Red Dwarf* (for cognoscenti). Literature abounds with dwarf protagonists: *Mendel's Dwarf* (Mawer 1999), *The Tin Drum* (Grass 1959), *Stones from the River* (Heigi 1994), and *The Dwarf* (1967), by the Nobel prize-winning author Pär Lagerkvist.

5 In part, Americans operationalize the push to perfectibility by relying on an ideology of exercising individual choice. Discussions of individualism have a long history in American studies, one that can be traced back to de Tocqueville, who identified individualism as a distinctively American characteristic (1835). C. B. Macpherson (1962) examined a more broadly Western notion of individualism in political theory. Linking individualism and capitalist accumulation, Macpherson describes a concept of "possessive individualism."

6 The field research on which this essay draws was supported by NIH/NHGRI/ELSI grant # 1RO1HG01582, for which we are deeply grateful.

7 McGill epidemiologist Abby Lippman labeled the process *geneticization* (Lippman 1991). In our fieldwork we have found that both this terrain and Lippman's concept itself are contested.

8 Veterans associations (Young 1995) and Alcoholics Anonymous (Powell 1987) provide examples of such sociality forged earlier in the twentieth century.

9 One encounter at an LPA session for parents also illustrates parental interest in limb lengthening. At a session billed as a "Teen Panel," at which short-statured teens answered questions from an audience of average-statured parents, one parent asked if any of the teens had considered, or would consider, limb lengthening. All four of the young women on the panel vigorously shook their heads no. One of them spoke quite emphatically, saying, "No, no way. I have too many things I want to do with my life. I don't have time."

10 We are indebted here to the sociologist Troy Duster (1990), who suggests that eugenics is already embedded in contemporary genetic practices through an ideology

of choice: with the new genetics, eugenics will come not through state policy but through "the back door," through individual choice.

11 Biotechnological individualism and the reign of free marketplace "choice" seems apparent in, for example, Eugenia Kaw's 1993 description of Asian American women, who may deeply identify with their cultural roots yet seek to transcend racial identity and exercise choice by choosing cosmetic surgery that anglicizes their eyes. In her work on changing attitudes toward the body, the historian Joan Brumberg (1988, 1997) describes a shift away from moral self-control to control of the unruly body. Especially for women, control over diet, exercise, and, for those who can afford it, plastic surgery enables individuals to choose the bodies they will accept as their own.

12 Biomedical and biotechnical interventions may well have other meanings in different national and local contexts. For example, Taussig's work concerning Dutch genetic medicine shows that normalcy, rather than perfectibility, is strongly marked and desired (1997). Lynn Morgan's 1997 analysis of sonography in Ecuador also points toward the context-specific interpretations attached to biotechnological interventions.

13 In this essay, we use only first names when we use pseudonyms.

14 On the hidden costs of standardization, see Starr (1991).

15 *LPA Today* 35, no. 3 (May–June 1998): 7.

16 *LPA Today* 35, no. 3 (May–June 1998): 7.

17 The molecular biotechnology lab where Deborah Heath carried out fieldwork in 1992 and 1994 was working on a prototype for the biochip at that time. Among rival groups working on the same technology was the biotechnology company Affymetrix, which is now in the forefront of microarray technology (www.affymetrix.com/technology/synthesis.html; accessed in June 1999).

18 Our debt to Labour and Woolgar (1979) should be evident here.

19 The ideology underlying contemporary genetic counseling, offered in a mode known as nondirective counseling, is one based on the idea that knowledge enables individuals to make informed choices. Taussig (1997) has argued that this knowledge is not always perceived as enabling choice and in some cases is experienced as constraining choice.

20 We and our informants have no evidence that there is any truth to such stories. In fact, the research position held by Clair Francomano, the physician whose story opens this essay, makes it very likely that she would know if any such cases had occurred.

References

Adoption and births
    1998.   LPA Today 35(3): 7.
Althusser, L.
    1971   Ideology and Ideological State Apparatuses. *In* Lenin and Philosophy and Other Essays. Pp. 121–173. New York: Monthly Review Press.
Barash, D.
    1998   DNA and Destiny. New York Times, November 16: A25.

Bellah, R., R. Madsen, W. Sullivan, A. Swidler, and S. Tipton
   1985   Habits of the Heart: Individualism and Commitment in American Life. New York: Perennial.
Berman, M.
   1982   All that is Solid Melts into Air: The Experience of Modernity. New York: Simon and Schuster.
Bevir, M.
   1999   Foucault and Critique: Deploying Agency against Autonomy. Political Theory 27(1): 65–84.
Brumberg, J.
   1988   Fasting Girls: The Emergence of Anorexia Nervosa as a Modern Disease. Cambridge, MA: Harvard University Press.
   1997   The Body Project: An Intimate History of American Girls. New York: Random House.
Canguilhem, G.
   1989[1966]   The Normal and the Pathological. New York: Zone.
Dagit, D.
   1998   From Russia with Love: An Adoption Adventure. LPA Today 35(3): 8.
Duster, T.
   1990   Backdoor to Eugenics. New York: Routledge.
Edwards, J., S. Franklin, E. Hirsch, F. Price, and M. Strathern
   1993   Technologies of Procreation: Kinship in the Age of Assisted Reproduction. Manchester: Manchester University Press.
Foucault, M.
   1988   Care of the Self: The History of Sexuality. New York: Random House.
Franklin, S.
   1997   Embodied Progress: A Cultural Account of Assisted Conception. New York: Routledge.
Friedman, L.
   1990   The Republic of Choice: Law, Authority, and Culture. Cambridge, MA: Harvard University Press.
Giddens, A.
   1984   The Constitution of Society. Berkeley: University of California Press.
Grass, G.
   1959   The Tin Drum. R. Manheim, trans. London: Secker and Warburg.
Heath, D.
   1998a   Locating Genetic Knowledge: Picturing Marfan Syndrome and its Traveling Constituencies. Science, Technology, and Human Values 23: 1.
   1998b   Bodies, Antibodies, and Modest Interventions: Works of Art in the Age of Cyborgian Reproduction. In Cyborgs and Citadels: Anthropological Interventions in the Borderlands of Technoscience. G. Downey and J. Dumit, eds. Santa Fe, NM: School of American Research.
Heigi, V.
   1994   Stones from the River. New York: Poseidon Press.
Hubbard, R.
   1990   The Politics of Women's Biology. New Brunswick, NJ: Rutgers University Press.

Hubbard, R., and E. Wald
  1993   Exploding the Gene Myth. Boston: Beacon.
Kaw, E.
  1993   Medicalization of Racial Features: Asian American Women and Cosmetic Sur-
    gery. Medical Anthropology Quarterly 7(1): 74–89.
Kicher, P.
  1992   Gene. *In* Keywords in Evolutionary Biology. E. F. Keller and E. A. Lloyd, eds.
    Pp. 125–28. Cambridge, MA: Harvard University Press.
Lagerkvist, P.
  1967   The Dwarf. London: Chatto.
Latour, B., and S. Woolgar
  1979   Laboratory Life: The Social Construction of Scientific Facts. Beverly Hills:
    Sage.
Lindee, M. S.
  2003   Provenance and the Pedigree: Victor McKusick's Fieldwork with the Old Order
    Amish. *In* Genetic Nature/Culture: Anthropology and Science beyond the Two-
    Culture Divide. A. H. Goodman, D. Heath, and M. S. Lindee, eds. Pp. 41–57.
    Berkeley: University of California Press.
Lippman, A.
  1991   Prenatal Genetic Testing and Screening: Constructing Needs and Reinforcing
    Inequities. American Journal of Law and Medicine 17(1–2): 15–50.
Macpherson, C. B.
  1962   The Political Theory of Possessive Individualism: Hobbes to Locke. Oxford:
    Oxford University Press.
Martin, E.
  1994   Flexible Bodies: Tracking Immunity in American Culture from the Days of
    Polio to the Age of AIDS. Boston: Beacon.
Mawer, S.
  1999   Mendel's Dwarf. New York: Penguin.
Morgan, L.
  1997   Imagining the Unborn in the Ecuadoran Andes. Feminist Studies 23(2):
    323–351.
Olby, R.
  1990   The Emergence of Genetics. *In* Companion to the History of Modern Science.
    R. C. Olby, G. N. Canton, J. R. R. Christie, and M. J. S. Hodge, eds. Pp. 521–536.
    London: Routledge.
Paul, D.
  1995   Controlling Human Heredity, 1865 to the Present. Atlantic Highlands, NJ:
    Humanities Press.
Portin, P.
  1993   The Concept of the Gene: Short History and Present Status. Review of Biology
    68: 172–222.
Powell, T.
  1987   Self-Help Organizations and Professional Practice. Silver Springs, MD: National
    Association of Social Workers Press.
Rabinow, P.
  1996   Essays on the Anthropology of Reason. Princeton: Princeton University Press.

Ragoné, H.
1994   Surrogate Motherhood: Conception in the Heart. Boulder, CO: Westview.
Rifkin, J.
1987   Time Wars. New York: Henry Holt.
Rothman, B. K.
1990   Recreating Motherhood: Ideology and Technology in Patriarchal Society. New York: Norton.
1998   Genetic Maps and Human Imaginations: The Limits of Science in Understanding Who We Are. New York: Norton.
Shiang, R., L. M. Thompson, Y. Z. Zhu, D. M. Church, T. J. Fielder, M. Bocian, S. T. Wonokur, and J. J. Wasmuth
1994   Mutations in the Transmembrane Domain of FGFR3 Cause the Most Common Genetic Form of Dwarfism, Achondroplasia. Cell 78(2): 335–342.
Starr, S. L.
1991   Power, Technologies, and the Phenomenology of Standards: On Being Allergic to Onions. *In* A Sociology of Monsters: Power, Technology, and the Modern World. J. Law, ed. Sociological Review Monograph no. 38. London: Routledge.
Strathern, M.
1992   Reproducing the Future. New York: Routledge.
Taussig, K. S.
1997   Normal and Ordinary: Human Genetics and the Production of Dutch Identities. PhD diss., Johns Hopkins University.
Taussig, K. S., R. Rapp, and D. Heath
1999   Translating Genetics: Crafting Medical Literacies in the Age of the New Genetics. Paper presented at the Annual Meeting of the American Anthropological Association, November 21, Chicago, Illinois.
Tocqueville, A. de
1945[1835]   Democracy in America. New York: Vintage.
Virilio, P.
1986   Speed and Politics. M. Polizzotti, trans. New York: Columbia University Press.
Weber, M.
1958[1904–05]   The Protestant Ethic and the Spirit of Capitalism. New York: Charles Scribner's Sons.
Young, A.
1995   The Harmony of Illusions: Inventing Post-Traumatic Stress Disorder. Princeton: Princeton University Press.

Part V
Necropolitical Projects

9

Life During Wartime:

Guatemala, Vitality, Conspiracy, Milieu

Diane M. Nelson

The mechanisms of power are addressed to the body, to life, to what causes it to proliferate, to what reinforces the species, its stamina, its ability to dominate, or its capacity for being used.

Michel Foucault

A Biopolitical Double Entendre

"The army gives water to the people!" read the slogan on a float at the Army Day parade, Guatemala City, 1992. Children dressed in indigenous clothing pumped actual water amid greenery and papier mâché structures meant to look like a highland Maya village. The float was sponsored by the S-5, army civil affairs, to highlight its community development work. "I wonder if they realize," said my Guatemalan friend as we watched the parade together, "that 'to give water' is slang for killing someone?" Potable water systems (and latrines) are centerpieces of late twentieth-century "development" and hygiene strategies, meant to improve life and health, whether sponsored by national, transnational, or NGO funds. But if " 'deduction' [taking life] has tended to be no longer the major form of power but merely one among others," as Foucault suggests about the transformation to biopower (1980: 136), then the float works as a perfect biopolitical double entendre.

Getting Smart with Biopolitics

Tom Tomorrow suggests that when smart bombs live up to their names they discuss Foucault's theories of power. Foucault's "power" is a complex idea,

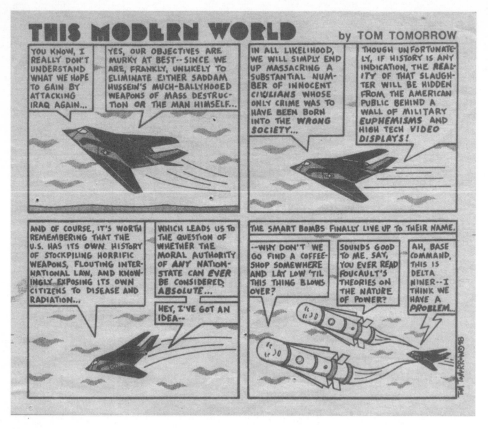

Used with kind permission. © Tom Tomorrow

developed through numerous books, lectures, and interviews, but I take him to mean that power does not repress an already existing subject. Instead, our experience of subjectivity itself is produced by power. Power may be expressed against our bodies in punishment, from Daddy spanking us to state-sanctioned capital punishment and wartime mass killings. But such power is relatively weak, only "the negative and emaciated form of prohibition" (Foucault 1980: 86). Power is also exercised productively, through each and every one of us when we pick up a pencil, strive to do well in school, turn to doctors for health, desire a sex partner, or engage in political activism. Power subjects us to capitalism, patriarchy, racism, and homophobia, but it also subjectivizes us, makes us who we are. To paraphrase Judith Butler, it is that without which we cannot think at all (1993: xi). Also described as capillary (like a bloodstream), this power is everywhere: inside us, around us, rather than somewhere else (like the White House or Wall Street).

In a very short passage (but one that has spawned a large literature[1]) of *The History of Sexuality* Foucault describes this power as a "biopolitics of the population." Working with anatomo-politics (centered on the body as a machine: its disciplining, the optimization of its capabilities, the extortion of its forces), the main role of biopolitics is "to ensure, sustain, and multiply life [*bios*], to put this life in order" (1980: 137–138). Health, the future of the species, the vitality of the social body, these are the sites and promises of *this* power.

I, and the others gathered in this volume, have found that Foucault offers useful tools for critical analyses of anthropology, modernity, and globalization (among other things). But his conception of power also makes many thoughtful people nervous. It seems pernicious, debilitating, or as Duccio Trombadori says, "there is no escaping the impression that Foucault, far from providing a new stimulus to demands for liberation, limits himself to describing a mechanism of pure imprisonment" (Foucault 1991: 20). A friend whose politics I much admire echoes this attitude: "The problem with Foucault is you don't see the stakes, you don't get a sense of what is being fought for. He's a conspiracy theorist without conspirators." I am torn between a Foucauldian hope that while power is as dangerous as a bomb it may also swerve off course, and the suspicion, expressed in Sam Gross's *New Yorker* cartoon, that maybe I'm the mouse in the wagon.

"*For God's sake, think! Why is he being so nice to you?*"

This essay grows out of my experiences of both solidarity and scholarly work on and between Guatemala and the United States, which have led me to ask: can one be a Foucauldian and an activist?[2] The second mouse, which sees through the cat's conspiracy of kindness, urges us to "think!" This is a global historical imperative as real-world smart bombs wreak havoc in Afghanistan and Iraq (and . . .?!). Yet I acknowledge that it is not easy to get smart with Foucault's injunction to cut off the king's head and think of power not as concentrated in one place like the state or the Pentagon but dispersed throughout individual and social bodies (especially since I personally don't feel very powerful!). I *do* find many conspiracy theories a useful way to understand the current conjuncture, but I am also convinced by Foucault's admonitions to question the productive role of any form of power/knowledge, i.e., what sort of subject do they assume (take for granted *and* create)? Is it as simple as the duped (the mouse enjoying the wagon ride) and nonduped (the mouse in the know)? To reset the terms of the famous debate (American liberal humanist versus French poststructuralist), will it just take more people reading Noam Chomsky to put the world right?[3] I'm a big fan of Chomsky but think we need to follow the swerving bomb of the cartoon to go somewhere else than the either/or of this duped-or-not binary structure (or the double entendre of the friendly face of the kitty [or S-5] versus its "true" intentions).

To understand biopolitics better I will draw on Foucault's notions of the right of death and power over life (1980) – and especially the role of vitality – to analyze life during wartime. We are all living that life, but I focus on Guatemala, specifically the genocidal civil war (1962 to 1996) and the war against malaria (1955 to the present). I structure this analysis around three tensions. One is this shuttling between my (and the mouse's) suspicious conspiracy theory and my (and Tom Tomorrow's) sense that Foucault *can* help us understand risks, stakes, and what is being fought over. (And he would push us to ask who, after all, is the cat?) This will entail some hard work to parse the vitality of power without the conspiratorial easy-out of assuming I am in the know while everyone else is duped. The second is a tension that Foucault is well aware of: the terrifying contradictions of twentieth-century ("modern") regimes that visit never-before-seen holocausts on their own populations, but simultaneously "now it is over life, throughout its unfolding, that power establishes its dominion" (1980: 137, 138). In fact it is this tension that he calls "biopolitics." The third is one of the central mysteries of anthropology: our relation to "culture" (aka the "social," "the state," "ideology," "hegemony," "collective consciousness," "power"). Foucault terms it the relation between the life of the individual and the life of the species. How can we feel like an individual (the "subject effect") while still being part of something larger? How do we come to be passionately attached to, say, political projects? What "makes" us activists, in the final measure willing to kill or die for something? How in turn is that "something larger" understood or known? Is "it" other people or does it include our own bodies, the environment, or even the past, and how all of these influence how we relate to the future, what we hope and struggle for – the goals of our activism? This leads me to focus on what might be called the milieu, or what lies between, in the tactics and strategies of Guatemala's civil war and the global campaign to eradicate malaria.[4] Addressing the milieu suggests, in turn, an unexpected link, a "preserved possibility" of Lamarckian eugenics that may be carried through biopolitics and may lend vitality to these struggles over life.

Removing the Water from the Fish, Giving Water to the People

Blood and Water

Like some other authors collected here, I will begin by waxing a bit confessional about my own encounter with Foucault's order of things in the production of my author-effect. In 1984 I became a conspiracy theorist when I discovered the US role in the violent regime-change of a democratically elected government in Guatemala (this knowledge changed me, as I began to see myself as an unconscious [duped?] conspirator in the resulting civil war). In 1954 a CIA-backed military coup overthrew the government of President Jacobo Arbenz who had sought to improve the lives of Guatemalans (some of the poorest people in the Western hemisphere) by setting up a (very) basic safety net including social security, workers' rights, the end of forced labor, and a mild land reform that bought unused land and distributed it to landless, primarily indigenous, peasants. In the midst of the Cold War Arbenz was labeled a Communist and this became one of many such overthrows orchestrated by the United States around the globe.

A military dictator was installed (except for a brief period, the army would rule Guatemala until 1986 and remains a major force), thousands of people were killed, and many were tortured (Gleijeses 1991; Kinzer and Schlesinger 1983). Most of the reforms were dismantled; land was returned to the United Fruit Company and wealthy Guatemalan landowners; unions were outlawed; and discussion of progressive social change stifled. The ten-year period of liberal nationalist reform (1944–54) known as the "Guatemalan Spring" gave way to a 40-year winter of discontent marked by civil war and the genocidal government counterinsurgency. "Knowing" about this, especially in the context of US foreign policy toward Central America in the 1980s, subjectivized me differently in relation to my national identity (that is, my milieu), and I began to identify as a human rights and solidarity activist.

In 1986 I had recently returned from my first research trip to Guatemala and was trying to write up the field report detailing army massacres of civilians, forced exile, the refugee camps in Mexico, and the "development poles" or army-run resettlement and re-education areas I had visited. These were some of the effects of the civil war in which over 200,000 people were killed, more than 400 villages massacred, and a million people displaced (CEH 1999) as the military state warred against an armed revolutionary movement, as well as anyone else it saw as a threat, including students, peasants, Mayan priests, newborn infants, health promoters, and anthropologists.

Guerrilla warfare is a "weapon of the weak." Rather than suicidally field a standing army against state-backed (and transnationally armed) soldiers, it relies on appropriated weapons, booby traps, local solidarity, word of mouth, and being able to melt into populations and uneven terrain like jungles, the folds of mountains, and through underpoliced borders. The state, with its warlike tactics undermined by such a moving target, attacks not the guerrillas but the population and the terrain. Massacres, scorched earth, displacement, defoliants, and resettlement are ways to control, monitor, reorganize, and redeploy insurgent networks and forces. If, as Mao Tse-Tung said, guerrillas move among the population like fish in water, Guatemalan counterinsurgency strategy, especially from 1978 to 1983, was to remove the water from the fish, to transform the milieu.

This was a time when movements for radical social change were doing pretty well, with the Sandinista triumph in 1979 following what looked like popular victories in Vietnam, Iran,[5] and in the African decolonization. Solidarnosc in Poland, the anti-apartheid movement in South Africa, nuclear freeze activism in the United States and Europe, and the FMLN in El Salvador were going strong. These new models of government promised to spread the fruits of modernity – education, health, economic development, and access to resources – to improve the lives of entire populations. "Schools not bombs!" we chanted. "Money for health care, not for war, US out of El Salvador!"

In Guatemala these hopes were expressed through the popular movement of students, workers, indigenous people, refugees, families of the disappeared, and the armed combatants of the URNG (Guatemalan National Revolutionary Unity). While I often felt overwhelmed with horror and pity at what Guatemalans were suffering, I also had a sneaking suspicion that part of the appeal of working in solidarity with them was because power relations seemed so much clearer there than in the United States. Guatemala looked pretty much cleanly divided between the corrupt elitist military state and the resisting people. Thanks to what appeared to be the state's psychotic refusal to acquiesce to any popular demands, Guatemalans seemed to have been spared the opiates of the welfare states that kept us citizens of the North blandly acquiescing. Of course, there were many people forced to participate in the army or civil patrols, and some misguided folks pursued their own selfish interests by way of the militarized situation (Paul and Demarest 1988), but the counterinsurgency was so overwhelming and brutal precisely because there was a strong movement threatening the state – the revolution was very close to succeeding. A common metaphor used in solidarity publications compared it to a river swelling as different streams joined it, to create an implacable force. While in the United States we were "working very well by ourselves"[6] in Guatemala people had to be beaten to be made to obey. Maybe they were "ahead" in seeing how oppressive power worked, because they were "behind."

One day I came home to find two books on my porch: Maribel Morgan's *The Total Woman* and Michel Foucault's *Discipline and Punish* (they were courtship gifts from a suitor experimenting with dialectical montage). Maribel was good for a laugh but I began to read the Foucault seriously. My goodness! but it was hard going. Not the bodies getting torn apart, which I found sick but kind of cool, but the way it shook up everything I thought I knew. I felt like I had to get into a Zen state to read it – letting go of how I understood power, the subject, resistance, everything that was most important to me. I still find it hard to read Foucault and to think of power as productive and not only repressive. But that reading helped me see, when I returned to Guatemala a few months later to study in more depth the army's resettlement villages, called "development poles," that the state was doing a lot more than exercising its right over death – it seemed to be using every trick in the Panopticon guide to population control. Not only was every prisoner made a warden through systems of "civil patrolling" and spy networks, but they were also "developing" different subjects through schools, clinics, sports, hygiene, urban planning, and new agricultural production techniques (Nelson 1988, 1999; see also Wilson 1995) – in addition to violence and terror. They were "modernizing." After 30 years of killing most anyone demanding health care, adequate housing, or education it seemed like the state was giving them what they asked for – it suddenly seemed very astute! Of course, discipline does not displace the power to take life in a progress narrative of history. Foucault (1979) helped me see these as overlapping and interacting. This is precisely the tension between the right of death and the administering of life he calls biopolitics. It also messes up any sense of "ahead" or "behind" or even "with" or "against."

Now I thought I was pretty smart to read cutting-edge Continental theory into the Guatemalan highlands (and I wasn't even in graduate school!). But about ten years later I was sitting in a downtown Guatemala City café with a Guatemalan friend. An acquaintance of his, another journalist, stopped by our table and I was introduced as "an anthropologist who wrote a book about Guatemala and Foucault." Shaking my hand the man smiled broadly and said, "Oh, I *love* Foucault! You must show me this book sometime." After he left my friend seemed somewhat uncomfortable. "That Cifuentes, he's not really my friend," he said. "I know him through the radio work, but he's with the Army. He's the designer of the development poles." While I tried on several occasions to interview Colonel Cifuentes he proved elusive so I can't really prove a nefarious connection between reading Foucault and masterminding the follow-up to genocidal counterinsurgency.[7] But might this justify people's suspicions that "biopolitics" is "really" a sly cover for social control? When the army "gives water" to the people (or food, or improved stoves, or any other "development assistance") by attending to their desperate needs (the same needs the state often *caused* by destroying people's homes, killing their animals, and displacing them!), is it just to buy docility or to serve as propaganda for outside observers?[8] Along with CIA torture manuals and guidelines for funding "assets" (Guatemalan nationals working as CIA informers), is Foucault just one more how-to book in the global diffusion of "modern" counterinsurgency?

Savoirs and Subjectivization

In his histories of science – of madness, health, prisons, sex – Foucault charts the emergence of these as objects of knowledge and of the simultaneous production of subjects judged capable of knowing them. Governments, political systems, and war itself, including its aftermath, have become objects of study for anthropology in the twentieth century and thereby formed the anthropologist as a subject presumed (although this is still highly contested!) to know about these issues. That's me, as I study and write about civil war in Guatemala. But Foucault (like many languages) differentiates between ways of knowing. In French, one is *connaissance*, "a" knowledge, "the process which permits the multiplication of knowable objects, the development of their intelligibility, the understanding of their rationality, while the subject doing the investigation always remains the same." *Savoir*, instead,

> is a process through which the subject finds himself [*sic*] modified by what he knows or rather by the labor performed in order to know. It is what permits the modification of the subject and the construction of the object.... It's a question, then, of understanding once more the formation of a knowledge (*connaissance*), that is, of a relation between a determinate subject and a determinate field of objects, and of grasping it in its historical origin, in that "movement of knowledge" (*savoir*) that renders it possible. Everything that I have occupied myself with up till now essentially regards the way in which people in Western societies have had experiences that were used in the process of knowing a determinate, objective set of things while at the same time constituting themselves as subjects under fixed and determinate conditions. (1991: 69–70)

At an emotional level it had been (and still is) satisfying to depict the Guatemalan army/military state as monolithically brutal, racist, violent, and thus easy to denounce. Denunciation (not only of human rights violations in Guatemala but also of militarization everywhere) is a vital task that I indulge in frequently. However, is it the only ethical way "to know"? I began to wonder if that depiction of Guatemala carried its own load of racist assumptions, positing Guatemala as somehow premodern, lacking a certain coevalness, and thereby *producing* me, the anthropologist, as modern, moral, righteous, and knowing.[9] Foucault's suggestion that modern power is never *only* about the power over death, but also about life, points toward more complex reasons people (including primarily indigenous soldiers and patrollers) would participate in the civil war. It helped me to think about villagers as not only passive victims waiting for the guerrillas (or me) to save them, or as the naive mouse being pulled around by the crafty kitty. This is not to underestimate the violence and terror produced through massacre, gruesome torture-murders, disappearances, and threats, but to struggle to understand the conditions of possibility for counterinsurgency and the tensions in "modern" power.

Foucault also pushes me to think about that tension between being subjected to counterinsurgency and how it subjectivizes or actively creates a sense of self. Guatemalan historian Matilde González's (2002) powerful study of one postwar highland town is called "*Se cambió el tiempo*." This is how the Sanbartolos she worked with describe the war, meaning "time changed," but also everything that time is connected to in Mayan cosmology: geographical and spiritual space, social relations and relations to nonhuman beings as well as to one's own body and the fragile parts of one's soul – i.e., the milieu. No one is the same after "knowing" such a thing, especially in a war that so thoroughly interpenetrated the roles of victim and victimizer (Zur 1998; Green 1999). (And this is not to say that state victory in the war was total – struggle goes on in many different forms on many terrains.)

The war challenges me as an anthropologist and activist. I think I "know" (*connaissance*) the state and army strategies as fixed objects, always bad, even when they seem to be doing good (giving [potable] water may seem like a vital public service but it's really a double entendre). But when I fix victims, victimizers, and survivors as unchanging entities, I also get to remain fixed. I have not had what Foucault calls "an experience that changes us, that prevents us from always being the same, or from having the same kind of relationship with things and with others that we had before" (1991: 41). Which, after all, is the whole point of participant-observation.

Life During "Post"-Wartime

By 1988 the guerrillas had definitely lost the armed battle, and had suffered major splits.[10] While a very strong ethos of sacrifice motivated many of the people struggling for a more just future, the counterinsurgency had "socialized risk" to such an extent that even hardened guerrilla commanders (like Mario Payeras [1997]) could no longer justify the death involved in their struggle for life (although by doing so they became "enemies" to their former companions). The late 1980s and early 1990s also saw an exodus of indigenous people from the armed struggle, complaining of racism in the ranks. What had looked like a unified movement seemed more and more multifaceted (which in turn was partly an effect of the war rather than a foregone conclusion). What would "national unity" or "liberation" look like? Some people began to imagine such concepts other-wise and to "organize differently" as they said, around indigenous identity and cultural rights, forming the Mayan movement that would rise to prominence in 1992 with the Columbus Quincentennial. Mayan activists worked for representation *in* the state and other sites of power like the school and the church (Cojtí Cuxil 1991, 1995; Bastos and Camus 1993, 1995, 2003; Fischer and Brown 1996; Warren 1998). Many on the left called them sell-outs. Women, both Mayan and non-indigenous (also called *ladina*), also began to organize and were also sometimes called traitors (Alvarez 1996; Nelson 2001).

Following the scorched earth of the early 1980s, the army's development pole strategies spread throughout the highlands. Minute attention to the details of everyday life – including deep ethnographic knowledge of Mayan lifeways, community divisions, and subtle shifts in people's loyalties – as well as desperately needed food aid, housing, and health care were institutionalized through the army's "civic action" arm as well as civilian government ministries (there were elections in 1985), Guatemalan Catholic and Protestant churches, and foreign aid (ranging from US, European, and Japanese government investment, to fundamentalist church programs, to progressive organizations like Oxfam). The army, the government, and transnational actors "gave water to the people," setting up sanitation systems and latrines as well as general "development" projects. Although there was constant organizing around human rights and over the terms of the emerging peace treaty (which took close to ten years to negotiate), the Guatemalan army had managed to make collaboration the only way to (maybe) survive.

People living in spaces that had seemed outside state power, like the refugee camps in Mexico and the Communities of Population in Resistance (groups hiding in the jungles and mountains of Northern Guatemala), were coming back "inside." With the peace treaty signed in 1996, even the URNG became, in ways, part of the state. The threat of violence remains and is sometimes actualized and life is extraordinarily risky in post-wartime Guatemala. Dozens of human rights activists have been murdered in the past few years, a number of people have gone into exile, mob violence and lynchings are frequent, and most military officers, even those indicted in high-profile assassinations, still enjoy court-approved immunity. The state is getting away with murder. It still enjoys the right of death. While this is far from the genocidal warfare of 20 years ago, the war for radical social change was lost and the US embassy counts "postwar" Guatemala one of its great success stories in Latin America.

But, after 1997, well-funded and energetic organizing to implement the peace accords flourished; Mayan claims became institutionalized through the state-funded ALMG (Mayan Language Academy) and COPMAGUA (Coordination of the Mayan People); and the government threw itself into infrastructure development like roads, potable water, sanitation, and schools. The health system was overhauled. Hundreds of NGOs were formed and foreign aid poured in. A historical accounting began with two "truth commission" reports (REMHI 1998, CEH 1999). Many of those involved in these projects understood themselves to be pursuing the same struggle by other means. As a Mayan woman and returned exile said to me, laughing: "When I go into the highlands to do these human rights and democracy workshops I am saying exactly the same things I said in the early 1980s when I was in the guerrillas. Only now I don't have to hide. *And* I'm getting paid."

Newer co-memorations of the civil war emphasize that army violence was excessive and in some cases genocidal, but also that, even when it seemed like a clear-cut battle between an illegitimate military dictatorship and a pure resisting people, things were not so simple. Can we understand all these processes in postwar Guatemala as hypocrisy, duping, selling out, giving up, betraying, donor fatigue, or naively taking a ride in the cat's little wagon? While Colonel Cifuentes devised the "development pole" strategy, can we "know" him or all the other people and institutions that deployed such strategies (including my returned exile friend, or me when I give money to Oxfam or collaborate with an NGO) via an analysis of this as a conspiracy, a humanitarian cover that simply hides the violence inherent in the system? "Life" during wartime – its prolifer-ation, its vicissitudes – radically complicates this knowledge.

"Schools not bombs! Money for health care not for war!," we chant. As many analyses of colonialism have described, schools, health care and other signs of "development" are as vital as bombs in acts of conquest and discipline. However, as Aimé Cesaire (1972) reminds us, colonized peoples now struggle *for* these very same techniques of oppression[11] and the former colonizers, in turn, are seen as cold and heartless when they refuse to provide them. They seem to be denying life and progress to the very people who need it most. Now that some of that *is* being provided in Guatemala, is it to be dismissed because it's not as I'd choose (via a revolutionary and thus "truly" popular government)? On the other hand, this small victory (that the state is assuming its responsibility to provide education and health) does not mean the struggle is over. Rather than a conspiracy to dupe, perhaps we can understand Cesaire, our chants, and the popular struggle for a more equitable distribution of the common wealth (in its multiple forms) as what Foucault calls a " 'reverse' discourse," one that demands "that its legitimacy be acknowledged, often in the same vocabulary, using the same categories by which it was . . . disqualified" (Foucault 1980: 101).[12]

These are the contradictions Foucault calls "politics" with its two poles of development: anatomo- with its attention to the individual body as a site of pain as well as vitality, and bio- the species body, and these are "linked together by a whole intermediary cluster of relations" (1980: 139). There are many "astonishments [in] a society in which political power had assigned itself the task of administering life" (1980: 139). While never denying that power is brutal and dangerous, Foucault's theories of biopolitics push us past an analysis of conspirators and duped, of crafty kitties and mice blind to their manipulations or even clear-cut wins and losses.

Rather than seeking to "know" whether a particular strategy is repressive or liberatory, perhaps we should question the appeal of fixed knowledges and even how we think at all (especially in such either/or forms). For example, how did repression or liberation come to form the very limits of our thought? How did we come to see the state as responsible for our health? What are the discursive waters that we, like little fishes (and guerrillas), swim in? And from there (rather than from an all-knowing, unchanging outside of those relations), how do we develop biopowerful strategies? To continue elaborating on these questions, and the tensions and swerves in power over life, I turn from a war that horrifies me to one most of us would support: the war to eradicate malaria, which was going on at the same time.

At the Juncture of the Body and the Population: The Capillary Power of Malaria

Malaria doesn't only kill, it enslaves the local population . . . malaria keeps its victims economically unproductive and is an epidemic disease that can depopulate entire areas of rich agricultural potential. We must cut the transmission chain, draining the sites of infection, overcoming the disease in those infected, and intercepting the mosquito vector so that the ill are no longer a danger for the collective.

Antonio Argueta, Guatemalan journalist, 1955[13]

It is a human right to be healthy. With malaria the problem is not limited to often-imprecise medicine. It is fundamentally an economic-social problem that gradually undermines the economy and the human status of nations. It is a barrier to the evolutionary march of improvement and progress. Ten to fifteen percent of infant mortality is attributed to malaria. This illness consumes and eliminates a considerable portion of the human group that constitutes the future of the nations. Each and every one of us, regardless of class or caste, must study how, through what attitudes, we can collaborate in its elimination, even minimally, given that every man is part of humanity and every contribution is clearly a contribution to our own protection and survival.

Werner Ovalle Lopez, Guatemalan journalist, 1960

In the Blood

In February 1955, in the midst of the post-Arbenz counterrevolution and martial law, the Guatemalan Health Ministry began a massive antimalaria campaign. While the previous democratically elected governments had antimalaria projects (as had the United Fruit Company and the infamous Ubico dictatorship in the 1930s), this was described as "all out war." Malaria was the number one health problem in 19 of the 22 departments (states) and Guatemala was reported to have the highest morbidity and mortality rates in the Americas (*Imparcial* February 29, 1960). Just as US officials described the coup as the first rollback of Communism in the hemisphere and declared Guatemala a showcase for the continent, Guatemala's malaria campaign became a pilot plan for the Global Malaria Eradication Program (organized by the World Health Organization [WHO] in 1958) that was the largest transnational public health project in history (Gladwell 2001: 47).

Malaria is a complex illness. The infamous and overwhelming fevers and chills that so stymied the colonial projects of the nineteenth century are caused by a parasite (not the *mal aires* or bad air from which it gets its name). Entering the bloodstream from a mosquito bite, the parasites migrate to the liver to replicate, forming a cyst, which bursts, sending parasites into the red blood corpuscles where they feed on hemoglobin (by this point the thirty or forty parasites deposited by the mosquito have become trillions). The parasite also makes the red blood cells sticky, forming a plaque that clogs the vascular system, including the capillaries of the brain. Malaria can kill you through anemia, organ failure from the fever (which can reach 106 degrees Fahrenheit), or from swelling and starvation of the brain. Those who survive experience a much-commented-upon listlessness and malaise. Mating and reproducing in the sufferer's body, the parasites pass through a number of developmental stages, making a medical "magic bullet" hard to develop (even now that the genome has been decoded). Their progeny may live in the body for years, causing periodic relapses (the "enslavement" Argueta describes). There are several forms of malaria plasmodium, four of which affect humans (*Plasmodium falciparum* is the most virulent and *Plasmodium vivax* the most common). They also develop immunity to the favored cures – quinine and its chemical replicants.

Malaria is a vector-transmitted disease, meaning the parasites are spread by mosquito bites from one human to another. Female mosquitoes ingest blood to fuel the production of eggs. Those that bite humans generally do so at night. Then, heavily laden, they sit on the nearest vertical surface to digest the meal and expel unneeded water. Later the female will lay her eggs in nearby standing water where they develop into larvae and then more mosquitoes. Sick people become a parasite reservoir the mosquitoes dip into then carry out into the world. With the vector's help, a single human carrier can infect over one hundred others.[14] Mosquitoes in their various forms – eggs, larvae, adults – seem to travel easily in ships and airplanes (as do the parasites, carried inside mosquito and human bodies moving about the globe). It's all about what's in between as a *New York Times* headline makes clear: "Hovering Where Rich and Poor Meet: The Mosquito" (McNeil 2000). There are some 60 species of *Anopheles* mosquitoes that carry malaria plasmodium. Like the parasites, mosquitoes also tend to develop immunities to the insecticides used against them. However, once malaria is eradicated in an area, humans tend to lose their immunity.

Malaria has been a big deal in human history, blamed for the fall of Rome and French failure to build the Panama canal, and might have been as decisive to Allied victory in World War II as breaking the Enigma code and the Russian sacrifice of millions of lives. The struggle to understand and control malaria was central to the colonial project and gave rise to the well-funded field of tropical medicine and several Nobel Prizes, awarded for the discoveries I've outlined above.

A Social Disease

With such a complex and mobile target, Guatemala's 1955 eradication campaign had to respond in kind. A special unit was created, the Servicio Nacional de Eradicación de la Malaria (National Service for Malaria Eradication) or SNEM, partly funded by the WHO, UNICEF, and later USAID. Curing those harboring the plasmodium was difficult enough. First, how to identify those suffering, who were often in the more remote areas of the country, with little in the way of public health infrastructure? Many, thankfully, recovered without benefit of medication, but they were still carriers (a "danger to the collective"). Second, the diagnosis. How to link the clinic (if those suffering even made it there) to the laboratory for analysis of the "*gota gruesa*," or blood sample, to ensure it was malaria? As one SNEM doctor put it, "this is the hardest and most delicate work. These are *complicadisimas* biological tests" (*Imparcial* March 11, 1957). Then there's the problem of distributing the medicine and getting people to take it. Chloroquine (and related drugs) is notoriously unpleasant to consume – foul tasting and with nasty side effects. Once fevers (which run in cycles) abate, many leave off the drugs (economizing by saving the pills for "next time"), which allows the stronger (increasingly resistant) plasmodium to survive.

Then, of course, there's the vector. Even in a small country like Guatemala (about the size of the state of Ohio) it's actually vectors since there are different kinds, with different habits, inhabiting various ecosystems (while they do not seem to transmit malaria, there are two species of *Anopheles* found only in Guatemala). In the words of Dr. Gehlert-Mata, former director of SNEM, "malaria is very, very social. It's all about the *ambiente* [environment, surroundings – social and physical]." Those dedicated to the eradication of malaria must combine the skills of phlebotomy and entomology (and anthropology). They must both take blood and catch mosquitoes. As a SNEM representative put it, "just finding out the current susceptibility of the *Anopheles* is so time consuming, it's almost an overwhelming task, completely fatiguing" (*Imparcial* February 4, 1957). Once the diagnosis is made, one site for attack is the standing water where eggs are laid and larvae develop. But this could mean anything from wetlands to limpid pools, from the small vases left in graveyards to hold flowers for the dead to footprints left by cattle in damp ground. Abandoned tires are favorite breeding grounds, as are soda cans. This means a massive intervention in the ecosystem, as wetlands are drained, rivers dammed, lake surfaces oiled and chemically treated, houses, yards, patios, and villages scoured for any offending containers. Then there is the mobile mosquito herself, notoriously hard to swat, who may hang out on walls, in the thatch of a hut's roof, on trees, and so on. Aerial insecticide spraying was deployed as well as house-to-house campaigns where Dieldrin and DDT were applied directly to all inside walls (which kills the mosquito while it is digesting its blood meal). While hard to believe for the post-*Silent Spring* generation, DDT was considered a miracle in the 1940s, the very sign of modernity.

In 1955 SNEM organized brigades to fan out across the countryside to test for malaria, hunt mosquitoes, destroy breeding areas, administer quinine for free, and spray down walls. This entailed a major investment in *savoirs* (knowledges) and techniques. Vehicles, spraying equipment, medicines and insecticides had to be bought and personnel trained in their use and surveilled in their practice. Just as only a few undisciplined patients resisting taking their drugs can maintain the hardy plasmodium in their bodies, ready to spread with any passing mosquito, so careless spraying – missing some buildings, skipping a wall, diluting the solution too much – can undermine the entire effort. Given the emerging proof that mosquitoes developed resistance to DDT within seven years, SNEM was also in a race against time. Areas had to be mapped, individuals identified, networks explored, movements analyzed, dangers accounted for, and this is where the anthropological *savoir* comes in.

Sorely lacking among the population, according to contemporary reports, was education and an understanding of what was at stake (in addition to basic sanitary infrastructure). "We must raise people's consciousness about the kind of enemy we are confronting. They must tell us if they are sick, they must get treatment, and not become a focal point for malaria transmission, feeding mosquitoes with their damaged blood" (*Imparcial* September 30, 1955). In one of the poorest countries in the hemisphere, where 22 languages are spoken, many people are monolingual in a Mayan language, and illiteracy rates were over 90 percent in some areas (not to mention that this occurred in the wake of a bloody coup), some frustration was to be expected. As Dr. Quintana, a SNEM collaborator, explained in the national newspaper, it takes not only the work of volunteers, researchers, epidemiologists, people skilled in taking and analyzing blood samples, DDT sprayers, doctors, and public health experts, but also a human touch. He wrote, "We have to understand that in rural areas there is good reason to mistrust those who come from outside, who are often arrogant. For the campaign to work people have to understand it, and we need to be conscious of their personal issues, learn their names" (*Imparcial* January 5, 1973).

Dr. Gehlert-Mata admitted some of the errors SNEM made.

We assured people that the medicine does not cause a stomach ache, that it doesn't cause miscarriages, or anything, but once I took the medicine and it gave me gastritis for four days! So you are saying things that aren't true, and when it causes suffering then they won't take the full eight-day treatment.... Another problem is that the DDT killed everything – the bugs and roaches and then the animals, the chickens that ate them, the cats, so there were rat invasions, and they ate the crops. This was a big problem that led people to refuse the fumigations. The director before me committed an error in a community that didn't want to allow it. They came out with sticks in the street when the brigade showed up and so the other director called out the military police and put them in front of the fumigators, they beat some people up. Yes, they managed to spray, but from that day on the people turned against the system of malaria. I practically had to go house to house in that community to convince them that despite what had happened we would respect them. There's a lot you can do, based on dialogue, methods you can take. It has to be based in respect. I think we've advanced in Guatemala, in a few things.

At the global level, William Gorgas (who eradicated yellow fever from Cuba and Panama in the early 1900s) said that in order to fight malaria you had to learn to think like a mosquito, but Fred Soper, who headed the WHO Global Eradication Program, disagreed. As Gladwell describes it, "Fighting malaria had very little to do with the intricacies of science and biology. The key was learning to think like the men he hired to go door-to-door and stream-to-stream, killing mosquitoes. His method was to apply motivation, discipline, organization, and zeal in understanding human nature" (2001: 44). As a WHO official said in 1957, "it's easy to write about eradication in countries where you just need to press a button to get everything moving, but not even the best informed understand how hard it is to get even the most rudimentary projects under way in those areas where malaria causes the worst ravages. We can rely on technical promise, but we will need a fundamental reorganization of existing services" (*Imparcial* January 20, 1957).

This would require careful systematization and subjectivization (*assujetisse-ment*). These knowledges (*connaissance*), carefully collated from around the globe and trailing the glory of Nobel Prizes, had to be incorporated into the most minute aspects of people's lives, activities, techniques, and selves. If people were to be saved from the scourge of malaria, these knowledges had to become *savoirs* in Foucault's sense: to "permit an alteration, a transformation, of the relationship we have with ourselves and our cultural universe: in a word, with our knowledge (*savoir*)" (1991: 37). These are examples of the microphysics of capillary power, defending the individual's blood meant acting through the social body's tiniest sites of flow and transfer. Sub-individual actants (mosquito larvae, the parasites) are thus "linked together by a whole intermediary cluster of relations" (Foucault 1980: 139) to super-body politics like the Guatemalan state, anthropology, and the World Health Organization via the individual, who thereby becomes an "effect" of power and "the element of its articulation" (Gordon 1980: 208).

Dr. Quintana outlined these biopolitical challenges in a series of articles in 1964 (just after the US Congress cut off funding to WHO). "To carry out the necessary organization in towns, villages, hamlets, even the tiniest parcels, we need courage! Optimism, energy, resources, executive support and sincere co-operation from everyone in the country. We need an extraordinary energy to eliminate the thousands of elements involved, but it is precisely in this that administration – in the modern sense of 'to administer' – consists!" (*Imparcial* January 15, 1964). In an article headlined "Guatemalans! If you are Patriotic, Don't be Lazy, Help Out!" he lists how you can: volunteer to discover malaria cases and make sure ("even if it means grabbing them by the hair") that sufferers take the full course of medicine, and keep up enthusiasm by talking about the importance of collaborating. Priests, pastors, teachers, journalists, soldiers, may-ors, business leaders, all must lend their aid. Without these steps, SNEM's entire project could fail, bringing international shame to Guatemala, decreasing worker efficiency, increasing risks for everyone of contracting malaria (in strains stronger than ever), and creating a serious obstacle to development (*Imparcial* January 8, 1964).

"To administer" the project, in 1960 volunteer brigades were set up making local people responsible for keeping track of each other. Volunteers were to identify those showing malarial symptoms, begin to treat them, and send a sample of their blood to the nearest laboratory. By special government decree, postage for the blood samples was free. According to a journalist who visited a brigade in 1964, the men and women of the Pro-Health Committee had donated land for a small office and it contained a welter of documents, maps, statistics, graphs, and charts showing all the water sources, houses, churches, and land parcels, and tracking registration, cooperation, and notifications of malaria cases. The an-onymous journalist said, "to the uninitiated in such paperwork, it was difficult to interpret. We were quite impressed with their rigor and exactitude" (*Imparcial* January 6, 1964).

Dr. Gehlert-Mata said,

we created a *mística*, yes. Back then the brigades looked great, all in their khaki uniforms, they had their hard hats, their yellow masks. I have a photo album of it all.[15] We had special jeeps. We also created maps of all the malaria regions of the country with each *house* drawn in. Around 100 maps. And this was long before there were satellites! They knew where the person lived when they took the blood sample, so if it came out positive they could be there within 24 hours with the medicine. There was a network of volunteers who indicated that there was a case that appeared to be malaria, a fever. I think they were trained to take blood themselves. It's really very simple – just a prick. *It was an entire social organization.* Now, of course this was all before the problems of the internal war that we lived through. This would have been *very* dangerous in those times, for one band, or for the other band, either for the government or the insurgency, to know the whereabouts of each and every person. They had even identified the little children. When you have to take the medicine every fourteen days, when it was the preventive medicine, you have to keep track.

Gehlert-Mata was proud that under his watch malaria cases dropped precipitously and *Falciparum* was practically eliminated.

As glowing reports on SNEM's progress frequently pointed out, the war on malaria was opening previously difficult-to-inhabit areas to commercial production, contributing to a surge in export crops, especially cotton (Humphreys 2001). While records of the time frequently criticize the cotton-growers for not doing enough in the malaria struggle, by the mid-1960s they too "realized it was better to cooperate than be indifferent." They began to keep track of work teams coming down from the highlands and set up medication sites and specialists to administer chloroprimaquine to each worker upon arrival (*Imparcial* January 6, 1964). Unfortunately, their massive use of DDT against cotton pests was simultaneously increasing mosquito resistance with remarkable speed.

For over one hundred years Guatemala's political economy has been based in the latifundia-minifundia system. Latifundias are vast tracts of land, usually in mid- to low-lying coastal areas (read malaria sites), producing primarily export crops like coffee, sugarcane, and bananas. Minifundias are tiny plots usually in highland areas, and often worked by indigenous subsistence farmers. Centuries of land shortages worsened by nineteenth-century government regulations giving communal land to nonindigenous (*ladinos*) for-profit producers mean that minifundistas are usually unable to grow enough corn and beans to sustain a family for a year. So they must migrate to pick export crops during harvest seasons, a nefarious scene of exploitative interdependence that was threatened by President Arbenz's land reform.

Malaria is an imperial disease.[16] It was brought to the Americas by the Spanish colonizers and it takes the heaviest toll on nonlocals in tropical areas, including highland Maya forced to descend to the tropics for work. In 1908 Brault wrote, "fever and dysentery are the 'generals' that defend hot countries against our incursions and prevent us from replacing the aborigines that we have to make use of" (in Latour 1988: 141). The French, British, and US race to find a cure in the late 1800s was meant to keep whites alive in their new milieu, and the legal and later virtual enslavement of Africans and their Caribbean descendents in the fever-ridden agro-export zones was justified by their supposed immunity. Creating transportation infrastructure like canals and railroads, stationing armies, clearing ground to plant and harvest tropical products, all had to confront (in addition to uprisings, escape, work slowdowns, and other human-level obstacles) the invisible microbial resistance and its effects. As Adams wrote in 1914:

> the natives would not work on plantations, and most of them still have an unconquerable aversion to sustained physical toil. The reason is not far to seek. The mosquitoes...have so inoculated them with their virus that they have neither the ambition nor the strength to compete with workers not thus afflicted. It is entirely possible that a generation of Central American natives of the laboring class might, if forced or persuaded to conform to modern sanitary science, surprise the world by displaying none of the laziness inherent in those who now inhabit mosquito-ridden sections. (267)

These biopolitical strategies of "modern sanitary science" – hygiene, medicine, health (what Latour calls Pasteurization or the S-5 might call "giving water") – are aimed at life. Their goal is both the life of the individual body – "the adjustment and economy of energies" (for Adams, the worker's body) – and the social body – "the regulation of populations, through the far-reaching effects of its activity" (Adams foresees entire classes and subsequent generations improved by these interventions). Like sex, malaria eradication "fitted in both categories at once, giving rise to infinitesimal surveillances, permanent controls, extremely meticulous orderings of space, indeterminate medical or psychological examinations, to an entire micro-power concerned with the body. But it gave rise as well to comprehensive measures, statistical assessments, and interventions aimed at the entire social body or at groups taken as a whole" (Foucault 1980: 145–146).

In 1957 an anonymous journalist compared Guatemala to the United States where malaria had been eradicated. "Their efficiency is helped by geography, organization, and education. Guatemala will require a lot of work, considerable investment and a limitless tenacity to achieve such coordination and systematization" (*Imparcial* January 11, 1957; see also Humphreys 2001). But the *savoirs* of science, technology, and human nature *did* seem to work. While in 1940 there were more than 30,000 cases of malaria and over 13,000 deaths, in 1963 no autochthonous cases were registered. People now remember the incredible spirit of the SNEM teams, their "*mística*," the organization, the discipline, the sense of mission (in fact the aging veterans still meet periodically to reminisce). The brigadistas seem to embody Foucault's pastoral power. As state representatives they crossed raging rivers, braved fever zones, fumigated in the heat, and cared for the flock, each and every one, thereby enacting the state's willingness to sacrifice for its people and not only demand sacrifice. Perhaps in response a *mística* also developed among the population. People proudly displayed the little papers that showed they'd been regularly fumigated, and participated in the immense, energetic network of volunteers who aided in mapping and then carefully administering their hamlets, seeking out feverish neighbors, ensuring they took the full course of medicine, attending to all the human and environmental sites that are "a danger for the collective" (Argueta 1955). As Rabinow would say, risk becomes socialized as each person's health becomes the responsibility of others (1989: 187). With this willingness to take responsibility they would seem to agree with Ovalle Lopez that "it is a human right to be healthy" (1960).

Redefining the Whole Caboodle

While I've definitely skewed my description toward a Foucauldian reading, it would be pretty easy to describe Guatemala's post-1954 coup WHO-supported malaria campaign point for point as a classic case of biopower on the loose. Governmental techniques of systematization are deployed throughout the social body and individuals are actively engaged in optimizing their health. You will also, no doubt, have noticed striking similarities between the strategies and tactics of the two wars I've been describing. As Dr. Gehlert-Mata acknowledges, SNEM's sophisticated mapping "would have been *very* dangerous . . . either for the government or the insurgency, to know the whereabouts of each and every person." (Of course the government *did* have such information, which is why the guerrilla so often burned down municipal archives.)

How might we think about the parallels between the two wars? While even the Guatemalan army admits that the civil war was a national tragedy, it's hard to dispute that eradicating malaria would be good for the world. This is true even if the eradication were instigated in order to support neocolonial capitalist assaults on resistant "unproductive" lowland environments, and on "lazy natives." So, was the campaign "just" a cover for the nefarious purposes of the Guatemalan military and a newly regnant United States? Does it matter that the counter-revolutionary government didn't "really" care about the wellbeing of its citizens, or that the plantation owners didn't "truly" give a damn about the health of the workers (outside of their ability to pick cotton)? Or, given the terrifying ease with which the target of such tactics can switch from *Falciparum* and mosquito to "Indian," activist (or terrorist, Jew, Palestinian, black, Tutsi, Timorese, and so forth), should the two wars be lumped together as the same thing? Should those of us "truly" invested in improving the world oppose them both?

Bruno Latour, keen on disputing the indisputable in investigations of the Pasteurization of France, warns (like Foucault) against any resting assured that we know (a *connaissance*, perhaps?) what "true" improvement might be. He records translations, displacements, strengthenings, and reorganizations that over time and through struggle produce a redefinition of the social. "We cannot reduce the action of the microbe to a sociological explanation, since the action of the microbe redefined not only society but also nature and the whole caboodle" (1988: 38). He might call the *savoirs* of the malaria eradication campaigns of the twentieth century a "strengthening," as new subjects are formed who understand and act on the "new facts" that standing water is dangerous, your neighbor needs to take her medicine, and so on. "This unexpected strengthening is not in itself 'reactionary,' as suggested by some authors who are used to speaking only of power and who see hygiene as a 'means of social control.' The allies of the microbe are to be found on the left as well as on the right.... It is often impossible to tell whether such wars serve the right or the left because the microbe, like other actors in such networks, 'renders unpredictable interests that would be too predictable without [them]' " (Latour 1988: 36–37).

The genocidal counterinsurgency definitely served the "right" in Guatemala, although often with unexpected consequences. While many in Guatemala were and are sympathetic to the aims of the guerrillas, the modernizing nationalist grid of intelligibility of their struggle has been critiqued as exclusionary of Maya, women, and others (many of whom, however, passed through the revolution, thereby redefining the whole caboodle) (see Hale 1994 on Nicaragua). Also, pursuing the unpredictable interests in wars against microbes is not to say that the plantation owners were not viciously exploiting the indigenous peasants who had no alternative to working for miserable wages in fever zones, or that the military state was not brutal when it beat up villagers who didn't want to be fumigated, and murdered coastal labor organizers struggling for higher wages, improved health care, and better working conditions.[17] In fact, these relations led directly to the second phase of the civil war in the late 1970s. Biopolitics however, like Latour's actor networks, push us to focus on relations (often violent, but not always), on what lies between minifundia and latifundia; between the Guatemalan state, local and transnational capital, *and* mosquitoes and indigenous workers; and between SNEM brigadistas and plasmodium, doctors, entomologists, soldiers, anthropologists, and others.

The productivity of power, the very subjectivization that works through these relational networks, suggests we are not actors in the liberal autonomous sense, but neither are we docile automatons. We are acting all the time (not only when taking up arms) in relations through which power always flows in more than one direction. Latour suggests

such distinctions among types of actors matter less than the fact that they are all renegotiating what the world is made up of, who is acting in it, who matters, and who wants what. They are all creating – this is the important point – *new sources* of power and new sources of legitimacy, which are irreducible to those that hitherto coded the so-called political space. They cannot be reduced to a "social or political explanation," since they are renewing the political game from top to bottom with new forces. (1988: 40)

I've been wagering that "getting smart" (like Tom Tomorrow's bombs) with Foucault's theories of power helps us resist reductions and instead work through the tensions between conspiracy theory and *savoirs* that subjectivize us, between the right of death and power over life, and between the life of the individual and the life of the species (rather than position ourselves only on one side, the other, or outside). Getting smart means thinking about "that without which I cannot think at all" and how, through that, to chart an ethical way to "make the world a better place." This entails, as Foucault suggests, attending to "subjugated knowledges," "preserved possibilities," and the "grid of intelligibility" (Gordon 1980; see also Stoler 1995) that makes improvement thinkable at all. He did this in his genealogies of fearless speech, pastoral power, confession, care of the self, and so forth. To move toward a conclusion, I'd like to address these "betweens" to quickly genealogize biopolitics and life during wartime through Lamarck.

Life and Lamarckian Interventions in the Milieu

Lamarckianism was the mechanism by which man's conscious social activities affected and effected his further physical evolution.... [It] expressed an almost pathetic yearning for the old belief...of the social worker [who] thinks that his efforts to help individuals are of social importance.

George Stocking

Lamarck? Isn't he the one from junior high biology who says that acquired traits are passed down? Like the old giraffe example? You know, an individual giraffe stretches to reach higher leaves, lengthening its neck slightly, then passes this trait on to her young, leading, after numerous generations of stretchers, to the giraffe of today, comfortably adapted to her niche. In junior high I was taught to giggle at this explanation and prefer the random workings of natural selection in Darwinian evolutionary theory. (Although Darwin was a Lamarckian!) After Mendel it became "aberrant" to believe in Lamarck (Stocking 1982: 253) and Arthur Kroeber called "heredity by acquirement...equally a biological and historical monstrosity" (in Stocking 1982: 259). But it turns out there may be more to Lamarck than my bio teacher let on. In fact, Lamarckianism may provide a grid of intelligibility that lends vitality to hopes and activism aimed at improving the world. *And* it may exist as a preserved possibility within the practices of biopolitics.

Around 1800 Lamarck articulated an evolutionary theory that undermined the then-current essentialist understanding of species as timeless ideal types.[18] Instead he focused on dynamic changes in creatures that would eventually lead to more widespread changes through which new species emerged. He developed the notion of *milieu* from its use in Newtonian physics to conceptualize an active relationship between an organism and its environment. He posited that when the body is faced with changing circumstances, its needs change. Attempting to fulfill these needs leads it to change how it acts, to transform its habits. By exercising different parts of the body – muscles, fluids, parts of the brain – those organs themselves change. It is a little unclear how this occurs, whether through fluids, electricity, or in part through what he called a *sentiment intérieur*, which Michael Ruse translates as "life force" (1999: 7). These changes would then be passed down to succeeding generations. It was believed that germ cells (egg and sperm) were produced from the whole body, including the brain, which is why the changes in such organs would be heritable (Ruse 1999: 153; see also Jordanova 1984; Rabinow 1989; Stepan 1991).

Lamarckianism is a behavioral and ecological theory of biological evolution. Rabinow says that "life was the central concept in Lamarck's system [but] he vigorously sought to strip the notion of any metaphysical or religious residues. Life was physical; matter was passive, life active" (1989: 135). Lamarck's notion of milieu, meaning literally in-between, is a mode of thinking about interactions among the natural environment, social elements, and individual humans. It insists on a relational system. Stocking says, "Lamarckianism helped to explain the evolution of races and the mental evolution of man in terms which gave what we would now call 'culture' a crucially determining role. It helped to explain and to validate the cultural progress of mankind in biological terms, at the same time that it freed man from the conservative implications of biological evolutionism" (1982: 256). By conservative he seems to mean that in traditional Darwinism the past determines the future, everything comes down to that bottleneck where egg and sperm meet and then you're done for (which may be why Foucault had to write a "history of sexuality").[19]

Stocking describes Lamarckianism influencing Auguste Comte, Herbert Spencer, Booker T. Washington (via the "uplift of the race"), the colonial sense of "the white man's burden," many socialist projects emphasizing cooperation rather than competition, and even some of Franz Boas's thinking. When United Fruit Company apologist Frederick Adams writes in 1914 of a generation of Central American natives surprising the world with their vitality (once they are subjectivized by modern sanitation), he is a Lamarckian. But of course, as I was taught in school, Lamarckianism is now *so* over. The growing popularity of Darwinist theories was reinforced by the rediscovery of Mendelian genetics in the early 1900s. Mendel's work with pea plants provided the random genetic mutations that scientifically explained "the descent of man" and August Weismann claimed to prove the continuity of germ plasm and its inability to acquire and pass on characteristics. This combined assault ensured the extinction of the increasingly unfit Lamarckian paradigm. A school of neo-Lamarckians emerged post-Weismann to argue that "the acquired characteristics they had in mind were . . . subtle, slow, internal, adaptive changes of the organism to the environment" (Stepan 1991: 69). But the blows delivered by Weismann, Boas, Kroeber, and others undermined the Lamarckian position so much that by the late 1910s in the United States and Britain it practically became a curse to accuse someone of holding such ideas. No one could plausibly argue that the net results of an individual's life had any effect upon germ plasm, especially not past the first generation.

Lamarckians were also weakened by their apparent obfuscation of the fundamental difference between race as a biological determinant and the new object of inquiry: culture. In fact, a mark of "modern," progressive Euro-American cultural anthropology became the steadfastness of its refusal of Lamarck and embrace of Darwin. (And not only anthropology defines itself this way. Think of the parking lot challenge posed to the Christian fish bumper ornament by its Darwinesque mimic with legs, as well as continuing battles over teaching evolution in US schools.[20]) In the hands of modern antiracists (like the much-missed Stephen Jay Gould) Darwinism is a powerful weapon.[21] But Stocking says it was not easy to give up Lamarck's theories, which legitimized "in *biological* terms the causal efficacy of *social* processes" (1982: 243). Nonetheless, by the 1930s the anti-biological tendencies in behavioral science were completely disseminated and Lamarck was finally done for, except for the pathetic yearnings of some backward-looking social workers (1982: 268).

However, Nancy Leys Stepan suggests that Lamarckianism retained aficionados in Latin America well past the mid-twentieth century.[22] Latin American neo-Lamarckians defined themselves as humane and sensible against Anglo-Saxon "practicality, materiality, and extremity" (1991: 19) and championed its progressive possibilities against social Darwinism's insistence that poverty, criminality, and other forms of "degeneration" were genetically determined and racially fixed. Lamarckianism was linked to hopes for modernity and progress through state intervention in sanitation (giving water to the people), hygiene, family and reproductive health, and exercise. (Here they mean sports and recreation but Stocking calls "exercise" the Lamarckian law: a change in circumstances creates a change in needs creates a change in exercise and action that leads to a change in the organism.) The doctors, activists, and state officials involved in Lamarckian eugenics linked "general hygiene, anti-alcohol campaigns, sports education, a minimum-wage law, and a reduction in the cost of living" (1991: 100) to improving the miserable conditions of their nation's citizens. Doctors and public health workers allied with the state gave Lamarckian theories a major role in struggles for the common good against both internal and external enemies. In postcolonial Latin America external aggression takes the form of military, political, and economic intervention, but it also attacks through aesthetico-scientific criteria. Euro-American social Darwinism blamed Latin American "backwardness" on the degeneracy caused by mixed unions or "miscegenation" (Young 1995). "As evidence that 'half-breeds' could not produce a high civilization, anthropologists pointed to Latin Americans who, they claimed, were now 'paying for their racial liberality' ... the 'promiscuous' crossings ... had produced a degenerate, unstable people incapable of progressive development" (Stepan 1991: 45).

Latin American Lamarckianism responded to these racist dismissals by empha-sizing nurture rather than nature and the importance of a collective antidote. It functioned as a *savoir* among socialist, anarchist, and feminist groups through-out the continent, even if it was often hidden or unconscious (Stepan 1991: 83, 95). But like Darwinism, Lamarckianism could be made an ally of racism, and it also legitimated fascist policies in the Southern Cone in the 1930s and 1940s. Similarly, in tracing the "French modern" Rabinow finds deep-seated and long-lasting Lamarckianism appealing to socialists *and* the soldiers engaged in pacifying colonial subjects (1989: 137–150). The deployment and alliance of Lamarckianism with a particular valence (left, right, racist, antiracist, insurgent, counterinsurgent) depended on its milieu, how it was exercised there, on what lay between it and the various actors struggling over its meaning, and over the strength it offered in particular moments. This also depended on its work as a *savoir*: changing and subjectivizing those who "knew" it. Lamarckianism con-tends that the collective body should manage life. It legitimates interventions that improve social conditions and strengthen both individual and social bodies. As such it functions as a grid of intelligibility enabling both the power over life *and* the right of death.

In 1931 a British reviewer critiqued Brazilian eugenics for being "more socio-logical than biological" (in Stepan 1991: 64). This was exactly the appeal and the terror of Lamarckianism according to Stocking: it was the last theoretical link between the biological and the social (1982: 265). But was it the "last?" Malaria eradication campaigns seem resolutely Lamarckian: they intervene to safeguard collective health and must pay attention to the milieu and its range of actors (social and biological) from plasmodium to standing water, from suspicious townspeople to global funding agencies, from screened houses to general pros-perity (Humphreys 2001). In 1976 *The History of Sexuality* is published, linking bio to politics (and thus becomes one of many "actors" struggling to relate these realms). In 2000 the progressive biologist Richard Lewontin declares himself decidedly non-Lamarckian: "There is no credible evidence that acquired charac-teristics can be inherited or that the process of gene mutation will produce enough of just the right variants at just the right moments to allow species to survive changing environments without natural selection. *But* the claim that the environment of an organism is causally independent of the organism, and that changes in the environment are autonomous and independent of changes in the species itself, is clearly wrong. It is bad biology" (48, emphasis added). By environment he seems to mean something very close to milieu, or even what the Maya understand as *tiempo* (González 2002): "the space defined by the activities of the organism itself" (Lewontin 2000: 53). Like SNEM brigadistas, like this famous biologist, like a French historian, like Guatemalan army counter-insurgency theorists, as I exercise my "self" as a "modern anthropologist" I have to deal with power: the mysterious relation between the life of the individual and the life of the species, the power over death and life, in other words with biopolitics – and with Lamarck. In this milieu I am subjectivized, *produced* by certain often-unacknowledged *savoirs* (including reverse discourses and preserved possibilities).

As you've probably noticed, I don't really think that Lamarck is over, even if, in this day and age, no one would ever admit to holding such "aberrant" views. Lamarckianism may undergird and animate the tensions with which I began this essay: how do I "get smart" with power? How do I understand the discourses that act like the water we swim in, the grid of intelligibility for my very sense of a "better world" and the value of intervention? How do I "know" that without which I would not be able to think at all? How do I bring bios (life) together with the political in an active productive relation?

UBthe*

In what way are those fundamental experiences of madness, suffering, death, crime, desire, individuality connected, even if we are not aware of it, with knowledge and power? I am sure I'll never get the answer; but that does not mean that we don't have to ask the question.

Michel Foucault

The Lamarckian milieu is a transformist conception that brings space and society together and is constantly changing. There is no fixed center, no graphic whole. It is a space of processes with nothing preordained, according to Rabinow (1989: 128–129). This suggests both Latour's description of the constant redefinition of "nature and the whole caboodle" and even more so Foucault's notion of *savoir* that, in the very practice of "knowing" something, produces the knower, and the known.

The Guatemalan army "won" the war, but by making the country into a pariah and destroying the economy. Now they are sharing power with the very people they would have killed 20 years ago and some soldiers are going to jail for their "victory." The war continues on other fronts, its meaning is constantly being remade. SNEM lost the war on malaria. Increased resistance in both mosquito and plasmodium, the DDT ban, lowered human immunity, and lack of medicine led cases to rise again in the 1970s and now they may be as high as ever. But no one really knows. The brigades and volunteer networks were disbanded under health guidelines drawn up to implement IMF support for the new civilian government in 1986. The latest malaria statistics available are from the mid-1990s.

Globalized neoliberal reforms have increasingly privatized risk, making it each person's individual responsibility to stay healthy and fit (Rose 1990; Castel 1991; Peterson and Bunton 1997). The careful if creepy attentions of biopolitical power (the infinitesimal surveillances, permanent controls, statistical assessments, and interventions aimed at the entire social body) seem to give way to the cynical graffiti warning from Pat Cadigan's cyberpunk novel *Synners*: "UBthe*" or you be the asterisk/ass to risk. Subjectivization has made you free, and now you're free to take care of yourself, as Thomas Osborne argues: patients must become entrepreneurs of their own health (1997: 186). The cat is no longer pulling the wagon, both the suspicious and the naive mice are uninsured, and it's darn scary. In response, I (and a lot of other people) have been spending time recently clashing with police at anticorporate-globalization protests because the WTO and G-8 are dismantling the world's welfare systems and environmental protections. As when I chanted "Money for health care not for war," I am still fighting "for" biopower.

But even in the neoliberal milieu, U and B are precisely what is at stake. They are what biopower is all about. It is exercise or struggle that pulls power "left" or "right." Milieu, remember, means what is in between. But as with all productive power, via *savoirs*, subjectivization, the moving internal frontier between individual and social bodies, between death and life, and the constantly changing whole caboodle, these directions are always unpredictable, veering off course, like the smart bombs inspired by Foucault's "theories of power." There are many questions left to be asked and preserved possibilities to be explored as we seek to understand and influence the control panel of smart bombs, deploying our bloody, capillary power. We're all conspirators in biopolitics. We cannot not be. But amidst all the risk we are also vitally unpredictable.

Notes

Acknowledgments: Fieldwork was funded by the National Science Foundation, Lewis and Clark College, and Duke University. I wouldn't have even embarked on it without Jorge Mario Aguilar Velásquez (and Amitav Ghosh). In it I am handing down ideas acquired in conversations with Anne Allison, Lee Baker, José García, Marcial Godoy-Anativía, Matilde González, Marcia Klotz, José Fernando Lara, Alejandro Lugo, Bill Maurer, Rubén Nájera, Liz Oglesby, Eric Worby, and Tomiko Yoda. Greg Grandin is responsible for the archive effect and other challenges. Donald Moore has feverishly supported this incipient project. Peter Redfield and Silvia Tomásková's skills in discipline *and* pleasure literally moved me forward. Jonathan Xavier Inda has labored patiently and pastorally to produce this new tool of power/knowledge and the anonymous reviewer offered very useful comments. Thanks to them, everyone in Guatemala, and especially that central relationship of my milieu, Mark Driscoll.

1 Exegeses of these passages have gone in a number of different directions with the idea of biopolitics, there being no one set definition of exactly what the term means. Some of the best-known deployments are by Agamben (1998, 2000), Hardt and Negri (2000), Rabinow (1989), and Stoler (1995).

2 This chapter draws on fieldwork conducted since 1985 in Guatemala, where I have spent more than four years all together. Where there is no citation, quotes are from author interviews. All translations from the Spanish are mine.

3 Rabinow (1984) describes this meeting of the minds.

4 Anthropology, of course, is the quintessence of the in-between as social science.

5 This was a struggle Foucault was especially interested in, visiting the country several times in the mid-1970s. On the conspiracy side, we *were* duped by Ollie North et al. on the milieu (in-betweens) of the Iran–Contra connections.

6 I'm paraphrasing Foucault's friend and teacher Althusser here (1971).

7 According to another anthropologist who has interviewed Cifuentes, "he knows a lot about the indigenous stuff. Army strategy was divided among either killing them all, ladinizing them, you know, assimilating them, *or* taking their culture into account. He was the spokesman for the latter. He said, in fact, that he was often distrusted within the army because he had these subversive ideas that they had to know their enemy" (personal communication). See also Schirmer (1998).

8 The development poles, like their predecessors – strategic hamlets created by the United States in Vietnam or the British during the Boer War, or the Potemkin villages under Stalinism – were often open to the public and the subject of glossy reports. I was easily able to acquire the Development Poles PR book after showing my passport and being registered at the Guatemala City army base. Full of photos, quotes from the Mayan sacred book *Popul Vuh*, and paeans to the soldiers who saved Guatemala from Communism, it reflects enormous pride in the resettlement areas (Government of Guatemala 1985).

9 On the delicate question of how certain forms and theories of power travel, please see Peter Redfield's nuanced interpretation of the penal colony (chapter 2, this volume). On coevalness and time itself as a form of power/knowledge, see Fabian (1983). While Latour argues that "we have never been modern" (1993), neither Guatemala nor any other colonized place has ever been "outside" modernity. (As I show later, the "modernizing" forms of power enacted in the development poles were already deployed in the 1950s in the war against malaria, and it would not be hard to find similar examples under the Estrada Cabrera dictatorship in the 1910s, or even earlier. We seem to have lingered for centuries on the "threshold of modernity.") Indeed, when we "reorient" our understandings of globalization it becomes clear that places like Guatemala are not only "laboratories of modernity" but indeed, that without which modernity itself cannot exist. *But* this does not mean that there is no difference. I meant to be a bit jokey about Guatemala being "ahead" because it's "behind." To argue that, despite government repression, Guatemalans may be more free precisely because they know they're not free is meant to upset the often maternalist sense that human rights work (like anthropology) is a gift the first world gives the third world. From "our" "developed" position in constitutional democracies where police brutality is supposedly the exception rather than the rule we can agitate for our sisters and brothers elsewhere to be treated just as nicely. Of course, human rights workers and anthropologists are not stupid. We know that our privilege is a function of a global system that unevenly distributes such "modern" enjoyments. But this is often a *connaissance* rather than a *savoir*.

10 While a peace treaty was not signed until 1996 between the government (responsible according to the UN CEH report [1999] for 96 percent of the war crimes they studied) and the guerrilla organization URNG, the worst of the scorched-earth violence had ebbed by late 1984 when, under international pressure, a slow return to civilian rule (not necessarily power) was begun. The numerous splits in the URNG reflect complex mixtures of competing strategies, philosophies, reactions to conditions of possibility,

and personalities. They also responded to structural aspects of the guerrilla organizations, especially the way ethnic difference, gender, and rural–urban identifications were conceived of and (often unconsciously) expressed. The biopolitical hopes that underwrote the struggle supposedly "waged on behalf of the existence of everyone" (Foucault 1980: 137) often retained exclusionary assumptions about which bodies and identities "mattered" (see Hale 1996; Arenas Bianchi et al. 1999; Bastos and Camus 2003; Nelson 2003). This is not to impugn the struggle itself or those who struggled. It is an ongoing process that may not transcend but certainly transforms conditions of possibility (see Žižek on Rosa Luxembourg 1989).

11   Which reminds me of the scene in Monty Python's *Life of Brian* set during the Roman Empire, when an underground anti-imperialist, Reg, declaims, "The Romans've bled us white . . . and what have they given us in return?" A henchman reluctantly offers, "The aqueduct." Reg must admit, "Oh yeah yeah, they did give us that, that's true." And again, "The sanitation." And another one chimes in: "Oh yeah, the sanitation, remember, Reg, what the city used to be like?!" Reg growls, "Alright, I'll grant you the aqueduct, the sanitation, the two things the Romans have done. . . ." "And the roads." "Well yeah, obviously the roads, the roads go without saying, don't they?" This goes on until Reg exclaims in exasperation: "Alright, apart from the sanitation, medicine, education, wine, public order, irrigation, roads, the fresh water system and public health, *what* have the Romans ever done for us?" More seriously, Streeter (2000) suggests that the nationalist army members who started the guerrillas in 1960 were disgruntled, in part, by the lack of health care provided by the Guatemalan military compared to the US soldiers they encountered while on the very international exchanges set up to consolidate the counterrevolution. The United Fruit Company makes much of its health contributions but many of the early labor actions taken against it were to demand improved and equitable health care for all employees (Dosal 1993).

12   "We must make allowance for the complex and unstable process whereby discourse can be both an instrument and an effect of power, but also a hindrance, a stumbling block, a point of resistance and a starting point for an opposing strategy. Discourse transmits and produces power; it reinforces it, but also undermines and exposes it, renders it fragile and makes it possible to thwart it. . . . There is not, on the one side, a discourse of power, and opposite it, another discourse that runs counter to it. Discourses are tactical elements or blocks operating in the field of force relations; there can exist different and even contradictory discourses within the same strategy; they can, on the contrary, circulate without changing their form from one strategy to another, opposing strategy" (1980: 101–102).

13   Page numbers for *El Imparcial* were not available.

14   This number is based on the notion of "basic reproduction number" or BRN, the number of additional infections that an originally infected person will generate under ideal conditions. By comparison, the highly contagious measles carrier tends to a BRN of 12 to 14, while AIDS transmission may have a BRN of only one (Spielman and D'Antonio 2001: 96). My description of malaria is deeply indebted to Gladwell (2001), Honigsbaum (2001), Humphreys (2001), and Spielman and D'Antonio (2001).

15   In 2002, to celebrate the 50th anniversary of the Pan-American Health Organization, the Banco de Café in upscale Zone 9 of Guatemala City sponsored a photo

exhibit in its lobby that featured a number of photos of the SNEM brigades standing proudly with their fumigating equipment or at work spraying down a wall.

16 "If it had been necessary to make colonial society only with masters and slaves, there would never have been any colonial society. It had to be made with microbes, together with the swarming of insects and parasites that they transported.... With only whites and blacks, with only miasmic regions and healthy or dangerous climates, that Colonial Leviathan which spread across the globe could never have been built" (Latour 1988: 144).

17 Matilde González (2002) powerfully describes these experiences from the point of view of the highland Maya.

18 Although George Stocking says that "the Lamarckian assumption had been part of the baggage of European thought for 2,000 years" (1982: 235).

19 Peter Redfield and Silvia Tomásková gave me this language, along with clarity on much else.

20 In October 2002 my personal sense of secular, progressive modernity got a blow to the gut as my home state of Ohio legalized teaching creationism in addition to Darwinism.

21 The social Darwinism that led to eugenics [race improvement] campaigns of sterilization and even mass murder in Nazi Germany are couched as an aberration of these theories.

22 The authors collected in Trigo (2002) provide similar insights on the deployment of Foucault in Latin America.

References

Adams, Frederick Upham
  1914   Conquest of the Tropics: The Story of the Creative Enterprises Conducted by the United Fruit Company. Garden City, NY: Doubleday, Page.
Agamben, Giorgio
  1998   Homo Sacer: Sovereign Power and Bare Life. Daniel Heller-Roazen, trans. Stanford: Stanford University Press.
  2000   Means Without End. Vincenzo Binett and Cesare Casarino, trans. Minneapolis: University of Minnesota Press.
Althusser, Louis
  1971   Ideological State Apparatuses: Notes Towards an Investigation. *In* Lenin and Philosophy and Other Essays. New York: Monthly Review Press.
Alvarez, Francisca
  1996   Las Mujeres Mayas Etnocidas. El Periodico Domingo, November 24.
Arenas Bianchi, Clara, Charles R. Hale, and Gustavo Palma Murga
  1999   ¿Racismo en Guatemala? Abriendo el debate sobre un tema tabú. Guatemala City: AVANCSO.
Argueta, Antonio
  1955   Malaria o paludismo, uno de los grandes peligros: El azote numero uno del pueblo guatemalteco. El Imparcial, June 16.

Bastos, Santiago, and Manuela Camus
  1993 Quebrando el silencio: Organizaciones del pueblo Maya y sus demandas (1986–1992). Guatemala City: FLACSO.
  1995 Abriendo caminos: Las organizaciones Mayas desde el Nobel hasta el Acuerdo de Derechos Indigenas. Guatemala City: FLACSO.
  2003 Entre el mecapal y el cielo: Desarrollo del movimiento Maya en Guatemala. Guatemala City: FLACSO and Cholsamaj.
Butler, Judith
  1993 Bodies that Matter: On the Discursive Limits of "Sex." New York: Routledge.
Cadigan, Pat
  1991 Synners. New York: Bantam Books.
Castel, Robert
  1991 From Dangerousness to Risk. In The Foucault Effect: Studies in Governmentality. Graham Burchell, Colin Gordon, and Peter Miller, eds. Chicago: University of Chicago Press.
CEH (Comisión para el Esclarecimiento Histórico/Commission for Historical Clarification)
  1999 Guatemala: Memory of Silence. Guatemala City: United Nations. Electronic document, hrdata.aaas.org/ceh/report.
Cesaire, Aimé
  1972 Discourse on Colonialism. New York: Monthly Review Press.
Cojtí Cuxil, Demetrio aka Waqi' Q'anil
  1991 Configuración del pensamiento Maya. Quetzaltenango, Guatemala: Academia de Escritores Mayas.
  1995 Ub'anik Ri Una'ooj Uchomab'aal Ri Maya' Tinamit: Configuración del pensamiento politico del pueblo Maya. Part 2. Guatemala City: Cholsamaj.
Dosal, Paul J.
  1993 Doing Business with the Dictators: A Political History of United Fruit in Guatemala 1899–1944. Wilmington, DL: Scholarly Resources Books.
Fabian, Johannes
  1983 Time and the Other: How Anthropology Makes Its Object. New York: Columbia University Press.
Fischer, Edward F., and R. McKenna Brown, eds.
  1996 Maya Cultural Activism in Guatemala. Austin: University of Texas Press.
Foucault, Michel
  1979 Discipline and Punish: The Birth of the Prison. New York: Vintage Books.
  1980 The History of Sexuality, vol. 1: An Introduction. Robert Hurley, trans. New York: Vintage Books.
  1991 Remarks on Marx: Conversations with Duccio Trombadori. New York: Semiotexte.
Gladwell, Malcolm
  2001 Annals of Public Health: The Mosquito Killer. The New Yorker, July 2: 42–51.
Gleijeses, Piero
  1991 Shattered Hope. Princeton: Princeton University Press.
González, Matilde
  2002 "Se cambió el tiempo": Conflicto y poder en territorio K'iche' 1880–1996. Guatemala City: AVANCSO.

Gordon, Colin, ed.
   1980   Power/Knowledge. New York: Random House.
Government of Guatemala
   1985   Polos de desarrollo y servicios: Historiagrafía institucional. Guatemala City:
      Editorial del Ejercito.
Green, Linda
   1999   Fear as a Way of Life: Mayan Widows in Rural Guatemala. New York: Columbia
      University Press.
Hale, Charles
   1994   Resistance and Contradiction: Miskitu Indians and the Nicaraguan State,
      1894–1987. Palo Alto, CA: Stanford University Press.
   1996   *Mestizaje*, Hybridity, and the Cultural Politics of Difference in Post-Revolution-
      ary Central America. Journal of Latin American Anthropology 2(1): 34–61.
Hardt, Michael, and Antonio Negri
   2000   Empire. Cambridge, MA: Harvard University Press.
Honigsbaum, Mark
   2001   The Fever Trail: In Search of the Cure for Malaria. New York: Farrar, Straus, and
      Giroux.
Humphreys, Margaret
   2001   Malaria: Poverty, Race and Public Health in the United States. New York:
      Farrar, Straus, and Giroux.
Jordovana, Ludmilla
   1984   Lamarck. New York: Oxford University Press.
Kinzer, Stephen, and Stephen Schlesinger
   1983   Bitter Fruit. New York: Doubleday Books.
Latour, Bruno
   1988   The Pasteurization of France. Cambridge, MA: Harvard University Press.
   1993   We Have Never Been Modern. Cambridge, MA: Harvard University Press.
Lewontin, Richard
   2000   The Triple Helix: Gene, Organism, and Environment. Cambridge, MA: Harvard
      University Press.
McNeil, Donald G.
   2000   Hovering Where Rich and Poor Meet. The New York Times: C1–3.
Nelson, Diane M.
   1988   Guatemala polos de desarrollo: El caso de la desestructuración de las comuni-
      dades indígenas, vol. 2. Mexico City: CEIDEC.
   1999   A Finger in the Wound: Body Politics in Quincentennial Guatemala. Berkeley:
      University of California Press.
   2001   Stumped Identities: Body Image, Body Politic, and the Mujer Maya as Pros-
      thetic. Cultural Anthropology 16(3): 314–353.
   2003   "The More You Kill the More You Will Live": The Maya, "Race," and Biopo-
      litical Hopes for Peace in Guatemala. *In* Race, Nature, and the Politics of Difference.
      Donald Moore, Jake Kosek, and Anand Pandian, eds. Durham, NC: Duke University
      Press.
Osborne, Thomas
   1997   Of Health and Statecraft. *In* Foucault, Health and Medicine. Alan Petersen and
      Robin Bunton, eds. London: Routledge.

Ovalle Lopez, Werner
    1960   Del día mundial de la salud: La erradicación del paludismo un reto al mundo. El Imparcial, April 8.
Paul, Benjamin, and William Demarest
    1988   The Operation of a Death Squad in San Pedro. *In* Harvest of Violence: The Mayan Indians and the Guatemalan Crisis. Robert Carmack, ed. Norman: University of Oklahoma Press.
Payeras, Mario
    1997   Los pueblos indígenas y la revolución guatemalteca: Ensayos etnicos. Guatemala City: Luna y Sol.
Peterson, Alan, and Robin Bunton, eds.
    1997   Foucault, Health, and Medicine. London: Routledge.
Quintana, Epaminondas
    1964   Guatemalense, si eres patriota no seas indolente, dá tu ayuda. El Imparcial, January 8.
Rabinow, Paul
    1989   French Modern: Norms and Forms of the Social Environment. Chicago: University of Chicago Press.
Rabinow, Paul, ed.
    1984   The Foucault Reader. New York: Pantheon.
REMHI (Recuperación de la Memoria Histórica)
    1998   Guatemala: Nunca Más. 4 vols. Guatemala City: ODHAG.
Rose, Nicholas
    1990   Governing the Soul: The Shaping of the Private Self. London: Routledge.
Ruse, Michael
    1999   The Darwinian Revolution: Science Red in Tooth and Claw. Chicago: University of Chicago Press.
Schirmer, Jennifer
    1998   The Guatemalan Military Project: A Violence Called Democracy. Philadelphia: University of Pennsylvania Press.
Spielman, Andrew, and Michael D'Antonio
    2001   Mosquito: The Story of Man's Deadliest Foe. New York: Hyperion.
Stepan, Nancy Leys
    1991   "The Hour of Eugenics": Race, Gender, and Nation in Latin America. Ithaca: Cornell University Press.
Stocking, George
    1982[1968]   Race, Culture, and Evolution: Essays in the History of Anthropology. Chicago: University of Chicago Press.
Stoler, Ann
    1995   Race and the Education of Desire: Foucault's History of Sexuality and the Colonial Order of Things. Durham, NC: Duke University Press.
Streeter, Stephen
    2000   Managing the Counterrevolution: The United States and Guatemala 1954–1961. Athens: Ohio University Press.
Trigo, Benigno, ed.
    2002   Foucault in Latin America. New York: Routledge.

Warren, Kay
    1998   Indigenous Movements and their Critics: Pan-Maya Activism in Guatemala. Princeton: Princeton University Press.

Wilson, Richard
    1995   Maya Resurgence in Guatemala: Q'eqchi' Experience. Norman: University of Oklahoma Press.

Young, Robert J. C.
    1995   Colonial Desire: Hybridity in Theory, Culture, and Race. London: Routledge.

Žižek, Slavoj
    1989   The Sublime Object of Ideology. London: Verso.

Zur, Judith N.
    1998   Violent Memories: Mayan War Widows in Guatemala. Boulder, CO: Westview Press.

10

Technologies of Invisibility:

Politics of Life and Social Inequality

João Biehl

The Dying City

I begin with three images. The first is that of a plagued city. Death has taken over Thebes, and Oedipus the King is frightened of losing power. Sophocles's tragedy opens with a lament and a request for action by the representative of the people (1984: 160–162):

> "Our city, look around you, see with your own eyes....
> Thebes is dying....
> You have the power, you must cure us of the plague....
> Rule our land, you know you have the power,
> but rule a land of the living, not a wasteland."

> "Curing you of the plague would be to my great benefit," [responded Oedipus]
> "for this plague that assails you, also assails me in my sovereignty."[1]

According to Michel Foucault, the Western antinomy between knowledge and power finds its mythical form in Sophocles's work: "When classical Greece appeared – Sophocles represented its starting date, its sunrise – what had to disappear for this society to exist was the union of power and knowledge" (2000: 32). In the classic tragedy, the plagued city becomes a conduit for a change in the ways power is conceived: the enunciation of truth shifts from a prophetic type of discourse to a retrospective one characterized by evidence. And as the tragedy comes to an end, truth doesn't belong to political power anymore. Power itself is blind. "From this time onward," writes Foucault, "the man of power would be the man of ignorance.... If there is a knowledge it must renounce power. Where knowledge and science are found in their pure truth, there can be no longer any political power. This great myth needs to be dispelled. Political power is not absent from knowledge, it is woven together with it" (2000: 32).

The second image is that of the West's most celebrated political icon: Thomas Hobbes's Leviathan. I want to note that in the image that introduces the text the city is emptied of people, with the exception of a few soldiers, and the population is present in the figure of the sovereign – their faces are actually inscribed in its figure – which rules in a ghost-like manner outside the city walls. Here power has to do with transforming people into a population embodied by the sovereign. The citizen is absent from the city and bodiless, one could say.[2] So, how are people made into absent things?

The dying city reappears in Foucault's *Discipline and Punish*. The measures brought into seventeenth-century European plague-ridden cities were a kind of precursor to the automatic functionings of power that Foucault exemplified in Bentham's panoptic model. "The registration of the pathological must be constantly centralized. The relation of each individual to his disease and to his death passes through the representatives of power, the registration they make of it, the decision they take on it" (1979: 197). In the eighteenth and nineteenth centuries, individual bodily discipline was increasingly combined with the regulation of the biological processes of populations, leading to emergence of what Foucault calls biopower: "If the old right of sovereignty consisted in killing or letting live, the new right will consist of making live and letting die. . . . The new right will not cancel the first, but will penetrate it, traverse it, change it" (1992: 172). Biopower is a "scientific power" which works continuously, changing scales, areas of action, and instruments of government. Government is no longer based only in the visible body but on living man as part of the species: "a new body emerges . . . a multiple body, with a numerous if not infinite quantity of heads. Biopolitics works with the notion of population . . . population as a biological problem, and as a problem of power" (1992: 176; see also Foucault 1991). Modern politics is increasingly played out in the physiology of the citizen: "modern man is an animal whose politics places his existence as a living being in question" (1980: 143). The question remains: Life for whom? Who is to be let die?

In this essay, I reflect on a new and emergent biopolitical paradigm: the Brazilian control of AIDS, which combines prevention with free distribution of antiretroviral therapies and is widely touted as a model for stemming the AIDS crisis in the developing world. Strands of these various political elements I alluded to are recombined in this policy, which came into existence through an assemblage of international financial institutions, commercial science, a reforming state, and nongovernmental mobilization – all in a context of deeply entrenched inequality. In the face of the devastation brought about by AIDS, the unlikely availability of a vaccine in the near future, and the relatively few interventions that seem replicable, this is a most welcome success story.[3] It emerges not out of utopian principles or privileged contexts but from being near to desperate realities and redirecting seemingly inflexible commercial scientific and state logics toward equitable outcomes. After briefly historicizing the development of this novel form of *biogovernmentality*, I will examine concrete situations in which the AIDS policy is involved and the ways in which it affects local trajectories of the epidemic both institutionally and in lived experience, particularly in urban poor contexts where AIDS is spreading most rapidly.[4] From the perspective of the marginal and poor people with AIDS living in the streets and in and out of pastoral institutions, we see that economic globalization, state and medical reform, and the acceleration of claims over human rights and citizenship coincide with a continuous local production of social death that remains by and large unaccounted for.

The AIDS Model

State, civil society, and market restructuring play an essential role in any understanding of the Brazilian AIDS model. In 1992 the World Bank and the Brazilian government approved an unprecedented 250 million dollars aid package for the creation of a National AIDS Program whose aim was to reverse what international experts were calling the "africanization" of AIDS in Brazil (*Isto É/Senhor* 1991: 52; Biehl 1999; Galvão 2000). AIDS activists, politicians, economists, and scientists organized an impressive governmental and nongovernmental administrative apparatus that is believed to have contained the epidemic's growth through massive and community-mediated prevention projects, with a particular focus on condom distribution, HIV testing, and behavioral change among the so-called high-risk groups (Coordenação Nacional de DST e AIDS 2000). In 1996 national data began to show a decrease in the epidemic's rate of growth. The National AIDS Program and the World Bank agree that half of the projected 1.2 million HIV cases have been averted. In November 1996, President Fernando Hénrique Cardoso signed a law that made anti-HIV drugs available to all registered AIDS cases. In the words of epidemiologist Pedro Cherquer, former National AIDS Coordinator and designer and implementer of this management: "This drug policy increased self-reporting and, as a result, we have achieved near universal registration" (personal communication, 2000). Approximately 135,000 patients are taking AIDS therapies today. The availability of the cocktail and laboratory testing, funded by the Brazilian government at an annual cost of 2,000 dollars per patient, has reduced the use of hospital services and AIDS mortality by more than 50 percent in São Paulo and Rio de Janeiro, the most affected areas of the country. Mother-to-child HIV transmission has been reduced by two-thirds.

As the Brazilian state renegotiates contracts with multinationals and threatens to overturn international patent laws in the name of protecting public health, this innovative program is also strengthening the country's scientific infrastructure and pharmaceutical industry. As Dr. Eloan Pinheiro, the former director of Far Manguinhos, the state's main pharmaceutical company that produces many of the generic antiretrovirals that are being consumed, explains: "We have reverse engineered two drugs that are under patent protection and we are ready to go into production if the government deems it necessary. The multinationals must become flexible, and we must all deal with the question of whether new technologies are going to benefit man or exclude him from the possibility of surviving" (personal communication, 2001). As to her way of doing science, Dr. Pinheiro does not agree that it is sheer copying: "We had to develop our own methods of analyzing the drugs. I traveled to China and India to learn and to buy salts from them.... Sometimes, if we want the species to survive, we have to regress from some advanced logics that are in place" (personal communication, 2001). Here, out of constraint and imagination, global market logics and the politics of science and technology are forced into explicitness and become a new and productive field of tension and negotiation.

This policy of biotechnology for the people is being hailed as "proof that poor nations can do it" and as "a model for treating AIDS worldwide" (Rosenberg 2001), and the Brazil story is now an important component of international medical activism (e.g., Doctors Without Borders, Oxfam, and Partners in Health). The Brazilian response to AIDS challenges the perception that it is impossible economically to even consider intervening in the pandemic's course in low-income countries, and calls our attention to the possible ways in which biotechnology can be integrated in public policy and can contribute to political and human advancement in developing contexts, even in the absence of an optimal health infrastructure. Affirming the need to combine prevention policies with treatment, this policy opens a political and moral debate on the role of industry, medical science, government, and philanthropy in providing medications to poor countries, and of the immediate and long-term implications of doing so.

From 1992 to 1997, and from 2000 to 2001, I carried out fieldwork in state, corporate, scientific, nongovernmental and local public health institutions, whose restructuring went hand in hand with what I call the Brazilian "AIDS transition." I also worked in community-run services and with marginal populations living with AIDS in the streets and without access to care in southern Porto Alegre and in northeastern Salvador. In my longitudinal ethnographic work, I charted the technical and political means through which such an innovative public health intervention has been engineered in a state marked by corruption, arbitrariness of resource allocation, inefficiency, and general inattention to abysmal social and health inequality. I am particularly interested in the ways in which populations are medically and bureaucratically restructured around this unique access to life-extending treatments.

My research concerns are situated in the fields of medical anthropology, science and technology studies, development, and international health. In the early 1990s, anthropologists began to closely follow the production of new bioscientific knowledge and the making of biotechnologies, inquiring into their multiple deployments and into their interactions with old and new forms of power relations (Strathern 1992; Rabinow 1996, 1999; Rapp 1999; Lock 2002; Fischer 2003). Rabinow (chapter 7, this volume), for example, notes a dissolution of the traditional social domain and the emergence of new forms of identity and moral reasoning around the technical possibility of the literal remodeling of life (what he calls "biosociality"). Medical anthropology has come a long way from its initial emphasis on ethnomedicine, which focused on folk categories of sickness and healing and counterposed them with Western biomedical diagnostics and treatment. The recent work of anthropologists Veena Das (1995, 1999), Arthur Kleinman (1999), and Nancy Scheper-Hughes (2000), to mention a few, shows how medical and technical interventions affect – sometimes for better, sometimes for worse – the etiology, experience, and course of disease. The appearance and distribution of disorders such as drug-resistant tuberculosis and AIDS are also closely correlated with poverty and social and technological inequality. They are "pathologies of power" (Farmer 1999, 2003) mediated by biological, social, and technical and political-economic mechanisms. Concrete biological phenomena are intertwined with environmental conditions that are part of a grander human life-context, and it is in this complicated web that the individual's illness experience is constituted.

Most social scientific accounts explain the Brazilian "antiretroviral revolution" in terms of the strength of social mobilization in Brazil. Gay activist groups and AIDS activists and experts working at the level of national and international mobilization and lawmaking played a great role in forcing the state to fulfill its constitutionally mandated health obligations (Galvão 2002). What remains largely unconsidered are other political and market forces that have been determinant to the AIDS policy's current form and course and which I briefly address in this essay. The main focus of the essay, however, is on the new fields of exchange and possibility that are generated as state actors and institutions reach out and so-called marginals leave (some successfully, some not) their predetermined place and face AIDS and its technical and political apparatuses.[5] What social capacities and institutions are instantiated? What destinies do marginals living in complex urban settings embrace as they are slated for intervention? More broadly, how are disease, misery, and marginality governed through the AIDS response? Throughout, I argue that selective life extension and social death are the two poles of a continuum through which the state, medicine, community, and the citizen empirically forge and modulate their existence today.

AIDS and Democratization

AIDS emerged in Brazil in the early 1980s, concurrently with the demise of a military state. Its growth coincided with the country's democratization amid a ruined economic and social welfare system (Parker and Daniel 1991; Parker et al. 1994; Galvão 2000). First reports showed that AIDS was most prevalent in urban centers, among men who had sex with men – but this epidemiological profile would rapidly and dramatically change (Bastos and Barcellos 1995, 1996). In

1985, 79 percent of the reported AIDS cases were individuals who had either finished high school or had a college education. Ten years later, 78 percent of the reported AIDS cases were illiterate or had only finished elementary school. In 1983, there were 40 men for 1 woman with AIDS; in 1990 the ratio was 6 : 1, in 1996 the ratio was already 3 : 1, and now it is almost 1 : 1. Amid panic, fear, and discrimination, the government's refusal to seriously address AIDS and its systematic nonintervention would play a determinant role in the unfettered course of the epidemic in the country (Scheper-Hughes 1994).

In those early years of AIDS and in the absence of international and national support, the response to the epidemic sprung from grassroots movements, most notably from gay activists who pressured local municipal and regional health services for information and treatment, and carried out prevention campaigns. In São Paulo, for example, such a mobilization led to the creation in 1983 of a state-wide public health AIDS Program, the first of this kind in Latin America (under the supervision of Dr. Paulo Teixeira who would later bring this know-how to the National Program). Here grassroots and regional state interventions were not antithetical to each other. They had in common a progressive political commitment and understood the need to integrate information and care and pragmatically established alliances with health technicians and philanthropic institutions (Teixeira 1997). The AIDS epidemic also occasioned the creation of several new nongovernmental organizations throughout the country.[6] These new social movements galvanized demands and actions aimed at securing citizenship and human rights mandated by the new progressive constitution of 1988 which made health everyone's right and the state's duty. This universal right would have to find ways to be realized amid the country's wholesale neoliberalization and state dismantling. AIDS activists representing socially vulnerable groups such as homosexuals and sex-workers developed a strong public voice in the dispute over access to ever scarcer public and medical resources. While the underfunded and understaffed state public health services were increasingly paralyzed in their capacity to address the growing complexities of AIDS, grassroot spaces of health care emerged and bore the medical and social burden of the AIDS crisis among the poorest.

In the 1990s, with AIDS increasingly viewed as a development problem and with World Bank funds available, activists became less antagonistic toward the state and became key advisors to the National AIDS Program. The role of NGOs was central to the new forms of governmentality sought by sociologist President Fernando Henrique Cardoso (1998). Activists along with managers and scientists constituted a new "epistemic community" within the state (Rosário Costa 1996). This community sought to produce a transparent and efficient system of coordination between international monitoring and regional demands for intervention. The Brazilian AIDS epidemic also served as a test case for the World Bank's development policies that called for institutional changes and a decentralized administration of well-targeted health-related projects for specified populations (World Bank 1993; see also Stiglitz 2002). The majority of funds were allocated to AIDS prevention, mostly through NGOs (which grew from 120 in 1993 to 480 in 1999) and to the institutional development of regional and municipal AIDS programs that operated like NGOs. On the one side, these technically construed and culturally sensitive prevention programs helped to create a new state credibility and a public discourse on sexuality and risk; on the other side, they failed to be integrated in the country's precarious universal health-care system. As the policy was being implemented, epidemiologists, demographers, and statisticians working within the Program and local health systems began to make the massive human scope of the epidemic legible.

By 1996, these interventions were said to be decreasing the epidemic's rate of growth. At this moment in the AIDS policy's course, we have afflicted populations represented by NGOs within the state and, at a local level, NGOs ruled by what anthropologist Jane Galvão calls "the dictatorship of projects" (2000). Also at local levels, we have religious and philanthropic organizations triaging AIDS patients' access to welfare and medical goods, a phenomenon I call the "pastor-alization of the social domain" (Biehl 1999). Paradoxically, by 1996, a World Bank-funded infrastructure that was initially guided by principles of decentralization and prevention rather than direct assistance created the conditions for the democratization of access to the new resources of AIDS science. Widespread access to anti-HIV drugs – which we could also call "a technological surprise" (Aron 1951) – redirected personal and political history and opened new markets. Indeed, as Sjaak van der Geest, Susan Reynolds Whyte, and Anita Hardon (1996) have pointed out, pharmaceuticals have a social life: they are part of booming economies and of novel political and symbolic actions.

I want to make the point that the developments around the AIDS policy dovetailed with former President Cardoso's efforts to internationalize Brazil's market. Not by chance, just a few months before the 1996 antiretroviral law was approved and succumbing to industry lobbying pressure, Brazil legalized patent protection for pharmaceuticals. Brazil signed the treaty on Trade-Related Aspects of Intellectual Property Rights (TRIPS) in 1995, and since the government was eager to attract new investments it allowed for immediate patent protection whereas other countries such as India and Argentina had until 2005 to conform to TRIPS. The Brazilian action led to a dramatic increase in the import of pharmaceutical products, making Brazil the largest pharmaceutical market in Latin America (and eighth largest in the world – see Bermudez 1995; Bermudez et al. 2000). It also led to a new form of leveraging power with big pharma. Pharmaceutical companies had already recouped their research investment on AIDS drugs, and with Brazil they enjoyed a new fixed market and unforeseen returns even in the face of lowered drug prices. Thus the Brazilian AIDS model has also become a model of developing new markets elsewhere. A pharmaco-economic report on emergent HIV/AIDS pharmaceutical markets, namely Brazil, Thailand, India, China, and South Africa, argues that even if these governments provided the simplest version of the cocktail to some 30 percent of the affected populations at 10 percent of the current US price, in 2004 the industry would still make some additional 11.2 billion dollars.

Through the AIDS policy, one sees that economic globalization does not necessarily limit states. Rather, it opens up new prospects for states, and allows states to experiment with new forms of regulating markets for life-saving treatments. Grassroots activities as well those of public opinion combined to maximize social equity in the face of the market's "inevitable" agency in resource allocation or denial. The work of nongovernmental organizations and their international counterparts gave voice to specific mobilized communities and helped to consolidate actions that were wider and more efficacious than state action alone. Empowered by the National AIDS Program, activists successfully forced the government to draft two additional legal articles that would allow compulsory licensing of patented drugs in a public health crisis, and this legislation created a venue for *state activism* vis-à-vis the pharmaceutical industry.

Internationally, the AIDS policy has also acquired a very powerful demonstrative power. Inspired on the Brazilian model, anthropologist-physicians Paul Farmer and Jim Kim and their Harvard-based organization Partners in Health have built up a pilot antiretroviral treatment project in impoverished Haiti (Farmer et al. 2001). They are now engaged with big pharma representatives and philanthropic institutions such as the Gates Foundation in thinking the cost and possibilities of such projects in large scale for the developing world. Jim Kim is now collaborating with Dr. Paulo Teixeira, the former coordinator of Brazil's AIDS Program at the World Health Organization, in among other things a project to bring AIDS therapies to at least 3 million people living in the poorest regions of the world by 2005.

Beyond such demonstrative power, however, I am concerned with how the AIDS policy coexists with historically entrenched mechanisms of social exclusion that continue to shape the course of life and death for Brazil's most vulnerable. As the lives of many poor AIDS patients are being extended and the international pharmaceutical contract and ethics are being rewritten, my ethnographic work in northeastern Brazil shows that a large number of poor and marginal AIDS victims are absent from epidemiological statistics and health care and, with no apparent rights, are allowed to die in abandonment. These persons live in the streets or abandoned buildings, before the eyes of the public. In their troubled existence with AIDS, they have sporadic contact with governmental services of testing and medical care or with nongovernmental forms of support, but no specific programs of prevention and treatment support them. Their experience of dying is simply ordinary and met with political and moral indifference. The invisibilization of death among the poorest with AIDS is concomitant with the successful control of mortality as articulated by Brazil's new biopolitical paradigm.

Science and Scarcity

These realities are neither the outcome of a simple progression nor are they absolutely new. So, before presenting some epidemiological and ethnographic data, let me briefly put these initial insights and arguments into historical perspective. Drawing from the past makes the present more comprehensible, and also illuminates how the current pharmaceutical regimes I am talking about are different from previous public health regimes. In this sense, the Brazilian experiment with AIDS reminds me of the much-celebrated technical control of yellow fever, the bubonic plague, and smallpox in Rio de Janeiro from 1903 to 1906, under the leadership of scientist-administrator Oswaldo Cruz.

In 1900, after returning from his microbiological studies at the Pasteur Institute in France, Cruz was given a position in the national Serum Therapy Laboratory, later named after him. The laboratory's growing technological and research base and rise to international fame with the discovery of Chagas's disease was closely connected to Cruz's successful public health campaign in Rio. As historian Nancy Stepan (1976) has shown, the need to halt disease in the capital was pressing not only in order to improve Brazil's public image abroad, but also to guarantee the flow of much-needed immigrants and capital. Cruz's program tested the nation's ability to be part of the modern world: it replaced the traditional solutions of fumigation and disinfection by a plan that was large scale and very expensive, including systematic extermination of *Aedes aegypti* mosquitoes, patient isolation, compulsory vaccination, and treatment with serums. Much of the efficacy of this short-lived intervention lay in strong federal financial support, the integration of laboratory science, experimental medicine and public health, and their urban targetedness. The rational-technical control of AIDS that I have been talking about follows this pattern: it integrates science into state policy and experiments with circumscribed populations – its economic sustainability is in question.

The optimism of successfully containing the plagues in Rio, and thereby engendering a limited reality that would stand for a healthy modern Brazil, was counterbalanced, however, by the shocking publication, in 1904, of Euclides da Cunha's classic *Os Sertões*, translated as *Rebellion in the Backlands* (1944). A military engineer and journalist, Euclides chronicled a war waged by the national army a few years earlier against an autonomous community made up of mostly landless peasants and former slaves led by a healer, Antonio Conselheiro, in the backlands of the northeastern state of Bahia. The ending of Canudos' settlement and the brutal elimination of thousands of *jagunços*, as they were called, played a key symbolic role in the spectacle of Brazil's turn of the century political modernization as well – the war was justified in the name of local order, democracy, and of militarily safeguarding the paths of progress.

For Euclides, the war itself became a source of intelligibility of the complex social order of which these abandoned people were a part. He took as his problem to understand and to indict what he called the "barbaric forces of civilization" inasmuch as they actively needed to leave "a third of our people in the heart of our country behind in centuries-old semi-darkness" (1944: 161), where any crime could be committed without being investigated or punished. Euclides counterposed that miserable society, in rags and self-sustaining, with the army of Brazil's modernization, backed by science, armaments, and arts of war derived from Europe. According to him, the same emancipatory science that helps to know and to improve life also helps to kill, particularly in the periphery of civilization, where that science is taken up as the norm by "the blind copyists that we are" (1944: 161). The wretched misery and violence witnessed by Euclides compelled him to question the determinism of a physical anthropology founded on the existence of a *homo americanus*, on the supposed degeneracy of "inferior mixed races," and on the destiny of environmental overdetermination: "There is not such a thing as a Brazilian anthropological type.... We are condemned to civilization.... Our biological evolution demands the guarantee of social evolution" (1944: 54).

How People Become Absent Things

Let me give you a brief sample of a social epidemiological study I carried out in the northeastern state of Bahia. Bahia is the largest state in the Northeast Region, with a population of 12.5 million. Salvador, the capital, has 2.5 million people and is a center of international tourism. Salvador concentrates 70 percent of the total AIDS cases in the state. In 1997, epidemiological reports were already citing a decrease in AIDS incidence in Bahia, and such a decrease was in line with the country's successful containment measures (Dourado et al. 1997a). The AIDS reality I saw exposed in the streets of Salvador and in community-run services contradicts this local and national optimistic epidemiological profile (Dourado et al. 1997b). I learned of a hidden AIDS epidemic by following Dona Conceição, a nurse who every Wednesday noon, aided by some of her religious friends, cooks large pots of food and distributes them to some 120 adults and children with AIDS, living in the abandoned buildings of downtown Salvador and surviving through marginal economies. As Dona Conceição says: "You know, the services never meet the demands, there is always lack." Most of her patients present "AIDS symptoms" and have either been treated in an emergency room, discharged without having recovered, or have received no assistance at all: "I have lost many, but others emerge."

As I was doing an ethnography of all state's AIDS services, out of curiosity I asked a nurse working in the state's surveillance service to check if some of Dona's Conceição's patients were registered in their database. They were not. I was challenged to investigate the public health machinery that structures this absence, all the while producing a rational-technical truth of decreases in AIDS incidence. I went to the state hospital where most of the *abandonados* aided by Dona Conceição try to get hospitalized. There, aided by two local epidemiologists, I counted all certificates of people who died with AIDS in the hospital from 1990 to 1996. In doing so, we were reconstructing what was happening in the present. We documented that only 26 percent of all AIDS-related deaths that took place there were actually registered as AIDS cases by the state's surveillance service.

I was able to identify a series of problems that are occurring at different levels of data collection and analysis, both in the hospitals and in the surveillance service. For example, even though doctors say that they are effectively registering all AIDS cases, many do not register due to sheer neglect or moral contempt. As the state has created a minimum infrastructure for AIDS care, it has not taken strategic steps to improve the sensitivity and speed of its surveillance activities. AIDS cases frequently get lost in the bureaucracy between hospitals and surveillance. In addition, political partisanships obliterate a good flow of information between technicians working at city, state, and national branches of the AIDS Program. Disagreements over diagnostic criteria also make AIDS cases disappear. Given the steady changes in the clinical biomedical knowledge about HIV/AIDS, there is an increasing discrepancy between what the health professionals understand as clinical AIDS and the criteria adopted by the Ministry of Health to define AIDS. Thus, quite often AIDS cases being treated in the public health services, even when they progress to death, are not acknowledged by the state as AIDS cases. Since surveillance technicians do not even keep track of all easily framed AIDS cases, they simply opt not to enter the questionable cases into the databank – thus making impossible even their a posteriori recovery.

The categories traditionally used by epidemiology and by the social sciences to map and interpret the impact of social and economic realities on health–disease–death processes (such as age, race, and individual risk factors, or gender inequalities, sexual culture, and social representations of risk and safety) are insufficient to account for the rational-technical dynamics at work here. Insights from the social studies of science are helpful, to a point (Latour 1987, 1990; Shapin and Schaffer 1985). Bruno Latour, for example, highlights the "cascading" power of scientific representations to socially "draw things together," thus allowing "harder facts" to be produced (1990: 40, 41). He explicates the "paradox" that "by working on papers alone, on fragile inscriptions that are immensely less than the things from which they are extracted, it is still possible to dominate all things and all people" (1990: 60). Thus, ideas and representations become social technologies in that they function for "accumulating time and space" (1990: 32), because they enable one to present (and therefore control) "absent things" (1990: 27) in a persuasive and efficient way. His caveat: "To take the existence of macro-actors for granted without studying the material that makes them 'macro,' is to make both science and society mysterious" (1990: 56). What is missing in a Latourian sociology of science is an account of how historically specific these transactions are, and how scientific and social technologies are combined into governance. The work of Ian Hacking comes to mind.

In his book *The Taming of Chance*, Ian Hacking (1990) points to the political and moral power of statistical representations, particularly with regards to medico-forensic-political language. Hacking builds upon Michel Foucault's notion that in modern societies there are two poles where politics takes place. One pole is the individual body, and the other is focused on the biological processes of populations. This polarity between human anatomics and the biopolitics of populations is linked together by intermediary relations. Hacking has identified scientific and technical dynamics that intermediate processes by which "people are made up" (1990: 3; 1999). Hacking's "dynamic nominalism" states that categories and counting define new classes of people, normalize their ways of being in the world, and also have "consequences for the ways in which we conceive of others and think of our own possibilities and potentialities" (1990: 6). If Hacking examines categories and statistics as making up people, I am concerned in this study with how technical and political dynamics make people invisible and how these dynamics literally impact dying, its experience, distribution, and social representation. As I found out in my ethnography, bureaucratic procedures, informational difficulties, sheer medical neglect and moral contempt, and unresolved disputes over diagnostic criteria all mediate the process by which these people are turned into "absent things." And I began to call these state and medical procedures and actions "technologies of invisibility."

Let me show you some numbers. We counted 571 AIDS deaths at the State Hospital between 1990 and 1996. We checked how many of those AIDS cases were registered by the state Surveillance Department. As I mentioned above, we found that only 150 (26 percent) of those AIDS cases were officially registered. The yearly notification rate has varied from 5.6 percent to 34.8 percent, and since 1992 has stabilized around 30 percent (immediately before the decrease of AIDS incidence was first reported; Dourado et al. 1997b). One can argue that this relatively stable registration rate of 30 percent represents the limited AIDS population that the state is ready to structure its services for (see Table 10.1).

Back to the death certificates. We were intrigued: what makes some of these AIDS cases officially visible and the majority not? Is there a bias of selection at work in their registration as AIDS cases?

The next table (see Table 10.2) compares the characteristics of the 150 patients who were registered with the characteristics of the 421 who were not.

I want to call your attention to three statistical facts:

1 Among the total cases analyzed, 297 (52 percent) died during their first hospitalization. One can argue that when these people finally have access to the hospital it is largely in order to die.

2 The percentage of those registered cases that died during the first hospitalization is very different from the percentage of those nonregistered cases that

Table 10.1 Number of deaths of AIDS patients at the AIDS Unit of the State Hospital between 1990 and October 1996, and breakdown by whether or not these patients were registered as AIDS cases by the Bahian Epidemiological Surveillance Service

| Year of hospitalization | Surveillance Service data | | TOTAL N |
	Registered N (%)	Nonregistered N (%)	
1990	3 (7.1)	39 (92.9)	42
1991	4 (5.6)	67 (94.4)	71
1992	33 (28.7)	82 (71.3)	115
1993	24 (28.9)	59 (71.1)	83
1994	32 (32.3)	67 (67.7)	99
1995	31 (34.8)	58 (65.2)	89
1996	23 (31.9)	49 (68.1)	72
TOTAL	**150 (26.0)**	**421 (74.0)**	**571**

Table 10.2 Comparison of characteristics of the 150 patients registered as AIDS cases by the state Surveillance Department with characteristics of the 421 not registered

Variables	Registered = 150 N (%)	Nonregistered = 421 N (%)	χ^2 (value of p)
1 Number of hospitalizations			
1 only	56 (37)	241 (57)	$p < 0.001$
2 or more	94 (63)	180 (43)	
2 Sex			
Total	150	421	
Male	109 (73)	344 (82)	$p < 0.02$
Female	41 (27)	77 (18)	
3 IDU	43 (29)	111 (26)	N.S.
4 Sexual transmission			
Total (male)	60	181	
Homosexual	14 (23)	101 (56)	$p < 0.001$
Heterosexual	34 (57)	62 (34)	$p < 0.002$
Bisexual	12 (20)	18 (10)	$p < 0.041$
5 Origin			
Total	139	381	
Salvador	124 (89)	290 (76)	$p \pm 0.001$
Interior of Bahia	15 (11)	91 (24)	
6 Age	29/34/40	29/35/40	N.S.

died during their first hospitalization. Among the registered cases, 56 (37 percent) died during the first hospitalization. By contrast, among the 421 nonregistered cases, 241 (57 percent) died during the first hospitalization. This is of very high statistical significance: $p < 0.001$. For people who are not familiar with statistical research, the *pi value* is the likelihood that the result of a comparison between two groups is not random – the lower the pi value, the more scientifically significant the difference is (at least in medical research). In this case, persons who died in their first and last hospitalization have fewer chances of being represented at all.

3   Regarding reporting on sexual behavior: among the 60 male cases who were registered, there is a greater percentage of individuals who reported hetero-sexuality (57 percent) and a lower proportion of individuals who reported homosexuality (23 percent). A reverse scenario is found among the male cases that were not registered (34 percent vs. 56 percent). This is also of high statistical significance: $p < 0.001$. These data indicate another bias of selec-tion: persons who reported themselves as homosexuals also have less chance of being epidemiologically represented.

Interestingly, the AIDS protocols we worked with had no social indicator such as level of education. But let me remind you that these are the poorest of the poor. As the unit's social worker put it: "These are the patients who live in the gutter.... Sometimes strangers send them here in a taxi, others are brought in by the police. They come in dying, they have bad skin lesions.... The ones who recover just return to the streets where they die.... They seldom come back for a follow-up. It is unrealistic to demand that a person who lives on the street adhere to treatment. They never heal."

To sum up the overall rationale at work here, these dynamics of minimum registration of around 30 percent produce norms of intervention aimed at a specific target group: a self-registered seropositive population. Specialized health care is provided to those who identify themselves as AIDS cases in an early stage of infection at a public institution, and who independently search for regular treatment. This specific population is, at the same time, conceived a priori and takes shape through this intervention – they are what I call AIDS or biomedical citizens. This is the reality that appears in the optimistic epidemiological reports showing a decrease of AIDS incidence in Bahia. Indi-viduals who cannot be framed within this planned demand and within this self-selecting conception of public health remain outside any official registers and do not receive intervention. The majority of these nonregistered cases are persons who are only identified as having AIDS when they are dying, in their first and last hospitalization. Meanwhile, the short-term care of these dying marginal patients is relegated to a mostly sporadic street charity, like that of Dona Conceição.

My colleagues and I submitted a report to the Bahian Health Division inform-ing them of this hidden AIDS epidemic. I learned later that this report was suppressed. It was within this kind of unreformed and publicly discredited regional politics that the antiretroviral policy came into effect; it is in these repressive local force fields and moral economies that the sustainability of the AIDS policy remains in question.

The Politics of Death

I am interested in the complexity that is revealed as the anthropologist returns to the field. Then one sees more clearly emerging changes and the making of intractable sameness. The returning longitudinal engagement is a key methodological and ethical move for anthropology, history, and critique. It clarifies how science and technology are integral with local worlds and politics. At stake is the temporality of knowledge, institutions, technology, money, and lives. In 2000 and 2001 I returned to Salvador where the antiretroviral mobilization and distribution system was also said to be operating well. Recall the three images I began with: the dying city, the absent people and bodiless citizens, and the disciplinary and automatic functionings of power. Juxtapose with those images the following ones. The central HIV testing center has been upgraded and there is a massive influx of poor and middle-class people, a new testing population. Next door, there is a new and sophisticated AIDS outpatient clinic under construction. Patients here, their social status known and ability to adhere proven, will be screened for all kinds of phase III and IV clinical trials run by new partnerships between the local Federal University and multinationals producing antiretrovirals. Back at the state's official AIDS unit, things are the same: still only 16 beds, care reduced to a minimum, and the dying in the corridors as in the streets is routine.

In this work, I am rethinking one of Foucault's maxims that biopower dominated mortality rather than death: "power does not know death anymore and therefore must abandon it" (1992: 177). As I have been demonstrating, the management of death among the poorest is concomitant with the successful control of mortality as articulated by Brazil's new biopolitics.[7] Here, letting die is a technical and political action, contiguous with the scientific, medical, and pastoral power that makes live.

Following Hannah Arendt and Michel Foucault, philosopher Giorgio Agamben argues that the original political element of sovereign power in Western democracies is "not simple natural life, but life exposed to death" (1998: 24). In *The Human Condition* (1958), Arendt argued that after World War II political action has been increasingly focused on the control of natural life, biological processes. *Homo faber* gave way to *homo laborans*, the being concerned with physiological existence. Science has played a key role in this transformation: "In other words, the process which, as we saw, invaded the natural sciences through the experiment, through the attempt to imitate under artificial conditions the process of 'making' by which a natural thing came into existence, serves as well or even better as the principle for doing in the realm of human affairs" (1958: 299). This happens within the fabric of Christian societies – and this is so because the fundamental belief in the sacredness of life has survived. "The only thing that could now be potentially immortal, as immortal as the body politic in Antiquity and as individual life during the Middle Ages, was life itself, that is, the possibly everlasting life process of the species mankind" (1958: 321). As Arendt concludes: "The loss of human experience involved in this development is extraordinarily striking" (1958: 321).

Agamben locates the beginnings of the structures of sovereign administration of bare life in ancient Roman law, particularly in the figure of *homo sacer*. The "sacred man" was the one convicted as a criminal, with the capacity to be killed (without legal charge of homicide) but not sacrificed. This particular form of life was caught in a double exception. "Just as the law, in the sovereign exception, applies to the exceptional case in no longer applying and in withdrawing from it, so *homo sacer* belongs to God in the form of unsacrificeability and is included in the community in the form of being able to be killed. Life that cannot be sacrificed and yet may be killed is sacred life" (1998: 82). Agamben argues that such an embodied violence, subtracted from human and divine law, opened up a new sphere of legitimate human action. This action is a human extension of the state of exception, that proper political space of the West: "The sovereign is the one with respect to whom all men are potentially *homines sacri*, and *homo sacer* is the one with respect to whom all men act as sovereigns" (1998: 84).

Agamben points out that the determinant structure of our modern inherited ways of ordering public spaces and political relations is in relation to a ban. "The ban is essentially the power of delivering something over to itself, which is to say, the power of maintaining itself in relation to something presupposed as nonrelational. What has been banned is delivered over to its own separateness and, at the same time, consigned to the mercy of the one who abandons it – at once excluded and included, removed and at the same time captured" (1998: 109–110). In the body of *homo sacer* political and social forms of life have entered into a symbiosis with death without it belonging to the world of the deceased. The original political element of sovereign power is "not simple natural life, but life exposed to death" (1998: 88).

As an anthropologist, I am particularly interested in the ability of medicine and politics to engender new sorts of populations in the field and to make some people an invisible part of the equation. As my Bahian investigation reveals, marginal and diseased groups are *included in the social order through their dying* and as if dying had been self-generated. By self-generated I mean that these noncitizens only become partially visible in the health system when they are dying; they are traced as "drug addicts," "robbers," "prostitutes," labels which allow them to be socially blamed for their dying. They have erased their origins as well as the complex social causes that exacerbate infections and immune depressions.

The existence of states of exception within the restructuring of Brazil's economy, state, and public health is a complex political and ethical question. In such states of exception, the person is presupposed as nonrelational and stays at the mercy of the individuals and institutions that at one point or another abandon him or her. He or she is, on the one hand, excluded from family and state action and, on the other, socially included either as a new epidemiological risk vector or through a public dying (Biehl 1999, 2001). The abandoned person with AIDS inhabits a zone of indifference in which the concept of the human is a posthumous one and the notion of a perpetrator or of accountability has been suspended.

In his insightful book *Seeing Like a State*, James Scott illustrates why some of the major projects to improve the human condition in the twentieth century have failed and produced tragedy: "The lack of context and particularity is not an oversight; it is the necessary first premise of any large-scale planning exercise" (1998: 346). "Making people invisible," I argue, has become an indispensable tool of containment (a structured nonintervention) within the calculations of life processes that are here and now at the center of governance: Who shall live? Who shall die? And at what cost?

Extending Life

A few of the AIDS *abandonados* are selected out for social regeneration in community-run sites called "houses of support." In order to uncover this different destiny, I undertook longitudinal work at Caasah, a community-based care center for some of the marginal and poor living with AIDS in Salvador (Biehl 1999). Caasah was founded in 1992, when a group of marginals squatted an abandoned maternity ward in the outskirts of Salvador. The squatters called themselves "revolutionary" and chose a trained nurse to administer their new house. City officials and local AIDS activists helped Caasah to gain legal status, and by 1993 it became a nongovernmental organization. With 30 inhabitants, Caasah then successfully applied with two projects to the National AIDS Program. The core maintenance of the institution, its technical upgrading and "civilizing processes" were now closely tied to the funds channeled from the World Bank loan. Indeed, Caasah and similar initiatives are actually being incorporated by the state and qualified as health services. Throughout the country, pastoral institutions such as Caasah triage AIDS pensions and antiretroviral therapies to some of the poorest with AIDS. As of 2000, 100 of the country's 480 AIDS NGOs were houses of support. The question of where to put the diseased poor has fallen out of the state's purview and has become a pastoral undertaking. In order to enter these institutions, the *abandonados* have to break with their past and addictions. They start to distinguish themselves from the "living dead" of the street environment they left behind and develop a biotechnical biography.

Over the years of my research, I produced an archive of Caasah's institutional history and recorded the inhabitants' collective and individual life histories. They experience accelerated time, in terms of both social and biological change. Beginning in 1994, strict disciplinary mechanisms led to the expulsion of unruly patients. A reduced group passed through an intense process of normalization coordinated by a therapist sent by the National AIDS Program in 1995. By the end of that year, concerns about internal violence, aggressions, and drug trade and consumption were replaced by concerns for hygiene and house maintenance. The next move involved medicalization, under the guidance of a newly hired nurse. He established an infirmary post with a pharmacy and a triage room.

Caasah had dramatically changed by 1996. The main corridor was now crowded with nursing trainees and volunteers wearing white lab-coats carrying trays with medicine to their patients. The marginal patients had either left or had died, and a higher number of working poor were now living there. The residents had acquired a new biomedical conscience – "culture," as Caasah's director told me – as they were managing their own health. "With time we domesticated them." I could see that the healthy patients followed very closely each other's debilitation process, and were actually obliged to help to care for the ones dying in the triage room. In this case, the dying *abandonados* still have a last social function: they are part of the *Bildung* (self-formation) process of the AIDS citizens. As the director puts it: "Handling the dying is helpful for the residents to see what will happen to them if they don't change their minds and follow their treatments." Dark-skinned and with contagious scabiosis, Evangivaldo understands himself as the pathogen of the healthy AIDS citizens: "I keep saying to myself, 'My God, I was not born like this, will this be my skin to the end?' I feel very isolated, as if I were in a prison. I see people passing by and wishing me dead. They give me tranquilizers. . . . All these things leave me in a sad psychosis."

As Caasah's inhabitants put their drives into place, so to speak, their biological condition becomes the locus of concentration and fabrication. Many refer to the HIV virus as "my little animal." Some patients used to say, "I want to let the little animal sleep in me." I frequently heard comments such as, "The moment you fall back into what you were and stop taking your treatment, the virus occupies your place. And the virus only occupies the place because you let it." Many live, in their own words, "in a kind of constant battle." They know they are trapped between two destinies: dying of AIDS like the poor and marginal, that is, "animalized," and the possibility of living pharmacologically into a future, thereby letting the animal sleep, and preventing it from consuming the flesh. With the availability of anti-HIV drugs, health is increasingly seen as a problem of treatment adherence or of individual misconduct.

Evilásio is a single man, illiterate, and a carpenter by profession. He said he did not know he had AIDS, even though he had been once to a hospital. As his body began to waste, he retreated into his shack and was found almost dead by neighbors, who finally dropped him at Caasah. Evilásio quickly learned the norms of the house and now "accumulates health": "The nurses have nothing bad to say about me.... I can tell you that for me Caasah is the house of God." Valquirene, Caasah's first patient to have successfully taken the combined therapies, knows that she is now "another person." As she puts it: "I have been born again; it is not such a bad thing to have HIV. It's like not having money. And in Brazil everybody experiences that."

The new medical and political reality lived by Caasah's inhabitants adds to Hannah Arendt's insights on the determinations of the present human condition. Arendt identified a modern political process that progressively eliminates the possibility of human fulfillment in the public realm, excluding masses and reducing them to the condition of *animal laborans*, whose only activity is that of biological preservation (1958: 320–325). This preservation is an individual concern; this metabolism is superfluous to the state and to society at large. "They begin to belong to the human race in much the same way as animals belong to a specific animal species" (1973: 302). I am telling a somewhat different story. What is distinctive in Caasah is that the diseased biology of these *abandonados* is also a technical means of social inclusion. While these people learn new scientific knowledge and navigate through new laboratories and treatment regimes, they force an inclusion into a very sophisticated and selective form of governance. Against an expanding discourse of human rights, we are here confronted with the limits of the official structures whereby these rights are realized, biologically speaking, but only on a selective basis, and the emergence of a new political economy of pharmaceuticals.

Pharmaceutical Futures

In spite of its internal paradoxes, the fact is that the Brazilian AIDS policy keeps thriving and it is now setting some of the terms of highly contested transnational economic processes, as well as informing new forms of pathbreaking international medical activism. In November 2001, the World Trade Organization (WTO) issued a declaration, originally proposed by Brazil, stating that the international protection of patents was indefensible in the face of public health crises. The declaration reads: "We are of the firm opinion that [TRIPS] should be interpreted and implemented in a way which is consistent with the right of WTO members to protect public health and in particular to assure medicines for all" (AIDS Imprensa 2001). The immediate implications of these new developments need to be carefully followed as they redefine the international pharmaceutical contract, as they challenge poor countries to work on their public health infrastructure to replicate the Brazilian model, as Brazil shares its AIDS managerial and technological know-how with Portuguese-speaking countries in Africa, and as they might also make possible for Brazil to secure new trade concessions from the United States, or even for India to become a key player in the global market of generic drugs. We are also challenged to continue to ethnographically chart, understand, and politicize the complex and often contradictory ways in which neoliberalizing policies, state presence, and health and wellbeing are forged in local worlds where biotechnology and scarcity exist side by side. The constitution of biomedical forms of citizenship[8] for marginal and poor AIDS patients happens within various networks of care (public/nongovernmental/pastoral) that are by and large reduced to triage, and the struggle over life extension and social death is played out on the very register of humanness. One's mere worthiness to exist, one's claim to life, and one's relation to what counts as the reality of the world passes through what is considered to be human now – and this is a site of intense medico-scientific and legal dispute, and of moral and subjective fabrication. Between the loss of an old working concept of humanness and of belonging, if solely to the streets, and the installment of a new one, the world is experienced as vanishing to many and to others as a pharmaceutical possibility.

Notes

1   This specific excerpt is taken from Michel Foucault's reading of Oedipus in "Truth and Juridical Forms" (2000).
2   I draw from Giorgio Agamben's interpretation of Leviathan's figure as presented in the seminar "Thresholds: Thinking in the State of Except" taught with Daniel Heller-Roazen at Princeton University in fall 2001.
3   Since AIDS first appeared in the early 1980s, the pandemic has killed approximately 22 million people worldwide, 17 million in Africa alone, and has produced more than 13 million orphans. In 2002 an estimated 36 million people were living with HIV, 95 percent of them in low-income countries; and 16 thousand new infections were occurring everyday worldwide. The pandemic has indeed become a major source of social, economic, and political instability, particularly in the developing world where therapies remain largely inaccessible. After the United States, Brazil has the second largest official number of HIV infections in the Western hemisphere.
4   For a detailed discussion of the governmental impact of neoliberalism see Nikolas Rose's book *Powers of Freedom* (1999).
5   See Caldeira (2000) for a discussion of democratization and human rights in Brazil and Paley (2001) for a discussion of health movements and democratization. See Das (1999) for a critique of the measures, practices, and values related to international health interventions and Appadurai (2002) for a discussion of the urban poor and new form of activism in India. See also Ferguson and Gupta (chapter 4, this volume) for a discussion of new forms of neoliberal governmentality.
6   In 1985, the first GAPA (Grupo de Apoio à Prevenção á AIDS) was created in São Paulo, and it would soon have independent extensions in Porto Alegre and Salvador, for example. GAPAs worked on prevention and also mediated the treatment and legal demands of AIDS victims. Also in São Paulo in 1985, transvestite Brenda Lee founded

the country's first *casa de apoio* (house of support) for dying patients. In 1986, activist Herbert Daniel created ABIA, the Brazilian Interdisciplinary AIDS Association, which played a key role in the production of AIDS knowledge and dissemination. In 1989, the group Pella Vida was formed in Rio de Janeiro and São Paulo (it was another very important outgrowth of the work of Daniel), composed mostly of HIV-positive people and aimed at their medical concerns.

7   Teresa Caldeira (2002) elaborates on police violence and on popular demands for the death penalty in light of Brazil's democratization and international cultures of human rights.

8   See Adriana Petryna's analysis of the emergence of biological forms of citizenship in the Chernobyl aftermath (2002).

References

Agamben, Giorgio
   1998   Homo Sacer: Sovereign Power and Bare Life. Daniel Heller-Roazen, trans. Stanford: Stanford University Press.
AIDS Imprensa
   2001   Coordenação nacional de DST/AIDS. Brasília: Ministério da Saúde.
Appadurai, Arjun
   2002   Deep Democracy: Urban Governmentality and the Horizon of Politics. Public Culture 14(1): 21–47.
Arendt, Hannah
   1958   The Human Condition. Chicago: University of Chicago Press.
   1973   The Origins of Totalitarianism. New York and London: Harvest/HBK.
Aron, Raymond
   1951   Les guerres en chaine. Paris: Gallimard.
Bastos, Francisco Inácio, and Christovam Barcellos
   1995   Geografia social da AIDS no Brazil. Revista de Saúde Pública 29(1): 52–62.
   1996   Redes sociais e difusão da AIDS no Brasil. Boletim da Oficina Sanitária Panamericana 121(1): 11–24.
Bermudez, Jorge
   1995   Indústria farmacêutica, estado e sociedade: Crítica da política de medicamentos no Brasil. São Paulo: Editora Hucitec e Sociedade Brasileira de Vigilância de Medicamentos.
Bermudez, J. A. Z., M. A. Oliveria, R. Epsztejn, and L. Hasenclever
   2000   Implicações do acordo TRIPS e da recente lei de proteção patentária no Brasil na produção local e no acesso da população aos medicamentos. Unpublished MS.
Biehl, João
   1999   Other Life: AIDS, Biopolitics, and Subjectivity in Brazil's Zones of Social Abandonment. Ann Arbor: UMI Services.
   2001   Vita: Life in a Zone of Social Abandonment. Social Text 68: 131–149.
Caldeira, Teresa
   2000   City of Walls: Crime, Segregation, and Citizenship in São Paulo. Berkeley: University of California Press.

2002   The Paradox of Police Violence in Democratic Brazil. Ethnography 3(3): 235–263.

Cardoso, Fernando Henrique
1998   Notas sobre a reforma do estado. Novos Estudos do CEBRAP 50: 1–12.

Coordenação Nacional de DST e AIDS
2000   The Brazilian Response to HIV/AIDS: Best Practices. Brasília: Ministério da Saúde.

Cunha, Euclides da
1944   Rebellion in the Backlands. Samuel Putnam, trans. Chicago: University of Chicago Press.

Das, Veena
1995   Critical Events: An Anthropological Perspective on Contemporary India. New Delhi: Oxford University Press.
1999   Public Good, Ethics, and Everyday Life: Beyond the Boundaries of Bioethics. Theme issue, "Bioethics and Beyond," Daedalus 128(4): 99–133.

Dourado, M. I. C., C. V. Noronha, A. Barbosa, and R. Lago
1997a   Considerações sobre o quadro da AIDS na Bahia. Boletim Epidemiológico do SUS. Brasília: Ministério da Saúde.

Dourado, M. I. C., M. L. Barreto, N. Almeida-Filho, J. G. Biehl, and S. Cunha
1997b   Região Nordeste. In Coordenação nacional de DST e AIDS. A epidemia da AIDS no Brasil: Situação e tendências. Pp. 123–143. Brasília: Ministério da Saúde.

Farmer, Paul
1999   Infections and Inequalities: The Modern Plagues. Berkeley: University of California Press.
2003   Pathologies of Power: Health, Human Rights, and the New War on the Poor. Berkeley: University of California Press.

Farmer, Paul, Fernet Léandre, Joia S. Mukherjee, et al.
2001   Community-Based Approaches to HIV Treatment in Resource-Poor Settings. The Lancet 358: 404–409.

Fischer, Michael M. J.
2003   Emergent Forms of Life and the Anthropological Voice. Durham, NC: Duke University Press.

Foucault, Michel
1979   Discipline and Punish: The Birth of the Prison. New York: Vintage Books.
1980   The History of Sexuality, vol. 1: An Introduction. New York: Vintage Books.
1991   Governmentality. In The Foucault Effect: Studies in Governmentality. Graham Burchell, Colin Gordon, and Peter Miller, eds. Pp. 87–104. Chicago: University of Chicago Press.
1992   Del poder de la soberanía al poder sobre la vida. In Genealogía del racismo. Buenos Aires: Editorial Altamira.
2000   Truth and Juridical Forms. In The Essential Works of Foucault, 1954–1984, vol. 3: Power. James D. Faubion, ed. Pp. 1–89. New York: New Press.

Galvão, Jane
2000   A AIDS no Brasil: A agenda de construção de uma epidemia. São Paulo: Editora 34.
2002   A política brasileira de distribuição e produção de medicamentos anti-retrovirais: privilégio ou um direito? Cadernos de Saúde Pública 18(1): 213–219.

Geest, Sjaak van der, Susan Reynolds Whyte, and Anita Hardon
  1996   Anthropology of Pharmaceuticals: A Biographical Approach. Annual Review of
    Anthropology 25: 153–178.
Hacking, Ian
  1990   The Taming of Chance. Cambridge: Cambridge University Press.
  1999   Making Up People. *In* The Science Studies Reader. Mario Biagioli, ed. New
    York: Routledge.
Isto É/Senhor
  1991   O sexo inseguro. November 20: 52.
Kleinman, Arthur
  1999   Experience and Its Moral Modes: Culture, Human Conditions, and Disorder.
    The Tanner Lectures on Human Values 20: 357–420.
Latour, Bruno
  1987   Science in Action. Cambridge, MA: Harvard University Press.
  1990   Drawing Things Together. *In* Representations in Scientific Practice. Michael
    Lynch and Steve Woolgar, eds. Cambridge, MA: MIT Press.
Lock, Margaret
  2002   Twice Dead: Organ Transplants and the Reinvention of Death. Berkeley:
    University of California Press.
Paley, Julia
  2001   Marketing Democracy: Power and Social Movements in Post-Dictatorship
    Chile. Berkeley: University of California Press.
Parker, Richard, and Herbert Daniel
  1991   AIDS: A terceira epidemia. São Paulo: Editora Iglu.
Parker, Richard, Cristiana Bastos, Jane Galvão, and José Stálin Pedrosa, eds.
  1994   A AIDS no Brasil. Rio de Janeiro: Relume Dumará, ABIA, IMS/UERJ.
Petryna, Adriana
  2002   Life Exposed: Biological Citizens After Chernobyl. Princeton: Princeton Uni-
    versity Press.
Rabinow, Paul
  1996   Essays on the Anthropology of Reason. Princeton: Princeton University Press.
  1999   French DNA: Trouble in Purgatory. Chicago: University of Chicago Press.
Rapp, Rayna
  1999   Testing Women, Testing the Fetus: The Social Impact of Amniocentesis in
    America. New York: Routledge.
Rosário Costa, Nilson
  1996   O Banco Mundial e a política social nos anos 90: A agenda para a reforma do
    setor saúde no Brasil. *In* Política de saúde e inovação institucional: Uma agenda para
    os anos 90. Nilson Rosário Costa and José Mendes Ribeiro, eds. Rio de Janeiro:
    Secretaria de Desenvolvimento Educacional/ENSP.
Rose, Nikolas
  1999   Powers of Freedom: Reframing Political Thought. Cambridge: Cambridge
    University Press.
Rosenberg, Tina
  2001   How To Solve the World's AIDS Crisis. The New York Times Magazine,
    January 28.

Scheper-Hughes, Nancy
  1994   An Essay: AIDS and the Social Body. Social Science and Medicine 39(7): 991–1003.
  2000   The Global Traffic in Human Organs. Current Anthropology 41(2): 191–211.
Scott, James C.
  1998   Seeing Like a State: How Certain Schemes to Improve the Human Condition Have Failed. New Haven: Yale University Press.
Shapin, Steven, and Simon Schaffer
  1985   Leviathan and the Air-Pump: Hobbes, Boyle and the Experimental Life. Princeton: Princeton University Press.
Sophocles
  1984   The Three Theban Plays. New York: Penguin Books.
Stepan, Nancy
  1976   The Beginnings of Brazilian Science: Oswaldo Cruz, Medical Research and Policy, 1890–1920. New York: Science History Publications.
Stiglitz, Joseph
  2002   Globalization and Its Discontents. New York: Norton.
Strathern, Marilyn
  1992   Reproducing the Future: Anthropology, Kinship, and the New Reproductive Technologies. New York: Routledge.
Teixeira, Paulo Roberto
  1997   Políticas públicas em AIDS. In Políticas, instituições e AIDS: Enfrentando a AIDS no Brasil. Richard Parker, ed. Rio de Janeiro: ABIA/J. Zahar Editor.
World Bank
  1993   The Organization, Delivery and Financing of Health Care in Brazil. (Study Document.)

Index